Police
Interrogations
and
False
Confessions

Police Interrogations and False Confessions

CURRENT RESEARCH, PRACTICE, and POLICY RECOMMENDATIONS

G. Daniel Lassiter and Christian A. Meissner

DECADE
of BEHAVIOR

2000-2010

AMERICAN PSYCHOLOGICAL ASSOCIATION
WASHINGTON, DC

Published by
American Psychological Association
750 First Street, NE
Washington, DC 20002
www.apa.org

To order
APA Order Department
P.O. Box 92984
Washington, DC 20090-2984
Tel: (800) 374-2721
Direct: (202) 336-5510
Fax: (202) 336-5502
TDD/TTY: (202) 336-6123
Online: www.apa.org/books/
E-mail: order@apa.org

In the U.K., Europe, Africa, and the Middle East, copies may be ordered from
American Psychological Association
3 Henrietta Street
Covent Garden, London
WC2E 8LU England

Typeset in New Century Schoolbook by Circle Graphics, Inc., Columbia, MD

Printer: Edwards Brothers, Ann Arbor, MI
Cover Designer: Berg Design, Albany, NY

The opinions and statements published are the responsibility of the authors, and such opinions and statements do not necessarily represent the policies of the American Psychological Association.

Library of Congress Cataloging-in-Publication Data

Police interrogations and false confessions : current research, practice, and policy recommendations / [edited by] G. Daniel Lassiter and Christian A. Meissner.
     p. cm. — (Decade of behavior)
  ISBN-13: 978-1-4338-0743-5
  ISBN-10: 1-4338-0743-2
  1. Police questioning—United States. 2. Confession (Law)—United States. I. Lassiter, G. Daniel, 1954- II. Meissner, Christian A. III. American Psychological Association.

  HV8073.3.P65 2010
  363.25'40973—dc22

                                                                    2009032819

British Library Cataloguing-in-Publication Data
A CIP record is available from the British Library.

Printed in the United States of America
First Edition

APA Science Volumes

Attribution and Social Interaction: The Legacy of Edward E. Jones

Best Methods for the Analysis of Change: Recent Advances, Unanswered Questions, Future Directions

Cardiovascular Reactivity to Psychological Stress and Disease

The Challenge in Mathematics and Science Education: Psychology's Response

Changing Employment Relations: Behavioral and Social Perspectives

Children Exposed to Marital Violence: Theory, Research, and Applied Issues

Cognition: Conceptual and Methodological Issues

Cognitive Bases of Musical Communication

Cognitive Dissonance: Progress on a Pivotal Theory in Social Psychology

Conceptualization and Measurement of Organism–Environment Interaction

Converging Operations in the Study of Visual Selective Attention

Creative Thought: An Investigation of Conceptual Structures and Processes

Developmental Psychoacoustics

Diversity in Work Teams: Research Paradigms for a Changing Workplace

Emotion and Culture: Empirical Studies of Mutual Influence

Emotion, Disclosure, and Health

Evolving Explanations of Development: Ecological Approaches to Organism–Environment Systems

Examining Lives in Context: Perspectives on the Ecology of Human Development

Global Prospects for Education: Development, Culture, and Schooling

Hostility, Coping, and Health

Measuring Patient Changes in Mood, Anxiety, and Personality Disorders: Toward a Core Battery

Occasion Setting: Associative Learning and Cognition in Animals

Organ Donation and Transplantation: Psychological and Behavioral Factors

Origins and Development of Schizophrenia: Advances in Experimental Psychopathology

The Perception of Structure

Perspectives on Socially Shared Cognition

Psychological Testing of Hispanics

APA Decade of Behavior Volumes

To my father, William James Lassiter
—*G. Daniel Lassiter*

To my loving wife, Dr. Amanda DeGraff
—*Christian A. Meissner*

Contents

Contributors

Ray Bull, PhD, School of Psychology/Forensic Section, University of Leicester, Leicester, England

Gregory DeClue, PhD, Sarasota, FL

Steven A. Drizin, JD, Center on Wrongful Convictions, Northwestern University School of Law, Chicago, IL

Ronald P. Fisher, PhD, Legal Psychology Program, Florida International University, North Miami

I. Bruce Frumkin, PhD, Forensic & Clinical Psychology Associates, South Miami, FL

Solomon M. Fulero, PhD, Department of Psychology, Sinclair College, Dayton, OH

Gisli H. Gudjonsson, PhD, Institute of Psychiatry, London, England

Saul M. Kassin, PhD, Department of Psychology, John Jay College of Criminal Justice, City University of New York

Jessica Kostelnik, MA, Department of Psychology, University of Virginia, Charlottesville

G. Daniel Lassiter, PhD, Department of Psychology, Ohio University, Athens

Kim D. Lassiter, PhD, Apex, NC

Sharon Leal, PhD, Department of Psychology, University of Portsmouth, Portsmouth, Hampshire, England

Richard A. Leo, PhD, JD, University of San Francisco School of Law, San Francisco, CA

Matthew J. Lindberg, MS, Department of Psychology, Ohio University, Athens

Samantha Mann, PhD, University of Portsmouth, Portsmouth, Hampshire, England

Jessica L. Marcon, PhD, Department of Psychology, University of Texas at El Paso

Christian A. Meissner, PhD, Department of Psychology, University of Texas at El Paso

Jessica Meyer, PhD, Connecticut Department of Children and Families, Middletown

Fadia M. Narchet, PhD, Department of Criminal Justice, Henry C. Lee College of Criminal Justice and Forensic Sciences, West Haven, CT

Jennifer J. Ratcliff, PhD, Department of Psychology, State University of New York at Brockport

Allison D. Redlich, PhD, School of Criminal Justice, State University of New York at Albany

N. Dickon Reppucci, PhD, Department of Psychology, University of Virginia, Charlottesville

Melissa B. Russano, PhD, School of Justice Studies, Roger Williams
    University, Bristol, RI
Stavroula Soukara, PhD, National Police Academy, Athens, Greece
Thomas P. Sullivan, LLB, Jenner & Block, Chicago, IL
Aldert Vrij, PhD, Department of Psychology, University of Portsmouth,
    Portsmouth, Hampshire, England
Lezlee J. Ware, PhD, Department of Psychology, Ohio University, Athens
Lawrence S. Wrightsman, PhD, Department of Psychology, University of
    Kansas, Lawrence

Foreword

In early 1988, the American Psychological Association (APA) Science Directorate began its sponsorship of what would become an exceptionally successful activity in support of psychological science—the APA Scientific Conferences program. This program has showcased some of the most important topics in psychological science and has provided a forum for collaboration among many leading figures in the field.

The program has inspired a series of books that have presented cutting-edge work in all areas of psychology. At the turn of the millennium, the series was renamed the Decade of Behavior Series to help advance the goals of this important initiative. The Decade of Behavior is a major interdisciplinary campaign designed to promote the contributions of the behavioral and social sciences to our most important societal challenges in the decade leading up to 2010. Although a key goal has been to inform the public about these scientific contributions, other activities have been designed to encourage and further collaboration among scientists. Hence, the series that was the "APA Science Series" has continued as the "Decade of Behavior Series." This represents one element in APA's efforts to promote the Decade of Behavior initiative as one of its endorsing organizations. For additional information about the Decade of Behavior, please visit http://www.decadeofbehavior.org.

Over the course of the past years, the Science Conference and Decade of Behavior Series has allowed psychological scientists to share and explore cutting-edge findings in psychology. The APA Science Directorate looks forward to continuing this successful program and to sponsoring other conferences and books in the years ahead. This series has been so successful that we have chosen to extend it to include books that, although they do not arise from conferences, report with the same high quality of scholarship on the latest research.

We are pleased that this important contribution to the literature was supported in part by the Decade of Behavior program. Congratulations to the editors and contributors of this volume on their sterling effort.

Steven J. Breckler, PhD
Executive Director for Science

Virginia E. Holt
*Assistant Executive Director
for Science*

Preface

For a subject as complex and controversial as false confessions, it is surprising that there is very little in the way of a comprehensive examination of the institutional and social psychological persistence (and pervasiveness) of the structural, interpersonal, and intrapersonal inducements and impediments that have informed law enforcement's interrogation techniques and the types of false confessions they encourage.

G. Daniel Lassiter's seminal volume *Interrogations, Confessions, and Entrapment* (2004) brought together for the first time the work of preeminent scholars in the area of interrogations and confessions. Six years have passed, and the growth of research and interest in the area has been exponential. It is our hope that the collection of chapters in this book will prove a valuable resource for years to come for scholars and practitioners alike and that it will spur continued progress toward a more complete understanding of the phenomenon of false confessions.

The impetus for the present volume was the first scientific conference devoted entirely to the topic of understanding and preventing false confessions. Although obviously long overdue, "Interrogations and Confessions: A Conference Exploring Current Research, Practice, and Policy," held in September 2007, was co-organized by the present volume's editors and made possible by support from the American Psychological Association, Ohio University, the University of Texas at El Paso, and the University of Texas at El Paso Center for Law and Border Studies. More than 200 academics, law enforcement personnel, prosecutors, public defenders, judges, clinical practitioners, and legislators attended, representing 15 states in the United States, as well as Canada, Great Britain, the Netherlands, Japan, and Australia. The resulting book provides a unique forum in which social scientists, legal scholars, and practitioners critically examine the current state of research on interrogations and confessions and assess whether policy recommendations might be developed or advocated on the basis of present knowledge.

It is obvious that the academic- and policy-oriented study of police interrogations and false confessions is so interdisciplinary that it poses quite a challenge to acknowledge the many scholars, practitioners, and organizations involved in this volume's undertaking. Yet that task is made somewhat easier by simply extending our profound thanks to the preeminent scholars and practitioners who presented their research at the El Paso conference, to the many attendees who came from afar to listen and contribute their thoughts on the issues, and most important, to those who worked behind the scenes at the University of Texas at El Paso and Ohio University. We are grateful for your contributions, and we hope that you and many others will enjoy and be inspired by the work presented in this volume.

Police
Interrogations
and
False
Confessions

Introduction: Police Interrogations and False Confessions—An Overview

G. Daniel Lassiter, Christian A. Meissner,
Lezlee J. Ware, Jessica L. Marcon,
and Kim D. Lassiter

> . . . and so the hour may be more favourable now for asking once more whether it is really 'inconceivable' that an innocent man can confess to a crime of which he is wholly ignorant.
>
> —Hugo Münsterberg, *On the Witness Stand,* 1908

The foregoing comment was made in regard to a murder case that took place at the turn of the 20th century in Chicago. Münsterberg, a pioneering scholar in applied psychology at Harvard, had been asked by a physician for his opinion about the man who confessed to and was convicted of the crime. A letter written to the physician in which Münsterberg expressed his view that the man was most certainly innocent somehow found its way to the newspapers of the day. Münsterberg's contention that the confession was untrue (based in part on proof of alibi) was met with scathing editorials and headlines such as "Harvard's Contempt of Court" and "Science Gone Mad." Münsterberg felt that this "noble outburst of feeling" was due to some extent to the fact that the people of Chicago were experiencing great fear and anxiety about the frequency of brutal murders occurring on their streets. The man whom Münsterberg believed confessed falsely was hanged a short time later, after a motion for supersedeas was denied by the Supreme Court. Münsterberg's search for a reason why the man was believed to be guilty of the heinous crime inevitably led to the oft-repeated statement that it would be "inconceivable that any man who was innocent of it should claim the infamy of guilt" (Münsterberg, 1908, p. 142). Several months after "the neck of the young man was broken," Münsterberg hoped (as expressed in the epigraph) that passions would have died down to a point at which a forthright discussion and exploration of the phenomenon of false confession was possible.

A century later, many people still cannot wrap their heads around the notion that innocent people sometimes admit to crimes they did not commit. However, today there exists a body of scholarship on the psychology of police interrogations that makes the concept of false confessions at least fathomable, if no less shocking. This volume brings together the most recent research by the preeminent scholars in this rapidly growing area of investigation. One aim in compiling this work was to provide the very latest findings for the benefit of the increasing number of researchers who have initiated their own systematic explorations of the problem of police-induced false confessions. An equally important objective was to provide sufficient background on the topic so that those who have not been directly immersed in the scholarship—particularly students, practitioners, and policymakers—could more clearly grasp the scope of the false confession phenomenon and see how scientific study can ultimately provide a solid empirical foundation for designing effective strategies to curb, if not eliminate, its occurrence. A final priority in developing this volume was to ensure that its content would be of value to scholars, students, practitioners, and policymakers associated with a range of pertinent disciplines, including social and forensic psychology, sociology, criminology, law enforcement, legal scholarship, and social justice. As we hope the following chapters will make abundantly clear, there is a need more than ever for a shift in the standard interrogation emphasis on, as Münsterberg (1908) put it, "bringing out the guilty thought" to one that "shall not bring it 'in' into an innocent consciousness" (p. 143).

To facilitate a broad audience's consumption of the material presented in this volume, we organized the 13 chapters (plus a conclusion by the coeditors and an afterword on the state of the literature by the field's leading scholar) into three thematic groupings. The first group, comprising chapters 1 through 5, focuses on establishing the extent of the problem of police-induced false confessions and on identifying the situational and dispositional factors that increase the risk that innocent suspects may incriminate themselves. The second group, comprising chapters 6 through 9, focuses on research programs and findings that suggest promising reforms to the criminal justice system that could eventually be implemented to minimize the occurrence of false confessions or, if they do occur, to better detect them before an innocent life is ruined by a wrongful conviction. The final group, comprising chapters 10 through 13, focuses on *Miranda* warnings and considers how experts might improve the implementation and effectiveness of this intended safeguard against compelled self-incrimination as well as more generally helping to educate judges and jurors regarding the reality of false confessions and their causes.

How Common Are Police-Induced False Confessions, Who Is Most Vulnerable, and What Aspects of Interrogations Are Most Problematic?

The first set of chapters begins appropriately with a contribution by Richard A. Leo and Steven A. Drizin, scholars who have been at the forefront of the movement to change the American justice system's current accusatorial approach to interrogating its citizens. It is appropriate that they identify what they consider to be the three critical errors in the standard interrogation process that are responsible for many instances of false confession: the misclassification error, the coercion error, and the contamination error. Leo and Drizin describe what each error is and cite anecdotal as well as research-based evidence for how these errors collectively can produce untrue confessions that invariably lead to wrongful convictions.

Chapter 2 is authored by Gisli H. Gudjonsson, one of the most renowned experts on the psychology of interrogations and confessions, who presents recent survey data relating to the incidence of false confession. Gudjonsson reviews growing evidence from prison inmates, police detainees, and community youths that false confession is a global phenomenon. Gudjonsson also describes a number of risk factors associated with false confessions, including the rate of delinquency, the number of delinquent friends, personality, mental state, and multiple exposures to unpleasant life events.

Allison D. Redlich follows in chapter 3 with the important insight that false guilty pleas (when innocents plead guilty despite having committed no crime) can also be construed as false confessions in that they are false admissions of guilt often accompanied by detailed allocutions. Despite their known existence and the striking similarities with false confessions, false guilty pleas have received little or no research attention. It is disturbing that Redlich notes that blatant threats or promises that would readily be recognized as illegal in an interrogation context occur frequently in a plea-bargaining context without raising as much as an eyebrow.

In chapter 4, N. Dickon Reppucci, Jessica Meyer, and Jessica Kostelnik focus on the interrogation of juveniles and children, who, psychological research shows, are especially susceptible to the tactics routinely used by police with detained suspects. In this regard, they report on the first standard, large-scale documentation of reported interrogation practices of law enforcement professionals, police beliefs about the reliability of these techniques, and their knowledge of child development. Reppucci and colleagues find that although police acknowledge some developmental differences between youth and adults and how these developmental limitations may affect the reliability of reports obtained from young suspects in interrogation, there are indications that police fail to apply this fundamental knowledge to their reported practices in the interrogation context. In general, police appear to believe that youths can be dealt with in the same manner as adults.

Ray Bull and Stavroula Soukara, in chapter 5, present data from actual police interviews as they occur today in England and Wales, two countries that over the past 2 decades have dramatically changed their approach to interrogation from one focused on obtaining a confession to one focused on maximizing information gathering that will make identifying the truly guilty more likely. Bull and Soukara report evidence that this desirable change is indeed occurring. For instance, they examined the extent to which a number of psychological tactics identified in the literature were actually used by a major English police force and found that coercive tactics were not often used and that tactics concerned with the seeking of information were common. The relationships between these findings and prior changes in relevant legislation and training are discussed by the authors, as are the implications for potential reform in other countries.

New Perspectives and Research to Serve as the Basis for Implementing Beneficial Changes to the Criminal Justice System

This second set of chapters begins with Aldert Vrij, a prolific scholar in the area of deception detection, and his colleagues Ronald P. Fisher, Samantha Mann, and Sharon Leal, who make an argument in chapter 6 for abandoning the assumption that liars are more uncomfortable than truth tellers in an interview setting and therefore more likely to display nervous behavior. They contend that this premise is theoretically weak and that the deception literature does not support it. Vrij et al. propose and provide empirical support for an alternative approach to detecting deception, namely, that lying is more cognitively demanding than truth telling. They also show how interviewers can exploit liars' diminished cognitive capacity to discriminate more effectively between liars and truth tellers.

Chapter 7, coauthored by Christian A. Meissner, Melissa B. Russano, and Fadia M. Narchet, reports on recent experiments that reveal that the information-seeking approach to interrogation adopted by England and Wales (described in chap. 5 by Bull and Soukara) provides superior diagnosticity to the accusatorial approach that is the norm in the United States. That is, guilty persons are more likely to confess and innocent persons are less likely to confess using an information-seeking approach than an accusatory approach. The authors appropriately emphasize the necessity of experimental tests of any proposed reforms designed to reduce the problem of false confessions.

In chapter 8, attorney Thomas P. Sullivan, who as cochair of the Illinois Commission on Capital Punishment played an important role in making Illinois the first state to pass legislation requiring electronic recording of custodial interrogations, writes on why an electronic-recording requirement (especially in videotape form) is a good thing for everyone concerned about the integrity of the criminal justice system. Partly on the basis of survey data, he specifically discusses the benefits obtained by both suspects and law enforcement when electronic recordings are made of custodial interrogations, from *Miranda* warnings to the end, as well as the dangers to both without complete recordings.

It is appropriate that Sullivan's chapter is followed by a chapter by G. Daniel Lassiter, Lezlee J. Ware, Matthew J. Lindberg, and Jennifer J. Ratcliff (chap. 9), who summarize 25 years of empirical studies regarding the circumstances under which evaluations of videotaped interrogations and confessions are likely to be unbiased and accurate. They glean from this body of work important recommendations that policymakers should take into account when developing any requirement that custodial interrogations be videotaped.

The Supreme Court's View of Interrogations, Making *Miranda* Warnings a More Effective Safeguard, and Educating With Expert Testimony

Chapter 10, the leadoff to the final grouping of contributions to this volume, is authored by Lawrence S. Wrightsman, perhaps the world's foremost authority on the psychology of the U.S. Supreme Court. Wrightsman notes that the two most important decisions by the Supreme Court relevant to police interrogations of suspects happened several decades ago: the establishment of *Miranda* warnings in *Miranda v. Arizona* in 1966 and the decision in *Frazier v. Cupp* in 1969 that implicitly accepted the use of deception by the police during an interrogation. Since then, various decisions have eroded the application of *Miranda* warnings, although the general procedure was upheld in *Dickerson v. United States* (2000). Wrightsman uses these decisions as a background to consider whether the continued use of deception by the police justifies another review by the Supreme Court.

Gregory DeClue writes in chapter 11 about two new tools to assist practitioners. The first is a checklist that clinical psychologists can use to facilitate their determination of whether suspects observed on videotape did indeed understand their *Miranda* rights at the time of questioning. The second was designed with law enforcement in mind. Specifically, DeClue describes a model presentation of the *Miranda* warnings that if delivered properly by police, would remove any doubt that suspects were adequately apprised of their constitutional rights to silence and to counsel.

I. Bruce Frumkin, in chapter 12, follows on this topic by focusing on frequent errors clinicians make when providing expert testimony. He focuses on two key issues: assessments pertaining to a defendant's ability to have made a knowing, intelligent, and voluntary waiver of rights at the time of the police questioning; and evaluations of psychological factors related to the voluntariness or credibility of a confession statement. Clinical practitioners especially will benefit from Frumkin's discussion of the misuse of specialized forensic tests in confession cases.

In chapter 13, Solomon M. Fulero notes that over the past 10 years attorneys have increasingly turned to psychologists to act as expert witnesses in cases involving claims of false confession. He then reviews the developing case law at both the federal and state levels as well as the content of expert testimony in this area. Fulero identifies five arguments that frequently arise for not admitting expert testimony and then suggests sound responses for refuting them.

The coeditors conclude the volume by identifying, on the basis of the previous chapters, critical recommendations for reforming police interrogation practice and policy. They also enumerate additional recommendations for better safeguarding false confessors once they reach the courtroom. Because our understanding of the problem of false confessions is an ever-evolving process of scientific inquiry, they also suggest several directions for future research.

This volume's coda comes in the form of a brief afterword by Saul M. Kassin, perhaps the most recognized scholar associated with the science of interrogations and confessions. Kassin first takes stock of the current state of research, policy, and practice in the area. He then offers suggestions on future directions, with the ultimate goal being that the criminal confessions that are the most compelling are those whose truthfulness has been rigorously assured.

References

Dickerson v. United States, 120 S.Ct. 2326 (2000).

Frazier v. Cupp, 394 U.S. 731 (1969).

Miranda v. Arizona, 384 U.S. 436 (1966).

Münsterberg, H. (1908). *On the witness stand: Essays on psychology and crime.* Garden City, NY: Doubleday.

1

The Three Errors: Pathways to False Confession and Wrongful Conviction

Richard A. Leo and Steven A. Drizin

On the morning of November 17, 1989, police in Peekskill, New York, discovered the body of 15-year-old Angela Correa, who had been raped and strangled. Peekskill Detectives Thomas McIntyre and David Levine, who had been assigned to lead the investigation into the murder, subsequently contacted Detective Raymond M. Pierce of the New York Police Department. Pierce was the founder of the department's Criminal Assessment and Profiling Unit and one of only a handful of officers who at the time had received training in criminal profiling by the Federal Bureau of Investigation (Wadler, 2000). After reviewing police reports, crime scene photos, and other information about the case, Pierce developed a detailed profile of the offender, a profile that in many ways would steer the course of the ensuing investigation (Snyder, McQuillan, Murphy, & Joselson, 2007). According to Pierce's profile, Correa's killer was a White or Hispanic male, less than 25 years of age and probably less than 19, who knew Correa. The killer was shorter than 5 ft.10 in. and was a loner who was not involved in school activities and who lacked confidence around women. He had a physical or mental disability and could have been a drug or alcohol abuser with a history of troublemaking or even assaultive behavior (Snyder et al., 2007).

With the profile in hand, the Peekskill police began their investigation by interviewing Correa's classmates at Peekskill High School. Jeffrey Deskovic, a 16-year-old student who was interviewed, seemed to fit Pierce's profile to a tee. He was a 5 ft.10 in. White male who was under the age of 19 and was described by his classmates as a "loner" and by unnamed sources as an "emotionally handicapped" young man who had on a prior occasion assaulted his mother. He became a suspect because he was allegedly absent from school on November 15 during the 3:30 to 4:30 p.m. time frame in which the medical examiner estimated Correa had died (Snyder et al., 2007). To police, Deskovic's behavior after Correa's death also raised suspicions. Deskovic had attended all three wakes for Correa and was seen crying uncontrollably. He seemed overly distraught for someone who only knew Correa casually and seemed obsessed with solving the crime. He had conducted his own investigation of the crime, had visited the crime scene, proffered his own theories of how the crime occurred, and in his early conversations with the police seemed to have intimate knowledge of the case (*People v. Deskovic,* 1994; Santos, 2007a). This unusual behavior led police to suspect that Deskovic was involved in Correa's slaying.

Shortly after meeting him for the first time, the investigating officers began to focus almost exclusively on Deskovic (Snyder et al., 2007). Between December 12, 1989, and January 25, 1990, detectives questioned Deskovic at least seven times. Throughout these contacts, the police used what they termed *passive/active* techniques, switching back and forth from low-key questioning to high stress, accusatory, and confrontational interrogation in an effort to get Deskovic to confess (Snyder et al., 2007). Despite their efforts, Deskovic refused to confess.

On January 25, 1990, Deskovic agreed to submit to a polygraph examination. He arrived at police headquarters by himself at 9:30 a.m., where he was met by Detectives Levine and McIntyre and driven to Brewster, New York, for the exam. Over the next 8 hours, in a 10 ft. × 10 ft. room, he was questioned repeatedly by the polygrapher, Investigator Stephens (Snyder et al., 2007). When Stephens's passive interrogation techniques failed to produce a confession from Deskovic, Stephens turned up the heat, telling Deskovic that he had failed the polygraph exam (Snyder et al., 2007). Detective McIntyre then entered the room and assumed the questioning, this time adopting a more aggressive and confrontational style. According to Deskovic, Detective McIntyre not only told him repeatedly that all the evidence, including the polygraph, conclusively established his guilt, he also used psychological coercion, threatening Deskovic that if he did not confess he would go to prison and promising that if he did confess, he would receive psychiatric treatment (and be allowed to go home; Santos, 2007c). Because McIntyre did not electronically record his interrogation (in fact, only snippets of the hours of interrogation over the seven different interrogations were recorded), the precise techniques he used to break down Deskovic's resistance are not known.

Deskovic finally confessed. According to McIntyre, Deskovic began by describing the acts committed by the perpetrator in the third person, switching to the first person at some point during the narrative (Snyder et al., 2007) when he told McIntyre that "I lost my temper" and hit Correa in the back of the head with a Gatorade bottle. Although he never confessed to raping Correa, Deskovic, now crying, then said that he put his hand over Correa's mouth and "may have left it there too long" (Bandler, 2006a, p. A1). According to Deskovic, he repeated back the details that the detectives had told him during the lengthy accusatorial interrogation (Santos, 2007c). "'I was tired, confused, scared, hungry— I wanted to get out of there,'" he recalled recently. "'I told the police what they wanted to hear, but I never got to go home. They lied to me'" (Santos, 2007c, p. A11). By the end of the interrogation, Deskovic was under the table, curled up in a fetal position, sobbing uncontrollably (Snyder et al., 2007). Solely on the basis of the confession, Deskovic was arrested and charged with the murder and rape of Angela Correa.

Prosecutors rushed to present their case against Deskovic to the grand jury, choosing to seek an indictment before receiving the results of DNA testing comparing Deskovic's blood with semen samples taken from vaginal swabs from Correa's body. Just 3 days after he was indicted by a grand jury, the FBI notified the district attorney that the semen did not belong to Deskovic (Snyder et al., 2007). As prosecutors prepared their case for trial, they received more bad news from results of additional DNA testing. The state's expert hair analyst also ruled Deskovic out as the source of several hairs found on the victim's body. One of the hairs, found on Correa's right foot, was determined to belong to an African American (Snyder et al., 2007).

Lacking DNA or any other forensic or physical evidence tying Deskovic to the crime scene, prosecutors relied exclusively on his confession to secure his conviction. To persuade the jury to convict Deskovic, police and prosecutors told the jury that Deskovic's statements were reliable because they contained details that only the true perpetrator could have known, including, for example, that there were multiple crime scenes and that the victim had written a note to a former boyfriend shortly before her death, a note that was found crumpled under Correa's body (Snyder et al., 2007). Police also attributed other details to Deskovic, including that Correa suffered a blow to the head, that he tore her clothes, that there was a struggle, and that he held his hand over her mouth. Throughout Deskovic's trial, police witnesses testified that they took precautions to prevent contaminating Deskovic's confession narrative by not disclosing any critical crime scene facts to Deskovic or to anyone else (Garrett, in press). Moreover, police and prosecutors relied heavily on one fact that was supposedly unknown to police prior to Deskovic's disclosure: a "Gatorade bottle" was used to strike the victim in the head. During closing argument, the district attorney emphatically highlighted this fact, noting that police found a Gatorade cap during a search conducted only after Deskovic had told them about the bottle and that injuries inflicted on Correa were consistent with a "heavy bottle" (Garrett, in press). Deskovic was convicted of Correa's murder and sentenced to 15 years to life.

Deskovic's conviction was affirmed on appeal, and efforts to get his conviction overturned through state appellate and federal habeas proceedings failed. The state appellate court found nothing wrong with the way in which police interrogated Deskovic and even went so far as to hold that the evidence against him was "overwhelming" and that his inculpatory statements were "corroborated" by physical evidence, such as the autopsy findings (*People v. Deskovic*, 1994; Snyder et al., 2007). After the Innocence Project agreed to take Deskovic's case in 2006, the semen from the rape kit was retested using newer technology. In September 2006, the DNA was matched to a convicted murderer named Steven Cunningham, who soon thereafter confessed to the crime. Deskovic was officially exonerated on November 2, 2006, after serving nearly 16 years in prison for a rape and murder he did not commit (Bandler, 2006b). Cunningham pled guilty to the murder and rape of Angela Correa on March 14, 2007 (Santos, 2007a).

The Jeffrey Deskovic case is not an isolated one. In recent years, police have elicited a substantial number of demonstrably false confessions from innocent individuals (Drizin & Leo, 2004; Gudjonsson, 2003). Many of these false confessions have led to erroneous prosecutions, and some have led to wrongful convictions and incarceration (Drizin & Leo, 2004; Leo & Ofshe, 1998). Some of the wrongfully convicted false confessors have spent many years unjustly incarcerated before being exonerated and released, whereas others remain behind bars (Drizin & Leo, 2004; Leo & Ofshe, 1998). A number of exonerated false confessors were convicted of capital crimes and sentenced to death (Cohen, 2003). One false confessor, Earl Washington, spent almost 10 of his more than 17 years of imprisonment on Virginia's death row and came within 9 days of being executed before being exonerated in 2001 (Edds, 2003). Researchers believe that several other innocent confessors have been executed: Edward Earl Johnson in 1987 (Lofquist & Harmon, 2008), Barry Lee Fairchild in 1995 (Leo & Ofshe, 1998, 2001), Leo Jones in 1998 (Lofquist & Harmon, 2008), and Dobie Gillis Williams in 1999 (Prejean, 2005).

Throughout American history, police-induced false confessions have been among the leading causes of miscarriages of justice (Borchard, 1932; Scheck, Neufeld, & Dwyer, 2000). Until the late 1980s, however, there were no systematic, social–scientific studies of the causes, patterns, and consequences of wrongful conviction in the United States. This changed with Hugo Bedau and Michael Radelet's (1987) landmark study of wrongful convictions in capital and potentially capital cases in the United States from 1900 to 1987, which found that false confessions played a causal role in 49 of 350 miscarriages of justice they had documented in these types of cases. Bedau and Radelet found that police-induced false confessions were the third leading cause—only behind perjury by prosecution witnesses and mistaken eyewitness identification—of wrongful conviction in their sample.

Only 2 years after Bedau and Radelet's (1987) article, in 1989, Gary Dotson became the first innocent prisoner exonerated by postconviction DNA testing (Doyle, 2005). The advent of DNA testing, and the window it opened onto the errors of the legal system, has permanently altered the nature and study of miscarriages of justice in the United States. Perhaps most important, DNA testing has established factual innocence with certainty in numerous postconviction cases. As a result, it is now widely accepted that wrongful convictions occur with troubling regularity in the U.S. criminal justice system, despite high-minded ideals and the many constitutional rights that are meant to safeguard the innocent. The DNA exonerations have led scholars and policymakers to focus not on whether wrongful convictions occur but on why they occur so frequently and what can be done to prevent and remedy them.

In recent years, scholars have documented and analyzed several hundred police-induced false confessions (Drizin & Leo, 2004; Garrett, 2008; Gross, Jacoby, Matheson, Montgomery, & Patel, 2005; Leo & Ofshe 1998, 2001; Scheck et al., 2000; Warden, 2003). In these studies, the percentage of miscarriages of justice involving false confessions range from 14% to 60%. These modern studies establish, once again, that the problem of false confession remains a leading cause of the wrongful conviction of the innocent. As the late Welsh White (2001) pointed out, "as soon as a police-induced false confession is accepted as true by the police, the risk that the false confession will lead to a wrongful conviction is substantial" (p. 185).

There is no single cause of false confession, and there is no single logic or type of false confession. Police-induced false confessions result from a multistep process and sequence of influence, persuasion, and compliance, and they usually involve psychological coercion (Ofshe & Leo, 1997; Zimbardo, 1971). Police are more likely to elicit false confessions under certain conditions of interrogation, however, and individuals with certain personality traits and dispositions are more easily pressured into giving false confessions (see chaps. 2 and 12, this volume). In the remainder of this chapter, we analyze the three sequential errors that occur in the social production of every false confession: (a) investigators first misclassify an innocent person as guilty; (b) they next subject him to a guilt-presumptive, accusatory interrogation that invariably involves lies about evidence and often the repeated use of implicit or explicit promises and threats, as well; and (c) once they have elicited a false admission, they pressure the suspect to provide a postadmission narrative that they jointly shape, often supplying the innocent suspect with the (public and nonpublic) facts of the crime. We refer to these as the *misclassification error,* the *coercion error,* and the *contamination error,* respectively (Leo, Costanzo, & Shaked, 2009). All of these errors featured prominently in the wrongful conviction of Jeffrey Deskovic.

Once these three errors combine to produce a false confession, however, the pathway from false confession to wrongful conviction is not yet complete. At least three other processes—misleading specialized knowledge, tunnel vision, and confirmation bias —usually pave the way to a wrongful conviction by convincing all of the criminal justice actors (defense attorneys, prosecutors, trial, and appellate court judges) to ignore the possibility that the confession is false. We also analyze these processes in this chapter and conclude with some recommendations designed to both reduce false confessions and to prevent them from leading to wrongful convictions.

The Misclassification Error

The first mistake occurs when detectives erroneously decide that an innocent person is guilty. As Davis and Leo (2006) pointed out, "the path to false confession begins, as it must, when police target an innocent suspect . . . . Once specific suspects are targeted, police interviews and interrogations are thereafter guided by the presumption of guilt" (pp. 123–124). Whether to interrogate is therefore a critical decision point in the investigative process. Without a classification error at this stage, there will be no false confession or wrongful conviction. In other words, if police did not erroneously interrogate innocent people, they would never elicit false confessions. Because misclassifying innocent suspects is a necessary condition for all false confessions and wrongful convictions, it is both the first and the most consequential error police will make. Yet it is also one of the least studied and thus least well understood.

There are several related factors that can lead police to mistakenly classify an innocent person as a guilty suspect. The first stems from poor and erroneous interrogation training. American police are trained, falsely, that they can become human lie detectors capable of distinguishing truth from deception at high rates of accuracy. Detectives are taught, for example, that subjects who avert their gaze, slouch, shift their body posture, touch their nose, adjust or clean their glasses, chew their fingernails, or stroke the back of their head are likely to be lying and thus guilty. Subjects who are guarded, uncooperative, and offer broad denials and qualified responses are also believed to be deceptive and therefore guilty. These types of behaviors and responses are merely a few examples from lengthy laundry lists of so-called nonverbal and verbal behavior symptoms of lying that police manuals, training materials, and trainers instruct detectives to look for when deciding whether to prejudge a suspect as guilty and subject him or her to an accusatorial interrogation (e.g., Inbau, Reid, Buckley, & Jayne, 2001). Although police trainers usually mention that no single nonverbal or verbal behavior is, by itself, indicative of lying or truth telling, they never-theless teach detectives that they can reliably infer whether a subject is deceptive if they know how to interpret his or her body language, mannerisms, gestures, and style of speech. In the absence of any supporting evidence, some police trainers boast of extraordinarily high accuracy rates: The Chicago-based firm Reid and Associates, for example, claims that detectives can learn to accurately discriminate truth and deception 85% of the time (Davis & Leo, 2006; Kassin & Gudjonsson, 2004).

The deeply ingrained police belief that interrogators can be trained to be highly accurate human lie detectors is both wrong and dangerous. It is wrong because it is based on inaccurate speculation that is explicitly contradicted by the findings of virtually all the published scientific research on this topic (Depaulo, Lindsay, Malone, Muhlenbruck, & Cooper, 2003; Vrij, 2000; chap. 6, this vol-ume). Social scientific studies have repeatedly demonstrated across a variety of contexts that people are poor human lie detectors and thus highly prone to error in their judgments about whether an individual is lying or telling the truth. Most people get it right at rates that are no better than chance (i.e., 50%) or the flip of a coin (Bond & DePaulo, 2006). Social scientific studies have also shown that even professionals who make these judgments on a regular basis—such as detectives, polygraph examiners, customs inspectors, judges, and psychiatrists (Ekman & O'Sullivan, 1991)—typically cannot distinguish truth tellers from liars at levels significantly greater than chance. Even specific studies of police interrogators have found that they cannot reliably distinguish between truthful and false denials of guilt at levels greater than chance; indeed, they routinely make erroneous judgments (Hartwig, Granhag, Stromwall, & Vrig, 2004; Meissner & Kassin, 2002; Vrij, 2004). The method of behavior analysis taught by Reid and Associates has been found empirically to actually lower judg-ment accuracy, leading Kassin and Fong (1999) to conclude that "the Reid tech-nique may not be effective—and, indeed, may be counterproductive—as a method of distinguishing truth and deception" (p. 512). According to Kassin and Gudjonsson (2004), police detectives and other professional lie catchers are accurate approximately 45% to 60% of the time.

The reasons police interrogators misclassify the innocent as guilty so often are not hard to understand. There is no human behavior or physiological response that is unique to deception and therefore no tell-tale behavioral signs of deception or truth telling (Lykken, 1998). The same behaviors, mannerisms, gestures, and attitudes that police trainers believe are the deceptive reactions of the guilty may just as easily be the truthful reactions of the innocent. As Kassin and Fong (1999) noted, "part of the problem is that people who stand falsely accused of lying often exhibit patterns of anxiety and behavior that are indistinguishable from those who are really lying" (p. 501). Police detectives acting as human lie detectors are therefore relying on cues that are simply not diagnostic of human deception (Vrij, Mann, & Fisher, 2006; chap. 6, this vol-ume). Instead, the manuals are replete with false and misleading claims—often presented as uncontested fact—about the supposed behavioral indicia of truth telling and deception. At least one prominent police trainer, Reid and Associates president Joseph Buckley, continues to insist "we don't interrogate innocent people" (Kassin & Gudjonsson, 2004, p. 36).

This police-generated mythology of the interrogator as human lie detector is not only wrong but also dangerous for the obvious reason that it can easily lead a detective to make an erroneous judgment about an innocent suspect's guilt on the basis of little more than his body language and then mistakenly subject him to an accusatorial interrogation that can lead to a false confession. For example, police in Escondido, California, decided that Michael Crowe was lying (and thus guilty of murdering his sister Stephanie) in large part because they believed he initially seemed "curiously unemotional" and thus, unlike other members of his family, wasn't grieving his sisters' death normally (White, 2001). In Illinois, McHenry County Sheriff's deputies decided that Gary Gauger was lying to them and thus guilty of brutally slaying both of his parents because of what they perceived to be his unemotional response to the bloody murders (Lopez, 2002). Peekskill, New York, detectives believed that Jeffrey Deskovic was lying and thus guilty of killing his high school classmate not because he was unemotional but because he was overly distraught at the classmate's death (Snyder et al., 2007). The Crowe, Gauger, and Deskovic cases are not exceptional: The social science research literature is replete with case examples of innocent suspects who were coercively interrogated (and ultimately confessed falsely) only after they were misclassified as guilty because detectives misinterpreted their nonverbal behavior and demeanor and thereafter erroneously presumed their guilt (Drizin & Leo, 2004; Leo & Ofshe, 1998).

The human lie detector mythology is dangerous not only because it leads police to mistakenly classify the innocent as guilty on the flimsiest of criteria (see Risinger & Loop, 2002) but also because it significantly increases detectives' confidence in the accuracy of their erroneous judgments (Kassin & Fong, 1999; Meissner & Kassin, 2002, 2004). Misplaced confidence in one's erroneous judgments is never a good thing, but that is especially true in investigative police work because the stakes—an innocent person's freedom and reputation and the guilty party's escape and ability to commit additional crimes—can be so high. Erroneous prejudgments of deception lead to what Meissner and Kassin (2002, 2004) have called the *investigator response bias* (i.e., the tendency to presume a suspect's guilt with near or complete certainty). The overconfident police detective who mistakenly decides an innocent person is a guilty suspect will be far less likely to investigate new or existing leads, evidence, or theories of the case that point to other possible suspects. As Kassin and colleagues have demonstrated, erroneous but confidently held prejudgments of deception also increase the likelihood that investigators will subject the innocent suspect to an accusatorial interrogation in which they seek to elicit information and evidence that confirm their prejudgments of guilt and discount information and evidence that do not (Kassin, Goldstein, & Savitsky, 2003; Meissner & Kassin, 2002, 2004).

The findings of Kassin and his colleagues are consistent with our own field observations. Detectives sometimes refer to their superior human lie detection skills as stemming from a "sixth sense" common to police detectives (Leo, 1996). The unfortunate effect is that interrogators will sometimes treat their hunch (or "gut reaction") as somehow constituting direct evidence of the suspect's guilt and then confidently move into an aggressive interrogation. In our analysis of both proven and disputed confession cases, we have found that interrogators are often more certain in their belief in a suspect's guilt than the objective evidence warrants and tenaciously unwilling to consider the possibility that their intuition or behavioral analysis is wrong (Drizin & Leo, 2004; Leo & Ofshe, 1998). These tendencies may be reinforced by an occupational culture that teaches police to be suspicious generally and does not reward them for admitting mistakes or expressing doubts in their judgments (Simon, 1991; Skolnick, 1966).

The human lie detector mythology is but one of many mythologies that can lead police officers to misclassify an innocent person as a suspect and then to subject that suspect to the kinds of confrontational and aggressive interrogation techniques that can lead to false confessions. Although this mythology played a role in the Deskovic case when Peekskill police jumped to the conclusion that Deskovic was lying because he was overly emotional in his grief, a second mythology—that trained police officers can create a detailed and accurate profile of a suspect by reading police reports and examining crime scene photographs and other evidence related to the crime—played an even greater role in the misclassification error. Deskovic appeared to police to be a near perfect match with the police-generated profile. He was the right race, the right age, the right height; he knew the victim; and he was a loner who lacked confidence around women and who had allegedly assaulted his mother.

Overreliance on the profile not only caused the officers to focus on Deskovic to the exclusion of all others but also may have influenced the questions they asked witnesses about Deskovic and the way they interpreted and recorded the answers of these witnesses in their police reports. Numerous police reports used words that seem to track the terms of the profile, describing Deskovic as "troubled," "prone to violence," and "hostile and agitated" (Snyder et al., 2007). The initial profile of the killer, however, turned out to be wrong in almost every respect. Steven Cunningham, the man who raped and killed Angela Correa, is African American, stands over 6 ft. tall, and was 29 years old at the time he committed these crimes (Santos, 2007b). He was also a total stranger to the victim (Snyder et al., 2007).

The Deskovic case is not the only case in the annals of false confessions in which a police profile was the source of the misclassification error. Nearly 3 months after Lori Roscetti was raped and murdered in 1986, Chicago detectives contacted FBI profiler Robert Ressler and asked him to create a profile of the man or men who had murdered Roscetti. Ressler opined that the crime was committed by three to six young black males between the ages of 15 and 20 years who had previously been incarcerated and had lived close to the spot where Roscetti's body had been found (Drizin & Leo, 2004). With Ressler's profile in hand, Chicago detectives focused in on three 17-year-old Black teenagers—Marcellus Bradford, Larry Ollins, and Omar Saunders—all of whom lived in the nearby housing project and had done time as juveniles. On January 27, 1987, detectives brought the boys in for questioning. More than 15 hours after the start of the interrogations, police emerged with a confession from Bradford that implicated himself, Larry Ollins, and Larry's 14-year-old cousin, Calvin, who had a learning disability, who police then picked up and grilled until he confessed (Drizin & Leo, 2004). Although early DNA testing of semen samples taken from the victim should have excluded the boys as the rapists, all four defendants were convicted at trial. Larry Ollins, Calvin Ollins, and Omar Saunders were sentenced to life in prison, whereas Marcellus Bradford, who agreed to plead guilty and testify against Larry

Ollins, was promised and received a 12-year sentence. In 2001, new DNA testing conclusively failed to link any of the defendants to the Roscetti rape and murder, and they were subsequently set free. Shortly afterward, police arrested Duane Roach and Eddie "Bo" Harris, who gave videotaped confessions to raping and murdering Roscetti and were later linked to the crime through fingerprint and DNA testing. Roach and Harris also did not fit Ressler's profile. Harris, who was 46 years old at the time of his arrest, would have been 31 when Roscetti was killed, whereas Roach, who was 38 years old at the time of his arrest, would have been 23. Police believe that Roach and Harris were the only two men involved in the crime, not six as Ressler had theorized (Possley, Ferkenhoof, & Mills, 2002).

Apart from their training, experience, and job culture, police detectives are, like everyone else, subject to normal human decision-making biases and errors that cause people to believe things that are not true (Gilovich, 1991; chap. 9, this volume). These decision-making biases include the tendency to attribute more meaning to random events than is warranted, to base conclusions on incomplete or unrepresentative information, to interpret ambiguous evidence to fit one's preconceptions, and to seek out information that confirms one's pre-existing beliefs while discounting or disregarding information that does not. All of these normal human decision-making biases are not only amply present in police work but compounded by the adversarial nature of American criminal investigation (Findley & Scott, 2006; Leo, 2008).

The Coercion Error

Once detectives misclassify an innocent person as a guilty suspect, they will often subject him or her to an accusatorial interrogation. This is because getting a confession becomes particularly important when there is no other evidence against the suspect, and typically no credible evidence exists against an innocent, but misclassified, suspect. Thus, detectives typically need a confession to successfully build a case. By contrast, when police correctly classify and investigate the guilty, there is often other case evidence, so getting a confession may be less important. Interrogation and confession taking also become especially important forms of evidence gathering in high-profile cases in which there is great pressure on police detectives to solve the crime and there is no other source of potential evidence to be discovered (Gross, 1996). Hence, the vast majority of documented false confessions cases occur in homicides and high-profile cases (Drizin & Leo, 2004; Gross et al., 2005).

Once interrogation commences, the primary cause of police-induced false confession is psychologically coercive police methods that sequentially manipulate a suspect's perception of the situation, expectations for the future, and motivation to shift from denial to admission (Ofshe & Leo, 1997). By *psychological coercion,* we mean either one of two things: police use of interrogation techniques that are believed to overbear a suspect's will (e.g., promises and threats) and are thus regarded as inherently coercive in psychology and law, or police use of interrogation techniques that cumulatively cause a suspect to perceive that he or she has no choice but to comply with the interrogators' demands. Usually, these amount to the same thing. Psychologically coercive interrogation techniques include some examples of the old "third degree," such as deprivations (e.g., of food, sleep, water, or access to bathroom facilities), incommunicado inter-rogation, and inducing extreme exhaustion and fatigue. In the modern era, how-ever, these techniques are rare. Instead, when today's police interrogators use psychologically coercive techniques, it usually consists of (implicit or express) promises of leniency and threats of harsher treatment. As Ofshe and Leo (1997) wrote, "the modern equivalent to the rubber hose is the indirect threat commu-nicated through pragmatic implication" (p. 1115). Threats and promises can take a variety of forms, and they are usually repeated, developed, and elabo-rated over the course of the interrogation. The vast majority of documented false confessions in the post-Miranda era either have been directly caused by or have involved promises or threats (Drizin & Leo, 2004; Leo & Ofshe, 1998).

The second form of psychological coercion—causing a suspect to perceive that he or she has no choice but to comply with the wishes of the interrogator—is not specific to any one technique but may be the cumulative result of the interroga-tion methods as a whole. The psychological structure and logic of contemporary interrogation can easily produce this effect. The custodial environment and phys-ical confinement are intended to isolate and disempower suspects. Interrogation is designed to be stressful and unpleasant, and it becomes more stressful and unpleasant the more intensely it proceeds and the longer it lasts. Interrogation techniques are meant to cause suspects to perceive that their guilt has been estab-lished beyond any conceivable doubt, that no one will believe their claims of inno-cence, and that by continuing to deny the detectives' accusations they will only make the situation (and the ultimate outcome of the case against them) much worse. Suspects may perceive that they have no choice but to comply with the detectives' wishes because they are fatigued or simply see no other way to escape an intolerably stressful experience. Some suspects, like Jeffrey Deskovic, come to believe that the only way they will be able to leave is if they do what the detectives say. Others comply because they are led to believe that it is the only way to avoid a feared outcome (e.g., same-sex rape in prison). When suspects perceive there is no choice but to comply, their resulting compliance and confession are, by defini-tion, involuntary and the product of coercion (Ofshe & Leo, 1997).

To better understand how the techniques and psychological dynamics of interrogation can become cumulatively coercive, it is helpful to view interroga-tion as a sequential two-step process of psychological pressure and persuasion (Davis & O'Donohue, 2004; Drizin & Leo, 2004; Ofshe & Leo, 1997; for a review, see Gudjonsson, 2003). In the first step of interrogation the investigator usually relies on several well-known interrogation techniques and strategies to persuade the suspect that he or she is caught and that he or she is powerless to change his or her situation. The investigator is likely to accuse the suspect of having com-mitted the crime, cut off the suspect's denials, roll past the suspect's objections, and interrupt or ignore the suspect's assertions of innocence. If the suspect offers an alibi, the interrogator will attack it as inconsistent, contradicted by all of the case evidence, implausible or simply impossible. The most effective technique used to persuade a suspect that his or her situation is hopeless is to confront him or her with seemingly objective and incontrovertible evidence of his or her guilt, whether or not any actually exists (Moston, Stephenson, & Williamson, 1992; Ofshe & Leo, 1997). American police often confront suspects with fabricated evidence, such as nonexistent eyewitnesses, false fingerprints, make-believe videotapes, fake polygraph results, and so on. The purpose of this technique is to convince the suspect that the state's case against him or her is so compelling and immutable that his or her guilt can be established beyond any possible doubt and that arrest, prosecution, and conviction are therefore inevitable. These techniques—accusation, cutting off of denials, attacking alibis, confronting the suspect with real or nonexistent evidence—are often repeated as the pressures of interrogation escalate. They are designed to reduce a suspect's subjective self-confidence that he or she will survive the interrogation without being arrested and thus that there is no way out of his or her predicament (Davis & O'Donohue, 2004; Drizin & Leo, 2004; Ofshe & Leo, 1997).

The second step of interrogation is designed to persuade the suspect that the benefits of compliance and confession outweigh the costs of resistance and denial and thus that the only way to improve the otherwise hopeless situation is by admitting to some version of the offense. In this part of the interrogation process, the investigator presents the suspect with inducements that communicate that he or she will receive some personal, moral, communal, procedural, materials, legal, or other benefit if he or she confesses but that he or she will experience some corresponding personal, moral, communal, procedural, material, legal, and other costs if he or she fails to confess. Ofshe and Leo (1997) suggested that these inducements can be arrayed along a continuum ranging from appeals to morality (at the low end), to appeals to how the criminal justice system is likely to react to the suspect's denial versus confession (in the mid-range), and to implicit or explicit promises or suggestions of leniency and threats of harsher treatment or punishment (at the high end). In most false confession cases, interrogators communicate—either indirectly through pragmatic implication (*minimization;* see Kassin & McNall, 1991) or more explicitly—that the suspect will receive more lenient treatment if he or she confesses but harsher punishment if he or she does not (Drizin & Leo, 2004). In some false confession cases, the coercion involves blatant threats of punishment or harm (e.g., threats of longer prison sentences, the death penalty, or harm to family members) or explicit promises of leniency or immunity (e.g., offers of outright release from custody, counseling instead of prison, or reduced charges). The innocent suspect typically confesses only after the techniques have persuaded him or her that—in light of what he or she perceives to be his or her limited options and the consequences of choosing denial over silence—confession is the most rational course of action. The psychological logic of modern interrogation is that it makes the irrational (admitting to a crime that will likely lead to punishment) appear rational (if the suspect believes that he or she is inextricably caught or perceives his or her situation as hopeless and that cooperating with authorities is the only viable course of action; Drizin & Leo, 2004; Ofshe & Leo, 1997).

The Contamination Error

A confession is more than an "I did it" statement. It also consists of a subsequent narrative that contextualizes and attempts to explain the "I did it" statement. Though it has not received the scholarly attention it deserves, the postadmission narrative and the interrogation process through which it is constructed are central to properly understanding and evaluating confession evidence (Leo & Ofshe, 1998; for a discussion of the distinction between a confession and an admission, see chap. 2, this volume). Psychologically coercive police methods (and how they interact with an individual's personality) may explain how and why a suspect is moved, often painstakingly, from denial to admission. But it is the postadmission narrative that transforms the fledgling admission into a fully formed confession. The postadmission narrative is the story that gets wrapped around the admission and thus makes it appear, at least on its face, to be a compelling account of the suspect's guilt. The content and rhetorical force of a suspect's postadmission narrative explains, in part, why confessions are treated as such powerful evidence of guilt and sometimes lead to the arrest, prosecution, and conviction of the innocent (Leo, 2008).

Police detectives understand the importance of the postadmission phase of interrogation. They use it to influence, shape, and sometimes even script the suspect's narrative. The detective's goal is to elicit a persuasive account that successfully incriminates suspects and leads to their conviction. A persuasive postadmission narrative requires a convincing story line; it must tell, or provide the elements of, a story that will cohere and make sense to the audience evaluating it. Either implicitly or explicitly, a persuasive postadmission narrative must have a believable plotline. Especially important is an explanation of the suspect's motive or motives for committing the crime. Interrogators are adept at inventing, suggesting, or eliciting an account of the suspect's motivation; indeed, the *theme development* technique is simply a method of attributing a motive to the suspect—typically one that minimizes his or her culpability—that the suspect agrees to and then repeats back, even if it is completely inaccurate. To incriminate the suspect, it is more important that the story be believable than that it be reliable (Leo, 2008). To bolster the believability and persuasiveness of confessions, detectives will seek to make the confession seem credible and authentic. They will encourage the suspect to attribute the decision to confess as an act of conscience, to express remorse about committing the crime, and to provide vivid scene details that appear to corroborate the suspect's guilty knowledge and thus confirm his or her culpability. Interrogators will also try to make the admission appear to be voluntarily given, portraying the suspect as the agent of his or her own confession and themselves merely as its passive recipients.

The detective helps create the false confession by pressuring the suspect to accept a particular account and suggesting crime facts to him or her. The detective in effect contaminates the suspect's postadmission narrative. Unless he or she has learned the crime scene facts from community gossip or the media, an innocent person will not know either the mundane or the dramatic details of the crime (Leo & Ofshe, 1998). Thus, the innocent suspect's postadmission narrative will be replete with errors when responding to questions for which the answers cannot easily be guessed by chance. Unless, of course, the answers are implied, suggested, or explicitly provided to the suspect, which, in fact, does occur, whether advertently or inadvertently, in many false confession cases (Leo, Drizin, Neufeld, Hall, & Vatner, 2006; Leo & Ofshe, 1998).

The contamination of the suspect's postadmission narrative is thus the third mistake in the trilogy of police errors that cumulatively lead to the elicitation and construction of a persuasive false confession. In Jeffrey Deskovic's case, contamination is the only explanation for how the absolutely innocent Deskovic learned details of the crime that only the true perpetrator could have known. Either police interrogators fed him these unique nonpublic crime facts, which he incorporated into his postadmission narrative, or they carelessly released these facts to the public. As a subsequent investigation of what went wrong in the Deskovic case put it: "If, as the prosecution contended, Deskovic had information about Correa's death that was not widely known, flaws in the investigation in some measure must be to blame" (Snyder et al., 2007, p. 19).

Given the specificity of the facts in Deskovic's confession, however, police contamination is the more likely source. Because Deskovic's interrogations were not fully recorded, however, one can never know with certainty whether and to what extent police contaminated his confession and made it appear truthful (even though it was actually false) to the jury that convicted him and the appellate courts that upheld his conviction. One thing, however, is certain: This contamination would never have been exposed were it not for the advent of DNA technology and its application to biological evidence that had been preserved in his case.

From False Confession to Wrongful Conviction

The process through which a false confession results in a wrongful conviction is far more complicated and less well understood than the processes through which police elicit and construct false confessions, for it involves multiple actors—not just police and suspects, but prosecutors, defense attorneys, judges, and juries—and thus multiple (psychological, sociological, and institutional) causes and errors. For a wrongful conviction based on a false confession to occur,

1. the police must misclassify an innocent person as a guilty suspect;
2. the police must subject that individual to an interrogation that results in a false confession;
3. the prosecution must decide to file charges against the false confessor, usually despite the lack of any other evidence against him;
4. the prosecution must convince a judge that probable cause exists to believe the innocent defendant committed the crime or crimes of which he stands accused;
5. the prosecution's case against the false confessor must survive any pretrial motions by the defense for exclusion of the confession evidence; and
6. assuming that the defense does not initiate or accept a plea bargain, a jury must unanimously agree that the innocent defendant is guilty beyond any reasonable doubt.

And for the wrongfully convicted false confessor to remain incarcerated, appellate courts must reject his postconviction counsel's procedural challenges to the erroneous verdict.

With so many points in the criminal process at which the case against an innocent person may become derailed and with the need for so many criminal justice professionals to be wrong in so many of their judgments, the process that produces a wrongful conviction is anything but simple. Though we are accustomed in the age of DNA testing and exoneration to witnessing wrongfully convicted individuals walk out of prison on a regular basis, the production of a miscarriage of justice is still stunning. Wrongful convictions represent a complete failure, if not breakdown, in the procedural safeguards and discretionary decision making of the criminal justice system. There is no outcome that the system is, in theory, more structured to avoid. It can only occur if there are multiple and conjunctural errors by numerous criminal justice officials and triers of fact who, at every stage of the criminal process, fail to identify, understand, and reverse the errors that occurred in the earlier stages.

Although the many cognitive errors (in perception, reasoning, and decision making) and erroneous actions that lead to wrongful convictions are beyond the scope of this chapter, we focus here on two fundamental processes that help transform a false confession into a wrongful conviction. The first is the use of what Gudjonsson (2003) has called *misleading specialized knowledge* to create the appearance that a false confession is true. The second is the more well-known and related problems of tunnel vision and confirmation bias that lead criminal justice officials and jurors to ignore the possibility that the confession is false.

Misleading Specialized Knowledge

The use of misleading specialized knowledge occurs when police investigators feed the suspect unique, nonpublic crime facts—facts that are not likely guessed by chance—and then insist that these facts originated with the suspect (Gudjonsson, 2003; Leo, 2008). Awareness of the facts is sometimes referred to as *guilty* or *inside* knowledge. When included in the suspect's postadmission narrative, the facts are believed to reveal that he or she possesses information that only the true perpetrator would know, and therefore, he or she must be guilty. Unlike true guilty knowledge, however, misleading specialized knowledge is pernicious because it is used so effectively to convict an innocent person. When police interrogators feed nonpublic crime facts to a false confessor and then insist, often under oath in courtroom testimony, that these facts originated with him, they are, in effect, fabricating evidence against him (Garrett, 2005).

Misleading specialized knowledge is powerful evidence because it appears to corroborate the defendant's confession. In many documented wrongful convictions, some or all of the following pattern emerges: When the reliability of the defendant's confession is called into question, police rely on misleading specialized knowledge to persuade prosecutors that the confession must be true; prosecutors rely on misleading specialized knowledge to persuade judges and juries that the confession must be true; defense attorneys rely on misleading specialized knowledge to persuade their clients to accept plea bargains; judges and juries rely on misleading specialized knowledge to convict false confessors; and appellate courts rely on misleading specialized knowledge to uphold their convictions.

Whether intentional or not, police use of misleading specialized knowledge poses a serious problem for the American criminal justice system because its presence in an unrecorded false confession virtually guarantees that the innocent defendant will be wrongfully convicted. Whether it is due to inadvertent influence, strong institutional pressure to solve cases (especially high-profile ones), or some other combination of factors, misleading specialized knowledge is present in many of the documented wrongful convictions based on police-induced false confessions. For example, in a study of the 34 DNA exonerations that involved false confessions, misleading specialized knowledge was used to convict innocent defendants in 31 of the 32 cases that went to trial and for which trial transcripts could be obtained (Garrett, in press).

Because misleading specialized knowledge is incorporated into the defendant's confession and taken by police and prosecutors as corroboration of the defendant's guilt, it is difficult to overcome. Take, for example, the well-documented cases of Earl Washington (Edds, 2003; Leo, 2008), Christopher Ochoa (Leo, 2008; Ochoa, 2005), and Joseph Giarratano (Gudjonsson, 2003; Leo & Ofshe, 2001). Earl Washington was only able to prove his innocence because of the advent of DNA testing that was not available at the time of his trial (Edds, 2003). Christopher Ochoa was only able to prove his innocence because the actual perpetrator, Achim Marino, found religion in prison, voluntarily confessed to the crime repeatedly, led police to evidence that corroborated his guilt, and was matched to DNA evidence left at the crime scene (Ochoa, 2005). Joseph Giarratano, however, has not been so lucky: Unlike Washington or Ochoa, Giarratano has not been able to affirmatively prove his innocence and remains incarcerated on a life sentence to this day (Leo & Ofshe, 1998, 2001).

Tunnel Vision and Confirmation Bias

Police-induced false confession is one of the most prominent and enduring causes of wrongful conviction, but there are others: eyewitness misidentification, perjured jailhouse "snitch" testimony, forensic fraud and error, and police and prosecutorial suppression of exculpatory evidence, for example (Christianson, 2004; Leo, 2005). The big picture studies of contemporary wrongful convictions typically aggregate documented cases of miscarriages of justice and then count the number and percentage of wrongful convictions attributable to each of these legal causes of error (Bedau & Radelet, 1987; Gross et al., 2005; Scheck et al., 2000).

The phenomena of tunnel vision and confirmation bias, however, cut across (and are thus present in) all of these types of legal error. *Tunnel vision* is the psychological process that causes an individual to focus exclusively on one possibility or outcome to the exclusion of all others (see Tavris & Aronson, 2007). In the criminal justice system, it is the tendency to "focus on a suspect, select and filter the evidence that will 'build a case' for conviction, while ignoring or suppressing evidence that points away from guilt" (Martin, 2002, p. 848). *Confirmation bias* is the psychological tendency to seek out and interpret evidence in ways that support existing beliefs, perceptions, and expectations and to avoid or reject evidence that does not (Gilovich, 1991). Tunnel vision and confirmation bias are pervasive in the criminal justice system and present in virtually all wrongful convictions (Findley & Scott, 2006; see Ask & Granhag, 2005, 2007). From a behavioral perspective, rather than a legal one, they are thus the leading cause of wrongful convictions in the United States and elsewhere (Findley & Scott, 2006; Martin, 2002). A closer look at tunnel vision and confirmation bias in the criminal process sheds light both on why the police interrogation process produces false confessions and on why false confessions often lead to wrongful convictions.

Tunnel vision and confirmation bias are involved in each of the multiple pathways through which police elicit and shape false confessions. The first error in the sequence of steps that leads to a false confession, as we have seen, is the misclassification of an innocent person as guilty. Police typically make this error based on hunches, erroneous assumptions (Ofshe & Leo, 1997), crime-related schemas or profiles (Davis & Follette, 2002), or a flawed training in behavioral analysis that encourages them to mistakenly believe that they can become highly accurate human lie detectors (Kassin & Fong, 1999; Meissner & Kassin, 2002, 2004; chap. 6, this volume). Tunnel vision may have already led investigators at this point to prematurely, but confidently, conclude that the innocent suspect is guilty. Confirmation bias then leads investigators to seek out information and evidence that affirms this belief and to reject or discount information and evidence that does not. The processes of tunnel vision and confirmation bias at this stage are compounded by the institutional pressures on police from multiple sources (their supervisors, prosecutors, victims, the community, politicians, officials, the media, as well as their high caseloads), especially in serious and high-profile cases, to solve crimes quickly (Findley & Scott, 2006).

The subsequent interrogation process involves tunnel vision and confirmation bias by definition: Interrogators assume guilt, seek only statements and information that confirm their assumption, and not only ignore but also discourage statements (e.g., denials, verbalizations of innocence, explanations) that do not. As Findley and Scott (2006) pointed out, the very notion of an interrogation, therefore, expressly embraces the foundational problems with tunnel vision: a premature conclusion of guilt and an unwillingness to consider alternatives. In this context, however, the tunnel vision is not inadvertent, but deliberate; police are taught that this is the way to advance their investigation. Cognitive biases are openly encouraged. That tunnel vision and confirmation bias can and do lead to false confessions—as well as the process through which they do so—has been repeatedly documented in aggregated case studies (Drizin & Leo, 2004; Leo & Ofshe, 1998), experimental studies (Kassin & Fong, 1999; Kassin et al., 2003; Meissner & Kassin, 2002), and documentary studies (Ofshe & Leo, 1997) of police interrogation and false confession.

The problems of tunnel vision and confirmation bias can also taint the postadmission process of interrogation. Indeed, police interrogation is just as rife with tunnel vision and confirmation bias in the postadmission phase as it is in the preadmission phase. Detectives rarely stop to consider the possibility that they are interrogating an innocent person and that the admissions they are eliciting may be false. Joseph Buckley's remarkable assertion that "we don't interrogate innocent people" (Kassin & Gudjonsson, 2004, p. 36) captures the problem of confirmation bias and tunnel vision. Once interrogators obtain an admission, they treat it as confirmation of their belief in the suspect's guilt rather than as a hypothesis to be tested against case evidence. As a result, they usually continue to interrogate in a manipulative, suggestive, and leading manner and shape the confession to successfully build a case against the suspect.

The problems of tunnel vision and confirmation bias do not end with police investigators, though. Prosecutors, defense attorneys, judges, and jurors are also subject to tunnel vision and confirmation bias, especially once they learn that someone has written or signed a confession statement that contains a plausible narrative of how and why the crime occurred as well as detailed knowledge of the crime facts. Once a suspect has confessed, the formal presumption of innocence is quickly transformed into an informal presumption of guilt that biases the subsequent decisions of fact finders and overrides their analysis of exculpatory evidence (Leo & Ofshe, 1998). In many false confession cases, prosecutors appear to seek out only information that is consistent with their belief in the defendant's guilt, often ignoring, dismissing, or even suppressing contradictory or exculpatory evidence. If the defendant is exonerated, they then frequently refuse to acknowledge his or her innocence or admit that any mistakes were made, even in the most egregious cases. As commentators have noted, the tunnel vision and confirmation bias of prosecutors stem from many sources: the institutional and political culture of their offices (Medwed, 2004), role pressures and "conviction psychology" (Findley & Scott, 2006; Fisher, 1988), and the problems of receiving one-sided and incomplete evidence from police investigators and only feedback that is consistent with their assessments of guilt (Findley & Scott, 2006). Even defense attorneys sometimes succumb to tunnel vision and confirmation bias once they learn that their client has confessed, ruling out the possibility of innocence, and pressuring their clients to plead guilty, as occurred in Christopher Ochoa's case (Ochoa, 2005). Juries, too, allow the power of confession evidence to bias their judgments (Kassin & Sukel, 1997); in false confession cases, they tend to selectively ignore and discount evidence of innocence (Leo & Ofshe, 1998).

In short, even when they are false, confessions appear to be such powerful evidence of guilt that they almost automatically trigger tunnel vision and confirmation bias among the criminal justice officials and jurors who must evaluate confessions, blinding them to the possibility of error.

Conclusion

The consequences of false confessions are predictable: As our research has demonstrated, false confessors whose cases are not dismissed pretrial will be convicted (by plea bargain or jury trial) 78% to 85% of the time, even though they are completely innocent (Drizin & Leo, 2004; Leo & Ofshe, 1998). Unless criminal justice officials and policymakers try to better understand why this occurs and change the system that regularly produces these outcomes, the status quo will persist. Poorly trained but confident police investigators will continue to misclassify innocent persons as guilty suspects; they will continue to deceptively, manipulatively, or coercively interrogate innocent suspects on the basis of an unwavering (yet mistaken) presumption of guilt; and they will continue to construct persuasive, if false, narratives of innocent suspects' culpability that are laced with misleading specialized knowledge. District attorneys will continue to prosecute innocent false confessors, who judges and juries will continue to wrongfully convict and incarcerate. It therefore behooves criminal justice officials not only to acknowledge and better understand the role that false confessions play in creating and perpetuating miscarriages of justice but also to introduce meaningful policy reforms that will prevent false confessions from occurring and leading to the wrongful conviction and incarceration of the innocent.

The policy implications of this chapter are clear: Police investigators, interrogators, and managers need to better understand how they may contribute to and perpetuate each of the three errors described in this chapter, and they need to learn when to intervene in actual cases to prevent the errors from snowballing into detailed and facially persuasive (but false) confessions that will almost certainly lead to wrongful convictions for those defendants' cases that go to trial. Because the three errors are sequential, the first one— the misclassification error—is the most important to prevent. To this end, police investigators and interrogators need better training and education about the sources of their mistaken judgments about whether a suspect is likely guilty or innocent. Police investigators and interrogators need to learn that the scientific research literature does not support their belief in their superior human lie detection abilities; they cannot reliably intuit whether a suspect is innocent or guilty on the basis of their perceptions of his or her demeanor, body language, and nonverbal behavior; their judgments of deception are highly prone to error; and they cannot accurately assess their own lie detection skills (see chap. 6, this volume). They also need to learn that their pseudoscientific training in behavior analysis falsely increases their confidence in their lie detection skills, rendering them even more certain in their erroneous judgments and thus more likely to mistakenly subject an innocent suspect to an accusatory guilt-presumptive interrogation that may ultimately lead to a false confession (Kassin & Fong, 1999; Meissner & Kassin, 2002, 2004). Perhaps most important, police need to be trained that no one should ever be interrogated unless there is a reasonable evidentiary basis for believing in his or her guilt. Speculative assumptions about a suspect's demeanor, gut hunches, and intuitive profiles are not sufficient as a basis for launching into a guilt-presumptive accusatory interrogation that endangers the innocent. Indeed, we would go further and join others in arguing that police should only be allowed to interrogate suspects for whom there exists probable cause of guilt (Covey, 2005; Davis & Leo, 2006; Leo, Costanzo & Shaked, 2009). To be effective, of course, a preinterrogation probable cause requirement must be formal, and there must be consequences for its violation. With better police training and knowledge of the scientific research literature and a probable cause requirement prior to interrogation, investigators should be able to substantially reduce misclassification errors.

But some misclassification errors will nevertheless continue to occur; the criminal justice system must therefore also do a better job of preventing coercion errors. Again, police need to receive better interrogation training. They need to be educated specifically about the empirical scientific research on the social psychology of police interrogation, how psychological interrogation techniques affect the perceptions and decision making of suspects, which techniques can be psychologically coercive and why, and how and why psychologically deceptive and coercive interrogation techniques such as promises and threats (whether delivered explicitly or implicitly, through pragmatic implication) can and sometimes do lead to false confessions from the innocent, especially from vulnerable suspects (Costanzo & Leo, 2007; Davis & O'Donohue, 2004; Kassin & Gudjonsson, 2004; Leo, 2008; Ofshe & Leo, 1997). Unless police interrogators learn more about how and why their interrogation techniques and behaviors sometimes cause innocent suspects to falsely say "I did it" or falsely agree to police-suggested scenarios that incriminate them, they will not be able to effectively prevent false confessions from innocent suspects. We believe trial judges could also benefit from the very same training that we are proposing for police, as they routinely fail to suppress false confessions that were the product of psychologically coercive police interrogation (Garrett, 2008, in press; Leo, 2008).

The third error—contamination—is perhaps the most dangerous of all because it is the least visible, and once a suspect's postadmission narrative has been contaminated by police scripting and feeding, the damage may be irreversible (Leo, 2008). People find detailed, vivid, and plausible confessions to be persuasive evidence of guilt, even when they turn out to be false (Garrett, in press; Kassin & Gudjonsson, 2004; Leo, 2008). Although investigators could benefit from better education and training, too, the only meaningful policy reform to counteract the problem of police contamination is mandatory electronic recording of interrogations in their entirety. Numerous scholars, including ourselves, have canvassed the many reasons why electronic recording of custodial interrogations is the most important reform to minimize police-induced false confessions and prevent them from leading to wrongful convictions (see Leo, 2008; chap. 8, this volume). We merely wish to point out here that electronic recording is the only way to create an objective, reviewable, and comprehensive record that will allow all outside observers—police supervisors, prosecutors, defense attorney, judges, juries, and others—to identify pre- and postadmission influence and contamination. If the entire interrogation is audio or video recorded, then it may be possible to trace, step by step, how and when the interrogator implied or suggested the correct answers for the suspect to incorporate into his postadmission narrative. If, however, the entire interrogation is not recorded—and the vast majority of documented false confession cases are not—then there may be no objective way to prove the interrogator contaminated the suspect's postadmission narrative (see Introduction and chap. 8, this volume). As Garrett (in press) has shown in cases involving DNA exonerations, virtually all false confessions leading to wrongful conviction have been the product of police contamination and feeding of unique, nonpublic crime facts that were later falsely attributed to the confessor (see also Leo et al., 2006).

More generally, by making transparent what occurs in the interrogation room both before and after a suspect's admission, electronic recording would also go a long way to preventing and recognizing the coercion error, as well. Had Jeffrey Deskovic's many interrogation sessions all been electronically recorded from start to finish, the coercive and contaminating methods of interrogation that his interrogators used may well have been exposed—long before DNA exonerated him and led police to the true perpetrator—and prevented Deskovic's nightmarish, 16-year ordeal of wrongful conviction and incarceration.

References

Ask, K., & Granhag, P. A. (2005). Motivational sources of confirmation bias in criminal investigations: The need for cognitive closure. *Journal of Investigative Psychology & Offender Profiling, 2,* 43–63.

Ask, K., & Granhag, P. A. (2007). Motivational bias in criminal investigators' judgments of witness reliability. *Journal of Applied Social Psychology, 37,* 561–591.

Bandler, J. (2006a, September 20). DNA clears Peekskill, N.Y. man after serving 15 years in prison. *The Journal News,* p. A1.

Bandler, J. (2006b, November 2). Wrongly imprisoned, Deskovic is formally cleared in slaying. *The Journal News,* p. A1.

Bedau, H. A., & Radelet, M. L. (1987). Miscarriages of justice in potentially capital cases. *Stanford Law Review, 40,* 21–179.

Bond, C. F., & DePaulo, B. M. (2006). Accuracy of deception judgments. *Personality & Social Psychology Review, 10,* 214–234.

Borchard, E. M. (1932). *Convicting the innocent: Errors of criminal justice.* New Haven: Yale University Press.

Christianson, S. (2004). *Innocent: Inside wrongful conviction cases.* New York: New York University Press.

Cohen, S. (2003). *The wrong men: America's epidemic of wrongful death row convictions.* New York: Carroll & Graf.

Costanzo, M., & Leo, R. A. (2007). Research findings and expert testimony on police interrogations and confessions to crimes. In M. Costanzo, D. Krauss, & K. Pezdek (Eds.), *Expert psychological testimony for the courts* (pp. 69–98). Mahwah, NJ: Erlbaum.

Covey, R. (2005). "Interrogation Warrants." *Cardozo Law Review, 26,* 1867–1946.

Davis, D., & Follette, W. (2002). Rethinking probative value of evidence: Base rates, intuitive profiling and the postdiction of behavior. *Law & Human Behavior, 26,* 133–158.

Davis, D., & O'Donohue, W. T. (2004). The road to perdition: "Extreme influence" tactics in the interrogation room. In W. T. O'Donohue & E. Levensky (Eds.), *Handbook of forensic psychology* (pp. 897–996). New York: Elsevier Academic Press.

Davis, D., & Leo, R. A. (2006). Strategies for preventing false confessions and their consequences. In M. Kebbell & G. Davies (Eds.), *Practical psychology for forensic investigations and prosecutions* (pp. 121–149). New York: Wiley.

DePaulo, B., Lindsay, J, Malone, B., Muhlenbruck, L., Charlton, K., & Cooper, H. (2003). Cues to deception. *Psychological Bulletin, 129,* 74–112.

Doyle, J. (2005). *True witness: Cops, courts, science, and the battle against misidentification.* New York: Palgrave Macmillan.

Drizin, S., & Leo, R. A. (2004). The problem of false confessions in the post-DNA world. *North Carolina Law Review, 82,* 891–1007.

Edds, M. (2003). *An expendable man: The near-execution of Earl Washington, Jr.* New York: New York University Press.

Ekman, P., & O'Sullivan, M. (1991). Who can catch a liar? *American Psychologist, 46,* 913–920.

Findley, K., & Scott, M. (2006). The multiple dimensions of tunnel vision in criminal cases. *Wisconsin Law Review, 2006,* 291–398.

Fisher, S. (1988). In search of the virtuous prosecutor: A conceptual framework. *American Journal of Criminal Law, 15,* 197–261.

Garrett, B. (2005). Innocence, harmless error, and federal wrongful conviction law. *Wisconsin Law Review, 2005,* 35–114.

Garrett, B. (2008). Judging innocence. *Columbia Law Review, 108,* 55–142.

Garrett, B. (in press). The substance of false confessions. *Stanford Law Review.*

Gilovich, T. (1991). *How we know what isn't so: The fallibility of human reason in everyday life.* New York: The Free Press.

Gross, S. (1996). The risks of death: Why erroneous convictions are common in capital cases. *Buffalo Law Review, 44,* 469–500.

Gross, S., Jacoby, K., Matheson, D., Montgomery, N., & Patel, S. (2005). Exonerations in the United States, 1989 through 2003. *Journal of Criminal Law & Criminology, 95,* 523–553.

Gudjonsson, G. H. (2003). *The psychology of interrogations and confessions: A handbook.* New York: Wiley.

Hartwig, M., Granhag, P. A., Stromwall, L., & Vrig, A. (2004). Police officers' lie detection accuracy: Interrogating freely vs. observing video. *Police Quarterly, 7,* 429–456.

Inbau, F., Reid, J., Buckley, J., & Jayne, B. (2001). *Criminal interrogation and confessions* (4th ed.). Gaithersburg, MD: Aspen.

Kassin, S. M., & Fong, C. T. (1999). "I'm innocent!" Effects of training on judgments of truth and deception in the interrogation room. *Law & Human Behavior, 23,* 499–516.

Kassin, S. M., Goldstein, C. J., & Savitsky, K. (2003). Behavioral confirmation in the interrogation room: On the dangers of presuming guilt. *Law & Human Behavior, 27,* 187–203.

Kassin, S. M., & Gudjonsson, G. (2004). The psychology of confessions: A review of the literature and issues. *Psychological Science in the Public Interest, 5,* 35–67.

Kassin, S. M., & McNall, K. (1991). Police interrogations and confessions: Communicating promises and threats by pragmatic implication. *Law and Human Behavior, 15,* 233–251.

Kassin, S. M., & Sukel, H. (1997). Coerced confessions and the jury. *Law & Human Behavior, 21,* 27–46.

Leo, R. A. (1996). Miranda's revenge: Police interrogation as a confidence game. *Law & Society Review, 30,* 259–288.

Leo, R. A. (2005). Re-thinking the study of miscarriages of justice: Developing a criminology of wrongful conviction. *Journal of Contemporary Criminal Justice, 21,* 201–223.

Leo, R. A. (2008). *Police interrogation and American justice.* Cambridge, MA: Harvard University Press.

Leo, R. A., Costanzo, M., & Shaked, N. (2009). Psychological and cultural aspects of interrogations and false confessions: Using research to inform legal decision-making. In J. Lieberman & D. Krauss (Eds.), *Psychology in the courtroom* (pp. 25–55). London: Ashgate.

Leo, R. A., Drizin, S., Neufeld, P., Hall, B., & Vatner, A. (2006). Bringing reliability back in: False confessions and legal safeguards in the twenty-first century. *Wisconsin Law Review, 2,* 479–539.

Leo, R. A., & Ofshe, R. (1998). The consequences of false confessions: Deprivations of liberty and miscarriages of justice in the age of psychological interrogation. *Journal of Criminal Law & Criminology, 88,* 429–496.

Leo, R. A., & Ofshe, R. (2001). The truth about false confessions and advocacy scholarship. *The Criminal Law Bulletin, 37,* 293–370.

Lofquist, W., & Harmon, T (2008). Fatal errors: Compelling claims of executions of the innocent in the post-*Furman* era. In C. R. Huff & M. Killias (Eds.), *Wrongful conviction: International perspectives on miscarriages of justice* (pp. 93–115). Philadelphia: Temple University Press.

Lopez, A. (2002). $10 and a denim jacket? A model statute for compensating the wrongly convicted. *University of Georgia Law Review, 36,* 665–722.

Lykken, D. (1998). *Tremor in the blood: Uses and abuses of the lie detector.* New York: Plenum.

Martin, D. (2002). Lessons about justice from the laboratory of wrongful convictions: Tunnel vision, the construction of guilt, and informer evidence. *UMKC Law Review, 70,* 847–864.

Medwed, D. (2004). The zeal deal: Prosecutorial resistance to post-conviction claims of innocence. *Boston University Law Review, 84,* 125–183.

Meissner, C. A., & Kassin, S. M. (2002). "He's guilty!": Investigator bias in judgments of truth and deception. *Law & Human Behavior, 26,* 469–480.

Meissner, C. A., & Kassin, S. M. (2004). "You're guilty, so just confess!": Cognitive and confirmational biases in the interrogation room. In G. D. Lassiter (Ed.), *Interrogations, confessions, and entrapment* (pp. 85–106). New York: Kluwer Academic.

Moston, S., Stephenson, G. M., & Williamson, T. (1992). The effects of case characteristics on suspect behaviour during police questioning. *British Journal of Criminology, 32,* 23–39.

Ochoa, C. (2005). My life is a broken puzzle. In L. Vollen & D. Eggers (Eds.), *Surviving justice: America's wrongfully convicted and exonerated* (pp. 13–46). San Francisco: McSweeney's Books.

Ofshe, R., & Leo, R. A. (1997). The decision to confess falsely: Rational choice and irrational action. *Denver University Law Review, 74,* 979–1122.

People of the State of New York v. Jeffrey Deskovic, 201 A.D. 2d 589 (1994).

Possley, M., Ferkenhoof, E., & Mills, S. (2002, February 8). Police arrest 2 in Roscetti case; Officials say tip led them to pair, who confessed. *Chicago Tribune,* p. 1.

Prejean, H. (2005). *The death of innocents: An eyewitness account of wrongful executions.* New York: Random House.

Risinger, M., & Loop, J. (2002). Three card monte, Monty Hall, modus operandi and offender profiling: Some lessons of modern cognitive science for the law of evidence. *Cardozo Law Review, 24,* 193–285.

Santos, F. (2007a, March 15). Inmate enters guilty plea in '89 killing. *New York Times,* p. B5.

Santos, F. (2007b, July 3). Playing down DNA evidence contributed to wrongful conviction, review finds. *New York Times,* p. B5.

Santos, F. (2007c, November 25). Vindicated by DNA but a lost man on the outside. *New York Times,* p. A11.

Scheck, B., Neufeld, P., & Dwyer, J. (2000). *Actual innocence: Five days to execution and other dispatches from the wrongly convicted.* New York: Random House.

Simon, D. (1991). *Homicide: A year on the killing streets.* Boston: Houghton Mifflin.

Skolnick, J. H. (1966). *Justice without trial: Law enforcement in a democratic society.* New York: Wiley.

Snyder, L., McQuillan, P., Murphy, W. L., & Joselson, R. (2007). *Report on the conviction of Jeffrey Deskovic.* Retrieved April 3, 2009, from http://www.westchesterda.net/Deskovic%20Comm%20Rpt%20Page.htm

Tavris, C., & Aronson, E. (2007). *Mistakes were made (but not by me): Why we justify foolish beliefs, bad decisions and hurtful acts.* New York: Harcourt.

Vrij, A. (2000). *Detecting lies and deceit: The psychology of lying and the implications for professional practice.* London: Wiley.

Vrij, A. (2004). Why professionals fail to catch liars and how they can improve. *Legal & Criminological Psychology, 9,* 159–181.

Vrij, A., Mann, S., & Fisher, R. P. (2006). An empirical test of the Behavioral Analysis Interview. *Law & Human Behavior, 30,* 329–345.

Wadler, J. (2000, March 29). Finding the criminal who fits the crime. *New York Times,* p. B2.

Warden, R. (2003). *The role of false confessions in Illinois wrongful murder convictions since 1970: Center on Wrongful Convictions research report.* Retrieved April 3, 2009, from http://www.law.northwestern.edu/depts/clinic/wrongful/FalseConfessions.htm

White, W. S. (2001). *Miranda's waning protections: Police interrogation practices after Dickerson.* Ann Arbor: University of Michigan Press.

Zimbardo, P. (1971). Coercion and compliance: The psychology of police confessions. In C. Perruci & M. Pilisuk (Eds.), *The triple revolution* (pp. 492–508). Boston: Little, Brown.

2

The Psychology of False Confessions: A Review of the Current Evidence

Gisli H. Gudjonsson

In the early 1980s, there was general skepticism among scientists and the legal profession that false confessions to serious crimes occurred and were worthy of study (Gudjonsson, 1992; Gudjonsson & MacKeith, 1982). This has now changed dramatically because of the large number of cases of proven false confessions to serious crimes in the United Kingdom and the United States since the 1980s. In the United Kingdom, Gisli Gudjonsson and James MacKeith identified and researched a number of cases of proven false confession (Gudjonsson, 2003b; Gudjonsson & MacKeith, 1990, 1994). In addition, a detailed description of their involvement in cases of miscarriage of justice in the United Kingdom and the impact of this work on legal judgments has been published (Elks, 2008; Gudjonsson, 2003b, 2006).

While Gudjonsson and MacKeith were studying false confessions in the United Kingdom, developing assessment tools for the psychological and psychiatric evaluation of disputed cases, and educating the legal profession and colleagues about the existence of the phenomenon (Gudjonsson, 2003a, 2003b), Saul Kassin and his colleagues were beginning to study false confessions in the United States. Particularly important was the development of a conceptualization of false confessions into three distinct psychological types—voluntary, coerced compliant, and coerced internalized (Kassin & Wrightsman, 1985; Wrightsman & Kassin, 1993). The impact was to draw attention to false confessions as a real and important phenomenon and to provide a framework for understanding and researching the psychological processes involved. Other American researchers, including Richard Ofshe and Richard Leo, began their important work on studying police-coerced false confessions and published extensively in the area (e.g., Leo, 2008; Leo & Ofshe, 1998; Ofshe, 1989, 1992; Ofshe & Leo, 1997a, 1997b). More recently, Drizin and Leo (2004) published a detailed account of 125 cases of proven false confession cases in the United States between 1971 and 2002, which is the largest sample ever studied (for a discussion of the errors contributing to such false confessions, see chap. 1, this volume). DeClue (2005) produced a manual for assessing disputed cases of false confessions, which is aimed at practitioners in the United States (see also chap. 11, this volume). By the middle of this decade, a seminal publication highlighting the breath of research on the topic of interrogations and confessions appeared (Lassiter, 2004). In an introductory chapter to this edited volume, Lassiter and Ratcliff (2004) argued that exposing subtle coercive influences in the criminal justice system should be a top priority of legal psychology in the 21st century.

In the 1980s, it was very difficult to ascertain factual innocence in most cases of disputed confessions. Typically, protestations of innocence were ignored by police, prosecutors, judges, and jurors. Suspects were assumed not susceptible to making false confessions to serious crimes, and often their only defense was psychological or psychiatric evidence (Gudjonsson, 1992). In the early 1990s, that predicament was to change dramatically in two fundamental respects. First, the flawed forensic evidence in the cases of the Birmingham Six and the Maguires (both in the United Kingdom) highlighted the fallibility of forensic evidence in police investigations (Walker & Stockdale, 1999). Second, and undoubtedly most important, innovative developments in DNA testing influenced investigations (Wambaugh, 1989) and led to numerous exonerations of people wrongly convicted; several of these cases involved false confessions (Scheck, Neufeld & Dwyer, 2000). According to the Innocence Project's Web site (as of April, 2009), there have been over 235 DNA exonerations in the United States. Almost all of these cases involved sexual assault or murder, which suggests that these cases are a selected sample and not representative of the majority of criminal cases going before the courts. Seventeen people had been sentenced to death before DNA evidence proved their innocence and resulted in their release.

On March 18, 2009, the Lord Chief Justice of England and Wales quashed the conviction of an innocent man, Robert Graham Hodgson, who had served 27 years in prison. The man had given a number of voluntary false confessions to a 1979 murder, which led to his conviction in 1982. DNA evidence exonerated the man, who had given important postconviction details of the murder to police, according to the prosecution evidence presented at trial. This case, like so many others (Garrett, in press; Gudjonsson, 2003b), demonstrates how misleading and dangerous it is to rely on apparent special knowledge to crime details presented by the prosecution at trial.

The high-profile cases involving DNA exonerations are unlikely to give a true picture of the frequency of false confessions within criminal justice systems in the United States and elsewhere. However, crucial developments in DNA have proved the presence of false confessions in many cases of miscarriage of justice, which is undoubtedly the single most effective way of influencing changes within the legal establishment and police practice.

The reasons why false confessions occur are multifaceted (i.e., they are usually due to a combination of factors rather than one single factor acting in isolation). They are the outcome of a dynamic and interactive social process. Gudjonsson (2003a) presented an interactive model of this process, which involves contextual factors (e.g., the nature and seriousness of the crime investigated, the strength of the police evidence, pressure on the police to solve the crime), custodial factors (i.e., the length and nature of the detention and interrogation), vulnerability factors (e.g., young age, mental illness or retardation, psychopathology, suggestibility, compliance), and support or protective factors (e.g., the presence of a lawyer or an independent person for vulnerable suspects—known in the United Kingdom as an *appropriate adult*—at the police station; see Medford, Gudjonsson, & Pearse, 2003). The focus of this chapter is principally false confessions and psychological vulnerabilities. For detailed reviews of police interrogation techniques within the English and American criminal justice systems, see Gudjonsson (2007) and Leo (2008; see also chaps. 1 and 5, this volume).

Confessions

Confessions are traditionally important in three different contexts: religion, psychotherapy, and criminal justice (Kassin & Gudjonsson, 2004). In this chapter, the focus is confessions within the criminal justice system. In its broadest sense, a *confession* is construed as "any statements which tend to incriminate a suspect or a defendant in a crime" (Drizin & Leo, 2004, p. 892), which on occasions include denials. Classifying a self-incriminating denial (e.g., denying having been to the scene of crime when the suspect's fingerprints are found there) as an admission is a problem and should be avoided (Gudjonsson, 2003b). Probably a better definition is to use *Black's Law Dictionary* to distinguish between a *confession* and an *admission*. It defines a *confession* as "a statement admitting or acknowledging all facts necessary for conviction of a crime" and an *admission* as "an acknowledgement of a fact or facts tending to prove guilt which falls short of an acknowledgement of all essential elements of the crime" (cited in Drizin & Leo, 2004, p. 892).

An admission, not amounting to the suspect accepting responsibility for the crime and giving a detailed narrative account of his or her actions, is not a proper confession. For example, a suspect may admit to having been in the vicinity of the crime or even claim to have witnessed it. Such admissions may be incriminating, but they should ideally be distinguished from confessions of culpability. Even the comment, "I did it," should be treated as an admission and not as a confession if there is no accompanying detailed explanation. Unfortunately, the distinction between admissions and confessions is difficult to distinguish in research papers because definitions vary across studies, and typically no distinction is made between these two terms.

Leo and Ofshe (1998) emphasized the importance of the *postadmission narrative* in validating the uttered words "I did it" in cases of disputed confessions. (Please note that in some cases, this type of special knowledge can be very misleading and result in a miscarriage of justice, because details were known to police and communicated either wittingly or unwittingly to suspects and in court were attributed to suspects as a way of strengthening the prosecution's case; see Garrett, in press; Gudjonsson, 2003b.)

According to Gudjonsson (2003b) and Kassin and Gudjonsson (2004), most interrogation-elicited statements fall into four groups: true confessions, false confessions, true denials, and false denials (though some are difficult to categorize as they may be partially true or partially false). Statements that consist only of "no comment" replies to questions cannot be classified into any of these four groups because such a suspect gives no account on which to base such a classification. This four-group classification is particularly useful when researching the psychological factors associated with each group (Gudjonsson, Sigurdsson, Bragason, Einarsson, & Valdimarsdottir, 2004; Gudjonsson, Sigurdsson, & Einarsson, 2004).

The problem with any research into confessions and denials is that the base rate of guilt (i.e., the proportion of those interrogated who are genuinely guilty of the offense of which they are suspected) is unknown. The base rate of guilt, using the above classification system, can be obtained for research purposes by combining the categories true confessions and false denials and dividing the number into the total number of interrogations (Gudjonsson, Sigurdsson, Asgeirsdottir, & Sigfusdottir, 2006), but, again, this base rate is obtained in a research setting. In real-life criminal cases, the base rate of guilt or innocence is rarely known and it is likely to fluctuate according to the nature of the case being investigated (Gudjonsson, 2003b). For example, in serious cases such as murder, or in terrorist cases, many innocent people may be arrested and interviewed as potential suspects, and this increases the risk of false confession.

The higher the base rate of guilt among those interrogated, the lower the risk of a false confession occurring. If the police interrogate only genuinely guilty suspects then there would be no false confessions! Indeed, one coauthor of an influential interrogation manual claimed at an international conference in 2004 that his or her technique did not result in false confessions, because "we don't interrogate innocent people" (Kassin & Gudjonsson, 2004, p. 36). The implication of this comment is that the interrogator is able, prior to interrogation, to distinguish with 100% accuracy between guilty and innocent suspects and only interrogate the guilty ones. The empirical evidence does not support such an unrealistic claim (Meissner & Kassin, 2002, 2004). In practice, the police are likely to interrogate many innocent suspects, and one will never know the true base rate of guilt, which is likely to be influenced by a number of factors, including the varied police practice in different jurisdictions and countries. If the police target the wrong suspects for interrogation, then the false confession rate is likely to rise (Steingrimsdottir, Hreinsdottir, Gudjonsson, Sigurdsson, & Nielsen, 2007).

Proportion of Young Persons Interrogated

Self-report questionnaires have shown that many crimes peak in the age group 15 to 18 years (Blackburn, 1993). It would therefore be expected that many young persons are arrested and interrogated by police. Table 2.1 gives the number of people in seven studies who report having been interviewed by police as suspects. Studies 1 through 4 involved students in higher education, whereas the last two studies (Gudjonsson, Sigurdsson, & Sigfusdottir, in press; Gudjonsson, Sigurdsson, & Sigfusdottir, 2009) involved students in the final years of compulsory education (i.e., a younger sample). Studies 1 through 5 were all conducted in Iceland. Studies 3 and 4 were the largest and involved national surveys among all secondary schools in Iceland and included 10,472 and 10,363 participants, respectively. These two samples are similar to that in Gudjonsson, Sigurdsson, Bragason, et al.'s (2004) study, but the lower frequency of interrogation (i.e., 19% and 20% vs. 25%) may be due, in part, to the fact that the two large national studies asked only for interrogations by police at a police station about a suspected offense, whereas Gudjonsson, Sigurdsson, Bragason, et al.'s (2004) and Gudjonsson, Sigurdsson, and Einarsson's (2004) studies were not restricted to interrogation at a police station (i.e., suspects may have been interviewed at a

Table 2.1. Base Rate of Guilt and False Confessions in Community Samples

Sample	N	Mean age (years)	Interrogated (%)	Base rate of guilt (%)	False confession of those interrogated (%)
Icelandic college students[a]	1,080	18	25	67	3.7
Icelandic university students[b]	666	24	25	66	1.2
Icelandic college students[c]	10,472	18	19	67	7.3
Icelandic college students[d]	10,363	18	20	—	8.8
Icelandic students[e]	7,149	15.5	11	65	11.3
European students[f]	24,627	15.5	11.5	44	13.8
Danish college students[g]	715	19	10	51	6.8

[a]Study 1; Gudjonsson, Sigurdsson, Bragason, Einarsson, & Valdimarsdottir (2004).
[b]Study 2; Gudjonsson, Sigurdsson, & Einarsson (2004).
[c]Study 3; Gudjonsson, Sigurdsson, Asgeirsdottir, & Sigfusdottir (2006).
[d]Study 4; Gudjonsson, Sigurdsson, Sigfusdottir, & Asgeirsdottir (2008).
[e]Study 5; Gudjonsson, Sigurdsson, & Sigfusdottir (2009).
[f]Study 6; Steingrimsdottir, Hreinsdottir, Gudjonsson, Sigurdsson, & Nielsen (2007).
[g]Study 7; Gudjonsson, Sigurdsson, & Sigfusdottir (in press).

crime scene or in settings other than a police station). In Iceland, suspects, as in the United States (e.g., Redlich, Silverman, Chen, & Steiner, 2004), are sometimes interviewed outside police stations (e.g., in police cars or at the scene of crime).

Study 5 involved 7,149 Icelandic students in the last 2 years of their mandatory education. The age group is similar to that in Study 6. Out of the total sample, 11% reported having been interrogated by police at a police station and of those, 11.3% reported a history of having made a false confession. In Study 6, the data were obtained from five European countries (cities are in parentheses): Iceland (Reykjavik), Norway (Oslo), Finland (Helsinki), Latvia (Riga), Lithuania (Vilnius, Kaunas, and Klaipedia), Russia (St. Petersburg), and Bulgaria (Sofia). The total sample comprised 24,627 participants. In each country, the school grades 8, 9, and 10 were randomly selected from each city (the last 3 years of compulsory schooling). The average age was 15.5 years (90% of the sample were aged 15 or 16 years). Here, the proportion interrogated was 11.5%, ranging from 6.4% (Russia) to 14.6% (Lithuania), using the broader definition of an interrogation context.

In the Danish study (Study 7), the proportion of college students interrogated was the lowest of all the studies (10%), even though the broader definition of interrogation was used (i.e., "Have you ever been interrogated by the police about a suspected offense?"). This result suggests that it is more than twice as common for students in Iceland, compared with Danish students, to report that the police had interrogated them. Steingrimsdottir et al. (2007) pointed out that this difference did not appear to be due to the rate of self-reported offending but was likely to reflect differences in police practice in these two Nordic countries.

These findings, although limited by their self-report status, suggest that at least in Iceland, Denmark, and a number of countries in Europe (mainly Eastern Europe and the Nordic countries), a substantial proportion of young adults report having been interrogated by the police as a suspect. For students in higher education, between 19% and 25% report being interrogated, though this figure is substantially lower (10%) in Denmark. Among the younger age group (i.e., students in the final years of their mandatory education), only about 11% report being questioned by police as suspects. The findings from these studies also show that there is a substantial variation across countries and possibly differences between jurisdictions within countries.

Base Rate of Guilt

Table 2.1 shows the base rate of guilt in the seven studies. The highest base rate of guilt is found in the five Icelandic studies (65% to 67%) and the lowest in the European study (44%), followed by the Danish study (51%). However, there was substantial variability across the seven European countries with the highest base rate of guilt being in Iceland (71%), followed by Finland (64%) and Norway (59%), and the lowest in Russia (35%), followed by Latvia (36%), Lithuania (37%), and Bulgaria (47%). What is striking is the consistency in the base rate of guilt in the Icelandic samples from six different studies. These findings suggest that police in Iceland are consistently targeting guilty individuals for interrogation. This may be partly due to Iceland having a relatively small population (only about 313,000 inhabitants) and crime possibly being more easily detected here than in the other countries.

Frequency of False Confessions

The frequency with which false confessions occur during interrogation in different countries is unknown. However, it is documented from anecdotal case histories and research on miscarriages of justice that false confessions do sometimes occur (Drizin & Leo, 2004; Gudjonsson, 2003b). Kassin and Gudjonsson (2004) commented: "As no one knows the frequency of false confessions or has devised an adequate method of calculating precise incident rates, there is perennial debate over the numbers" (p. 48). The problem with high-profile cases is that they undoubtedly represent only the tip of the iceberg and focus primarily on the most serious cases, such a murder, rape, and terrorism (Gudjonsson, 2003b). There is evidence from self-report studies that false confessions are commonly reported in studies conducted among prisoners (Gudjonsson, Sigurdsson, Einarsson, Bragason, & Newton, 2008), young persons (Gudjonsson et al., in press), and those with mental disorders (Redlich, 2007). Experimental studies (e.g., Blair, 2007; Horselenberg et al., 2006) using the classic *Alt* key paradigm introduced by Kassin and Kiechel (1996) have shown that false confessions can be readily elicited by false accusations, psychological manipulation, and interrogative pressure (see chap. 7, this volume).

The seven studies listed in Table 2.1 show that the rate of false confessions in these studies among 55,072 young adults range from 1.2% (university students, who are older and have achieved a higher level of educational attainment than other college students listed in Table 2.1) to 13.8% (European students in the last years of their compulsory education). Two factors appear to explain the differences in the false confession rate between studies: age and educational attainment. The university students were the oldest and the most educated, whereas the European students were the youngest and the least educated. The college students in Studies 1, 3, 4 and 6 fall in between the university students (Study 2) and the students in compulsory education (Studies 5 and 7) in terms of the rate of false confession. Among the European group, many of those in the study would not go on to further education, and the false confession rate was significantly higher among those boys who intended not to go on to further education (Gudjonsson et al., in press). No significant difference was found for girls, which means that there may be gender differences in the relationship between further education and false confessions. Certainly pupils who do not complete their compulsory education at the age of 15 years and those who do not attend further education are likely to have more involvement with police than those who enter further education (Stattin & Klackenberg-Larsson, 1993). This increased police contact will augment their risk of making a false confession to the police. Age when interrogated may also be a significant risk factor in its own right (Redlich & Goodman, 2003; Redlich et al., 2004). In the first national Icelandic study (Gudjonsson et al., 2006), those aged 17 years and below were significantly more likely to report a false confession than were older students (the false confession rates were 9% and 5.7%, respectively).

In the first two community studies (Gudjonsson, Sigurdsson, Bragason, et al., 2004; Gudjonsson, Sigurdsson, & Einarsson, 2004), the most common reason given for making a false confession was to protect a peer. This is evident in about 60% of cases. In terms of personality, antisocial personality disorder traits and the extent and seriousness of self-reported offending were the best predictors of a history of false confession in these studies. In the two Icelandic national studies (Studies 3 and 4 in Table 2.1) and the European study (Study 6 in Table 2.1), participants were not asked about the reason for having made a false confession, but in both studies the highest rate of false confession was found among those who had been interrogated more than once.

Gudjonsson, Sigurdsson, Sigfusdottir, and Asgeirsdottir (2008; Study 4 in Table 2.1) asked about the type of offense to which individuals falsely confessed. These were most commonly property offenses, serious traffic violations, and violent offenses. The reasons given for the false confessions were mainly protecting a peer and wanting to escape from custodial and interrogative pressures. It is important that over one third (37.1%) of the participants who reported a history of false confession said they had been wrongfully convicted of the offense. This suggests that false confessions do have important consequences for the individuals concerned and the criminal justice system (see also Drizin & Leo, 2004).

Table 2.2 provides false confession rates reported among Icelandic prisoners (Gudjonsson & Sigurdsson, 1994; Gudjonsson, Sigurdsson, Einarsson, et al., 2008; Sigurdsson & Gudjonsson, 1996), suspects detained at Icelandic police stations (Sigurdsson, Gudjonsson, Einarsson, & Gudjonsson, 2006), Icelandic adolescents given a conditional discharge (Sigurdsson & Gudjonsson, 1996),

Table 2.2. Reported False Confessions Among Prisoners, Suspects Interviewed at Police Stations, and Persons With Serious Mental Illness

Sample	N	Mean age (years)	False confession of those interrogated (%)
Icelandic prisoners[a]	229	30	12
Icelandic prisoners[b]	509	31	12
Icelandic prisoners[c]	90	30	24
Suspects at Icelandic police stations[d]	47	31	19
Icelandic adolescent offenders given a conditional discharge[e]	108	18	0
Persons with mental illness[f]	1,249	37	22
English forensic adolescents[g]	60	15	23
U.S. forensic adolescents[h]	152	15	6

[a]Gudjonsson & Sigurdsson (1994).
[b]Sigurdsson & Gudjonsson (1996).
[c]Gudjonsson, Sigurdsson, Einarsson, Bragason, & Newton (2008).
[d]Sigurdsson, Gudjonsson, Einarsson, & Gudjonsson (2006).
[e]Sigurdsson & Gudjonsson (1996).
[f]Redlich (2007).
[g]Richardson (1991).
[h]Viljoen, Klaver, & Roesch (2005).

persons with serious mental illness in institutions in the United States (Redlich, 2007), an English forensic adolescent sample (Richardson, 1991), and a U.S. forensic adolescent sample (Viljoen, Klaver, & Roesch, 2005).

The first two prison studies, which were conducted in the early 1990s, show a 12% prevalence rate of false confession (i.e., having ever confessed falsely to the police in their lives). The more recent Icelandic prison study (Gudjonsson, Sigurdsson, Einarsson, et al., 2008) shows a confession rate of 24%, twice the rate recorded in the two previous studies. This suggests either that the false confession rate among Icelandic prisoners has increased during the past decade or that prisoners are now more aware of the phenomena of false confessions and therefore more likely to report it. There is evidence that the Icelandic prison population has changed markedly since the 1990s, with the less serious prisoners now being able to serve their sentences in the community, which could explain the higher false confession rate in the most recent prison study (Sigurdsson, 2007). In the early studies, false confessions were associated with more serious offending (Sigurdsson & Gudjonsson, 2001).

The small Icelandic police stations study (Sigurdsson et al., 2006) shows a 19% lifetime prevalence rate for false confession (the rate was 9% for current interrogation). The two main reasons given for providing a false confession in these Icelandic studies were avoiding custodial pressure (i.e., interrogation and confinement) and wanting to protect a peer. In terms of the relative importance of psychological, criminological, and substance use variables, antisocial personality disorder traits, elevated compliance (measured by the Gudjonsson Compliance Scale; GCS; Gudjonsson, 1997), substance abuse and involvement in offending were all significant discriminators. Interrogative suggestibility and confabulation were found to be elevated among the coerced-internalized type of false confessor (Sigurdsson & Gudjonsson, 2001).

Sigurdsson and Gudjonsson (1996) asked 108 young, first-time offenders who had been given a conditional discharge for minor criminal offenses if they had ever provided a false confession to the police. None of them reported having given a false confession to police, and this is the only study in Table 2.2 that documents a zero false confession rate. A 5-year follow-up study of these young offenders showed that 41% of them committed serious offenses during the follow-up period (Sigurdsson, Gudjonsson, & Peersen, 2001). The resisters were superior to the re-offenders in their intellectual and memory abilities and were significantly more prosocial and compliant in terms of temperament. In view of the high rate of re-offending, which is similar to the 48% conviction rate over 5 years for adult Icelandic prisoners (Peersen, Sigurdsson, Gudjonsson, & Greatarsson, 2004), it is surprising that none of these young offenders reported a history of false confession. Part of the reason may be the relatively late onset of their official offending (the average age at the time of the offending was 18 years). In addition, the data were collected in the early 1990s (Sigurdsson, 1998) when the phenomenon of false confession was not well known. The methodology used was the same as that used in the two Iceland prison samples in which false confession rates of 12% were reported (Studies 1 and 2 in Table 2.2).

The false confession rate of 22% reported by Redlich (2007) among patients with serious mental illness reveals a similar life-time prevalence rate to the recent Icelandic prison and police station studies (when adjusted for number of interrogations, the rate dropped to 4%). Richardson (1991) asked 60 juveniles living in a residential home in England if they had ever made a false confession to the police. Fourteen (23%) claimed to have made a false confession to the police. The main reason given for having made a false confession was to protect a peer. Viljoen et al. (2005) assessed 152 adolescent defendants who resided in a pretrial detention facility in the state of Washington. Out of those, 9 (6%) reported that they had at some time in their lives falsely confessed to police. The most common reason given for the false confession was that they did so to protect others (78%). It is interesting that in this study, defendants who reported a history of false confession did not differ from the nonfalse confessors in terms of demographic and criminological variables, the understanding of their legal rights, or cognitive abilities and psychopathology. The problem with this study is that the number of participants who had reported a false confession was very small ($n = 9$) and no statistical analyses could be carried out on the data to provide meaningful information on the differences between the two groups.

In addition to evidence of false confessions from anecdotal case histories and self-report studies, surveys among police investigators illustrate the existence of false confessions during interrogation. For example, respondents in a recent U.S. survey of 631 police investigators estimated from their own experience that 4.8% of innocent suspects make a false confession during interrogation (Kassin et al., 2007).

Models of False Confession

Why do people confess to crimes they have not committed? Gudjonsson (2003a) argued that this is typically due to a combination of factors that are associated with the circumstances and nature of the custodial confinement and interrogation, the suspect's psychological vulnerabilities, and the absence of support (e.g., a lawyer, appropriate adult). Most typically, however, it seems to be the inability of suspects to cope with the custodial and interrogative environment or protecting a peer (this seems to be the main reason among young persons admitting to minor crimes). As the case becomes more serious (e.g., murder, sexual offenses), greater pressure may be placed on the suspect in the interview, thereby increasing the risk that suspects will break down and give a false confession (Pearse & Gudjonsson, 1999). Individual differences in suggestibility and compliance are typically important in cases in which there is evidence of leading questions and custodial pressure.

There are a number of theories or models of false confession, which were developed on the basis of observations of anecdotal cases reported in the literature or a series of individual case studies (Gudjonsson, 2003b). Munsterberg (1908) was the first to provide a conceptual framework for understanding false confessions. He viewed false confessions as a normal reaction to unusual circumstances, such as the emotional shock of being arrested, detained, and interrogated. As noted earlier, Kassin and Wrightsman (1985) developed a more sophisticated model, which suggested three psychologically distinct types of false confession, referred to as *voluntary, coerced-compliant,* and *coerced-internalized* types. More recently, Ofshe and Leo (1997a, 1997b) have proposed a modified five-level model that distinguishes between coerced and non-coerced compliant and persuaded confessions. Their model applies to both true and false confessions. I proposed a refinement of the Kassin and Wrightsman model (Gudjonsson, 2003b). First, the term *coerced* should be substituted by the term *pressured* to overcome problems related to legal definitions and applications of the term *coercion.* Second, I recommend a bivariate classification system that distinguishes between the three types of false confessions (i.e., voluntary, compliant, and internalized) and categorizes the source of pressure (i.e., internal, custodial, and noncustodial).

Risk Factors

The evidence that some people are vulnerable to giving a false confession during questioning or confrontation (i.e., the role of individual differences) comes from four main sources: (a) anecdotal case histories (e.g., Drizin & Leo, 2004; Gudjonsson, 2003b, 2006; Leo & Ofshe, 1998); (b) self-report studies among prisoners and college student samples (see Gudjonsson, 2003b, for a review of this methodology); (c) laboratory paradigms (Kassin & Kiechel, 1996), which usefully complement the other two kinds of studies in understanding the psychology of false confessions; and (d) surveys among police investigators illustrating the existence of false confessions (Kassin et al., 2007; chap. 4, this volume).

Kassin and Gudjonsson (2004) suggested that the risk or vulnerability associated with false confessions can be separated into personal and situational factors. Personal risk factors are those associated with the individual character-istics of the suspect (e.g., low intelligence), personality (e.g., suggestibility and compliance), youth, and psychopathology. Young persons are clearly most vulnerable, but so are those who are of limited intelligence, are highly sug-gestible and compliant in their temperament, and have mental health problems (Gudjonsson, 2003b, 2006).

Redlich (2007) suggested that persons with serious mental illness are vul-nerable to giving false confessions to police, but more evidence is needed to demonstrate that they are more vulnerable than other persons who have contact with the police (e.g., prisoners). The lifetime rate of false confessions in Redlich's (2007) study is similar to that found among prison inmates in Iceland, and it may be that their false confessions have more to do with antisocial personality traits and substance use than mental illness (Sigurdsson & Gudjonsson, 2001).

However, some clinical groups may also be more susceptible than others to giving false confession during interrogation. For example, in a recent study among Icelandic prisoners, Gudjonsson, Sigurdsson, Einarsson, et al. (2008) found that participants reporting symptoms of attention-deficit/hyperactivity disorder (ADHD) in adulthood were significantly more likely than the other par-ticipants to claim that they had made a false confession to police at some time in their lives (41% vs. 18%, respectively). Childhood symptoms that have been out-grown did not discriminate between the two groups, which suggests that it is the current symptoms that are of primary importance. Gudjonsson, Young, and Bramham (2007) had previously found that people with a diagnosis of ADHD respond to questioning by giving a disproportionate number of "don't know" replies, rather than merely yielding to suggestions and interrogative pressure, which might lead the police to misconstrue their replies as being due to evasive-ness. ADHD symptoms are also associated with emotional liability and poor behavioral inhibition (Gudjonsson, Sigurdsson, Young, Newton, & Peersen, 2009), which may impair capacity to cope with police interrogation.

The findings from the large Icelandic national study (Gudjonsson et al., 2006) show that false confessions can form part of a criminal lifestyle, the delinquency of friends, poor self-esteem, and depression (Gudjonsson et al., 2006). However, the findings also suggest that multiple exposures to unpleasant or traumatic life events are associated with false confessions (Gudjonsson et al., 2007; Gudjonsson, Sigurdsson, Sigfusdottir, & Asgeirsdottir, 2008). These were largely associated with multiple victimization (e.g., being a victim of bullying, loss of a significant other to death, being a victim of violence) and substance abuse (i.e., having attended substance abuse treatment, having used LSD) experiences. These find-ings have been replicated in our large European study (Gudjonsson et al., in press). They suggest the importance of a history of victimization and substance abuse among some adolescents in relation to giving a false confession. However, the nature and relative importance of psychological vulnerabilities depends on the individual case and needs to be interpreted within the totality of the case.

Situational risk factors include contextual factors (e.g., seriousness of the offense, strength of the evidence), physical custody and isolation, the nature of the interrogation techniques used, the process of confrontation, and the social support system available during the custodial confinement and interrogation (Gudjonsson, 2003a). Sleep deprivation also increases psychological vulnerability to giving in to suggestions and interrogative pressure (Blagrove, 1996; Blagrove & Akehurst, 2000). There have been a number of experimental studies following the innovative study of Kassin and Kiechel (1996), which have demonstrated that the presentation of false evidence can lead some vulnerable people to make a false admission of guilt of crashing a computer, internalize responsibility for the act, and confabulate details (Blair, 2007; Forrest, Wadkins, & Larson, 2006; Forrest, Wadkins, & Miller, 2002; Horselenberg, Merckelbach, & Josephs, 2003; Horselenberg et al., 2006; Klaver, Lee, & Rose, 2008; Redlich & Goodman, 2003). These laboratory paradigms, although having little in common with real-life interrogations, demonstrate that false confessions can be readily elicited from many apparently normal individuals using subtle tactics. The relationship with personality traits such as suggestibility and compliance has been mixed in these studies, perhaps because of the nature of the samples studied (i.e., they are mainly undergraduate university students) and the low level of pressure in the paradigms used. Redlich and Goodman (2003) demonstrated the role of age and suggestibility as vulnerability factors. In one study, fantasy proneness was associated with false confessions (Horselenberg et al., 2006), whereas in another locus of control, anxiousness, and authoritarian personality traits were related to internalized false confessions (Forrest et al., 2006).

In a relatively large experiment, Blair (2007) used the classic Kassin and Kiechel (1996) experimental design to investigate the relationship between false confessions and three types of variables (interrogation tactics, perceptions, and compliance). A total of 196 participants were assigned to four different equal-sized experimental conditions (false evidence vs. no false evidence, minimization/maximization statements vs. no minimization/maximization statements) following Ofshe and Leo's (1997b) model of interrogation. Two types of perceptions were measured by specially developed scales: the unavoidability of consequences (i.e., that he or she was going to be held responsible for the computer crash) and the severity of consequences. Compliance was measured using the GCS (Gudjonsson, 1997). Out of all participants, 54 (27.6%) signed a false confession statement, but there was no significant effect across experimental conditions suggesting that the interrogation manipulation was ineffective in producing a higher rate of false confession. The unavoidability of consequences did significantly differentiate between the false confessors and nonfalse confessors, but the GCS was the single most powerful predictor of false confession and explained 25% of the variance. Blair (2007) pointed to methodological limitations in previous experimental studies in which the GCS failed to discriminate between false confessors and nonfalse confessors and emphasized the importance of individual differences identified by Gudjonsson (2003b).

Klaver et al. (2008), using the Kassin and Kiechel (1996) paradigm, studied with 219 undergraduate students the effects of personality (i.e., compliance, self-esteem, locus of control, and interrogative suggestibility), type of interrogation technique (i.e., minimization vs. maximization), and the extent of plausibility of the allegations on false confession. An increased likelihood of false confession was associated with a higher Shift score on the Gudjonsson Suggestibility Scale (Gudjonsson, 1997; for a discussion of this scale, see chap. 12, this volume), the use of minimization interrogation techniques, and high plausibility of the allegations. Some ethnic differences were found, in which Caucasians who signed a false confession were significantly more compliant than those who did not, whereas Asians, Shift, external locus of control, and low self-esteem were associated with the signing of a false confession. This suggests that different factors may be associated with the signing of a false confession for people from different ethnic backgrounds.

Conclusions

We have come a long way since the early 1980s, when the knowledge of false confessions, and its legal acceptance, was in its infancy. There has been a sufficiently large number of proven cases of false confession to serious crimes to alert the scientific community and the legal establishment to the genuine phenomenon of false confessions. This has been a major achievement. However, in the vast majority of cases of disputed confessions, there is no forensic evidence to prove or disprove the confession. True confessions are sometimes retracted when defendants realize that there is no other tangible evidence against them and do not want to face the consequences of their actions (Gudjonsson, 1994). There are many others who are genuinely trying to prove their factual innocence and who struggle for years to find the evidence required for their conviction to be overturned (Drizin & Leo, 2004; Elks, 2008; Gudjonsson, 2006). High-profile cases, which almost exclusively involve very serious crimes—such as murder, rape, and terrorist offenses— do not give a representative picture of false confessions. In serious cases, pressure in an interview is likely to peak (Pearse & Gudjonsson, 1999), and this is where difficulties in coping with the police and custodial pressure become a key issue (Gudjonsson, 2006). This is why the empirical measurement of suggestibility and compliance is important. However, we should keep in mind that custodial interrogation is a dynamic process that involves a number of interacting factors (e.g., the nature and seriousness of the crime, the strength and nature of the evidence, the suspect's perceptions of the evidence, the nature and extent of the custodial environment, pressure in interview, idiosyncratic psychological vulnerabilities, presence of support in the interview by a person who is independent of the police). Accordingly, false confessions typically result from a combination of factors rather than from one factor acting in isolation (Gudjonsson, 2003a). To develop a complete picture of the nature of false confessions and their prevalence, researchers need evidence from a variety of sources (i.e., detailed individual case studies; surveys among offenders, young persons, and the general public; police investigators; and experimental studies). Experimental research is particularly helpful in studying the conditions under which people make false confessions and allow the researcher to control for ground truth, but this kind of research has little ecological validity in terms of applying it to real-life individual cases.

In many anecdotal case studies, ground truth is difficult to ascertain (Ofshe & Leo, 1997a, 1997b). Similarly, in studies of false confessions among prisoners and community samples, the genuineness of the false confession is nearly impossible to corroborate. The prison and police station studies discussed in this chapter involved the researcher interviewing each participant in detail about the false confession and its circumstances. In the larger surveys (Gudjonsson et al., 2006, in press), this was not possible. In spite of the limitations of these self-reported false confession studies, there is some consistency indicating that the reporting of false confessions is not uncommon among prisoner samples and young persons in the community.

This review has a number of implications for criminal justice systems and policy. First, false confessions to serious crimes do happen more commonly than previously thought. Anecdotal cases and numerous DNA exonerations provide strong evidence for this. This needs to be acknowledged by the legal establishment, and appropriate steps should be taken to prevent future miscarriages of justice (e.g., the first step is to educate police officers, lawyers, judges, and mental health professionals about the phenomena and the risk of false confessions). It is important to realize that the problem with false confessions is not just a quantitative one; regardless of the rate, the fact that people are wrongfully convicted of serious crimes on the basis of false confessions suggests serious problems in the administration of justice.

Second, the blind faith of the legal establishment regarding apparent special knowledge in postadmission narratives needs to be urgently addressed. The prosecution and the courts need to be much more cautious in their acceptance of special knowledge confessions unless they involve information that was not in the possession of the police (i.e., discovery of new evidence, which can be independently corroborated).

Third, individual differences are important in the way suspects cope with the pressure of custody and interrogation. Psychological vulnerabilities (e.g., mental retardation, suggestible and compliant temperament) are important in many of the cases involving a false confession. In general, younger suspects are at the greatest risk of false confession because they are the age group most likely to be arrested by police, and once arrested and interrogated they cope less robustly during interrogation. However, psychological vulnerabilities should not be viewed in isolation of the other salient components of the investigative process (e.g., contextual, custodial, interrogative, situational, support factors). Psychological vulnerabilities have to be relevant and appropriately interpreted in the broader context of the case.

Finally, learning what happens behind the closed door of the interrogation room is essential for the administration of justice. The mandatory electronic recording of all interrogations of suspects in the United Kingdom has been a great success and should be a lesson to other countries, including the United States.

References

Blackburn, R. (1993). *The psychology of criminal conduct: Theory, research and practice.* Chichester, UK: Wiley.

Blagrove, M. (1996). Effects of length of sleep deprivation on interrogative suggestibility. *Journal of Experimental Psychology: Applied, 2,* 48–59.

Blagrove, M., & Akehurst, L. (2000). Effects of sleep loss on confidence-accuracy relationships for reasoning and eyewitness. *Journal of Experimental Psychology: Applied, 6,* 59–73.

Blair, J. P. (2007). The role of interrogation, perception, and individual differences in producing compliant false confessions. *Psychology, Crime & Law, 13,* 173–186.

DeClue, G. (2005). *Interrogations and disputed confessions: A manual for forensic psychological practice.* Sarasota, Florida: Professional Resource Press.

Drizin, S. A., & Leo, R. A. (2004). The problem of false confessions in the post-DNA world. *North Carolina Law Review, 82,* 891–1007.

Elks, L. (2008). *Righting miscarriages of justice? Ten years of the Criminal Review Commission.* London: Justice.

Forrest, K. D., Wadkins, T. A., & Larson, B. A. (2006). Suspect personality, police interrogations, and false confessions: Maybe it is not just the situation. *Personality & Individual Differences, 40,* 621–628.

Forrest, K. D., Wadkins, T. A., & Miller, R. L. (2002). The role of pre-existing stress on false confessions: An empirical study. *Journal of Credibility Assessment & Witness Psychology, 3,* 23–45.

Garrett, B. L. (in press). The substance of false confessions. *Stanford Law Review.*

Gudjonsson, G. H. (1992). *The psychology of interrogations, confessions and testimony.* Chichester, UK: Wiley.

Gudjonsson, G. H. (1994). Confessions made to the expert witness: Some professional issues. *Journal of Forensic Psychiatry, 5,* 237–247.

Gudjonsson, G. H. (1997). *The Gudjonsson Suggestibility Scales manual.* Hove, UK: Psychology Press.

Gudjonsson, G. H. (2003a). Psychology brings justice: The science of forensic psychology. *Criminal Behaviour & Mental Health, 13,* 159–167.

Gudjonsson, G. H. (2003b). *The psychology of interrogations and confessions: A handbook.* Chichester, UK: Wiley.

Gudjonsson, G. H. (2006). Disputed confessions and miscarriages of justice in Britain: Expert psychological and psychiatric evidence in court of appeal. *The Manitoba Law Journal, 31,* 489–521.

Gudjonsson, G. H. (2007). Investigative interviewing. In T. Newburn, T. Williamson, & A. Wright (Eds.), *Handbook of criminal investigation* (pp. 466–492). Devon: Willan.

Gudjonsson, G. H., & MacKeith, J. A. C. (1982). False confessions: Psychological effects of interrogation. In A. Trankell (Ed.), *Reconstructing the past: the role of psychologists in criminal trials* (pp. 253–269). Deventer, The Netherlands: Kluwer.

Gudjonsson, G. H., & MacKeith, J. A. C. (1990). A proven case of false confession: psychological aspects of the coerced-compliant type. *Medicine, Science & the Law, 30,* 329–335.

Gudjonsson, G. H., & MacKeith, J. A. C. (1994). Learning disability and the Police and Criminal Evidence Act 1984. Protection during investigative interviewing: A video-recorded false confession to double murder. *Journal of Forensic Psychiatry, 5,* 35–49.

Gudjonsson, G. H., & Sigurdsson, J. F. (1994). How frequently do false confessions occur? An empirical study among prison inmates. *Psychology, Crime, & Law, 1,* 21–26.

Gudjonsson, G. H., Sigurdsson, J. F., Asgeirsdottir, B. B., & Sigfusdottir, I. D. (2006). Custodial interrogation, false confession and individual differences. A national study among Icelandic youth. *Personality & Individual Differences, 41,* 49–59.

Gudjonsson, G. H., Sigurdsson, J. F., Asgeirsdottir, B. B., & Sigfusdottir, I. D. (2007). Custodial interrogation: What are the background factors associated with claimed false confessions? *Journal of Forensic Psychiatry & Psychology, 18,* 266–275.

Gudjonsson, G. H., Sigurdsson, J. F., Bragason, O. O., Einarsson, E., & Valdimarsdottir, E. B. (2004). Confessions and denials and the relationship with personality. *Legal & Criminological Psychology, 9,* 121–133.

Gudjonsson, G. H., Sigurdsson, J. F., & Einarsson, E. (2004). The role of personality in relation to confessions and denials. *Psychology, Crime, & Law, 10,* 125–135.

Gudjonsson, G. H., Sigurdsson, J. F., Einarsson, E., Bragason, O. O., & Newton, A. K. (2008). Interrogative suggestibility, compliance and false confessions among prisoners and their relationship with attention deficit hyperactivity disorder (ADHD) symptoms. *Psychological Medicine, 38,* 1037–1044.

Gudjonsson, G. H., Sigurdsson, J. F., & Sigfusdottir, I. D. (2009). *False confessions among 15 and 16 year olds in compulsory education and their relationship with adverse life events.* Manuscript submitted for publication.

Gudjonsson, G. H., Sigurdsson, J. F., & Sigfusdottir, I. D. (in press). Interrogations and false confessions among adolescents in seven countries in Europe. What background and psychological factors best discriminate between false confessors and non-false confessors? *Psychology, Crime, & Law.*

Gudjonsson, G. H., Sigurdsson, J. F., Sigfusdottir, I. D., & Asgeirsdottir, B. B (2008). False confessions and individual differences. The importance of victimization among youth. *Personality & Individual Differences, 45,* 801–805.

Gudjonsson, G. H., Sigurdsson, J. F., Young, S., Newton, A. K., & Peersen, M. (2009). Attention deficit hyperactivity disorder (ADHD). How do ADHD symptoms relate to personality among prisoners? *Personality & Individual Differences, 47,* 64–68.

Gudjonsson, G. H., Young, S. & Bramham, J. (2007). Interrogative suggestibility in adults diagnosed with attention-deficit disorder (ADHD). A potential vulnerability during police questioning. *Personality & Individual Differences, 43,* 737–745.

Horselenberg, R., Merckelbach, H. & Josephs, S. (2003). Individual differences and false confessions: A conceptual replication of Kassin and Kiechel (1996). *Psychology, Crime, & Law, 9,* 1–18.

Horselenberg, R., Merckelbach, H., Smeets, T., Franssens, D., Peters, G.-J. Y., & Zeles, G. (2006). False confessions in the lab: Do plausibility and consequences matter? *Psychology, Crime & Law, 12,* 61–75.

Kassin, S. M., & Gudjonsson, G. H. (2004). The psychology of confessions: A review of the literature and issues. *Psychological Science in the Public Interest, 5,* 33–67.

Kassin, S. M., & Kiechel, K. L. (1996). The social psychology of false confessions: Compliance, internalization, and confabulation. *Psychological Science, 7,* 125–128.

Kassin, S. M., Leo, R. A., Meissner, C. A., Richman, K. D., Colwell, L. H., Leach, A.-M., & La Fon, D. (2007). Police interviewing and interrogation: A self-report survey of police practices and beliefs. *Law & Human Behavior, 31,* 381–400.

Kassin, S. M., & Wrightsman, L. S. (1985). Confession evidence. In S. M. Kassin & L. S. Wrightsman (Eds.), *The psychology of evidence and trial procedure* (pp. 67–94). Beverly Hills, CA: Sage.

Klaver, J. R., Lee, Z., & Rose, V. G. (2008). Effects of personality, interrogation techniques and plausibility in an experimental false confession paradigm. *Legal & Criminological Psychology, 13,* 71–88.

Lassiter, G. D. (Ed.). (2004). *Interrogations, confessions, and entrapment.* New York: Kluwer Academic/Plenum Publishers.

Lassiter, G. D., & Ratcliff, J. J. (2004). Exposing coercive influences in the criminal justice system: An agenda for legal psychology in the 21st century. In G. D. Lassiter (Ed.), *Interrogations, confessions, and entrapment* (pp. 1–8). New York: Kluwer Academic/Plenum Publishers.

Leo, R. A. (2008). *Police interrogation and American justice.* Cambridge, MA: Harvard University Press.

Leo, R. A., & Ofshe, R. J. (1998). The consequences of false confessions: Deprivations of liberty and miscarriages of justice in the age of psychological interrogation. *Journal of Criminal Law & Criminology, 88,* 429–496.

Medford, S., Gudjonsson, G. H., & Pearse, J. (2003). The efficacy of the appropriate adult safeguard during police interviewing. *Legal & Criminological Psychology, 8,* 253–266.

Meissner, C. A., & Kassin, S. M. (2002). "He's guilty!": Investigator bias in judgments of truth and deception. *Law & Human Behavior, 26,* 469–480.

Meissner, C., & Kassin, S. M. (2004). "You're guilty, so just confess!" Cognitive and confirmational biases in the interrogation room. In G. D. Lassiter (Ed.), *Interrogations, confessions, and entrapment* (pp. 85–106). New York: Kluwer Academic.

Munsterberg, H. (1908). *On the witness stand.* Garden City, NY: Doubleday.

Ofshe, R. J. (1989). Coerced confessions: the logic of seemingly irrational action. *Cultic Studies Journal, 6,* 1–15.

Ofshe, R. J. (1992). Inadvertent hypnosis during interrogation: False confessions due to dissociative state: Misidentified multiple personality disorder and the Satanic cult hypothesis. *Journal of Clinical & Experimental Hypnosis, 40,* 125–156.

Ofshe, R. J., & Leo, R. A. (1997a). The decision to confess falsely: rational choice and irrational action. *Denver University Law Review, 74,* 979-1122.

Ofshe, R. J., & Leo, R. A. (1997b). The social psychology of police interrogation. The theory and classification of true and false confessions. *Studies in Law, Politics, & Society, 16,* 189–251.

Pearse, J., & Gudjonsson, G. H. (1999). Measuring influential police interviewing tactics: A factor analytic approach. *Legal & Criminological Psychology, 4,* 221–238.

Peersen, M., Sigurdsson, J. F., Gudjonsson, G. H., & Greatarsson, S. J. (2004). Predicting re-offending: A five-year prospective study of Icelandic prison inmates. *Psychology, Crime, & Law, 10,* 197–204.

Redlich, A. D. (2007, September). *False confessions in interrogations and in plea arrangements*. Paper presented at the International Conference on Interrogations and Confessions, University of Texas at El Paso, TX.

Redlich, A. D., & Goodman, G. S. (2003). Taking responsibility for an act not committed: The influence of age and suggestibility. *Law & Human Behavior, 27,* 141–156.

Redlich, A. D., Silverman, M., Chen, J., & Steiner, H. (2004). The police interrogation of children and adolescents. In G. D. Lassiter (Ed.), *Interrogations, confessions, and entrapment* (pp 107–125). New York: Kluwer Academic.

Richardson, G. (1991). *A study of interrogative suggestibility in an adolescent forensic population.* Unpublished thesis, University of Newcastle, Newcastle, United Kingdom.

Scheck, B., Neufeld, P., & Dwyer, J. (2000). *Actual innocence.* Garden City, NY: Doubleday.

Sigurdsson, J. F. (1998). *Alleged false confessions among Icelandic offenders: An examination of some psychological, criminological and substance use factors that are associated with the reported false confessions.* Unpublished dissertation, King's College, University of London, United Kingdom.

Sigurdsson, J. F. (2007). Iceland. In H. J. Salize, H. Dreßing, & C. Kief (Eds.), *Mentally disordered persons in European Prison Systems—Needs, programmes and outcome (EUPRIS)* (pp. 172–184). Mannheim, Germany: Central Institute of Mental Health.

Sigurdsson, J. F., & Gudjonsson, G. H. (1996). Psychological characteristics of false confessors: A study among Icelandic prison inmates and juvenile offenders. *Personality & Individual Differences, 20,* 321–329.

Sigurdsson, J. F. & Gudjonsson, G. H. (2001). False confessions: The relative importance of psychological, criminological and substance abuse variables. *Psychology, Crime, & Law, 7,* 275–289.

Sigurdsson, J. F., Gudjonsson, G. H., Einarsson, E., & Gudjonsson G. (2006). Differences in personality and mental state between suspects and witnesses immediately after being interviewed by the police. *Psychology, Crime, & Law, 12,* 619–628.

Sigurdsson, J. F., Gudjonsson, G. H., & Peersen, M. (2001). Differences in the cognitive ability and personality of desisters and re-offenders: A prospective study. *Psychology, Crime, & Law, 7,* 33–43.

Stattin, H., & Klackenberg-Larsson, I. (1993). Early language and intelligence development and their relationship to future criminal behavior. *Journal of Abnormal Psychology, 102,* 369–378.

Steingrimsdottir, G., Hreinsdottir, H., Gudjonsson, G. H., Sigurdsson, J. F., & Nielsen, T. (2007). False confessions and the relationship with offending behaviour and personality among Danish adolescents. *Legal & Criminological Psychology, 12,* 287–296.

Viljoen, J. L., Klaver, J., & Roesch, R. (2005). Legal decisions of preadolescent and adolescent defendants: Predictors of confessions, pleas, communication with attorneys, and appeals. *Law & Human Behavior, 29,* 253–277.

Walker, C., & Stockdale, R. (1999). Forensic evidence. In C. Walker & K. Starmer (Eds.), *Miscarriages of justice: A review of justice in error* (pp. 119–150). London: Blackstone Press Limited.

Wambaugh, J. (1989). *The blooding.* London: Bantam Press.

Wrightsman, L., & Kassin, S. (1993). *Confessions in the courtroom.* Newbury Park: age.

3

False Confessions, False Guilty Pleas: Similarities and Differences

Allison D. Redlich

To many, it is unfathomable that an innocent individual would admit guilt for a crime he did not commit, particularly murder or rape. However, false confessions and false guilty pleas are not uncommon, and of identified proven cases, murder and rape are quite prevalent. Christopher Ochoa is one example. In the late 1980s, Mr. Ochoa and his friend Richard Danziger were accused and convicted of raping and murdering Nancy DePriest at a Texas Pizza Hut. Because of Ochoa's false confession and false guilty plea, they spent 12 years imprisoned before the real perpetrator confessed. Achim Marino, a serial killer in prison serving three life sentences, reportedly underwent a religious conversion. Feeling compelled to come forward, he wrote to several officials with claims that he alone murdered DePriest. Although his claims were first ignored, police began to investigate, and eventually DNA testing revealed that Ochoa and Danziger were innocent.

Why did Ochoa falsely implicate himself and Danziger? After being inter-rogated for a total of 24 hours in which he was deceived, denied an attorney, and repeatedly threatened with the death penalty, an exhausted Ochoa falsely confessed (Wisconsin Criminal Justice Study Commission, 2007). Ochoa's false confession to the police, however, did not take the death penalty off the table: In exchange for a life sentence and his testimony against Danziger, Ochoa continued his false claims and pleaded guilty despite actual innocence. It was inconceivable to Ochoa's court-appointed attorney that his client had con-fessed to a brutal rape and murder he did not do. As a result, Ochoa's attorney did not conduct an investigation and was instrumental in getting Ochoa to accept the plea offer. Danziger, who claimed he was with his girlfriend at the time of the crime and could offer no explanation for Ochoa's false claims, was convicted at trial on the basis of Ochoa's testimony. In prison, Danziger suffered irreversible brain damage as the result of a severe beating.

Although Ochoa's is an extreme case of misconduct, there are hundreds of proven cases of persons falsely confessing to the police or pleading guilty to crimes they did not do (Davis & Leo, 2006; Drizin & Leo, 2004; Gross, Jacoby, Matheson, Montgomery, & Patil, 2005). At the time of this writing, the Innocence Project has been instrumental in exonerating 209 wrongfully convicted individuals, approximately 25% of whom were convicted by false confessions or false admissions (Innocence Project, 2007; see also Garrett, 2008); this rate includes persons who falsely confessed to the police, persons whose codefendants falsely confessed, and those who falsely admitted guilt through the acceptance of a plea offer.

This chapter compares and contrasts false confessions and false guilty pleas, paying particular attention to their estimated prevalence and the contexts in which they arise. A false confession is defined here as a statement provided to the police in which the person partially or fully admits guilt, or otherwise takes responsibility, for a crime he or she did not commit. A false guilty plea is defined as the acceptance of a plea offer from the prosecutor for a crime the person did not commit. Like false confessions, guilty pleas are acknowledgments for responsibility for the crime, particularly when the defendant has to allocute as a condition of the plea deal.

False confessions and false guilty pleas are theoretically similar in their nature (i.e., taking responsibility for a noncommitted criminal act), underlying motivations, and often their consequences (e.g., a criminal record). However, there are qualitative differences between them as well. Although great strides have been made in understanding false confessions (e.g., Kassin & Gudjonsson, 2004; Lassiter, 2004), the topic of false guilty pleas has received almost no research attention, despite their known existence. Thus, an additional goal of this chapter is to spark empirical work on false guilty pleas, a problem arguably even larger than false confessions.

False Confessions

As noted throughout this book, false confessions are a serious problem for the criminal justice system: They greatly increase the risk of incarcerating and convicting innocent persons and allow actual perpetrators to go free. Judges and juries alike find it quite difficult to acquit when there is confession evidence, even when the interrogation techniques used to procure the confession are perceived as questionable or inappropriate (Kassin, 2005).

The Problem

False confessions are not a new phenomenon (e.g., see Borchard, 1932). What is new is the accumulation of evidence indicating the phenomenon is not as rare as once believed. Many proven false confessions cases have been identified, most of which involve murder and rape. These two serious crimes occur much less frequently than other crimes: Of all felony cases from the 75 largest U.S. counties, murder accounted for 0.8% and rape 1.8% (Cohen & Reaves, 2006). Thus, the opportunity to falsely confess to a murder would be significantly lower than the opportunity to falsely confess to a theft, for example. Indeed, in one study (Sigurdsson & Gudjonsson, 1996b) of self-reported false confessors, 58% claimed to have made false confessions for property offenses, whereas only 7% and 3% did so for violent and sexual offenses, respectively. Of importance, the detection of wrongful convictions in lower severity cases is also less imperative than in severe cases. Often, the person's incarceration time has been served and the motivation from the innocent himself and the motivation of persons in positions to help (e.g., attorneys) are lacking.

Related to the severity of the crime is the motivation behind the false confession. To date, the majority of identified false confession cases are the result of police coercion and improper interrogation techniques (Drizin & Leo, 2004). However, across several studies, Gudjonsson and his colleagues (Sigurdsson & Gudjonsson, 1996a, 1996b, 1996c, 1997) have noted that the "great majority of false confessions . . . are aimed at protecting somebody else rather than resulting from external pressure and coercion" (Gudjonsson, Sigurdsson, & Einarsson, 2004, p. 133).

Another reason to suspect that the prevalence of false confession is much higher than uncovered to date is subjectively reported false confession rates. Among samples of adult Icelandic prisoners, 12% claimed to have falsely confessed in their lifetime (Sigurdsson & Gudjonsson, 1996a, 1996b). Among a sample of more than 10,000 Icelandic college students, of those who had been interrogated by police, 7% claimed to have falsely confessed (Gudjonsson, Sigurdsson, Asgeirsdottir, & Sigfusdottir, 2006). Gudjonsson and colleagues have extended these studies to other European countries and have found similar self-reported rates of false confessions (e.g., Steingrimsdottir, Hreinsdottir, Gudjonsson, Sigurdsson, & Nielson, 2007). Further, Sigurdsson and Gudjonsson (1996a, 1996b) found that of those who claimed to have made a false confession, only 33% reported officially retracting the confession.

False confessions that have been objectively proved and those that have been self-reported appear different. In brief, objectively proved false confessions (e.g., those in Drizin & Leo, 2004) are primarily of the coerced-compliant form, are for serious crimes, and have been retracted. In contrast, self-reported false confessions are primarily voluntary (i.e., protecting the actual perpetrator), are for less serious but more prevalent crimes than murder and rape, and may or may not be retracted. Certainly, one explanation for these disparities is that all the self-proclaimed false confessors are lying, and this is why objective and subjective false confessions differ. However, this explanation cannot be the entire story: For one, all objectively proven false confessors were once self-reported false confessors themselves. More likely, the explanation is that the qualities associated with objectively proven false confessions—coercion, crime severity, and retraction—are also the factors that influence their identification.

For these and other reasons, the number of identified false confessions to date is surely the tip of the iceberg. In mid-2005, there were 2,186,230 U.S. prisoners or sentenced jail inmates (Harrison & Beck, 2006). If only half a percent (0.5%) had falsely confessed, there would be almost 11,000 false confessions, and this represents only one point in time, persons who were convicted and incarcerated, and one false confession per person and is quite a conservative estimate. Regardless of how many people have falsely confessed, the salient question is why people falsely confess.

The Context

Over the past 2 decades, psycholegal scholars have conducted groundbreaking studies on police interrogations and false confessions (for reviews, see Gudjonsson, 2003; Kassin & Gudjonsson, 2004; Leo, 2008). The primary question of why a person would admit to criminal acts not committed (and most often heinous crimes) can generally be answered with two complementary explanations: situational factors of the interrogation (e.g., the setting, the techniques themselves, the context of the crime) and dispositional factors inherent to the suspect.

Regarding situational factors, police interrogation tactics rely with near exclusivity on psychological manipulation and the betrayal of trust (including feigned sympathy and friendship) and minimization scenarios that reduce or shift blame (Inbau, Reid, Buckley, & Jayne, 2001; Leo, 1996a, 2008). One particularly controversial, but legal, interrogation technique is lying to, or otherwise deceiving, suspects. In police surveys, this technique has been found to be somewhat common (Kassin et al., 2007; Meyer & Reppucci, 2007), and in laboratory experiments it has been found to increase false confession rates (Kassin & Kiechel, 1996; Redlich & Goodman, 2003). There are several notable false confession cases in which lies and deception appeared to be the main reason for the false admissions of guilt. Nonetheless, with the exception of some egregious lies, courts consider the use of trickery and deception legally permissible interrogation tactics (see chap. 10, this volume).

There are, however, constraints on the police that in part are intended to guard against coerced and false confessions. Perhaps most notable is the *Miranda v. Arizona* decision by the Supreme Court in 1966. Prior to an interrogation (which is distinct from an interview; see Inbau et al., 2001), law enforcement must inform suspects of their rights against self-incrimination and to (free) counsel. Suspects can then decide to invoke or waive their rights, though this decision is required to be voluntary, knowing, and intelligent. Some research has indicated that *Miranda* warnings are often passed off as a mere formality (Leo, 1996b, 2008) rather than a protection. Similar to the psychological manipulation underlying interrogation techniques used to obtain confessions, the police have developed equally effective ways to obtain waivers of *Miranda*.

Another constraint on police interrogators is that they are not allowed to offer explicit promises of leniency, issue explicit threats of harm or punishment, or inflict actual harm or punishment. For example, as noted by Reid and Associates on its Web site, impermissible interrogative statements include, "You're not leaving this room until you confess" and "With the evidence that we have, there's no doubt you will be convicted of this. The only question is how long you are going to sit in jail." That is, because confessions should be voluntary, overt references to jail, the death sentence, loss of liberty, and so on are disallowed. However, a common element in many, if not all, false confessions is implicit promises of leniency or threats of punishment (and sometimes explicit, despite their illegality, such as in the Ochoa case). In other words, police imply that outcomes will be better for suspects if they cooperate or that things will be worse if they do not. Kassin and McNall (1991) examined this notion of pragmatic implication and indeed found explicit promises and minimization techniques that only imply leniency were perceived similarly and had indistinguishable effects on the likelihood of guilty verdicts. Russano, Meissner, Narchet, and Kassin (2005) also found that offering leniency to guilty and innocent suspects in a laboratory study increased both the true and false confession rates. Overall, although there are constraints on police interrogators that exist to reduce the likelihood of coerced and false confessions, contemporary interrogation techniques often skirt these constraints. Whereas most interrogators follow the letter of the law (see Leo, 1996a), the spirit behind these legal constraints is arguably less regarded.

In addition to the situational factors related to the interrogation, dispositional factors inherent in the suspect have been identified as contributing to false confessions. The two groups most commonly cited as at risk are juveniles (Owen-Kostelnik, Reppucci, & Meyer, 2006; Redlich, 2007; Redlich & Drizin, 2007) and persons with mental impairment (persons with mental illness and with developmental disabilities; Fulero & Everington, 2004; Redlich, 2004), although certainly other vulnerability factors exist (Gudjonsson, 2003). In brief, immature development, impulsivity, obedience to and desire to please authority, inability to consider long-term consequences, and deficits in executive functioning are some of the factors that can be present in these populations and that can affect decision making and the likelihood of false confession in interrogation settings (see Appelbaum & Appelbaum, 1994; Owen-Kostelnik et al., 2006; Perske, 2004; Redlich & Drizin, 2007). These limitations are most often discussed in relation to the situational aspects of interrogation, and it is clear that contemporary interrogation tactics are neither developmentally appropriate nor altered for persons with vulnerabilities (Meyer & Reppucci, 2007; chap. 4, this volume).

False Guilty Pleas

Another burgeoning problem for the criminal justice system is that of false guilty pleas (Bikel, 2004). According to one legal scholar, "Very few issues in the American criminal justice system generate such fierce controversy as plea bargaining—and very few allegations against the practice are as severe as the assertion that it leads to the conviction of innocent defendants" (Gazal-Ayal, 2006, p. 103). Despite this fierce debate and the tragic consequences of false guilty pleas, virtually no psychological research exists.

The Problem

As defined here, false guilty pleas are when innocent persons agree to plead guilty, usually in response to plea deals or bargains offered by prosecutors. There are dozens of known cases, and if conventional estimates existed, they would probably show many more. Of the 209 Innocence Project exonerees to date, 11 (5%) pleaded guilty (see Table 3.1); of the 340 Gross et al. (2005) exonerees, 20 (6%) pleaded guilty; and of the 125 proven false confessors from Drizin and Leo's (2004) sample, 14 (11% of total sample or 32% of those convicted) pleaded guilty. Note, however, that these false guilty pleaders overlap between samples, and numbers should not be summed. There have also been mass exoneration cases—in which many of the defendants pleaded guilty (see Gross et al., 2005)—and other individually highlighted cases such as the Lackawanna Six (Powell, 2003) and two of the Norfolk Four defendants (Wells & Leo, 2008). It is also important to note the direct role of plea deals involving informants, snitches, and codefendants in wrongful conviction cases: For the

Table 3.1. Characteristics of 11 False Guilty Plea Takers From the Innocence Project

Name (state)	Crime, plea, and sentence	False confession (Yes/No)
Larry Bostic (FL)	• Pleaded guilty to sexual battery and robbery • Faced possible life sentence at trial • Received 8-year sentence • Served 3 years (though re-imprisoned on new charges and probation violation of this crime, spending a total of 17 years in prison)	No
Marcellius Bradford (IL)	• Pleaded guilty to aggravated kidnapping • Murder, rape, and armed robbery charges dropped • Had to agree to testify against co-defendant • Received 12-year sentence • Served 6.5 years	Yes Claim of police coercion Juvenile
Keith Brown (NC)	• Pleaded guilty to second degree rape and second degree sexual offense • Received 35-year sentence • Served 4 years	Yes Mentally retarded
John Dixon (NJ)	• Pleaded guilty to sexual assault, kidnapping, robbery, and unlawful possession of a weapon • Claimed he pleaded guilty because he feared the jury would convict and receive a harsher sentence • After entering his guilty plea, asked the Judge to withdraw his plea and perform DNA testing. The Judge denied his request. • Received 45-year sentence • Served 10 years	No
Anthony Gray (MD)	• Pleaded guilty to murder and rape • Received two life sentences • Served 7 years	Yes Borderline retarded Police deception
Eugene Henton (TX)	• Pleaded guilty to sexual assault • Received 4-year sentence • Served 18 months	No

Table 3.1.   Characteristics of 11 False Guilty Plea Takers From the
Innocence Project (Continued)

Name (state)	Crime, plea, and sentence	False confession (Yes/No)
Christopher Ochoa (TX)	• Pleaded guilty to murder and sexual assault, reportedly to avoid death sentence • Had to agree to testify against codefendant • Received life sentence • Served 11.5 years	Yes Police pressure Threatened with death penalty
James Ochoa (CA)	• Pleaded guilty to carjacking and armed robbery • DNA had excluded Ochoa prior to the trial, but "prosecutors were sure he did the crime" • Judge allegedly threatened Ochoa with a sentence of 25 years to life • Received 2-year sentence • Served 10 months	No
Jerry Frank Townsend (FL)	• Tried and convicted of two murders, acquitted of one murder • Pleaded guilty to two murders and one rape, and no contest to two other murders • Received seven life sentences • Served 21.5 years	Yes Mentally retarded; mental capacity of an 8-year-old Wanting to please authority
David Vasquez (VA)	• Pleaded guilty to homicide and burglary • Received 35-year sentence • Served 4 years	Yes Borderline mentally impaired Dream Statement Confession
Arthur Lee Whitfield (VA)	• Tried and convicted on first rape charge, received 45 years • Pleaded guilty to second rape charge, receiving a lighter sentence (18 years to run consecutively with the 45 years) and had other charges dropped • Received a total sentence of 63 years • Served 22.5 years	No

most part, it is not malicious intent that makes a jailhouse snitch lie and claim that an innocent person confessed; rather, it is the promise of a reduced sentence or some other reward from the state.

These identified cases are, again, likely to represent the tip of the iceberg: Rates of 5% to 11% are most probably a gross underestimation of the extent of the problem. First, guilty pleas constitute nearly all (95%) of convictions (Cohen & Reaves, 2006). Second, guilty pleas occur more often for less serious crimes, and the majority of identified injustices are for the serious crimes of rape and murder; for example, 44% of accused murderers took their case to trial, whereas trial rates for all other crimes (including rape) were 9% or lower (Cohen & Reaves, 2006). Third, because plea bargains do generally shorten the time of incarceration or even eliminate it, the motivation to correct the injustice and be set free is not present. And fourth, guilty pleas are difficult to withdraw and appeal, and thus the wrongful conviction may never be recognized and righted.

In addition, estimating rates of false guilty pleas using samples of officially exonerated individuals can be misleading. By definition, persons who plead guilty are convicted of crimes, and attempting to assert actual innocence after entering a plea is notoriously difficult. As established by the Federal Rules of Evidence, guilty pleas are extremely difficult to withdraw (Weaver, 2001–2002), especially after sentencing. The two Norfolk Four defendants who had pleaded guilty attempted to withdraw their pleas later but were not allowed (Wells & Leo, 2008). Thus, those who plead falsely may never receive an official determination of legal innocence. Kerry Max Cook is one such example (Cook, 2007). Cook spent 21 years on death row and eventually accepted a plea of no contest in exchange for time served. His case, highlighted in the popular play and movie *The Exonerated,* however, is not included in Gross et al.'s (2005) sample of 340 exonerees. Gross and colleagues included only official declarations of exoneration, and because Cook pleaded no contest, his case did not qualify. Nonetheless, 22 years after the commission of the crime and a mere 2 months after accepting the plea, DNA from the crime exculpated Cook. Cook was released from prison, yet he retains the legal status of convicted murderer.

Another reason pointing to larger numbers of false guilty pleas than those presently known is the lack of safeguards in the plea process. When a defendant pleads guilty, institutionalized trial safeguards like burden of proof and cross-examination are absent. Consider that a defendant who pleads guilty may know that an eyewitness exists against him and will consider this risk when opting to plead guilty; a defendant who goes to trial may also hold this knowledge but has the opportunity to challenge the eyewitness, bring in expert witnesses, and have a jury or judge decide the credibility of the witness. As Bibas (2004) pointed out, because of rules of discovery, innocent defendants are especially disadvantaged in not knowing the evidence that exists against them (as in theory there should be no factual evidence). To be sure, in the wrongful conviction cases that went to trial, the safeguards meant to identify the causal factors (e.g., eyewitness misidentification, false confessions) failed. However, in the wrongful conviction cases that culminated in a plea bargain, the causal factors never had the opportunity to undergo scrutiny or challenge. As such, the factors identified as contributing to wrongful convictions by trial are likely to be even more prevalent in wrongful convictions by guilty plea.

For example, Alschuler (1986) convincingly argued why the plea bargaining system promotes inadequate representation, or "bad lawyering," one of the main causes of wrongful convictions (see also Bibas, 2004). In brief, defense attorneys working within the plea bargaining system, most of whom are overburdened, are subject to many temptations that serve to seek quick solutions and reduce the likelihood of acting in clients' best interests. Exacerbating the problem is that ineffective assistance of counsel is virtually undetectable in the guilty plea system, as the system is characterized by secrecy, confidential conferences, and unwritten rules (Alschuler, 1986). Trials create a basis and a record for appeal, whereas pleas are more secret endeavors (with the exception of plea discussions; see below). The Innocence Project exonerees convicted at trial had the opportunity to argue that trial errors were committed or that information not presented to the jury has since come to light. Persons who plead guilty have much less of a basis from which to argue. In essence, plea arrangements, which account for 95% of convictions, create situations in which the identified contributors of wrongful convictions (e.g., eyewitness misidentification, false confessions, bad lawyering) are more likely to be present (than at trials) and to be present without dispute, scrutiny, or public review.

The Context

When addressing the question of why innocent persons would plead guilty to crimes they did not commit, it is important to address the plea process itself. Since the inception of the plea bargaining process in the mid-1800s, the possibility of innocents pleading guilty has been recognized (*State v. Kaufman,* 1879). Indeed, the *Alford plea* is an explicit endorsement of innocents who would rather plead guilty than risk their fates at trial. Henry Alford, a defendant accused of first-degree murder, testified that he did not commit the murder but was pleading guilty because of the threat of death penalty if he lost at trial (*North Carolina v. Alford,* 1970). Today, defendants can enter Alford pleas when innocent but perceive their chances at trial to be too much of a risk (Bibas, 2003). Redlich and Ozdogru (2009) reported that more than 76,000 state prison inmates incarcerated in 2004 were estimated to have entered Alford pleas.

The main arguments for plea bargaining is that it empowers choice on the defendant and that it saves the courts time and money. Many contend that the U.S. criminal justice system could not operate without plea bargains or without the high frequency of plea bargains (see Bibas, 2003). The main argument against plea bargaining is that it is a coercive choice and eschews the standard safeguards built into the trial process. When guilty pleas are in place, the state does not have to prove the charge against the defendant beyond a reasonable doubt and the defendant loses the presumption of innocence, the rights to confront persons against him and present evidence in his defense, and all other constitutionally afforded safeguards. As Gazal-Ayal (2006) argued, it is often in the weaker cases that the prosecutor offers a deal because the state knows or suspects that they cannot prove their case beyond a reasonable doubt at trial (see also Bibas, 2004). Thus, assuming that innocent defendants have weak evidentiary cases, plea bargains may be more readily offered to innocents and offered with increased incentives. A caveat to this, however, is that innocents who falsely confess may not be offered plea bargains because of the seemingly strong evidence against them (see Drizin & Leo, 2004). Though, as I discuss later, some false confessors surely are offered plea deals.

Regardless of guilt or innocence, there are powerful inducements to plead guilty, particularly when pitted against remaining in jail pretrial or risking a conviction with a stiffer sentence at trial. For the most part, plea arrangements do reduce the charges and the time in jail or prison and potentially have other consequences (e.g., having to register as a sex offender). It is common knowledge that many defendants plead guilty to get out of jail and receive reduced sentences or probation (Gross et al., 2005). In a study of actual prosecutorial decisions, detained defendants were more likely to be offered pleas than defendants who had been released. Indeed, the authors viewed detention as a way to encourage or coerce pleas (Kellough & Wortley, 2002).

Many scholars posit this choice between remaining in jail awaiting a trial (in which they are likely to be found guilty) and having a reduced sentence or probation via a guilty plea as one of coercion (e.g., Langbein, 1992). A watershed case concerning the coerciveness of pleas is *Bordenkircher v. Hayes* (1978; see Lynch, 2003). In this case, the prosecutor attempted to pressure the defendant into pleading guilty by offering him a deal of 5 years (for the crime of passing a forged check for $88.93) to "save the court the inconvenience and necessity of a trial" (Lynch, 2003, p. 25) or by charging the defendant as a habitual offender, for which he would serve a mandatory life sentence. Hayes opted for his constitutional right to a jury trial and lost. In 1978, Hayes's case was heard by the U.S. Supreme Court, who approved the prosecutor's actions and upheld Hayes' life sentence.

For persons who are innocent, the choice to plead is arguably even more coercive. Although there is a lack of empirical studies on guilty pleas, generally, and false guilty pleas, specifically, studies have been conducted comparing guilty and innocent subjects. In one set of studies, Gregory, Mowen, and Linder (1978) asked male college students to imagine they were guilty or innocent of armed robbery, listen to a tape of the defense attorney's arguments, and then reject or accept a plea offer. The number of charges and the sanction severity were also manipulated. They found that when the number of charges was high versus low (four vs. one charge) and when the sanctions were high versus low (10–15 vs. 1–2 years in prison), both guilty and innocent participants were more likely to plead: 100% for guilty and 33% for innocents. In a separate experiment, Gregory et al. (1978) manipulated the guilt or innocence of subjects in regard to cheating on a test. After all the participants (16 male college students) were accused of cheating, they were told they would have to go before the department ethics committee, and if the committee determined the subject had cheated, his final grade in the class would be dropped. However, the subject was told that if he admitted guilt, the experimenter would be willing to drop the matter and forgo the committee. Of the 8 innocent subjects, none accepted the deal. In comparison, 6 of the 8 guilty subjects admitted to cheating.

In a similar study with more participants, Russano et al. (2005) varied the use of minimization (i.e., lessening the seriousness of the offense) and the use of a deal with subjects who were either guilty or innocent of cheating on a problem-solving task. In the deal condition, guilty and innocent subjects were offered the following options: sign the statement (false confession) to "settle things quickly" and receive research credit for that day, but also agree to return and not receive additional credit; or not sign the statement, in which the "supervising professor" would be called with the "strong implication being that the consequences would be worse if the professor became further involved" (p. 483). They found that when subjects were guilty, and when minimization and the deal were used in conjunction, 87% signed the statement. When subjects were innocent, almost half (43%) took responsibility when both techniques were used. Unlike Gregory et al.'s (1978) findings, the deal alone was sufficient to induce some (14%) of the innocent subjects to admit guilt. Although Russano et al.'s (2005) study was framed as a false confession study, the implications for false guilty pleas are clear. Indeed, whether the acceptance of the deal is labeled a false confession or a false guilty plea is immaterial.

Similarities and Differences Between False Confessions and False Guilty Pleas

False confessions and false guilty pleas share several aspects: the false admission of guilt, the techniques used to obtain them, the rationales behind them, and potentially the dispositional traits of those who utter them. Of particular note, false confessions often precipitate false guilty pleas for the same crime.

On their face, false confessions and false guilty pleas both represent taking responsibility for criminal acts not committed. False confession statements can range from a mere "I did it" without further explanation to seemingly detailed rich accounts of the crime (Gudjonsson, 2003). Similarly, plea arrangements are often conditioned on the defendant admitting guilt in open court and allocuting to details (Wrightsman, Nietzel, & Fortune, 1998). Like false confessions, there have been instances in which allocutions consist of inaccuracies, inconsistencies, and details supplied by someone other than the defendant (see Bikel, 2004).

Though there is a dearth of research on the techniques prosecutors use to secure guilty pleas, at first glance, interrogation and prosecutorial techniques overlap. Both use social influence–gaining tactics, such as scarcity (e.g., "This is a one-time offer"; "I can only help you now"), authority, reciprocity, and social validation (Cialdini, 2001). One common interrogation technique is bluffing about the evidence against suspects (Inbau et al., 2001). Bibas (2004) stated, "Prosecutorial bluffing is likely to work particularly well against innocent defendants, who are on average more risk averse than guilty defendants" (p. 2495). Thus, like false confessors, false guilty pleaders may be misled about the strength of the evidence against them, which in turn produces the false taking of responsibility. The perceived strength of evidence is a leading reason behind true and false confessions (Gudjonsson, 2003) and contributes to true and false guilty pleas as well (Redlich, Summers, & Hoover, in press).

The proximate reason for most coerced false confessions and false guilty pleas is the need to extricate oneself from the situation, such as the need to simply have the questioning stop or to get out of jail. False confessors and false guilty pleaders are confronted with a Hobson's choice, that is, an apparently free choice that offers no real alternative. The Hobson's choice for the false confessor is to continue denials and thus continue the interrogation or to confess and have the interrogation end. Similarly in false guilty pleas, often the decision is between pleading guilty, receiving time served for the days already spent incarcerated, and being allowed to walk out of jail; or pleading not guilty, awaiting trial in jail, and risking a much greater sentence (possibly death) if adjudged guilty. The case of Robert H. illustrates this point (Alschuler & Deiss, 1994). Robert H. spent 6 months in jail without being charged before first meeting his public defender, who reportedly handled more than 500 cases that year. The lawyer recommended that Robert plead guilty and explained that if he pleaded guilty, he could go home that day, or if he chose, he could go to trial but spend up to another year in jail. Although Robert pleaded guilty, it was later discovered that he had been confused with someone else and was innocent.

The same traits that place persons at risk for false confession may also place persons at risk for false guilty pleas. The same rationales underlying juveniles' risk for false confession (see Owen-Kostelnik et al., 2006; Redlich, 2007), for example, are likely to also underlie risks for false guilty pleas. That is, juveniles' impulsivity, immaturity, and possible impairments in decision-making capabilities can also influence the decision to accept plea offers when truly innocent. Further, findings from the adjudicative competence literature are highly relevant here, as understanding and appreciation of the adjudication process pertains most to pleas, not trials. Juveniles and persons with mental illness and with mental retardation are significantly more likely to have deficits in competence than their adult and nondisordered counterparts (Appelbaum & Appelbaum, 1994; Grisso et al., 2003; Hoge et al., 1997; Viljoen, Roesch, & Zapf, 2002). Thus, as argued in regard to police interrogations and false confessions (Redlich, 2004; Redlich, Silverman, Chen, & Steiner, 2004), individuals who do not understand and appreciate the plea process may be more likely to falsely plead guilty.

Finally, though not a similarity per se, it is important to recognize that false confessions and false guilty pleas are often present for the same crime. This is important because the driving factor behind the false guilty plea may be the false confession itself (supported by the strength of the evidence). Among the 125 proven false confessors reported by Drizin and Leo (2004), who were subsequently convicted, 32% pleaded guilty despite their innocence, a rate higher than the 5%–6% rates seen in samples of exonerations of all causes (i.e., Gross et al., 2005; Innocence Project, 2007).

Table 3.1 lists the to-date 11 false guilty pleaders from 209 exonerees identified by the Innocence Project. The most striking pattern among these individuals is the presence of false confessions: Of the 11 who falsely pleaded guilty, 6 (54.5%) had also falsely confessed. Of the 198 exonerees who did not falsely plead guilty, only 26 (13%) had also falsely confessed. Similarly, of those who falsely confessed, 6 of 32 (19%) pleaded guilty. Of the 177 who did not falsely confess, only 5 (3%) pleaded guilty. Although it is difficult to draw conclusions from 11 persons, it is telling that more than half of the false guilty pleaders had falsely confessed and therefore knew that their self-incriminating statements would be used at trial. It is quite possible that because confession evidence is perceived as one of the strongest forms of evidence (if not the strongest), these 11 false guilty pleaders presaged the trial outcome and did not risk harsher sentences. Future research should focus on the situational and dispositional differences between false confessors who do and do not plead guilty.

Though false confessions and false guilty pleas share the above commonalities, there are apparent differences. The differences concern perceived versus actual leniency, the legalities of promising leniency, and the appearance of coercion. First, a notable difference between false confessions and false guilty pleas is that whereas innocents who plead guilty receive a reduced sentence or probation, innocents who confess and who choose to go to trial are treated quite harshly (Drizin & Leo, 2004; Kassin, 2005). However, false confessors, especially those pressured by police, perceive lenient treatment to be forthcoming. Though the police are not allowed to explicitly promise leniency, as mentioned, implied leniency (via pragmatic implication; Kassin & McNall, 1991) is an extremely common interrogation tactic, and one that is evident in almost all false confessions. Many false confessors have self-reported that they believed they could go home after telling the police what they wanted to hear (Drizin & Leo, 2004; Kassin & Gudjonsson, 2004; Redlich et al., 2004). Thus, although the leniency associated with false guilty pleas is perceived and actual, the leniency associated with false confessions may only be perceived.

A second and related difference between false confessions and false guilty pleas are the techniques considered legally permissible in interrogations versus plea bargains. Interrogation confession statements stemming from explicit promises of leniency or threats of punishment are in theory inadmissible in court and cannot be used against defendants. In contrast, the basis of the plea bargaining system is predicated on promises of leniency, and to some, threats of harm. In essence, many of the same actions and statements that lend themselves to false confessions and are impermissible for police interrogators because of the risk of false confessions—such as explicit threats of punishment (including death) and promises of leniency—are standard practice for prosecutors to use in obtaining plea agreements, and they are deemed legal by our highest courts (*Bordenkircher v. Hayes,* 1978). Again, Christopher Ochoa's case serves as an example. The threats of the death penalty in the interrogation room, as reported by Ochoa, were a primary factor for his proven false confession. The threat of the death penalty from the prosecutor was a primary factor for his false guilty plea. Whereas the threats in the interrogation were illegal, the threats in the plea offer were not. From a theoretical standpoint, this distinction between legal and illegal inducements offered in the interrogation room versus the prosecutor's office makes little sense.

A third difference between false confessions and guilty pleas has to do with the appearance of coercion and how it is handled. Although electronic recording of interrogation is becoming more common among law enforcement (Sullivan, 2005; chap. 8, this volume), for the most part, interrogations take place in secrecy. Suspects or defendants who claim to have confessed in response to coercion often endure a credibility battle in which the police interrogator's version of events is pitted against the suspect's version (Redlich & Meissner, 2009). It is not surprising that police officers are often found more credible, and suppressed confessions on the basis of coercion are uncommon.

In contrast, persons who plead guilty usually undergo a *plea colloquy* or *plea discussion.* Generally, this refers to a series of questions asked by the judge of the defendant aimed at determining whether the guilty plea was made voluntarily, knowingly, and intelligently. This discussion serves as the formal record of the plea. The American Bar Association (ABA; 1999) specified the legalities surrounding receiving and acting on a guilty plea, withdrawal of the plea, plea discussions and agreements, and diversion and other alternative resolutions (Standards 14-1.1–14-4.1). The Standards require that prior to taking the plea, defendants be advised of the nature and elements of the offense, the terms and conditions of the plea, the maximum sentence on the charge, the rights they are waiving, and other things that may affect, or be affected by, the plea (e.g., defendant's past criminal history or immigration status). In contrast, in regard to one's rights when arrested, the ABA states on its Web site, "The police do not have to tell you the crime for which they are arresting you, though they probably will" (ABA, n.d.).

Several states have developed statewide forms that standardize the plea discussion process. Minnesota developed a four-page form (http://www.courts. state.mn.us/forms), which includes 28 items (many with subparts) to help the court ensure that the guilty plea was not coerced or ill-informed. For example, Point 3 is "I understand the charge(s) made against me in this case." Point 12 is "I do/do not make the claim that the fact I have been held in jail since my arrest and could not post bail caused me to decide to plead guilty in order to get the thing over with rather than waiting my turn at trial." Similarly, Idaho uses a seven-page form with nearly 50 questions asked of the defendant prior to the plea (Idaho Criminal Rules, Rule 11, 2007).

On the one hand, a comparably detailed conversation (or written agreement) is unlikely to take place between law enforcement and an alleged confessor after the confession is obtained. One could argue that the *Miranda* warning prior to interrogation has a similar intent, but reading the four or five *Miranda* components aloud (or having suspects read the warning themselves) does not replicate the detailed plea questions recommended by the ABA or those seen within statewide plea discussion documents. Additionally, some jurisdictions' warnings are ambiguous. For example, Rogers, Harrison, Shuman, Sewell, and Hazelwood (2007) examined 560 *Miranda* warnings and found that only 32% explicitly informed suspects that if indigent, legal services were free.

On the other hand, it is unclear whether these plea discussions serve as true safeguards or whether they are indeed mere formalities. Without further research, it is difficult to say. However, once defendants have negotiated a plea and accepted the offer informally prior to coming before the judge, it is probable that some defendants will answer the questions in the plea discussion to ensure that the plea bargain goes through rather than to state the truth. There is a wealth of empirical research demonstrating that individuals who commit to a position are much more willing to comply with future requests for the same or similar positions, especially when the commitments are made publicly (see Cialdini, 2001). Thus, in an overcrowded criminal justice system in which almost all convictions are the result of guilty pleas, plea discussions may be a formality that better protect the court than the defendant.

Conclusion

A goal of this chapter was to introduce a new topic for research, that of false guilty pleas, by comparing and contrasting them with false confessions. Given the sheer number of pleas that occur each day and the potential for error and abuse inherent within our criminal justice system, false guilty pleas pose a large problem, a problem most deserving of research. Though it is premature to recommend specific policy reforms, the implications of allowing innocents to plead guilty to crimes they did not commit are clear. In addition to the immorality of imprisoning innocent individuals, there are public safety and cost-related concerns. True perpetrators are allowed to go free and commit crimes, and given the perennial problem with correctional overcrowding, jail and prison beds should be reserved for the truly guilty.

Several issues described in this chapter stand out. First, allowing promises of leniency and threats of punishment in the plea context but not in the interrogation context is nonsensical from a psychological standpoint. When innocent, promises of leniency and threats of harm increase the likelihood of false admissions, regardless of the context. Second, the trend that false confessions and false guilty pleas often occur for the same crime is in need of further study. Studies could examine the differences between false confessors who do and do not accept pleas as well as the confession cases in which pleas are and are not offered. Third, the techniques used to secure guilty pleas as well as the purported reasons for taking them have not been thoroughly examined. Fourth, the area of plea discussions is ripe for research, including the extent of the questioning and information provided by attorneys and judges, the extent to which such questions and information are understood by the defendant, and whether the discussion promotes voluntary and knowing pleas as intended. The steady attention paid to false confessions, such as at the El Paso conference (from which this volume is derived), has highlighted plausible and practical reforms. Although some of the problems with false guilty pleas are systemic, an increased attention to the problem can shed light on policy reforms that could be implemented and effective.

With each passing year, the number of identified miscarriages of justice increases. From 2000 to 2007, the Innocence Project exonerated an average of 18 persons per year. False confessions and false guilty pleas play a role in one quarter of these miscarriages. As Borchard (1932) noted 75 years ago, "sheer good luck" has much to do with the uncovering of these wrongs, which is readily apparent today as well. The serendipitous nature of detecting wrongful arrests and convictions, although sure to continue, can be decreased with increasing knowledge and insight into their causes.

References

Alschuler, A. W. (1986). Personal failure, institutional failure, and the sixth amendment. *New York University Review of Law & Social Change, XIV,* 149–156.

Alschuler, A. W., & Deiss, A. G. (1994). A brief history of the criminal jury in the United States. *The University of Chicago Law Review, 61,* 867.

American Bar Association. (1999). *ABA standards for criminal justice, pleas of guilty* (3rd ed.). Washington, DC: American Bar Association.

American Bar Association. (n.d.). *The police and your rights: What procedures must the police follow while making an arrest?* Retrieved December 16, 2007, from http://www.abanet.org/publiced/practical/criminal/arrest_procedures.html

Appelbaum, K. L., & Appelbaum, P. S. (1994). Criminal justice-related competencies in defendants with mental retardation. *Journal of Psychiatry & Law, 22,* 483–503.

Bibas, S. (2003). Harmonizing substantive criminal law values and criminal procedure: The case of Alford and Nolo Contendere pleas. *Cornell Law Review, 88,* 1361–1412.

Bibas, S. (2004). Plea bargaining outside the shadow of trial. *Harvard Law Review, 117,* 2463–2547.

Bikel, O. (Producer). (2004, June 17). *Frontline's The Plea.* [Television broadcast]. Boston, MA: WGBH Educational Foundation. Retrieved April 28, 2007, from http://www.pbs.org/wgbh/pages/frontline/shows/plea/

Borchard, E. M. (1932). *Convicting the innocent: Sixty-five actual errors of criminal justice.* New Haven, CT: Yale University Press.

Bordenkircher v. Hayes, 434 U.S. 357 (1978).

Cialdini, R. B. (2001). *Influence: Science and practice.* New York: Harper Collins.

Cohen, T. H., & Reaves, B. A. (2006). *Felony defendants in large urban counties, 2002.* Washington, DC: U.S. Department of Justice, Office of Justice Programs, Bureau of Justice Statistics.

Cook, K. M. (2007). *Chasing justice: My story of freeing myself after two decades on death row for a crime I did not commit.* New York: Harper Collins.

Davis, D., & Leo, R. (2006). Strategies for preventing false confessions and their consequences. In M. R. Kebbell, & G. M. Davies (Eds.), *Practical psychology for forensic investigations and prosecutions* (pp. 121–149). Chichester, England: Wiley.

Drizin, S. A., & Leo, R. A. (2004). The problem of false confessions in the post-DNA world. *North Carolina Law Review, 82,* 891–1008.

Fulero, S. M. & Everington, C. (2004). Mental retardation, competency to waive *Miranda* rights and false confessions. In G. D. Lassiter (Ed.), *Interrogations, confessions, and entrapment* (pp. 163–179). New York: Kluwer Academic/Plenum.Garrett, B. L. (2008). Judging innocence. *Columbia Law Review, 100,* 101–190.

Gazal-Ayal, O. (2006). Partial ban on plea bargains. *Cardozo Law Review, 27,* 101–155.

Gregory, W. L., Mowen, J. C., & Linder, D. E. (1978). Social psychology and plea bargaining: Applications, methodology, and theory. *Journal of Personality & Social Psychology, 36,* 1521–1530.

Grisso, T., Steinberg, L., Woolard, J., Cauffman, E., Scott, E., Graham, S., et al. (2003). Juveniles' competence to stand trial: A comparison of adolescents' and adults' capacities as trial defendants. *Law & Human Behavior, 27,* 333–363.

Gross, S. R., Jacoby, K., Matheson, D. J., Montgomery, N., & Patil, S. (2005). Exonerations in the United States 1989 through 2003. *The Journal of Criminal Law & Criminology, 95,* 523–560.

Gudjonsson, G. H. (2003). *The psychology of interrogations and confessions.* Chichester, England: Wiley.

Gudjonsson, G. H., Sigurdsson, J. F., & Einarsson, E. (2004). The role of personality in relation to confessions and denials. *Psychology, Crime, & Law, 10,* 125–135.

Harrison, P. M., & Beck, A. J (2006). Prison and jail inmates at mid-year 2005. *Bureau of Justice Statistics Bulletin.* Washington, DC: U.S. Department of Justice, Office of Justice Programs.

Hoge, S. K., Poythress, N. G., Bonnie, R. J., Monahan, J., Eisenberg, M., & Feucht-Haviar, T. (1997). The MacArthur adjudicative competence study: Diagnosis, psychopathology, and competence-related abilities. *Behavioral Sciences & the Law, 15,* 329–345.

Idaho Criminal Rules, Rule 11. (2007). *Optional guilty plea advisory form—Effective July 1, 2007.* Retrieved December 16, 2007, from http://www.isc.idaho.gov/rulesfrm.htm

Inbau, F. E., Reid, J. E., Buckley, J. P., & Jayne, B. C. (2001). *Criminal interrogation and confessions* (4th ed.). Gaithersburg, MD: Aspen.

Innocence Project. (2007). *200 exonerated: Too many wrongfully convicted.* New York: Benjamin N. Cardozo School of Law, Yeshiva University.

Kassin, S. M. (2005). On the psychology of confessions: Does innocence put innocents at risk? *American Psychologist, 60,* 215–228.

Kassin, S. M., & Gudjonsson, G. H. (2004). The psychology of confessions: A review of the literature and issues. *Psychological Science in the Public Interest, 5,* 33–67.

Kassin, S. M., & Kiechel, K. L. (1996). The social psychology of false confessions: Compliance, internalization, and confabulation. *Psychological Science, 7,* 125–128.

Kassin, S. M., Leo, R. A., Meissner, C. A., Richman, K. D., Colwell, L. H., Leach, A. M., & La Fon, D. (2007). Police interviewing and interrogation: A self-report survey of police practices and beliefs. *Law & Human Behavior, 31,* 381–400.

Kassin, S. M., & McNall, K. (1991). Police interrogations and confessions: Communicating promises and threats by pragmatic implication. *Law & Human Behavior, 15,* 233–251.

Kellough, G., & Wortley, S. (2002). Remand for plea: Bail decisions and plea bargaining as commensurate decisions. *British Journal of Criminology, 42,* 186–210.

Langbein, J. H. (1992). On the myth of written constitutions: The disappearance of criminal jury trial. *Harvard Journal of Law & Public Policy, 15,* 119–127.

Lassiter, G. D. (Ed.). (2004). *Interrogations, confessions, and entrapment.* New York: Kluwer.

Leo, R. A. (1996a). Inside the interrogation room. *Journal of Criminal Law and Criminology, 86,* 266–303.

Leo, R. A. (1996b). *Miranda's* revenge: Police interrogation as a confidence game. *Law and Society Review, 30,* 259–288.

Leo, R. A. (2008). *Police interrogation and American justice.* Cambridge, MA: Harvard University Press.

Lynch, T. (2003). The case against plea bargaining. *Regulation, 26,* 24–27.

Meyer, J. R., & Reppucci, N. D. (2007). Police practices and perceptions regarding juvenile interrogation and interrogative suggestibility. *Behavioral Sciences & the Law, 25,* 1–24.

North Carolina v. Alford, 400 U.S. 25 (1970).

Owen-Kostelnik, J., Reppucci, N. D., & Meyer, J. R. (2006). Testimony and interrogation of minors: Assumptions about maturity and morality. *American Psychologist, 61,* 286–304.

Perske, R. (2004). Understanding persons with intellectual disabilities in the criminal justice system: Indicators of progress? *Mental Retardation, 42,* 484–487.

Powell, M. (2003, July 29). No choice but guilty: Lackawanna case highlights legal tilt. *Washington Post,* p. A1.

Redlich, A. D. (2004). Mental illness, police interrogations, and the potential for false confession. *Psychiatric Services, 55,* 19–21.

Redlich, A. D. (2007). Double jeopardy in the interrogation room: Young age and mental illness. *American Psychologist, 62,* 609–611.

Redlich, A. D., & Drizin, S. (2007). Police interrogation of youth. In C. L. Kessler & L. Kraus (Eds.), *The mental health needs of young offenders: Forging paths through reintegration and rehabilitation* (pp. 61–78). Cambridge, England: Cambridge University Press.

Redlich, A. D., & Goodman, G. S. (2003). Taking responsibility for an act not committed: The influence of age and suggestibility. *Law & Human Behavior, 27,* 141–156.

Redlich, A. D., & Meissner, C. A. (2009). True lies: The psychology of false confessions. In J. Skeem, K. Douglas, & S. Lilienfeld (Eds.), *Psychological science in the courtroom: Controversies and consensus* (pp. 124–148). New York: Guilford Press.

Redlich, A. D., & Ozdogru, A. A. (2009). Alford pleas in the age of innocence. *Behavioral Sciences and the Law, 27,* 467–488.

Redlich, A. D., Silverman, M., Chen, J., & Steiner, H. (2004). The police interrogation of children and adolescents. In G. D. Lassiter (Ed.), *Interrogations, confessions, and entrapment* (pp. 107–126). New York: Kluwer Academic/Plenum Publishers.

Redlich, A. D., Summers, A., & Hoover, S. (in press). Self-reported false confessions and false guilty pleas among offenders with mental illness. *Law and Human Behavior.*

Rogers, R., Harrison, K. S., Shuman, D. W., Sewell, K. W., & Hazelwood, L. L. (2007). An analysis of Miranda warnings and waivers: Comprehension and coverage. *Law & Human Behavior, 31,* 177–192.

Russano, M. B., Meissner, C. A., Narchet, F. M., & Kassin, S. M. (2005). Investigating true and false confessions within a novel experimental paradigm. *Psychological Science, 16,* 481–486.

Sigurdsson, J. F., & Gudjonsson, G. H. (1996a). Illicit drug use among "false confessors": A study among Icelandic prison inmates. *Nordic Journal of Psychiatry, 50,* 325–328.

Sigurdsson, J. F., & Gudjonsson, G. H. (1996b). The psychological characteristics of false confessors: A study among Icelandic prison inmates and juvenile offenders. *Personality & Individual Differences, 20,* 321–329.

Sirgudsson, J. F., & Gudjonsson, G. H. (1996c). The relationship between types of claimed false confession made and the reasons why suspects confess to the police according to the Gudjonsson Confession Questionnaire. *Legal & Criminological Psychology, 1,* 259–269.

Sigurdsson, J. F., & Gudjonsson, G. H. (1997). The criminal history of "false confessors" and other prison inmates. *The Journal of Forensic Psychiatry, 8,* 447–455.

State v. Kaufman, 51 Iowa 578 (1879).

Steingrimsdottir, G., Hreinsdottir, H., Gudjonsson, G. H., Sigurdsson, J. F., & Nielsen, T. (2007). False confessions and the relationship with offending behavior and personality among Danish adolescents. *Legal & Criminological Psychology, 12,* 287–296.

Sullivan, T. P. (2005). Electronic recording of custodial interrogations: Everybody wins. *The Journal of Criminal Law & Criminology, 95,* 1127–1144.

Viljoen, J. L., Roesch, R., & Zapf, P. A. (2002). An examination of the relationship between competency to stand trial, competency to waive interrogation rights, and psychopathology. *Law & Human Behavior, 26,* 481–506.

Weaver, K. D. (2001–2002). A change of heart or a change of law? Withdrawing a guilty plea under federal rule of criminal procedure 32(e). *Journal of Criminal Law & Criminology, 92,* 273–306.

Wells, T., & Leo, R. A. (2008). *False confessions: Murder and injustice in Virginia.* New York: The New Press.

Wisconsin Criminal Justice Study Commission. (2007). *Position paper on false confessions.* Retrieved December 3, 2007, from http://www.wcjsc.org/Position_Paper_on_False_Confessions.pdf

Wrightsman, L. S., Nietzel, M. T., & Fortune, W. H. (1998). *Psychology and the legal system* (4th ed.). Pacific Grove, CA: Brooks/Cole.

4

Custodial Interrogation of Juveniles: Results of a National Survey of Police

N. Dickon Reppucci, Jessica Meyer, and Jessica Kostelnik

Obtaining confessions from criminal suspects is a common way in which law enforcement officers incriminate those suspected of committing a crime (Gudjonsson, 2003). The general assumption is that police do not want to obtain confessions from innocent suspects and that most innocent suspects do not purposefully incriminate themselves. However, it is clear that many documented cases of false confessions have led to conviction of innocent suspects (see chaps. 1 and 2, this volume). For example, Drizin and Leo's (2004) review suggests that false confessions were a leading cause in wrongful conviction in 14% to 25% of the cases. In addition, Scheck, Neufeld, and Dwyer (2000) found that about 23% of individuals in the United States who were exonerated by DNA evidence had provided false confessions before they were wrongfully convicted.

Until recently (Kassin et al. 2007; Meyer & Reppucci, 2003, 2007), law enforcement officers had not been questioned about their perceptions of the likelihood of false confessions or the types of interrogation strategies they use and what they believe about their effectiveness. Because they are the interviewers and interrogators, it seems obvious that they should be key informants as to what they actually do. But as legal scholar Yale Kamisar (2003) recently wrote, "We know little more about actual police interrogation practices than we did at the time of *Miranda* [in 1966]."

We have tried to remedy this issue over the past several years by surveying police, including patrol officers and detectives, at several departments throughout the United States. Our specific goal, however, was not a general survey about interrogation per se but rather to focus on reported interrogation strategies of police officers and their beliefs about the reliability of these techniques as used with young suspects in comparison with adults. Our pursuit of this more narrow focus has been strengthened by Drizin and Leo's (2004) findings that juveniles may be especially vulnerable to the pressures of interrogation and the potential for falsely confessing. In fact, in studies of wrongful convictions, false convictions are more common among younger exonerees; for example, in a descriptive study of 328 exoneration cases, 44% of the juvenile exonerees falsely confessed, compared with 13% of the adults, and among the youngest juveniles (aged 12 to 15 years), 75% falsely confessed (Gross, Jacoby, Matheson, Montgomery, & Patil, 2005).

This pattern has held up in experimental studies. Using the *Alt* key paradigm developed by Kassin and Kiechel (1996), Redlich and Goodman (2003) found marked developmental differences in rates of false confessions between participants of different ages: The 12- and 13-year-olds were more likely to confess (78% compliance rate) than were the 15- and 16-year-olds (72% compliance rate), who in turn were more likely to confess than were the young adults (59% compliance rate). In addition, our goal was to document the beliefs of law enforcement officers about the differences between youths and adults concerning susceptibility to suggestive questioning and general developmental capacities. This chapter addresses interrogation techniques only to the extent that they are clearly related to understanding the national survey, which is the substance of this chapter.

False Confessions and Their Consequences

A few case examples are worth noting to highlight coercive and deceptive interrogation strategies and the dangers inherent in their use. Two boys aged 7 and 8 years were charged with murder of an 11-year-old girl after Chicago police authorities claimed to have both physical evidence of the children's guilt and valid confessions that contained information that only the perpetrators could have known (Kotlowitz, 1999). The two boys were interrogated without the presence of their parents or lawyers and changed their stories multiple times. One of the boys had significant cognitive deficits and often repeated and incorporated what he heard into his stories. Ultimately, all charges were dropped when physical evidence was discovered exonerating the boys of criminal responsibility. Similarly in California, 14-year-old Michael Crowe was charged with the brutal murder of his sister on the basis of a confession he made that was later proven to be false. Contributors to Crowe's false confession included prolonged questioning over several days without the presence of parents or a lawyer, implications of leniency, and the presentation of false evidence. In New York, the infamous 1989 Central Park jogger rape case was reopened in 2002, more than a decade after five teenagers were convicted of the crime on the basis of their videotaped confessions. DNA evidence and a confession incriminated a previously convicted rapist and murderer, who claimed that he committed the crime alone. Apparently, the convicted adolescents falsely confessed.

These cases vividly illustrate the consequences that may result from the use of repeated, suggestive, and psychologically coercive interrogation techniques with juveniles. In particular, these cases expose a pressing concern regarding the welfare of youths: Is consideration given to the developmental immaturity of youths and its impact on the reliability of juveniles' confessions? Perhaps explaining the disproportionate rates of false confessions given by juveniles in both reviews of actual exonerations (e.g., Drizin & Leo, 2004; Gross et al., 2005) and in experimental studies (e.g., Redlich & Goodman, 2003), research results strongly suggest that youths are more likely to provide unreliable reports (including false confessions) during suggestive questioning than adults (Ceci, 1994; Dunn, 1995; Leo, 1994; Loftus, 1979; Richardson, Gudjonsson, & Kelly, 1995). This vulnerability is especially problematic because many juveniles are now being tried as adults, and youths who confess to committing felony crimes often suffer similar, if not harsher, sanctions as those afforded to adults (Feld, 1999). Police interrogation tactics in the United States are largely based on training known as the *Reid technique,* developed by Inbau, Reid, Buckley, and Jayne (2001), in which more than 500,000 law enforcement officers have been trained over the past several decades. Because this technique is a central focus of several chapters in this book, the particulars are not reviewed here, other than to note that not only have the authors of this chapter read their manuals but one of them (Jessica Meyer) also participated in a full 4-day, 32-hour Reid & Associates "Interviewing and Interrogation" training program before the authors began this research. Such direct involvement has revealed that the training is almost exclusively focused on adult suspects; in fact, only 10 minutes of instruction were dedicated to youths, and this was to advocate for the use of the same strategies with youths as with adults. The participants were taught that "the principles discussed with respect to adult suspects are just as applicable for use with young ones" (Inbau et al., 2001, p. 298), and even included encouragement of the use of adult language with youths. There was no discussion of developmental issues that may affect the reliability of deceptive and psychologically coercive interrogation techniques.

What is important is that the Reid training totally neglects the vast amount of social science literature that indicates these tactics may not be appropriate, especially for use with young suspects. The main concerns are the following:

- The influence of suggestive, leading and repeated questioning on the reliability of reports from young suspects. Evidence suggests that children are more suggestible than adults; may easily be influenced by questioning from authority figures; and may provide inaccurate reports when questioned in a leading, repeated, and suggestive fashion (Ceci, 1994; Ceci & Bruck, 1993; Owen-Kostelnik, Reppucci, & Meyer, 2006).
- The influence of adult language, confusing questioning, and trickery on the ability of young suspects to comprehend police questioning and thus respond reliably. Comprehension research has demonstrated that questions that include multiple parts, negatives, double negatives, and difficult vocabulary often lead to inaccurate reports by minors of all ages (Perry et al., 1995; Saywitz, Jaenicke, & Camparo, 1990; Walker, 1994).
- The influence of psychologically coercive questioning, including presentation of false evidence and minimizing the moral seriousness of the crime, on the decision-making process and the reliability of reports from young suspects who manifest diminished psychosocial maturity, such as being more influenced by short-term (e.g., wanting to go home) than by long-term consequences (e.g., spending significant time incarcerated), being eager to please, having a lack of self-confidence, as well as demonstrating increased obedience to authority, a desire to impress peers, and limited perspective-taking abilities.
- The fallibility of the interrogator's deception detection regarding the behavior of young suspects. Although there is abundant research on deception detection in adults, fewer studies have evaluated the accuracy

of deception detection in youths (e.g., DePaulo & Jordon, 1982; Vrij, Akehurst, Brown, & Mann, 2006) This is especially problematic because many juveniles demonstrate behaviors labeled as deceptive by Reid and Inbau (2000) in their everyday behaviors: for example, slouching in their seats, making less eye contact, using I swear statements, and having more liberal responses to questions about punitive sanctions.

Research on Police Practices and Beliefs

In a pilot study, Meyer and Reppucci (2007) examined reports from Baltimore County police about their use of interrogation tactics with children, adolescents, and adults; their beliefs about the reliability of these techniques; and their beliefs about general child development issues. Participants were 132 law enforcement officers from multiple ranks—including majors, colonels, detectives, and officers—who completed a 49-item survey about criminal interrogation (Police Interrogation Survey; PIS), a 20-item child development survey (Developmental Knowledge Survey; DKS), and nine demographic questions. Each participant received one of three versions of the PIS (about children under the age of 14 years, youths between 14 and 17 years, or adults 18 years and older) and one of two versions of the DKS (about children or youths). Different versions were used so that age comparisons could be made. The surveys were specifically designed for this investigation because there were no historical data collection instruments on either topic. The surveys were developed after extensive review of relevant literature and consultation with local police departments, police organizations, academic scholars, and pretests. In addition, 197 doctoral-level developmental psychologists completed the same surveys so that their answers could serve as the standard for developmental knowledge.

Principal axis factoring was conducted separately on each of the two surveys for both the police and psychologist samples to confirm the number of factors that provided the best fit to the Likert-scale data; three factors were confirmed for the PIS (Suggestibility, Comprehension, and Detection of Deception) but none for the DKS. Analyses of the PIS revealed that between 16% and 85% of our sample used various Reid interrogation techniques, including psychological coercion, trickery, deceit, and suggestion. There were no significant differences between survey versions in response to any of the actual interrogation practices, indicating that police use the same techniques with younger children, older youths, and adult suspects.

Results on the DKS indicated that although police understand some differences related to child development between children, youths, and adults, they seem to lack fundamental knowledge and awareness of how various interrogation techniques may be inappropriate for use with juveniles, in that such techniques may be particularly harmful to the reliability of reports given by children and youths. Police answers to the DKS (the developmental questions) were significantly different from those of psychologists on 16 of the 20 DKS questions. If we assume that the developmental psychologists do, in fact, have more accurate assessments on these matters, then police could clearly benefit from exposure to more knowledge of developmental psychology.

Overall, results indicated that whereas police acknowledge some developmental differences between juveniles and adults, there were gaps in police knowledge of child development and about reliable ways to apply developmental knowledge to the interrogation context. There were also indications that how police perceive juveniles in general and how they perceive and treat them specifically in the interrogation context may be contradictory in that police often believe that juveniles can be dealt with in the same manner as adults in interrogation contexts but not in others. Note also that participants' ethnicity, gender, level of education, age, and status as a parent were not related to any views about suggestibility and immaturity of youths. Participants' rank and years of experience were related to a few perceptions: Specifically, detectives and those with more work experience were less aware or less likely to acknowledge the fallibility of interrogation with juveniles than nondetectives and those with less work experience.

The National Survey

On the basis of the results from the pilot study (Meyer & Reppucci, 2007), the National Science Foundation provided funding (Grant SES-0423332) to determine their generalizability to other police departments. The goal was to document the police officers' reported interrogation practices, their beliefs about the reliability of these techniques, and their beliefs about the differences between juveniles and adults concerning susceptibility to psychologically coercive questioning and general developmental capacities. We now summarize a portion of the more consequential findings from this national survey.

Participants

Our final sample included 1,828 law enforcement officers recruited from 10 police agencies of various sizes and in various parts of the country: Oakland, California; Minneapolis, Minnesota; Dallas, Texas; Mesa, Arizona; Santa Ana, California; Washington, D.C.; Raleigh, North Carolina; Montgomery County, Maryland; Albemarle County, Virginia; and Oconee County, Georgia. There were no selection criteria within each agency because the pilot study suggested that the overwhelming majority of police (97%) within an agency have some experience questioning suspects. The officers presented a range of ranks and responsibilities: 60.4% were patrol officers, 22.8% were detectives (investigators), 10.9% were other ranks and 5.9% did not provide the information. Approximately 93% had experience questioning adults and 87% questioning juveniles. The gender of participants was 77.7% men, 14.7% women, and 7.7% did not provide that information. The racial mixture was 52.2% Caucasian, 18.5% African American, 10.7% Latino, 2.4% Asian American, and 16.2% other or no information. Average age was 36.8 years and average number of years of experience was 11.8 years; 63.6% had children, and 29.4% did not. The predominant educational level was a bachelor's degree (44.4%). In each department, the percentage of sworn officers who were asked to participate and did ranged from 90.5% to 100%, with a mean of 97%.

Survey Instruments

The PIS assesses law enforcement officers' reports of (a) interrogation practices used and (b) beliefs concerning interrogation procedures that affect the reliability of reports and confessions. The survey comprises 65 interrogation questions and 10 demographic questions. Participants received one of three versions of the survey, which contain the same questions about interrogation concerning (a) children under 14 years of age ($n = 600$), (b) youths 14 to 17 years of age ($n = 619$), or (c) adults 18 years and older ($n = 609$). Questions about young suspects were separated into two surveys (children and youths) because much of the literature suggests that there are developmental differences between those 13 years old and younger and those 14 to 17 years old (Grisso, 1981; Scott, Reppucci, & Woolard, 1995) and because the majority of states have set 14 years as the lowest age at which a youth can be transferred and tried as an adult. The survey developed for the Baltimore County pilot study (Meyer & Reppucci, 2007) was modified slightly for the National Study. All open-ended questions were removed because they were seldom completed in the pilot, and 16 more questions that were based on discussions with Baltimore police administrators were added to provide clarity. The survey took approximately 15 to 25 minutes to complete.

The DKS assesses law enforcement officers' general developmental knowledge concerning children and youths and comprises 26 items addressing perceptions of developmental differences among children, youths, and adults. All of the survey statements are rated on 6-point Likert response scales, ranging from strongly disagree to strongly agree. Survey items include developmental issues that may relate to interrogation practices, such as behaviors that are often used in behavioral symptom analysis of deception detection (e.g., gaze aversion, slouching posture). Participants received one of two versions of the survey that contained the same questions concerning either developmental differences between the following: (a) children (under 14 years of age) and adults ($n = 903$), or (b) youths (ages 14–17 years) and adults ($n = 925$). Six items were added to the DKS after the pilot study. The survey took about 5 minutes to complete.

Procedures for Survey Distribution

To obtain police participation, we initially contacted 54 police agencies around the nation. We mailed packets containing a cover letter describing the purpose and procedure of the study, a letter of support from the Baltimore County Police Department, and copies of the surveys to the chiefs of each department. Fourteen agencies (26%) indicated a willingness to participate, and three more expressed interest with further questions. Because of funding limitations, data were collected from only 10 departments.

Two of the authors, Meyer and Kostelnik, traveled to each police agency to personally distribute the surveys. Upon arrival, they met with the department chief or personnel director to review project procedures and discuss agency interrogation policies. Then the researchers attended several of the agencies' patrol and detective roll calls to recruit participants and provide the explanation and rationale for the study. Questions were often asked that suggested possible skepticism and distrust of research, and the investigators spent ample time alleviating concerns of officers about anonymity, confidentiality, and voluntariness of participation. Each person received one of the four versions of the survey packets: child PIS and child DKS, youth PIS and youth DKS, adult PIS and child DKS, or adult PIS and youth DKS. The two surveys were stapled together, counterbalanced such that half of the participants received the PIS first and half the DKS first. Once the participant completed his or her packet, he or she returned it directly to the researcher. Upon completion, each participant received a written debriefing statement that explained the purpose of the study.

Data Analysis

Initial analyses revealed order effects (which survey was completed first) in two instances: Police primed to think about interrogation (those who completed the PIS first) were less prone to acknowledge developmental limitations of juveniles in general, and police primed with developmental issues (those who completed the DKS first) were more prone to acknowledge suspects' diminished comprehension. As a result, survey order was used as a covariate in subsequent analyses.

Structural factor analysis was conducted on each of the two surveys (PIS and DKS) separately to confirm the latent factors represented by the observed survey items. The PIS factors found in the pilot study were confirmed, and factorial invariance was found for each of the factors, indicating that the same constructs were measured in child, youth, and adult versions of the survey. Table 4.1

Table 4.1. Police Interrogation Survey (PIS) Factor Items and Loadings

Factor and item	B	B
Suggestibility factor		
The reports of events given by children are more susceptible to suggestion by interviewers than are those given by adults.	1.00	.66
Children are more likely to confess to crimes they did not commit than adults.	0.97	.56
Compared to adults, children are more easily influenced by trickery during interviewing.	0.91	.58
Children incorporate elements of stories told by police into their own reports when they are interviewed for more than a couple of hours.	0.78	.49
Comprehension factor		
Children do not understand their right to an attorney.	1.00	.90
Children do not understand their right to remain silent.	0.96	.81
Miranda rights are well understood by children.	0.91	.84
Children do not understand the intent of a police interview.	0.59	.57
Detection of Deception factor		
Only guilty children react defensively to questions.	1.00	.92
Only guilty children react with discomfort to questions.	0.97	.88
Only innocent children are cooperative during interviewing.	0.79	.68
Only innocent children produce direct responses to questions.	0.60	.52

Note. B = Unstandardized factor loadings; B = Standardized factor loadings.
The term *children* is used, although *youth* or *adult* was also used depending on the version of the survey.

presents items in the three PIS factors—Suggestibility, Comprehension, Detection of Deception—and corresponding unstandardized and standardized factor loadings. The standardized indicator loadings that were estimated for each latent factor were all above .40, and all were statistically significant. Two factors were confirmed in the DKS—Suggestibility and Psychosocial Immaturity—and factorial invariance was again found for each factor. Table 4.2 presents items in the DKS factors and corresponding factor loadings.

To determine whether police perceive children or youths as developmentally different from adults and whether they use different interrogation techniques with them, we examined mean group differences on the DKS and the PIS using structural equation modeling (SEM) comparison of means tests for the factors, analysis of variance or analysis of covariance for continuous items, chi-square tests for dichotomous items, and logistic regression for dichotomous items with covariants. Demographic characteristics were also examined, and no substantive differences on the DKS factors were linked to them. For the PIS, there were meaningful effects for years of experience and frequency of interviewing youth, so these variables were entered as covariates into analyses predicting PIS factors. Finally, all analysis of variance and SEM regression analyses indicated no interaction effects involving demographics and survey versions.

We examined several hypotheses, which we present with summaries of our findings but without multiple tables of results because of page limitations.

Hypothesis 1: *Police will demonstrate some knowledge of child development and some areas of deficit in developmental knowledge, particularly regarding developmental differences between young children and adolescents.*

Overall, police demonstrated adequate recognition of both children's and youths' developmental capacities outside of the interrogation context. The vast majority of police officers agreed that in comparison with adults, children and youths were more suggestible, more immature in a psychosocial sense, and less

Table 4.2. Developmental Knowledge Survey (DKS) Factor Items and Loadings

Factor and item	B	B
Suggestibility factor		
Children will say untruthful things if they feel pressured by adults to do so.	1.00	.70
Children will say untruthful things to please adults.	0.98	.74
Children will say untruthful things if they feel pressured by parents to do so.	0.87	.65
Children will often repeat things that adults say.	0.70	.57
Psychosocial Immaturity factor		
Compared to adults, children are more concerned with immediate outcomes than with future outcomes.	1.00	.61
Children are intimidated by authority figures.	0.75	.44
Children are frequently unaware of long-term consequences of their actions.	0.73	.46
Children are more impulsive than adults.	0.72	.48

Note.   B = Unstandardized factor loadings; *B* = Standardized factor loadings.
The term *children* is used, although *youth* was also used depending on the version of the survey.

able to comprehend language. Most police officers acknowledged typical nonverbal behavior patterns of juveniles, noting that young individuals readily display lack of eye contact and slouching (behaviors indicative of deception according to Reid & Inbau, 2000). These results correspond to the substantive literature regarding what is known about youths' heightened suggestibility (Ceci & Bruck, 1993, 1998), limited decision-making capacities (Fried & Reppucci, 2001; Scott et al., 1995), and deficits in psychosocial maturity (Steinberg & Cauffman, 1996). Although there were no mean differences between responses regarding the younger children and responses regarding the youths or adolescents, a higher percentage of police officers agreed that younger children demonstrate diminished capacities in comparison with youths or adolescents.

Hypothesis 2: *Police will fail to apply their developmental knowledge to the interrogation context, which will be demonstrated by a lack of recognition of the suggestibility and malleability of youthful suspects in interrogation as well as a lack of relationship between developmental knowledge and interrogation survey factor scores.*

Police officers endorsed some overlap between their developmental knowledge of children in general and children in interrogation contexts. For example, on average police officers agreed that children were more susceptible to the provision of false confessions and unreliable reports when exposed to suggestion, trickery and lengthy interrogations. About half of the police officers (48.8%) acknowledged that young children do not comprehend *Miranda* warnings and police intent during interrogation. However, they were less likely to acknowledge the suggestibility of youth or adolescent and adult suspects. More than half (54.4%) disagreed that adolescent suspects were suggestible in comparison with adults, and the vast majority disagreed that adolescent (78.2%) and adult (90%) suspects fail to comprehend elements of interrogations. In addition, whereas most respondents agreed that children and youths are suggestible outside of the interrogation context (93.9% and 84.6%, respectively), a much lower percentage agreed that children and youths are suggestible in the interrogation context (67.5% and 45.6%, respectively). These results suggest that at least in terms of suggestibility and comprehension abilities, many police officers viewed adolescent suspects (aged 14–17 years) as able to respond reliably to interrogative questioning and as similar to adults.

With regard to behaviors typically thought to be indicative of deception, most police officers disagreed that suspects of all ages behave in prescribed manners according to their actual guilt or innocence. On average, police officers believed they were reliable at deception detection using behavioral cues 65% of the time, which is closer to the scientific literature's findings of 45% to 60% accuracy than to Reid and Inbau's (2000) 85% accuracy claim; however, this belief was far from universal among the police. A sizable minority (24%) claimed 85% or more accuracy at deception detection using speech, eye movements, and body language with suspects of all ages. Moreover, given their responses to the DKS, one might have expected differentiation of age groups, but they indicated no differences in reliability of behavioral analysis among suspects of various ages.

With regard to false confessions, 77% say that they do occur, with the most common response being 10% of the time. However, as a result of the pilot study, to clarify this response we had added a question that asked about their own behavior as well as about police behavior in general. Indeed, 69% indicated that they personally elicit false confessions 0% of the time. Also, the most common response among police officers was that 90% of the time police can determine if a suspect's confession is false regardless of the suspect's age. These findings substantiate Kassin and colleagues' (Kassin, Meissner, & Norwick, 2005; Meissner & Kassin, 2002) assertions that law enforcement personnel are often more confident about their own abilities and judgments than about others. Finally, the individual difference factors that relate to beliefs about false confessions are numerous: Minorities, women, and nondetectives acknowledged a greater occurrence of false confessions and were more likely to endorse a decreased ability to identify unreliable confessions.

Hypothesis 3: *Police will report receiving no interrogation training regarding juvenile suspects and therefore indicate use of similar interrogation practices (including psychologically coercive and deceptive tactics) with children, adolescents, and adults.*

With regard to training, approximately 24% of all respondents and 54% of the detectives indicated having received instruction on the Reid method of interrogation. Of all respondents, 36% (44% of detectives) indicated they had received instruction specific to interrogating youth; however, the majority (53%) stated that it consisted of 10 hours or less.

Using a checklist format, participants were asked to indicate whether they used certain techniques during interrogations in the past year and if they had not done any interrogations during that year (about 37% of the sample) to indicate what techniques they would have used. As can be seen in Table 4.3, police

Table 4.3. Percentage of Police Endorsing Use of Various Interrogation Techniques

Interrogation technique	Participants who interrogated in past year (%)			Participants who had not interrogated in past year (%)		
	C	Y	A	C	Y	A
Observe body language to detect deception	92	91	92	83	85	83
Observe body language to detect deception and make decision to begin interrogation	54	55	60	32	37	37
Observe speech patterns to detect deception	62	65	64	58	63	58
Observe speech patterns to detect deception and make decision to begin interrogation	42	44	47	24	29	25
False evidence[a]	23	25	31	11	17	13
Deceit	32	34	39	15	23	24
Discouraging denials	25	30	32	18	22	13
Repeated questioning[b]	58	57	67	51	45	52
Suggest what may have happened	42	47	47	28	35	34
Alternative questioning	22	22	29	15	20	21

Note. C = child survey version; Y = youth survey version; A = adult survey version.
[a,b]Omnibus group effects found for these tactics for participants who interrogated in the past year. Chi-square tests indicate significant differences in adult versus child and adult versus youth comparisons.

officers who interrogated suspects in the past year reported higher endorsement of most interrogation strategies. Depending on the particular technique, 22% to 92% (of those who interrogated during the past year) and 11% to 85% (of those who said what they would have used) endorsed use or willingness to use Reid techniques with children and adolescents as well as adults. The only techniques for which there were significant differences between adults and youths were the use of false evidence and the use of repeated questioning.

Note that a higher percentage of detectives endorsed use of every technique in comparison with patrol officers. It is not surprising that those detectives who had received Reid training were more likely to endorse many of the tactics in comparison with non-Reid-trained detectives. One of the most striking findings was that a higher percentage of police officers who reported having had interrogation training about youths endorsed every Reid tactic with child and adolescent suspects in comparison with those reporting no training regarding youths at all. This finding raises questions as to whether the training being received was based on the Reid approach instead of a developmentally sensitive curriculum.

It should also be noted that no relationship existed between beliefs on the DKS and interrogation practices. The only PIS factor related to interrogation practices was the Comprehension factor: A lower percentage of police officers who acknowledged suspects' comprehension difficulties reported use of suggestive, deceitful, and deception detection interrogation tactics than police officers who disagreed that suspects demonstrate comprehension difficulties. Finally, when asked more directly whether the same interrogation techniques should be used with adults and youth or children, police officers tended to slightly agree or remained somewhat neutral.

Hypothesis 4: *Police will indicate a need and a desire for additional interrogation training regarding youths and children.*

About 76% of police officers endorsed a need for more training regarding interrogation of youths or children, and 60% endorsed the need to use more standard procedures with them.

Hypothesis 5: *A higher percentage of law enforcement officers from agencies located in areas with high crime rates will report use of coercive and deceptive interrogation techniques as compared with police from agencies in low crime areas. Similarly, police who work in high crime areas will view suspects as hardened criminals with less tendency to be suggestible and malleable to police questioning.*

To test this hypothesis, we compared means of the PIS Suggestibility, Comprehension, and Detection of Deception factors as a function of crime rates in the location of the agencies, using SEM comparison of means tests after accounting for relevant demographics. To our surprise, no relationships were found between reported practices and crime rates in locations of agencies.

Hypothesis 6: *Despite the location of the police department, law enforcement professionals will demonstrate similar levels of knowledge about child development and understanding of the relationship between developmental capacities and the reliability of reports obtained.*

To test this hypothesis, we compared means of the DKS Suggestibility and Immaturity factors as a function of crime rates in the agencies' locations using SEM comparison mean tests. As expected, there were no differences found.

Summary and Implications

Overall, the most important conclusions that can be drawn from the national survey are the following: (a) Police officers demonstrate adequate knowledge of child development and some knowledge of the unreliability of reports obtained from young suspects; yet (b) police officers do not seem to apply this fundamental developmental knowledge to their reported practices in the interrogation context; and (c) police officers demonstrate a general view that youths can be dealt with in the same manner in interrogations as adults, especially those officers who have received Reid training. It is unclear whether police officers fail to apply basic developmental knowledge because of their desire to conduct interrogations in prescribed ways; whether they fail to make the connection between developmental information and its applicability in the interrogation context or whether they make the connection but consider immaturity to be an advantage in extracting a confession; whether they believe that youths suspected of involvement in criminal activities are unlike typical youths; or whether they believe such applications are unnecessary for their own behavior or practices because they would know if they obtained an unreliable admission or a false confession. Of interest regarding these questions is one anecdotal piece of information that the researchers often heard during data collection: that the youths police see in interrogations are not like normal kids but are more like adults.

Our goal has been to stimulate research by increasing understanding of police beliefs and reported practices concerning the interrogation of juveniles. We hope this first effort at documenting the problem of false confessions through the lens of law enforcement will have the potential to enhance criminal justice operations and to encourage other investigators to do the same. Moreover, as Wells et al.'s (1998) research has been used to develop guidelines to improve eyewitness identification, and Lassiter and colleagues' (Lassiter & Irvine, 1986; Lassiter, Slaw, Briggs, & Scalan, 1992; chap. 9, this volume) findings on the importance of equal focus on both suspect and investigator in interrogations have stimulated the introduction of legislation to require videotaping, we hope that findings such as ours will encourage a public policy that mandates training in developmental differences among children, youths, and adults and in the relationship between youthful capacities and the use of various interrogation techniques in order to achieve a more equitable and fairer justice system.

References

Ceci, S. J. (1994). Cognitive and social factors in children's testimony. In B. Sales & G. VandenBos (Eds.), *Psychology in litigation and legislation* (pp. 14–54). Washington, DC: American Psychological Association.

Ceci, S. J., & Bruck, M. (1993). Suggestibility of the child witness: A historical review and synthesis. *Psychological Bulletin, 113,* 403–439.

Ceci, S. J., & Bruck, M. (1998). Children's testimony: Applied and basic issues. In W. Damon, I. E. Sigel, & K. A. Renniger (Eds.), *Handbook of child psychology* (5th ed., pp. 713–773). New York: Wiley.

DePaulo, B. M., & Jordon, A. (1982). Age changes in deceiving and detecting deceit. In R. S. Feldman (Ed.), *Development of nonverbal behavior in children* (pp. 151–180). New York: Springer-Verlag.

Drizin, S. A., & Leo, R. A. (2004). The problem of false confessions in the post-DNA world. *North Carolina Law Review, 82,* 891–1007.

Dunn, A. R. (1995). Questioning the reliability of children's testimony: An examination of problematic events. *Law & Psychology Review, 19,* 203–215.

Feld, B. (1999). *Bad kids: Race and the transformation of the juvenile court.* Oxford: Oxford University Press.

Fried, C. S., & Reppucci, N. D. (2001). Criminal decision making: The development of adolescent judgment, criminal responsibility, and culpability. *Law & Human Behavior, 25,* 45–61.

Grisso, T. (1981). *Juveniles' waiver of rights: Legal and psychological competence.* New York: Plenum.

Gross, S., Jacoby, K., Matheson, D., Montgomery, N., & Patil, S. (2005). Exonerations in the United States 1989 through 2003. *Journal of Criminal Law and Criminology, 95,* 523–560.

Gudjonsson, G. H. (2003). *The psychology of interrogations and confessions.* London: Wiley.

Inbau, F. E., Reid, J. E., Buckley, J. P., & Jayne, B. C. (2001). *Criminal interrogation and confessions* (4th ed.). Gaithersburg, MD: Aspen.

Kamisar, Y. (2003). Interrogating suspects: Limit police secrecy. *The National Law Journal.* Retrieved November 5, 2005, from http://www.nacdl.org/sl_docs.nsf/freeform/Mandatory:151?Open Document

Kassin, S. M., & Kiechel, K. L. (1996). The social psychology of false confessions: Compliance, internalization, and confabulation. *Psychological Science, 7,* 125–128.

Kassin, S. M., Leo, R. A., Meissner, C. A., Richman, K. D., Colwell, L. H., Leach, A., & Fon, D. L. (2007). Police interviewing and interrogation: A self-report survey of police practices and beliefs. *Law & Human Behavior, 31,* 381–400.

Kassin, S. M., Meissner, C. A., & Norwick, R. J. (2005). "I'd know a false confession if I saw one": A comparative study of college students and police investigators. *Law & Human Behavior, 29,* 211–227.

Kotlowitz, A. (1999, February 8). The unprotected. *The New Yorker,* pp. 42–53.

Lassiter, G. D., & Irvine, A. A. (1986). Videotaped confessions: The impact of camera point of view on judgments of coercion. *Journal of Applied Social Psychology, 16,* 268–276.

Lassiter, G. D., Slaw, R. D., Briggs, M. A., & Scanlan, C. R. (1992). The potential for bias in videotaped confessions. *Journal of Applied Social Psychology, 22,* 1828–1851.

Leo, R. A. (1994). Police interrogation and social control. *Social & Legal Studies, 3,* 93–120.

Loftus, E. (1979). *Eyewitness testimony.* London: Harvard University Press.

Meissner, C. A., & Kassin, S. M. (2002). He's guilty! Investigator bias in judgments of truth and deception. *Law and Human Behavior, 26,* 469–480.

Meyer, J. R. & Reppucci, N. D. (2003, April). *Police perceptions of youth interrogative suggestibility and false confession rates.* Poster presented at the Society for Research in Child Development, Tampa, FL.

Meyer, J. R. & Reppucci, N. D. (2007). Police practices regarding juvenile interrogation and interrogative suggestibility. *Behavioral Sciences & the Law, 25,* 757–780.

Owen-Kostelnik, J., Reppucci, N. D., & Meyer, J. (2006) Testimony and interrogation of minors: Assumptions of immaturity and immorality. *American Psychologist, 61,* 286–304.

Perry, N. W., McAuliff, B. D., Tam, P., Claycomb, L., Dostal, C., & Flanagan, C. (1995). When lawyers question children: Is justice served? *Law & Human Behavior, 19,* 609–625.

Redlich, A. D., & Goodman, G. S. (2003). Taking responsibility for an act not committed: The influence of age and suggestibility. *Law and Human Behavior, 27,* 141–156.

Reid, J. E., & Inbau, F. E. (2000). *The Reid technique of interviewing and interrogation.* Chicago: Reid Associates.

Richardson, G., Gudjonsson, G. H., & Kelly, T. P. (1995). Interrogative suggestibility in an adolescent forensic population. *Journal of Adolescence, 18,* 211–216.

Saywitz, K., Jaenicke, C. & Camparo, L. (1990). Children's knowledge of legal terminology. *Law & Human Behavior, 14,* 523–525.

Scheck, B., Neufeld, P., & Dwyer, J. (2000). *Actual innocence* (1st ed.). New York: Doubleday.

Scott, E. S., Reppucci, N. D., & Woolard, J. L. (1995). Evaluating adolescents' decision making in legal contexts. *Law & Human Behavior, 19,* 221–244.

Steinberg, L., & Cauffman, E. (1996). Maturity of judgment in adolescence: Psychosocial factors in adolescent decision making. *Law & Human Behavior, 20,* 249–272.

Vrij, A., Akehurst, L., Brown, L., & Mann, S. (2006). Detecting lies in young children, adolescents and adults. *Applied Cognitive Psychology, 20,* 1225–1237.

Walker, A. G. (1994). *Handbook on questioning children: A linguistic perspective.* Washington, DC: American Bar Association Center on Children and the Law.

Wells, G., Small, M., Penrod, S., Malpass, R., Fulero, S., & Brimacombe, C. (1998). Eyewitness identification procedures: Recommendations for lineups and photospreads. *Law & Human Behavior, 22,* 603–647.

5

Four Studies of What Really Happens in Police Interviews

Ray Bull and Stavroula Soukara

Surprisingly, there exist rather few published studies of what actually takes place during police interviews with suspects. Only a proportion of this small sample has provided data concerning the various tactics and skills used by such interviewers, and almost no studies have examined the possible relationship between actual tactic and skill usage and the elicitation of confessions (but see Pearse & Gudjonsson, 1999). The present chapter describes four interrelated studies that provide a significant addition to this limited literature. These four studies were conducted several years after a very major initiative was undertaken in England and Wales to improve and change the way police conduct interviews with suspects, witnesses, and victims.

Background to the Present Investigations

In England and Wales since the mid-1980s it has been mandated by law that all police interviews with suspects be fully recorded on videotape or more typically audiotape (for more on this legislation, see Zander, 1990). Such recordings have permitted research to be conducted on how well interviews are actually conducted. However, of course, such interviews constitute sensitive material to which research access has been limited. Nevertheless, a small number of relevant studies (some with large samples) were conducted (for a review, see Milne & Bull, 1999; for a pioneering study in the United States, see Leo, 1996).

A consistent finding across these early studies was that the introduction of mandatory recording (and of other factors in the relevant legislation that emphasized that confessions must be voluntary) had resulted in few interviews being coercive or oppressive. However, it was also clear from these data that at that time officers' relevant skills were deficient. For example, Baldwin (1993) analyzed several hundred interviews with suspects and found them generally to be of a surprisingly poor standard. He noted that in most, the interviewers made no serious challenge to what the suspects were saying (perhaps because of the new legislation, including its requirement for electronic recording). He also noted that the majority of suspects who confessed did this very near to the beginning of the interviews (when all the evidence against them was usually revealed, perhaps because, for them, the evidence was strong). Almost no suspects moved during the interviews from denial to confession, thus demonstrating that what the interviewers did throughout most of the interview had no impact. Similarly, Moston, Stephenson, and Williamson (1992) found (in a very large sample of audio recorded interviews) that interviewers devoted little time to trying to obtain an account from suspects but instead almost straightaway and in an accusatory way revealed all the evidence against the suspect and demanded that he or she confess. (Such a strategy is not likely to be that successful if the evidence is perceived by the suspect to be weak.)

The Association of Chief Police Officers (for England and Wales; ACPO) took note of the rather devastating findings of these studies; though published in the early 1990s, they were of interviews conducted in the early years after electronic recording became common practice. One probable explanation of the generally poor interviewing was that at that time and hitherto, police officers in England and Wales had received minimal relevant training. Such a lack of relevant, comprehensive training continued, however, for only a few years, and in 1992 the ACPO in consultation with the relevant part of the government (i.e., the Home Office) introduced a new, nationwide training initiative based on an updated philosophy relating to such interviews. This novel approach was deemed so important that in 1992 every police officer in England and Wales (approximately 127,000) was issued two booklets to read on the topic. Also, from 1992 onward, over the ensuing years every police officer would receive substantial training regarding this new approach, starting with those who interview most frequently (i.e., experienced detectives).

This new approach, called PEACE by the police service, has been fully described elsewhere (e.g., Milne & Bull, 1999). The acronym stands for the following:

- *P*lanning and Preparation
- *E*ngage and Explain
- Obtain an *A*ccount
- *C*losure
- *E*valuation

These five crucial aspects of interviewing relate to the national seven principles of investigative interviewing (Milne & Bull, 1999), which include the following:

- The role of interviewers is to obtain reliable and accurate information.
- Interviewers should be open-minded.
- Interviewers must act fairly.
- Interviewers ask questions to establish the truth.

The PEACE approach, clearly, was (and is) not in line with what has been advocated in many other countries (e.g., in the United States, where the Reid technique predominates; see chap. 1, this volume), although recently some countries have decided to adopt the PEACE approach nationally (e.g., New Zealand, Norway). Given that the PEACE approach and its training constituted a major and very expensive development, it was deemed important both by ACPO and the government to examine, after it had been in place for some years, the extent to which interviewers' beliefs and their actual interviewing were now in line with the PEACE philosophy. However, to date only a few investigations have examined this. One was by Bull and Cherryman (1996), parts of which are briefly described in this chapter. Another, which looked at interviews with witnesses as well as interviews with suspects, was by Clarke and Milne (2001), which we return to in the Conclusion section.

We now present four interrelated studies that were designed to examine not only the extent to which interviewers' beliefs and interviewers' actual performance were in line with PEACE but also which aspects of their performance (e.g., tactics, skills) might relate to suspects giving a confession. Given the limited number of relevant prior studies of actual police interviews and the few laboratory or experimental studies of sufficient relevance and quality (see chap. 7, this volume), the new research studies to be reported in this chapter were exploratory in nature. That is, too little was already known to allow a predictive or inductive approach.

Study 1: Belief in the New Approach

Soon after the introduction in 1992 of the PEACE approach, Ray Bull was asked by the relevant part of the government to conduct several studies to determine to what extent those who were the first to receive training regarding this new approach (i.e., experienced detectives) were able to conduct interviews in line with its philosophy (Bull & Cherryman, 1996; for a fuller account, see Milne & Bull, 1999). An important aspect of the initial investigations was to determine what those who regularly interview suspects were willing to indicate as the most necessary skills. These turned out to be preparation, knowledge of topic, rapport, listening, questioning, flexibility, open-mindedness, and compassion or empathy.

Several years later, we again asked a different sample of experienced detectives from a relatively large police force in England for their views on issues pertaining to the interviewing of suspects (Soukara, Bull, & Vrij, 2002). This more recent investigation formed Study 1 of the set of four interrelated studies that are reported in the present chapter (which constitute Soukara's, 2005, doctoral thesis). This study found that 60% of the participants (mean length of police service was over 20 years) indicated that good interviewing skills can be acquired only via specialized training, with only 5% asserting that experience alone is sufficient. More than 70% of these detectives also indicated that planning and preparation for the interview was, in their opinion, the most important aspect of interviewing (i.e., the P in PEACE). When asked what tactics or techniques they had used in a successful interview with an initially uncooperative suspect, detectives mostly said that the use of evidence played the main role. Their responses also emphasized the role of flexibility in terms of the conducting of interviews and that this flexibility should be influenced by the nature of the alleged offense and the individual characteristics of the suspect.

When asked to indicate on a 5-point scale, "How important do you think it should be for an interviewing officer to obtain a confession?" almost all respondents chose "Not at all important." However, in response to the question, "How often do you think interviewing officers enter the interview room with an assumption that the suspect is guilty?" the mean response was 3.28 (but with quite a high standard deviation). Nevertheless, in response to "How important do you think it is for the interviewing officer not to assume guilt when entering the interview room?" the mean response was 4.28 (5 = *very important*). Thus, although these experienced detectives' beliefs were in line with the philosophy of the PEACE approach, they indicated that some interviewers nevertheless do enter the interview room with a degree of guilt assumption. With regard to assuming guilt or innocence on the basis of suspects' behavior (e.g., part one of the Reid approach; see chap. 6, this volume), these detectives indicated clearly that in their view interviewers are not influenced by this. That is, in response to the question, "To what extent do you think interviewers' approach towards suspects is influenced by how guilty or innocent the suspect looks/behaves?" the mean response was 1.68 (1 = *never,* 5 = *always*).

The results of Study 1 (for more, see Soukara et al., 2002) seem to indicate that these experienced detectives expressed views largely in line with the PEACE approach. (For views in Finland, see Hakkanen, Ask, Kebbell, Alison, & Granhag, 2007; in North America, see Kassin et al., 2007.) However, would interviews conducted by members of their force actually also be in line with the PEACE philosophy? Studies 2 and 3 were conducted, in part, to answer this crucial question.

Study 2: Tactic Usage and Confession

For this investigation, a random sample of 80 of the 200 interviews made available by the police was selected. (Some of the remainder were used in Study 3.) Listening to these audiotaped interviews revealed that they were concerned with 22 different types of alleged offenses that ranged from murder, rape, fraud, and sexual offenses against children to shoplifting, burglary, and reckless driving. Eight of the suspects were women, and 72 were men. Some of the interviews lasted as long as 4 hours, and a few lasted only about 10 minutes.

Five raters, experienced with the topic of interviewing suspects from their academic work and research, independently listened to and evaluated the interviews. One main rater evaluated all 80, and the other four each evaluated five different interviews (to provide a sample of 20 with which to assess the interrater reliability of the main rater). The raters were instructed (a) to listen to the whole of each interview before finally evaluating it and (b) that they could stop the recording and replay a part whenever they wished. The rating and evaluation sheets were designed to incorporate the major tactics most commonly mentioned in previous publications on the interrogating and interviewing of suspects. Table 5.1 lists these 17 tactics along with brief descriptions of each (which were provided to the raters).

Each of the 80 interviews evaluated the following:

- whether each of the 17 tactics was present or not;
- if a tactic was used, the degree to which in each interview it was used;

Table 5.1. The Tactics and Their Descriptions

Tactic	Description
1. Disclosure of evidence	Revealing evidence regarding the offense
2. Maximization of offense	Exaggerating the significance or seriousness of an action, in order to facilitate an admission
3. Minimization of offense	Reducing the significance of an action in order to facilitate admission
4. Emphasizing contradictions	Pointing out inconsistencies in the suspect's account
5. Positive confrontation	Directly accusing the suspect regarding his or her involvement to the crime
6. Gentle prods	Trying to make the suspect reveal information by encouraging him or her to continue speaking
7. Concern	Showing concern or empathy toward the suspect
8. Interruptions	Continuing to interrupt the suspect when he or she tries to answer the questions
9. Silence	Maintaining silence after the suspect has said something
10. Repetitive questioning	Repeating the same questions over and over again
11. Leading questions	Asking questions in a way in which the answer is suggested
12. Open questions	Asking the suspect to give his or her account of events
13. Intimidation	Accusing the suspect of being a liar, or laughing at the person
14. Suggest scenario	Interviewer tries to give his or her side of the story, suggesting possible scenarios of what happened
15. Handling the suspect's mood	Recognizing changes in the suspect's mood and reacting accordingly
16. Challenging the suspect's account	Revealing evidence that counters what the suspect has said, implying that it is not the truth.
17. Situational futility	Telling the suspect that the truth will come out one day, pointing out negative consequences resulting from continuous denial

- the extent to which each suspect moved (or not) toward an admission or confession (using a 5-point scale; 1 = *no change,* 5 = *moved from denial to confession*); and
- whether a confession occurred.

Interrater agreement (significant correlations or Cohen's kappas) was found (save for the degree of usage of *concern* and *silence;* for more on this study, see Soukara, Bull, Vrij, Turner, & Cherryman, 2008).

Use of Each of the 17 Tactics

On the basis of the main rater's data, the following was determined.

1. The tactics that were most frequently used (to some extent) were
    -   disclosure of evidence and open questions (used in all but 1 interview),
    -   leading questions (used in 73 of the 80 interviews), and
    -   repetitive questioning (used in 67).
2. The other tactics used in at least 50% of the interviews were
    -   emphasizing contradictions,
    -   positive confrontation, and
    -   challenging the suspect's account.
3. The tactics used in less than 50% were
    -   gentle prods,
    -   handling suspect's mood,
    -   suggest scenario,
    -   interruptions,
    -   concern, and
    -   silence.
4. The tactics that were never or almost never used were
    -   maximization (in only one interview),
    -   minimization (never),
    -   intimidation (never), and
    -   situational futility (never).

Confessions

Of the 80 interviews, 31 involved a confession. However, unlike in the few previous studies of confessions occurring in an interview (all seem to have involved audiotaped interviews in England or Wales), the majority of the confessions were not at or near to the beginning of the interviews. Instead, only 5 of these 31 confessions occurred in the first third of the interviews' duration. Of the confessions, 15 were in the middle third, and 11 were in the final third.

That the majority of the confessions did not occur near the beginning of the interviews allows for the examination of the possible relationships or correlations between interviewer tactic usage and the extent to which confessing suspects moved from denial to confession. However, several of the tactics were rarely used in these 31 interviews. The tactics that occurred in most of the confession interviews were disclosure of evidence, open questions, positive confrontation, leading questions, emphasizing contradictions, challenging suspect's account, and repetitive questioning. (However, many of these tactics also occurred in the no confession interviews.) For the tactics that had a frequency of usage that allowed a correlation to be calculated between their usage and confessing, none produced a positive correlation (even though the usage of positive confrontation, silence, leading questions, and suggest scenario was more frequent in the confession interviews). In fact, the only correlation that exceeded the critical value required for statistical significance was negative (i.e., for challenge the suspect's account), and negative correlations were not predicted. What this negative correlation suggests is that the tactic of challenging the suspect's account was used to a lesser degree in interviews that involved a greater shift to confessing. Although this tactic was used in 26 of the 31 confession interviews, it was also used in 31 of the 49 no-confession interviews. Indeed, in these no-confession interviews the degree of usage of this tactic was stronger than in the confession interviews (as was the case for eight other tactics). What this suggests, of course (with the benefit of hindsight), is that interviewers will use certain tactics even more strongly in interviews during which the suspect does not confess (cf. Kassin, Goldstein, & Savitsty, 2003; Meissner & Kassin, 2004).

Although this Study 2 did not find a simple relationship between degree of tactic usage and extent of shift to confessing, it did find that the tactics of greatest concern to most psychologists (i.e. minimization, maximization, intimidation, and situational futility) were not used. This would be in line with the philosophy of the PEACE approach, as would be the frequent use of tactics such as disclosure of evidence, emphasizing contradictions, and challenge account. However, the frequent use of leading questions and repetitive questioning is not in line with the PEACE approach. Nevertheless, that emphasizing contradictions and challenge account had the largest difference in average degree of usage between no confession and confession interviews suggests that interviewers especially used these two tactics more with suspects who were not confessing. This would seem to be in line with the PEACE approach.

Study 3

For this study, an additional 50 of the audiotaped interviews made available by the police were randomly selected (i.e., this sample of 50 is different from the 80 used in Study 2, discussed previously). Listening to these audiotapes revealed that the interviews were concerned with the following alleged offenses: fraud, murder, indecent assault, assault resulting in bodily harm, cruelty, criminal damage, sexual offenses against children, vehicle theft, theft, physical assault of children, drug dealing, arson, burglary, handling of stolen goods, possession of firearms, public order offenses, shoplifting, reckless driving, and neglect. Five of the suspects were women, and 45 were men. Some of the interviews lasted as long as 3 hours, and a small number lasted only 5 minutes or so. This variability across interviews in the nature of the crime or accusation, interview length, and probably the strength of the evidence (and other factors) was unavoidable. However, such variability probably aids generalizability.

Five raters, experienced with the topic of investigative interviewing from their academic work and research, independently listened to and evaluated the audiotaped interviewers. One main rater evaluated all 50, and the other four each evaluated four different interviews (to provide a sample of 16 to assess the interrater reliability of the main rater). As in Study 2, the raters were instructed (a) to listen to the whole of each interview before finally evaluating it and (b) that they could stop the recording and replay a part whenever they wished.

In light of Holmberg and Christianson's (2002) suggestion that suspects' perception of and response to how they are interviewed may well influence their decision whether to confess, in this study we tried to evaluate a number of suspect behaviors, a rather novel thing to attempt. For this sample of 50 interviews, in addition to the 17 interviewer tactics listed in Table 5.1, the following six interviewer skills (among those found important by Bull & Cherryman, 1996; see earlier) were also evaluated on 5-point scales: rapport building, communication, open-mindedness (willingness to listen to what suspect says), presumptiveness (assuming guilt), flexibility (extent to which interviewer changes to suit suspect's behavior or attitude), and responsiveness to interviewee (extent of positive reaction to suspect's behavior or attitude). The following suspect behaviors were also evaluated: cooperation, responsiveness to interviewer (extent of positive reaction to interviewer's behavior or attitude), plausibility of account, and resistance (unwillingness to answer questions; see Pearse & Gudjonsson, 1999).

Each of the 50 interviews was evaluated using 5-point scales to determine the extent to which each of the 17 tactics was used, the extent to which each of the six interviewer skills was present, the extent to which each of the four suspect behaviors was present, and the extent to which each suspect moved toward an admission or confession (1 = *no change,* 5 = *moved from denial to an admission/confession*). Interrater agreement was demonstrated by significant correlations or Cohen's kappas for each of the tactics, skills, and behaviors.

Relationships Between Interviewer Tactics and Skills

Across the 50 interviews, there were no strong simple relationships between each of the interviewers' skills and the degree to which each of the tactics were used. In part, this is due to several of the tactics rarely being used. Nine tactics were used in more than 10 of the 50 interviews (in the order of the number of interviews in which they were used): open questions, disclosure of evidence, repetitive questioning (repeating the same questions over and over again), leading questions, handling mood (focusing the suspect on possible reasons for committing the crime), positive confrontation (directly accusing the suspect), emphasizing contradictions, and interruptions. Three of these tactics (open questions, disclosure of evidence, and emphasizing contradictions) are emphasized by the PEACE training philosophy as being appropriate, but five are not.

For each interview, the proportion of the tactics used that was inappropriate was calculated. The possible relationships were examined between this proportion and the extent to which each of the six interviewer skills was present. Significant negative correlations were found for communication and for responsiveness to suspect, indicating that interviews containing more of these two skills involved a lower proportion of inappropriate tactics.

Relationships Between Interviewer Skills and Suspect Behaviors

Several significant relationships were found between the four suspect behaviors and the six interviewer skills:

1. Suspect responsiveness to interviewer was significantly and positively correlated with interviewer
   - communication,
   - open-mindedness,
   - flexibility,
   - rapport building, and
   - responsiveness to suspect.
2. Suspect cooperation was significantly and positively correlated with interviewer
   - open-mindedness,
   - flexibility,
   - rapport building, and
   - responsiveness to suspect;
   and significantly negatively correlated with interviewer presumptiveness.
3. Suspect resistance was significantly and positively correlated with interviewer
   - open-mindedness, and
   - rapport building;
   and significantly negatively correlated with interviewer
   - presumptiveness and
   - responsiveness to suspect.

The first 10 relationships above make sense (i.e., more suspect responsiveness and cooperation when skills emphasized by the PEACE approach or philosophy were present, and less suspect cooperation with interviewer presumptiveness). The relationships between greater suspect resistance and more rapport, open-mindedness, less presumptiveness, and responsiveness to suspect initially might seem difficult to explain. However, when suspects were resistant, perhaps this caused the interviewers to demonstrate more rapport and a greater willingness to listen to whatever the suspect was willing to say. Similarly, when suspects were resistant, perhaps this caused the interviewers to be less presumptive (i.e., of guilt) and less responsive (to such suspects). (*Caused* is used tentatively here because this research does not allow causation to be determined.)

Interviewer Skills Associated With Confession and No-Confession Interviews

Previous studies (see earlier in this chapter) of tape-recorded, real-life suspect interviews in the United Kingdom noted that at that time (i.e., prior to the PEACE philosophy being introduced), if a confession occurred this would usually be very early on or at the beginning of the interviews (e.g., Baldwin, 1993). This may well have been due to the police strategy in those days of revealing at the beginning of the interview all of the evidence against the suspect. As stated previously, if such evidence was strong, more confessions occurred (Moston et al., 1992).

An evolving aspect of the PEACE approach has been to obtain an account from the suspect before revealing all the evidence (although appropriate disclosure by the police to the suspect's legal representative of the evidence is an issue). In these 50 interviews, 19 suspects confessed, but only 7 of these did so during the first third of their interview. Three confessed in the final third of their interview, and nine confessed in the middle third of their interview. (The PEACE approach encourages continuing with the interview once a confession has occurred if more information is needed to support or verify the confession.) That over 60% of the confessions did not occur in the first third of the interviews would possibly allow effects of interviewer skills to be manifest.

The 19 confession interviews were compared with the 31 no-confession interviews with regard to the six interviewer skills (described earlier). Only for interviewer rapport building was there a significant difference found (perhaps because these analyses combined all the 19 confessions into one group). With regard to suspect behaviors, only suspect responsiveness was found to differ significantly across confession and no-confession interviews. This latter finding suggests that in part confessing is related to how suspects choose to behave. (Furthermore, it was noted above that the extent of suspect responsiveness was positively correlated with five of the six interviewer skills.) Thus, even though the sample sizes are rather small (e.g., probably in only 12 of the interviews could the six interviewer skills have an effect), it is possible that a relationship did actually exist between confessing or not and some aspects of interviewer skill. (The effect for interviewer flexibility would also have been significant for a one-tailed hypothesis.)

Study 4: The Timing of Tactics

> You just work on making the suspect open up and start talking. It is often a "trial and error" situation—you try something and if it doesn't work then you move on to something different. No one says it's easy, all you need is patience and keep trying . . . . (an extract from an experienced detective's reply while being interviewed for Study 1, reported earlier).

Almost no publications have examined at what times during interviews various tactics are used, and almost none have examined the possible relationships between the timing of tactics and the timing of a change within interviews from denial to confession. The study by Pearse and Gudjonsson (1999) is a rare exception in which they examined a special sample of 18 confessions. In our Study 4, we examined not only the use and timing of various tactics within interviews but also the possible relationships between the timing of tactics and the timing of confessions. To achieve the latter, we selected from the available sample of 200 interviews 40 in which a confession occurred, but not near to the beginning. (Some, but not all, of these 40 interviews formed parts of Studies 2 and 3.) These 40 interviews had a duration of between 15 and 60 minutes. They involved the following alleged offenses: arson, assault resulting in bodily harm, criminal damage, vehicle theft, drug dealing, burglary, handling of stolen goods, possession of firearms, public order, fraud, reckless driving, and neglect. Each interview was divided into a number of 5-minute slots.

For each 5-minute slot, the coder of these audiorecorded interviews noted whether each of 17 interviewer tactics (that had formed part of Studies 2 and 3 above, in which she was a rater) had been used. The actual timing of the confession was also noted. (Although it was not that difficult to determine the timing of the actual confessions, they typically did not suddenly happen but were preceded by related matters such as the suspect revealing bits of relevant information.)

It is not surprising (because some of these 40 interviews were included in Studies 2 and 3) that the tactics of minimization, maximization, and intimidation were never used. The percentage of interviews involving the following tactics were disclosure of evidence (100%), open questions (100%), repetitive questions (93%), leading questions (75%), handling suspect's mood (73%), contradictions (65%), positive confrontation (60%), interruptions (55%), silence (35%), challenge account (28%), suggest scenario (20%), gentle prods (15%), concern (10%), and situational futility (3%).

Table 5.2 presents for the consecutive 5-minute time slots how many of the 40 interviews lasted that long, and the number of the interviews in which each tactic was used in each time slot.

Table 5.2 reveals some aspects of the timing of tactics but not their possible relationships to confessing. Information relevant to confessing is provided in Table 5.3, which focuses not only on the 5-minute time slot in which the 40 confessions occurred but also the two prior time slots.

Table 5.3 reveals that 7 of the 14 tactics were used (remembering that minimization, maximization, and intimidation were never used) in the minutes prior to more than half of the 40 confessions, that 4 of other 7 tactics were used in the prior minutes in less than a quarter of these confessions interviews, and 3 tactics were used in the prior minutes in between a quarter and a half of these interviews. If (and it probably is a rather big "if," given that tactics used earlier on can set the scene for later ones to be effective) confessing is most influenced by the interviewer tactics used in the preceding 10 to 15 minutes, then the most influential tactics would seem to be disclosure of evidence, open questions, and repetitive questions followed by leading questions, handling suspect's mood, pointing out contradictions, and positive confrontation.

However, Study 2 found that only two of the above tactics (i.e., positive confrontation and leading questions) were more frequent in the confession interview. But the analyses in Study 2 did not take note of when during the interviews, in relation to confessing, the tactics were used. Study 4 does demonstrate that the tactics of suggest scenario, gentle prods, concern, and situation futility rarely occurred in the minutes leading up to the confessions, and they therefore could be of limited general utility when interviewing suspects. However, suggest scenario (i.e., interviewer suggests possible scenarios) and situational futility (i.e., pointing out negative consequences of denial) may have rarely been used because they are not part of the PEACE approach. Thus, their possible relationships with confessing could not be effectively studied. Gentle prods (i.e., encouraging suspect to speak) and the showing of concern to the suspect fit better with the PEACE approach but also were rarely used.

The main point that Study 4 suggests (and a stronger verb should not be used) is that suspects' ongoing decisions whether to confess during interviews

Table 5.2. The Timing of Tactics Within the Interviews

Tactic	Time from start of interview (in minutes)										
	5 (n = 40)	10 (n = 40)	15 (n = 40)	20 (n = 38)	25 (n = 32)	30 (n = 25)	35 (n = 21)	40 (n = 13)	45 (n = 26)	50 (n = 2)	55 (n = 2)
Disclosure of evidence	15	35	40	38	28	23	12	5	3	2	1
Open questions	40	40	40	38	31	23	17	10	1	0	0
Repetitive questions	3	26	37	29	18	11	3	2	0	0	0
Leading questions	4	20	30	27	16	9	3	0	0	0	0
Handling mood	3	18	29	25	17	5	3	1	0	0	0
Contradictions	1	13	26	21	15	4	0	0	0	0	0
Positive confrontation	2	15	24	24	14	5	2	0	0	0	0
Interruptions	0	11	22	18	9	2	0	0	0	0	0
Silence	1	5	14	13	5	1	0	0	0	0	0
Challenge account	0	10	11	10	4	0	0	0	0	0	0
Suggest scenario	1	8	7	2	1	1	1	0	0	0	0
Gentle prods	0	6	6	3	0	0	0	0	0	0	0
Concern	0	3	4	2	0	0	0	0	0	0	0
Situational futility	0	1	1	0	0	0	0	0	0	0	0

Note. n = number of interviews still in progress.

Table 5.3.   Tactic Usage Just Prior to Confessing

Tactic	Time slot relative to confessing		
	Two time slots prior	Immediately prior time slot	Time slot of confession
Disclosure of evidence	31	40	39
Open questions	38	40	40
Repetitive questions	26	33	26
Leading questions	21	26	21
Handling mood	20	28	24
Contradictions	18	23	15
Positive confrontation	14	24	20
Interruptions	14	16	15
Silence	8	11	10
Challenge account	11	9	3
Suggest scenario	3	5	6
Gentle prods	3	7	5
Concern	2	2	2
Situational futility	0	1	1

may to some extent be influenced by the police tactics of disclosure of evidence, open questions, and repetitive questions. However, these three tactics were used in several time slots within the interviews, and so their proximity to the moment of confessing may have been coincidental. The first two of these three tactics could not be considered to be directly contrary to the PEACE approach, but the third (repeating the same questions over and over again) definitely is (having been the subject of Courts' criticisms of police interviewing; Gudjonsson, 2006).

Conclusion

Published studies of what really happens in police interviews with suspects are exceedingly rare. Even rarer are publications concerning the actual relationships between the tactics and skills used by police interviewers and the behaviors of suspects (e.g., their cooperation, resistance, confessing). This chapter has presented a unique set of studies on such topics. Study 1 found that the views of experienced interviewers and detectives in England appeared to be in line with the new approach (referred to as *investigative interviewing*) and its evolving training program (called PEACE). One major aim of Studies 2 and 3 was to determine if actual police interviewing of suspects was in line with the philosophy behind investigative interviewing. These two studies found this to be the case to a considerable extent (e.g., the absence of oppressive coercive tactics), which clearly suggests that the PEACE approach can be accepted and used by police officers. However, some inappropriate tactics were used in a considerable number of interviews (e.g., leading questions, repeating the same questions, positive confrontation), although Clarke, Milne, and Bull (2009) found fewer leading questions.

Studies 3 and 4 also had the major aim of trying to determine whether interviewer use of tactics and skills bore any relationship to the suspect confessing. Interviews largely using the noncoercive PEACE investigative interviewing approach still resulted in confessions. Contrary to what the limited previous research had found (e.g., Baldwin, 1993), most of the suspects who confessed did not do so very early on. This allowed, almost for the first time, examination of whether the interviewer's behavior influences confessing (as suggested by convicted persons in studies by Holmberg & Christiansson, 2002; Kebbell & Hurren, 2006). Of course, in our research studies it was not possible to determine whether use of the PEACE approach results in fewer false confessions.

Whereas the use of some tactics clearly seemed to bear no relationship to confessing, the presence and timing of others (e.g., open questions, disclosure of evidence, repetitive questioning) possibly was important. To complicate matters, when suspects were not confessing, interviewers used tactics more strongly—such as emphasizing contradictions and challenge account—that recently are being recommended in relevant literature that is well-informed by psychology, for example, the SUE technique (Granhag, Stromwall, & Hartwig, 2007; i.e., informing suspects of the incriminating information or evidence not at the beginning of the interview but Strategically Using such Evidence only after they have provided an account) and the GRIMACE approach (Milne & Bull, 2009; involves devoting resources to the Gathering of Reliable Information before interviewing, then interviewing in a manner that Motivates suspects to provide an Account, and only then Challenging this Effectively with that information). Study 3 specifically also examined other aspects of suspects' behavior, such as responsiveness, cooperation, and resistance. These behaviors were found to be significantly related to some of the six interviewer skills (rather than tactics), including that less cooperation and more resistance occurred in interviews in which the interviewer demonstrated more presumptiveness. However, we must not ignore the likely possibility that any causality between interviewer use of skills or tactics and suspect behavior is to some extent reciprocal in nature.

Overall, this chapter demonstrates that when a sufficiently good relationship can be established (taking many years), enlightened police officers and police organizations are sometimes willing to allow comprehensive scrutiny of their interviewing performance by psychologists. Perhaps they had the confidence to do this because a national policy plus a comprehensive training program (i.e., PEACE) had been in place for several years, and they therefore thought that the interviews in their fairly large police force would be, at least, of reasonable standard. If so, they were correct. The tactics of greatest concern to some eminent psychologists (e.g., Gudjonsson, 2003; chap. 2, this volume) were very rarely present, though some that are likely to be unreliable (e.g., leading questions) were often used, perhaps because of their probable high frequency in everyday life. Thus, the new research presented in this chapter could be taken to suggest that police organizations around the world actively consider adopting the PEACE approach and associated training programs.

References

Baldwin, J. (1993). Police interview techniques. Establishing truth or proof? *British Journal of Criminology, 33,* 325–352.

Bull, R., & Cherryman, J. (1996). *Helping to identify skills gaps in specialist investigative interviewing: Enhancement of professional skills.* London: Home Office.

Clarke, C., & Milne, R. (2001). *National evaluation of the PEACE investigative interviewing course.* London: Home Office.

Clarke, C., Milne, R., & Bull, R. (2009). *Interviewing suspects of crime: How good are we?* Manuscript submitted for publication.

Granhag, P. A., Stromwall, L., & Hartwig, M. (2007). The SUE technique: The way to interview to detect deception. *Forensic Update, 88,* 25–29.

Gudjonsson G. (2003). *The psychology of interrogations and confessions.* Chichester, England: Wiley.

Gudjonsson, G. (2006). The psychology of interrogations and confessions. In T. Williamson (Ed.), *Investigative interviewing: Rights, research and regulation* (pp. 123–146). Cullompton: Willan.

Hakkanen, H., Ask, K., Kebbell, M., Alison, L. & Granhag, P.A. (2007, July). *Police officers' views of effective interview tactics with suspects.* Paper presented at the Third International Congress of Psychology and Law, Adelaide, Australia.

Holmberg, U., & Christiansson, S.-A. (2002). Murderers' and sexual offenders' experiences of police interviews and their inclination to admit or deny crimes. *Behavioral Sciences & the Law, 20,* 31–45.

Kassin, S., Goldstein, C., & Savitsky, K. (2003). Behavioral confirmation in the interrogation room: On the dangers of presuming guilt. *Law & Human Behavior, 27,* 187–203.

Kassin, S., Leo, R., Meissner, C., Richman, K., Colwell, L., Leach, A.-M., & La Fon, D. (2007). Police interviewing and interrogation: A self-report survey of police practices and beliefs. *Law & Human Behavior, 31,* 381–400.

Kebbell, M., & Hurren, E. (2006). Improving the interviewing of sex offenders. In M. Kebbell & G. Davies (Eds.). *Practical psychology for forensic investigations and prosecutions* (pp. 103–119). Chichester, England: Wiley.

Leo, R. (1996). Inside the interrogation room. *Journal of Criminal Law & Criminology, 86,* 266–303.

Meissner, C. A., & Kassin, S. M. (2004). "You're guilty, so just confess!": Cognitive and confirmational biases in the interrogation room. In G. D. Lassiter (Ed.), *Interrogations, confessions, and entrapment* (pp. 85–106). New York: Kluwer Academic.

Milne, R. & Bull, R. (1999). *Investigative interviewing: Psychology and practice.* Chichester, England: Wiley.

Milne, R. & Bull, R. (2009). *Investigative interviewing: Psychology and practice* (2nd ed.). Manuscript in preparation.

Moston, S., Stephenson, G., & Williamson, T. (1992). The effects of case characteristics on suspect behaviour during police questioning. *British Journal of Criminology, 32,* 23–40.

Pearse, J., & Gudjonsson, G. (1999). Measuring influential police interviewing tactics: A factor analytic approach. *Legal & Criminological Psychology, 4,* 221–238.

Soukara, S. (2005). *Investigative interviewing of suspects: Piecing together the picture.* Unpublished doctoral dissertation, University of Portsmouth, England.

Soukara, S., Bull, R., & Vrij, A. (2002). Police detectives' aims regarding their interviews with suspects: Any change at the turn of the millennium? *International Journal of Police Science & Management, 4,* 101–114.

Soukara, S., Bull, R., Vrij, A., Turner, M., & Cherryman, J. (2008). *The relationships between police interviewers' skills, the tactics they use, suspects' behaviours, and confessions.* Manuscript in preparation.

Zander, M. (1990). *The police and criminal evidence act.* London: Sweet and Maxwell.

6

Lie Detection: Pitfalls and Opportunities

Aldert Vrij, Ronald P. Fisher,
Samantha Mann, and Sharon Leal

With current concerns over security, it is becoming increasingly important to discriminate between suspects who lie versus those who tell the truth. Nevertheless, a substantial empirical base shows that laypeople and even trained investigators (e.g., police) are often poor at discriminating between truth tellers and liars (Vrij, 2004, 2008). Vrij (2008) reviewed 107 lie detection studies (79 studies with laypeople and 28 studies with trained investigators) in which observers attempted to detect truths and lies told by people they did not know. The observers did not have any factual evidence to rely on and had to base their judgments solely on the nonverbal and verbal behavior displayed by the truth tellers and liars. The accuracy rates obtained by laypeople (54.27%) and trained investigators (55.91%) were similar and only just above the accuracy rate that could be expected by merely tossing a coin (50%). (O'Sullivan & Ekman, 2004, and O'Sullivan, 2005, 2007, claim to have discovered 29 individuals with superior lie detection skills after having tested over 12,000 professionals for their expertise in lie detection. They call them "wizards." See Bond & Uysal, 2007, for a statistical critique of the evidence for this claim.)

One important difficulty observers face is that the act of lying per se does not result in any nonverbal or speech-related cues to deceit (DePaulo et al., 2003; Vrij, 2008). In other words, reliable cues to deception, akin to Pinocchio's growing nose, do not exist; therefore, there is no cue that the lie detector can truly rely on. In this light, the Screening Passengers by Observation Technique introduced at airports in the United States and soon to be introduced in United Kingdom airports can be seen as limited. Screening Passengers by Observation Technique teams look for signs of erratic behavior among passengers and thus assume that the mere fact of hiding something, or other forms of lying, result in unique patterns of behavior displayed by passengers. (This is based largely on the work of Paul Ekman, who claims that aspects of facial communication are beyond control and can betray a deceiver's true emotion via micro-expressions [lasting 1/25 to 1/5 of a second] of that emotion; Ekman, 2006; Porter & Ten

The project described in this chapter was sponsored by grants from the Economic and Social Research Council (RES-000-23-0292 and RES-000-22-1632).

Brinke, 2008, in press. The published research to date has not really supported this claim. In their experiment, Porter and Ten Brinke found that microexpressions only occurred in 14 out of the 697 analysed expressions and that 6 of those 14 expressions were displayed by truth tellers.) Rather than passively observing people, which characterizes many unsuccessful lie detection approaches, this chapter argues that it is more effective to intervene actively to try to elicit differences between liars and truth tellers.

The Dominant Approach: Concern-Based Interventions

The dominant intervention approach to detecting deception is based on the theory that liars will be more concerned about their responses than will truth tellers. According to this concern-based approach, liars are more uncomfortable than truth tellers in an interview setting, resulting in them being more likely to display nervous behavior. The Behavior Analysis Interview (BAI) is a prime example of such an intervention. The groundwork for the BAI was carried out by Frank Horvath, who conducted a field study in which he examined the verbal and nonverbal responses of examinees when answering a set of questions prior to their polygraph examinations (Horvath, 1973). The BAI protocol, a modification of the set of questions tested by Horvath, is among the most commonly taught questioning methods in the United States (Colwell, Miller, Lyons, & Miller, 2006) and is described in detail in the manual written by Inbau, Reid, Buckley, and Jayne (2001).

Inbau et al. (2001) described the core of the BAI as "the asking of behavior-provoking questions that are specifically designed to evoke behavioral responses" (p. 173). The BAI purportedly interprets nonverbal and verbal responses of interviewees. In this chapter, however, we restrict ourselves to the nonverbal responses. The BAI protocol includes asking an open-ended question that invites suspects to describe their activities during a specific period of time (e.g., "What did you do between 3 pm and 4 pm?") which is then followed by a series of standardized questions, such as "Did you take the money?" (in the case of an alleged theft of money) and "Do you know who took the money?" Inbau et al. (2001) reported that liars feel less comfortable than truth tellers in an investigative interview situation. As a result, guilty suspects are more likely to display nervous behavior, such as crossing their legs, shifting about in their chair, and performing grooming behavior while answering the question, whereas innocent suspects are more likely to lean forward, establish eye contact, and use illustrations to reinforce their confidence in their statements. In addition, according to Inbau et al., guilty suspects are more likely to answer quickly, and their answers will sound less sincere. Finally, guilty suspects are more likely to exhibit anxiety-reducing behavior such as shifting posture in their chair.

We tested the working of BAI, and our results directly refuted Inbau et al.'s (2001) predictions: In fact, liars were less likely to cross their legs and less likely to shift posture than truth tellers (Vrij, Mann, & Fisher, 2006a). In a subsequent lie detection experiment, we showed observers these videotaped BAI interviews. The observers were unable to distinguish the truth tellers from the liars (Vrij, Mann, Kristen, & Fisher, 2007). Moreover, in their experiment Kassin and Fong

(1999) taught some observers the visual cues that Inbau et al. discuss in their manual. The trained observers' performance on a subsequent lie detection test was worse than the performance of untrained participants. In other words, endorsing the information about visual cues to deception discussed in Inbau et al.'s manual is counterproductive and makes people worse lie detectors. In accord with the National Research Council (2003), we believe that there is a plausible theoretical explanation as to why the BAI may not work: Liars are not necessarily less comfortable (or more concerned) than truth tellers. In situations in which the consequences of being disbelieved are severe (often the case in criminal investigations), truth tellers will also be concerned about being disbelieved. Merely being spoken to accusingly, or concern about being unable to convince an interviewer of their innocence, could make truth tellers feel uncomfortable. (The most widely used polygraph test, the Control Question Test and Voice Stress Analysis, is based on the same premise as BAI. This explains why the Control Question Test leads to relatively high percentages of falsely accused truth tellers and why Voice Stress Analysis is an ineffective lie detection tool; Gamer, Rill, Vossel, & Gödert, 2006; Porter & Ten Brinke, in press; Vrij, 2008.)

The notion that liars will show more nervous behavior than truth tellers, which derives from the concern-based intervention approach, is not unique to the BAI. It is emphasized in every single police manual of which we are aware (for reviews of such manuals, see Vrij, 2008; Vrij & Granhag, 2007). In particular, the notion that liars look away and display nervous behavior during interviews is mentioned often. But there is no evidence that liars actually display such behavior. Both laboratory research (for reviews, see DePaulo et al., 2003; Vrij, 2008) and analyses of police–suspect interviews (Mann, Vrij, & Bull, 2002) have shown that eye contact does not differentiate truth tellers from liars and that liars tend to make fewer, rather than more, movements than truth tellers. (This is not the same as Pinocchio's growing nose, as not every single lie a person tells is associated with a decrease in movements.) At least two explanations for these findings sound plausible. First, liars often have to think harder than truth tellers (more about this in the following), and research has demonstrated that the cognitive load associated with lying reduces tonic arousal in liars (Leal, Vrij, Fisher, & van Hooff, 2008). When their levels of tonic arousal are low, liars are unlikely to display nervous behavior. Second, liars take their credibility for granted less than truth tellers (DePaulo et al., 2003; Kassin, 2005; Kassin & Gudjonsson, 2004; Kassin & Norwick, 2004), among other reasons, because truth tellers typically assume that their innocence shines through (Granhag, Strömwall, & Hartwig, 2007; Kassin, 2005; Kassin & Gudjonsson, 2004; Kassin & Norwick, 2004; Vrij, Mann, & Fisher, 2006b). As such, liars will be more inclined than truth tellers to monitor and control their demeanor to appear honest to the lie detector (DePaulo & Kirkendol, 1989), and this may result in liars, more than truth tellers, attempting to reduce their nervous behavior and, subsequently, show fewer nervous behaviors.

Why is the notion that liars show more nervous behavior than truth tellers so dominant, given the lack of evidence? Charles Bond believes that a moral explanation is responsible (The Global Deception Team, 2006). The stereotypical view among people is that lying is bad (Vrij, 2008) and the belief that liars avoid eye contact fits well with the stereotype that lying is bad (The Global Deception Team, 2006). If lying is bad, then people should feel ashamed when they lie. People often avert their gaze when they feel ashamed (DePaulo et al., 2003). Moreover, if lying is bad, then people should feel nervous about getting caught when they lie. This should result in signs of nervousness, such as avoiding eye contact and making fidgety movements.

The moral argument may account for the original belief, but why does this endure, given the lack of supporting evidence? From social psychology research, we know that once incorrect beliefs have been established, they are difficult to overturn. Illusory correlations (i.e., perceiving relationships that do not actually exist), confirmation bias (i.e., a tendency to seek information that confirms existing beliefs), belief perseverance (i.e., a tendency to disregard evidence that opposes existing beliefs), and the power of thinking (i.e., thinking about evidence and reasons that support someone's beliefs) are some explanations as to why incorrect beliefs will endure (Vrij, 2008). The combination of how incorrect beliefs originate (i.e., moral explanation) and why they endure can explain why incorrect beliefs about cues to deception appear in many police manuals. We have no doubt that the authors of these manuals believe that their claims are correct, that is, liars are nervous and their behavior will reflect this. However, such views are based on the authors' own or other police officers' impressions about how suspects behave and what they say during police interviews rather than on systematic research.

An Alternative Approach: Cognitive-Based Interventions

Given the limitations of the concern-based intervention approach, we developed an alternative approach to discriminate between truth tellers and liars (Vrij, Fisher, Mann, & Leal, 2006, 2009; Vrij, Mann, Fisher, Leal, Milne, & Bull, 2008). We assume that lying is sometimes more cognitively demanding than truth telling. Lie detectors could exploit the increase in cognitive load that liars experience by introducing mentally taxing interventions. Liars, who require more cognitive resources than truth tellers to produce their statements, will have fewer cognitive resources left over to address these mentally taxing interventions than will truth tellers. This should result in more pronounced differences between liars and truth tellers in terms of displaying signs of cognitive load, for example, stutters, pauses, slower speech, a decrease in movements, less quality details, when these cognitively demanding interventions are introduced than when such interventions are not introduced.

Our approach will be effective only when lying is more cognitively demanding than truth telling and when it is incorporated in an interview protocol. Before describing our approach in more detail, we explain why lying is cognitively more demanding than truth telling, provide examples of when lying is more cognitively demanding than truth telling, and discuss which interview protocol is best suited for lie detection.

Why Is Lying Cognitively More Demanding Than Truth Telling?

We believe that six aspects of lying contribute to an increase in mental load. First, formulating the lie itself may be cognitively demanding. Liars need to invent a story and must monitor their fabrication so that it is plausible and adheres to everything observers know or might find out. In addition, to maintain consistency, liars must remember what they have said and to whom. Liars should also avoid making slips of the tongue and refrain from providing new leads (Vrij, 2008).

A second aspect of lying that adds to mental load reflects that liars are typically less likely than truth tellers to take their credibility for granted (DePaulo et al., 2003; Kassin, 2005; Kassin & Gudjonsson, 2004; Kassin & Norwick, 2004). As such, liars will be more inclined than truth tellers to monitor and control their demeanor so that they will appear honest to the lie detector (DePaulo & Kirkendol, 1989). Monitoring and controlling their own demeanor should add cognitive demand for liars. Third, because liars do not take credibility for granted, they may monitor the interviewer's reactions more carefully to assess whether they appear to be getting away with their lie (Buller & Burgoon, 1996; Schweitzer, Brodt, & Croson, 2002). Carefully monitoring the interviewer also requires cognitive resources.

Fourth, liars may be preoccupied by the task of reminding themselves to act and role-play (DePaulo et al., 2003), which requires extra cognitive effort. Fifth, liars have to suppress the truth while they are lying, and this is also cognitively demanding (Spence et al., 2001). Finally, although activating a truthful idea often happens automatically, activating a lie is more intentional and deliberate and thus requires mental effort (D. T. Gilbert, 1991; Walczyk, Roper, Seemann, & Humphrey, 2003; Walczyk, Schwartz, Clifton, Adams, Wei, & Zha, 2005).

When Is Lying Cognitively More Demanding Than Truth Telling?

The six reasons why lying is more cognitively demanding could give us insight into when it is more cognitively demanding. That is, lying is more cognitively demanding than truth telling to the degree that these six principles are in effect. For example, lying is likely to be more demanding than truth telling only when interviewees are motivated to be believed. Only under those circumstances can it be assumed that liars take their credibility for granted less than truth tellers and hence will be more inclined than truth tellers to monitor their own behavior or the interviewer's reactions. Second, for lying to be more cognitively demanding than truth telling, liars must be able to retrieve from memory their truthful activity easily and have a clear image of it. Only when liars' knowledge of the truth is easily and clearly accessed will it be difficult for them to suppress the truth. On the other side of the equation, truth tellers need to have easy access to the truth for their task of truthfully reporting an event to be relatively undemanding. If truth tellers have to think hard to remember the target event (e.g., because it was not distinctive or it occurred long ago), their cognitive demands may be as difficult as the liars' task of fabricating a story.

In experimental studies, researchers ensure that interviewees are motivated (typically by giving them a reward for making a credible impression) and
that the target event is easily retrieved (typically by interviewing the suspects
shortly after informing them about the target event). In those experiments,
lying has been found to be more demanding than truth telling in various settings. Participants who have directly assessed their own cognitive load report
that lying is more cognitively demanding than truth telling. This occurred
when lengthy, elaborative responses were required (Granhag & Strömwall,
2002; Hartwig, Granhag, Strömwall, & Kronkvist, 2006; Strömwall, Hartwig,
& Granhag, 2006; Vrij, Edward & Bull, 2001; Vrij & Mann, 2006; Vrij, Mann,
& Fisher, 2006b; White & Burgoon, 2001) and also when short responses were
sufficient (Caso, Gnisci, Vrij, & Mann, 2005; Vrij, Mann, & Fisher, 2006b; Vrij,
Semin, & Bull, 1996). In functional magnetic resonance imaging (fMRI) deception research, lying and truth telling are differentiated only by the act of pressing either a "lie" or "truth" button. Nevertheless, reviews of fMRI deception
research (Langleben, 2008; Spence, 2008; Spence et al., 2004) reveal that deception generally activates the higher centers of the brain, which are typically associated with cognitive demand.

In forensic settings, we can reasonably assume that interviewees are
motivated to be believed, but we cannot assume that interviewees are always
able to easily retrieve from memory the target event, as this varies from one
case to another. Analyses of police interviews with real-life suspects, however,
suggests that lying is often more cognitively demanding than truth telling in
the forensic setting. First, in those police interviews, lies were accompanied by
increased pauses, decreased blinking, and decreased hand and finger movements, all of which are signs of cognitive load (Mann et al., 2002; Vrij & Mann,
2003). Second, police officers who saw videotapes of these suspect interviews
(but did not know when the suspects were lying or truth telling) reported that
the suspects appeared to be thinking harder when they lied than when they
told the truth (Mann & Vrij, 2006).

Which Interview Protocol Is the Best Protocol for Lie Detection Purposes?

Interrogators commonly use a mixture of two types of interview styles: information gathering and accusatory. In the *information-gathering* style, interviewers
request suspects to give detailed statements about their activities through open
questions (e.g., "What did you do yesterday between 3 pm and 4 pm?"; "You just
mentioned that you went to the gym. Who else was there?"). By comparison, in the
accusatory style, interviewers confront suspects with accusations (e.g., "Your
reactions make me think that you are hiding something from me"). Information-
gathering interviews encourage interviewees to talk, whereas accusatory
interviews often yield short denials (e.g., "I am not hiding anything"). Therefore,
information-gathering interviews typically elicit more information about an event
and result in longer responses than accusatory interviews (Fisher, Brennan, &
McCauley, 2002; Vrij, Mann, & Fisher, 2006b; Vrij et al., 2007).

The information-gathering interview style is desirable for lie detection
purposes for several reasons. First, a good lie detection strategy is to check the

factual information provided by an alleged liar with the available evidence (Vrij, 2008). An information-gathering interview is likely to result in the interviewee providing more factual information, and hence more opportunities for the lie detector to check the facts. Second, information-gathering interviews result in more nonverbal cues to deceit than accusatory interviews (Vrij, 2006). Longer statements, which are most likely to occur in information-gathering interviews, typically reveal more nonverbal cues to deception than shorter statements because the more someone talks, the more opportunity there is for nonverbal cues to deception to occur. By comparison, being accused of wrongdoing (i.e., accusatory interview style) is likely to affect the behavior of both truth tellers and liars in a similar way (Bond & Fahey, 1987), and the accusation has a stronger impact on someone's nonverbal behavior than the act of lying. Consequently, differences in nonverbal behavior between truth tellers and liars are overshadowed by the accusation (Vrij, 2008).

The third advantage of an information-gathering interview is that it results in more verbal cues to deceit (Vrij et al., 2007). The more words included in a statement, the more opportunities for verbal cues to deceit occur, because words are the carriers of such cues. Fourth, because information-gathering interviewing does not involve accusing interviewees of any wrongdoing or any other tactics designed to make them feel discomfort, it may be a safeguard against false confessions because innocent people do sometimes falsely confess when they feel uncomfortable (Gudjonsson, 2003). Finally, our cognitive-based intervention approach is easier to use in information-gathering interviews than in accusatory interviews.

Magnifying the Differences Between Truth Tellers and Liars

Although liars should sometimes experience more cognitive load than truth tellers, the differences in their nonverbal and verbal cues may be relatively small and perhaps not readily discernable by observers (DePaulo et al., 2003). Our goal, therefore, was to magnify the differences between truth tellers and liars. This might be accomplished by devising interventions that pose excessive cognitive demands on the interviewees. The underlying assumption is that such interventions will be particularly debilitating for liars, whose cognitive resources have already been partially depleted by the cognitively demanding task of lying. The following analogy may make our approach clearer. Suppose that in the gym two people cycle on an exercise bike at the same speed, but one cyclist is using a higher resistance than the other. How could one discover which of the two cyclists is using the highest resistance? With our approach, we would ask both cyclists to increase their speed. This would lead to a difference between the two because eventually the cyclist with the higher resistance will not be able to increase his or her speed, whereas the cyclist with the lower resistance will.

Increasing cognitive demand can be implemented by instructing interviewees to recall a story in reverse order. It should do so because it runs counter to the natural forward-order coding of sequentially occurring events (J. A. E. Gilbert & Fisher, 2006; Kahana, 1996), and it disrupts reconstructing events from a schema (Geiselman & Callot, 1990). Empirical support that reverse order recall is resource-demanding derives from a time-sharing study in which perform-ance on a concurrent psychomotor task declined when a memory list was recalled in reverse order rather than in forward order (Johnston, Greenberg, Fisher, & Martin, 1970).

We examined the impact of telling a story in reverse order on lying and lie detection in two experiments (Vrij et al., 2008). In Experiment 1A, 80 mock sus-pects took part. Truth tellers participated in a staged event and were instructed to report in as much detail as possible what happened during the event. Liars did not participate in this event, but they received a detailed description of the event. The liars were then instructed to report in as much detail as possible what hap-pened during the event, pretending that they had actually participated in it. Furthermore, half of the liars and half of the truth tellers were instructed to recall the event in reverse order (no instruction was given to the remaining half of par-ticipants). Our predictions were guided by two assumptions: Lying is cognitively more demanding than truth telling in the present task, and telling a story in reverse order is cognitively more demanding than telling a story in chronological order. We therefore expected liars to display more cues to cognitive load than truth tellers and, most important, that this pattern would be most striking in the reverse order condition. In Experiment 1B, we showed 55 police officers a selec-tion of those interviews, and examined their ability to discriminate between liars and truth tellers in the reverse order and control conditions. On the basis of our anticipated outcome of Experiment 1A, we expected truth and lie detection to be superior in the reverse order condition. See Vrij et al. (2008) for more details about these two experiments.

As predicted, many more cues to deceit emerged in the reverse order condi-tion (nine cues) than in the control condition (one cue), and most of the cues that distinguished liars from truth tellers in the reverse order condition were signs of cognitive load. In the reverse order condition, liars displayed the following signs of cognitive load. Liars described fewer auditory details (details about what they heard) and contextual embeddings (details referring to space, e.g., "He walked behind me," and time, e.g., "We played a game for 3 minutes") in their statements than truth tellers. Liars also recalled their stories in chrono-logical order more than truth tellers. As such, liars performed worse than truth tellers, because participants were requested to tell their stories in nonchrono-logical order. The level of performance on this request thus gives insight into deception in this experiment. In addition, liars included more cognitive opera-tions in their statements than truth tellers. Cognitive operations include descriptions of inferences based on perceptual information (e.g., "She seemed to enjoy herself") rather than descriptions of the perceptual information itself (e.g., "She was smiling a lot"). Moreover, liars included more speech hesitations (say-ing "uhm" and "err") and speech errors (stutters) in their statements and spoke more slowly than truth tellers.

Liars not only revealed more signs of cognitive load than truth tellers, they also made more leg and foot movements than truth tellers, and they blinked more. These are signs of nervousness, rather than signs of cognitive load. It thus appears that the instruction to tell a story in reverse order not only made the participants have to think harder, it also made them more nervous. We can only speculate about why this is the case. Telling a story in reverse order is certainly an unusual activity, and, as such, participants may not have had any experience in doing this. They may have thought that they did not perform well in this task, and liars in particular may have had doubts about their performance given that lying is more mentally taxing than truth telling. This may have contributed to their anxiety.

Participants in the control condition displayed only one cue to deceit: Liars moved their hands and fingers less than truth tellers. This cue has emerged as a sign of deceit in many of our previous studies (for reviews, see DePaulo et al., 2003; Vrij, 2008) and is one of the most consistent cues to deceit in our deception research. Yet, very few other researchers have examined these movements (DePaulo et al., 2003; Vrij, 2008).

In Experiment 1B, we showed 55 police officers (mostly general uniformed officers with an average 2.82 years of work experience) a random sample of these reverse order and control interviews. One group of 31 officers saw six deceptive and six truthful interviews told in reverse order, whereas the remaining 24 officers saw six deceptive and six honest control interviews, which were all told in chronological order. After each interview, the officers were asked, among other questions, to answer the following two questions: (a) Do you think that the suspect is telling . . . (dichotomous answer, the truth or a lie?) and (b) Is the person lying? (Likert-scale response, ranging from 1 = *definitely not* to 7 = *definitely*.)

Lie accuracy (i.e., correct classification of lies) in the reverse order condition (60%) was significantly higher than lie accuracy in the control condition (42%). Lie accuracy in the reverse order condition was significantly above the level of chance, whereas lie accuracy in the control condition was significantly below the level of chance. Although the truth accuracy (i.e., correct classification of truths) was also higher in the reverse order condition (56%) than in the control condition (50%), this difference was not significant. In other words, instructing interviewees to tell their stories in reverse order led to higher lie accuracy without impairing truth accuracy. The lie accuracy rate in the reverse order condition (60%) may not appear impressive. However, one should take into account that the lie accuracy rate in the control condition was very low (42%) and that an increase from 42% to 60% is a considerable improvement.

In the reverse order condition, participants could discriminate truths from lies via Likert-scale judgments, with liars ($M = 4.34$, $SD = 0.6$) appearing to be more deceptive than truth tellers ($M = 3.84$, $SD = 0.6$). In the control condition, the Likert-scale judgments also revealed a significant effect, however: The mean scores indicate that the participants' decisions were erroneous as they perceived liars ($M = 3.78$, $SD = 0.6$) as less deceptive than truth tellers ($M = 4.27$, $SD = 0.8$). The results thus revealed that participants discriminated between truths and lies considerably better when they judged reverse order than control interviews. In other words, instructing liars and truth tellers to tell their stories in reverse order benefits lie detection.

Another intervention that should increase cognitive demand in interviewees is the instruction to maintain eye contact with the interviewer (Beattie, 1981). When people have to concentrate on telling their stories, which is likely when they are requested to recall what has happened, they are inclined to look away from their conversation partner (typically to a motionless point) because maintaining eye contact with the conversation partner is distracting (Doherty-Sneddon,

Bruce, Bonner, Longbotham, & Doyle, 2002; Doherty-Sneddon & Phelps, 2005).
When interviewees are instructed to maintain eye contact, their concentration on
telling their stories is therefore likely to be hampered, and because lying is more
mentally taxing than truth telling, this should impair the storytelling of liars
more than the storytelling of truth tellers.

We examined the impact of maintaining eye contact on lying and lie detection in two experiments (Vrij, Mann, Leal, & Fisher, in press). The experiments
were very similar to the reverse order experiments described previously. The
only difference was that rather than recall the story in reverse order, half of the
liars and half of the truth tellers were instructed to maintain eye contact with
the interviewer. No instruction was given to the other half of participants.
Three cues (verbal cues and all signs of cognitive load) differentiated liars from
truth tellers in the eye contact condition: Liars included fewer spatial and tem-
poral details in their stories than truth tellers, and liars recalled their stories
in chronological order more than truth tellers. In the control condition, liars
moved their hands and fingers less than truth tellers.

We then showed 46 university students a selection of those interviews
and examined their ability to discriminate between liars and truth tellers.
Truth accuracy and lie accuracy did not differ from each other in the eye contact and control conditions. Truth accuracy in the eye contact condition (59%)
was significantly above the level of chance, whereas the lie accuracy score in
the eye contact condition and the truth and lie accuracy scores in the control
condition did not differ from chance. However, in the eye contact condition
participants could discriminate truths from lies via Likert-scale judgments,
with liars appearing more deceptive ($M = 4.10$, $SD = 0.8$) than truth tellers
($M = 3.65$, SD = 0.7), whereas participants in the control condition could not
discriminate between truths and lies. In other words, the Likert-scale judgments suggest that instructing interviewees to maintain eye contact benefits
lie detection.

A comparison between the reverse order and maintaining eye contact
experiments shows that instructing liars and truth tellers to recall their stories
in reverse order improved ability to distinguish between lies and truths more
than instructing liars and truth tellers to maintain eye contact. We tentatively
offer a few explanations for this difference. First, the instruction to maintain eye
contact resulted in fewer observable differences between liars and truth tellers
than the instruction to recall a story in reverse order, providing the lie detectors
in the former group with fewer opportunities to distinguish between liars
and truth tellers. Fewer differences may have emerged because maintaining
eye contact may not be as cognitively demanding as recalling a story in
reverse order. Unlike recalling a story in reverse order, maintaining eye contact
is something people do regularly, for example, when attempting to persuade
others. Frequent practice may reduce cognitive load. Second, the ability to
detect truths and lies in the eye contact condition may not yet have reached its
full potential. We cannot rule out the possibility that maintaining eye contact
confused the observers in the lie detection experiment. That is, observers tend
to (erroneously) rely heavily on eye movements while making veracity judgments (Strömwall, Granhag, & Hartwig, 2004; Taylor & Hick, 2007; Vrij, 2008;
Vrij, Akehurst, & Knight, 2006), and the eye movements shown by participants

in the eye contact condition were unnatural because of the instruction to maintain eye contact. Perhaps observers would fare better in the eye contact condition if they listen to audiotapes rather than watch videotapes.

Another, yet untested, manner of imposing cognitive load on interviewees is asking them to carry out a secondary task at the same time as recalling their stories. For example, interviewees could be asked to recall their stories while conducting a computer driving simulation task at the same time. This means that interviewees would have to divide their attention between the storytelling task (i.e., truth telling or lying) and the driving task. Because of the additional resources that are needed for telling the lie, liars may find this dual tasking more cognitively difficult than truth tellers and may perform worse than truth tellers. Because of liars' keenness to be believed, we expect that they will focus their attention primarily on the storytelling task. As a consequence, the predominant differences between truth tellers and liars will occur in the driving task (i.e., liars will perform worse at the driving task than truth tellers). However, if the salience of complying with the additional request increases (i.e., interviewees are informed that mistakes on the task are viewed as suspicious), this strategy of neglecting the additional request will become less viable, and consequently liars' storytelling may become impaired.

Conclusion

Detecting deception on concern-based techniques yields woefully poor performance. Therefore, we proposed another approach to discriminate between liars and truth tellers on the basis of analyses showing that lying can be more mentally taxing than truth telling. The aim is to magnify the differences between liars and truth tellers in situations in which lying is more cognitively demanding than truth telling by using interventions that impose cognitive load on interviewees during information-gathering interviews. Several laboratory experiments showed that these kinds of manipulation enlarged the differences between liars and truth tellers and, more important, facilitated lie detectors' ability to discriminate between the two. The effects were moderate, but this is not surprising given that these are only preliminary experiments that test a whole new lie detection approach. Therefore, although we are reluctant to recommend that practitioners put our approach into practice at this point, we do however encourage practitioners and other researchers to explore the potential of this novel approach to detecting deception.

References

Beattie, G. W. (1981). A further investigation of the cognitive interference hypothesis of gaze patterns during conversation. *British Journal of Social Psychology, 20,* 243–248.

Bond, C. F., & Fahey, W. E. (1987). False suspicion and the misperception of deceit. *British Journal of Social Psychology, 26,* 41–46.

Bond, C. F., & Uysal, A. (2007). On lie detection "wizards." *Law & Human Behavior, 31,* 109–115.

Buller, D. B., & Burgoon, J. K. (1996). Interpersonal deception theory. *Communication Theory, 6,* 203–242.

Caso, L., Gnisci, A., Vrij, A., & Mann, S. (2005). Processes underlying deception: An empirical analysis of truths and lies when manipulating the stakes. *Journal of Interviewing & Offender Profiling, 2,* 195–202.

Colwell, L. H., Miller, H. A., Lyons, P. M., & Miller, R. S. (2006). The training of law enforcement officers in detecting deception: A survey of current practices and suggestions for improving accuracy. *Police Quarterly, 9,* 275–290.

DePaulo, B. M., & Kirkendol, S. E. (1989). The motivational impairment effect in the communication of deception. In J. C. Yuille (Ed.), *Credibility assessment* (pp. 51–70). Dordrecht, the Netherlands: Kluwer.

DePaulo, B. M., Lindsay, J. L., Malone, B. E., Muhlenbruck, L., Charlton, K., & Cooper, H. (2003). Cues to deception. *Psychological Bulletin, 129,* 74–118.

Doherty-Sneddon, G., Bruce, V., Bonner, L., Longbotham, S., & Doyle, C. (2002). Development of gaze aversion as disengagement of visual information. *Developmental Psychology, 38,* 438–445.

Doherty-Sneddon, G., & Phelps, F. G. (2005). Gaze aversion: A response to cognitive or social difficulty? *Memory & Cognition, 33,* 727–733.

Ekman, P. (2006, October 29). How to spot a terrorist on the fly. *The Washington Post.* Retrieved August 21, 2009, from http://archive.gulfnews.com/articles/06/11/03/10079485.html

Fisher, R. P., Brennan, K. H., & McCauley, M. R. (2002). The cognitive interview method to enhance eyewitness recall. In M. L. Eisen, J. A. Quas, & G. S. Goodman (Eds.), *Memory and suggestibility in the forensic interview* (pp. 265–286). Mahwah, NJ: Erlbaum.

Gamer, M., Rill, H. G., Vossel, G., & Gödert, H. W. (2006). Psychophysiological and vocal measures in the detection of guilty knowledge. *International Journal of Psychophysiology, 60,* 76–87.

Geiselman, R. E., & Callot, R. (1990). Reverse and forward order recall of script based text. *Journal of Applied Cognitive Psychology, 4,* 141–144.

Gilbert, D. T. (1991). How mental systems believe. *American Psychologist, 46,* 107–119.

Gilbert, J. A. E., & Fisher, R. P. (2006). The effects of varied retrieval cues on reminiscence in eyewitness memory. *Applied Cognitive Psychology, 20,* 723–739.

Granhag, P. A., & Strömwall, L. A. (2002). Repeated interrogations: Verbal and nonverbal cues to deception. *Applied Cognitive Psychology, 16,* 243–257.

Granhag, P. A., Strömwall, L. A. & Hartwig, M. (2007). The SUE technique: The way to interview to detect deception. *Forensic Update, 88,* 25–29.

Gudjonsson, G. H. (2003). *The psychology of interrogations and confessions.* Chichester, UK: Wiley.

Hartwig, M., Granhag, P. A., Strömwall, L., & Kronkvist, O. (2006). Strategic use of evidence during police interrogations: When training to detect deception works. *Law & Human Behavior, 30,* 603–619.

Horvath, F. (1973). Verbal and nonverbal cues to truth and deception during polygraph examinations. *Journal of Police Science & Administration, 1,* 138–152.

Inbau, F. E., Reid, J. E., Buckley, J. P., & Jayne, B. C. (2001). *Criminal interrogation and confessions* (4th ed.). Gaithersburg, MD: Aspen.

Johnston, W. A., Greenberg, S. N., Fisher, R. P., & Martin, D. W. (1970). Divided attention: A vehicle for monitoring memory processes. *Journal of Experimental Psychology, 83,* 164–171.

Kahana, M. J. (1996). Associate retrieval processes in free recall. *Memory & Cognition, 24,* 103–109.

Kassin, S. M. (2005). On the psychology of confessions: Does innocence put innocents at risk? *American Psychologist, 60,* 215–228.

Kassin, S. M., & Fong, C. T. (1999). "I'm innocent!": Effects of training on judgments of truth and deception in the interrogation room. *Law & Human Behavior, 23,* 499–516.

Kassin, S. M., & Gudjonsson, G. H. (2004). The psychology of confessions: A review of the literature and issues. *Psychological Science in the Public Interest, 5,* 33–67.

Kassin, S. M., & Norwick, R. J. (2004). Why people waive their Miranda rights: The power of innocence. *Law & Human Behavior, 28,* 211–221.

Langleben, D. D. (2008). Detection of deception with fMRI: Are we there yet? *Legal and Criminological Psychology, 13,* 1–10.

Leal, S., Vrij, A., Fisher, R., & van Hooff, H. (2008). The time of the crime: Cognitively induced tonic arousal suppression when lying in a free recall context. *Acta Psychologica, 129,* 1–7.

Mann, S., & Vrij, A. (2006). Police officers' judgments of veracity, tenseness, cognitive load and attempted behavioral control in real life police interviews. *Psychology, Crime, & Law, 12,* 307–319.

Mann, S., Vrij, A., & Bull, R. (2002). Suspects, lies and videotape: An analysis of authentic high-stakes liars. *Law & Human Behavior, 26,* 365–376.

National Research Council. (2003). *The polygraph and lie detection.* Washington, DC: The National Academic Press.

O'Sullivan, M. (2005). Emotional intelligence and deception detection: Why most people can't "read" others, but a few can. In R. E. Riggio & R. S. Feldman (Eds.), *Applications of nonverbal communication* (pp. 215–253). Mahwah, NJ: Erlbaum.

O'Sullivan, M. (2007). Unicorns or Tiger Woods: Are lie detection experts myths or rarities? A response to "On lie detection 'wizards'" by Bond and Uysal. *Law & Human Behavior, 31,* 117–123.

O'Sullivan, M., & Ekman, P. (2004). The wizards of deception detection. In P. A. Granhag & L. A. Strömwall (Eds.), *Deception detection in forensic contexts* (pp. 269–286). Cambridge, UK: Cambridge University Press.

Porter, S., & Ten Brinke, L. (2008). Reading between the lies: Identifying concealed and falsified emotions in universal facial expressions. *Psychological Science, 19,* 508–514.

Porter, S., & Ten Brinke, L. (in press). The truth about lies: What works in detecting high-stakes deception? *Legal & Criminological Psychology.*

Schweitzer, M. E., Brodt, S. E., & Croson, R. T. A. (2002). Seeing and believing: Visual access and the strategic use of deception. *The International Journal of Conflict Management, 13,* 258–275.

Spence, S. A. (2008). Playing devil's advocate: The case *against* fMRI lie detection. *Legal & Criminological Psychology, 13,* 11–26.

Spence, S. A., Farrow, T. F. D., Herford, A. E., Wilkinson, I. D., Zheng, Y., & Woodruff, P. W. R. (2001). Behavioral and functional anatomical correlates of deception in humans. *Neuroreport: For Rapid Communication of Neuroscience Research, 12,* 2849–2853.

Spence, S. A., Hunter, M. D., Farrow, T. F. D., Green, R. D., Leung, D. H., & Hughes, C. J. (2004). A cognitive neurobiological account of deception: Evidence from functional neuroimaging. *Philosophical Transactions of the Royal Society of London, 359,* 1755–1762.

Strömwall, L. A., Granhag, P. A., & Hartwig, M. (2004). Practitioners' beliefs about deception. In P. A. Granhag & L. A. Strömwall (Eds.), *Deception detection in forensic contexts* (pp. 229–250). Cambridge, UK: Cambridge University Press.

Strömwall, L. A., Hartwig, M., & Granhag, P. A. (2006). To act truthfully: Nonverbal behavior and strategies during a police interrogation. *Psychology, Crime, & Law, 12,* 207–219.

Taylor, R., & Hick, R. F. (2007). Believed cues to deception: Judgments in self-generated serious and trivial situations. *Legal & Criminological Psychology, 12,* 321–332.

The Global Deception Team. (2006). A world of lies. *Journal of Cross-Cultural Psychology, 37,* 60–74.

Vrij, A. (2004). Invited article: Why professionals fail to catch liars and how they can improve. *Legal & Criminological Psychology, 9,* 159–181.

Vrij, A. (2006). Challenging interviewees during interviews: The potential effects on lie detection. *Psychology, Crime, & Law, 12,* 193–206.

Vrij, A. (2008). *Detecting lies and deceit: Pitfalls and opportunities.* Chichester, England: Wiley.

Vrij, A., Akehurst, L., & Knight, S. (2006). Police officers', social workers', teachers' and the general public's beliefs about deception in children, adolescents and adults. *Legal & Criminological Psychology, 11,* 297–312.

Vrij, A., Edward, K., & Bull, R. (2001). Stereotypical verbal and nonverbal responses while deceiving others. *Personality & Social Psychology Bulletin, 27,* 899-909.

Vrij, A., Fisher, R., Mann, S., & Leal, S. (2006). Detecting deception by manipulating cognitive load. *Trends in Cognitive Sciences, 10,* 141-142.

Vrij, A., Fisher, R., Mann, S., & Leal, S. (2009). Increasing cognitive load in interviews to detect deceit. In B. Milne, S. Savage, & T. Williamson (Ed.), *International developments in investigative interviewing* (pp. 176–189). Uffculme: Willan.

Vrij, A., & Granhag, P. A. (2007). Interviewing to detect deception. In S. A. Christianson (Ed.), *Offenders' memories of violent crimes* (pp. 279–304). Chichester, England: Wiley.

Vrij, A., & Mann, S. (2003). Deception detection. In P. W. Halligan, C. Bass, & D. A. Oakley (Eds.), *Malingering and illness deception* (pp. 348–362). Oxford, England: Oxford University Press.

Vrij, A., & Mann, S. (2006). Criteria-based content analysis: An empirical test of its underlying processes. *Psychology, Crime, & Law, 12,* 337–349.

Vrij, A., Mann, S., & Fisher, R. (2006a). An empirical test of the Behavior Analysis Interview. *Law & Human Behavior, 30,* 329–345.

Vrij, A., Mann, S., & Fisher, R. (2006b). Information-gathering vs. accusatory interview style: Individual differences in respondents' experiences. *Personality & Individual Differences, 41,* 589–599.

Vrij, A., Mann, S., Fisher, R., Leal, S., Milne, B., & Bull, R. (2008). Increasing cognitive load to facilitate lie detection: The benefit of recalling an event in reverse order. *Law & Human Behavior, 32,* 253–265.

Vrij, A., Mann, S., Kristen, S., & Fisher, R. (2007). Cues to deception and ability to detect lies as a function of police interview styles. *Law & Human Behavior, 31,* 499–518.

Vrij, A., Mann, S., Leal, S., & Fisher, R. (in press). "Look into my eyes": Can an instruction to maintain eye contact facilitate lie detection? *Psychology, Crime, & Law.*

Vrij, A., Semin, G. R., & Bull, R. (1996). Insight into behavior during deception. *Human Communication Research, 22,* 544–562.

Walczyk, J. J., Roper, K. S., Seemann, E., & Humphrey, A. M. (2003). Cognitive mechanisms underlying lying to questions: Response time as a cue to deception. *Applied Cognitive Psychology, 17,* 755–744.

Walczyk, J. J., Schwartz, J. P., Clifton, R., Adams, B., Wei, M., & Zha, P. (2005). Lying person-to-person about live events: A cognitive framework for lie detection. *Personnel Psychology, 58,* 141–170.

White, C. H., & Burgoon, J. K. (2001). Adaptation and communicative design: Patterns of interaction in truthful and deceptive conversations. *Human Communication Research, 27,* 9–37.

7

The Importance of a Laboratory Science for Improving the Diagnostic Value of Confession Evidence

Christian A. Meissner, Melissa B. Russano, and Fadia M. Narchet

In 1989, the brutal assault and rape of a young White female jogger shocked the city of New York. Five Hispanic and Black teenage boys eventually gave detailed confession statements indicating involvement in the crime. Despite the fact that all the teenagers later retracted their confessions and that no other physical evidence conclusively linked them to the crime, the five boys were ultimately convicted of committing the attack and served up to 12 years in prison, all the while maintaining their innocence. In January 2002, a convicted serial rapist and murderer, Matias Reyes, came forward and confessed to attacking the jogger. He claimed to have acted alone, and DNA tests of semen and pubic hair found at the scene of the crime later confirmed that Reyes had, in fact, committed the attack (McFadden & Saulny, 2002). Their convictions were overturned, and the boys were officially exonerated in December 2002.

The False Confession Phenomenon and Its Consequences

Wrongful detainment and conviction of the innocent is likely the most egregious error that can occur in the criminal justice system, not only for the life-altering consequences it may have on an innocent person but also for the potential harm caused by the actual perpetrator of the crime who remains at large. Although it is generally believed that such instances of wrongful conviction are relatively rare, exonerations of the innocent through DNA testing are increasing at a rate that few in the criminal justice system might have speculated (Scheck, 2001; Scheck, Neufeld, & Dwyer, 2000). A variety of factors have been shown to be associated with such wrongful convictions, including false confessions. As a result of the growing realization of this false confession phenomenon, social scientists have begun to examine factors that may lead a person to implicate themselves in a crime that he or she did not commit (Gudjonsson, 2003; Kassin, 2005; Kassin & Gudjonsson, 2004).

Reliable confession evidence is important not only to the criminal justice system but also to U.S. security agencies (Evans, Meissner, Brandon, Russano,

& Kleinman, in press; Redlich, 2007). With the dawn of increased security and intelligence activity following the 9/11 attacks, it would appear that the elicitation of *diagnostic* information (i.e., a greater likelihood of true vs. false information) from interrogations would prove instrumental in preventing future terrorist activity. As the political debate surrounding the use of torture with terrorist suspects illustrates, there is a pressing need to identify noncoercive, evidence-based techniques that will yield diagnostic information (Evans et al., in press; Meissner & Albrechtsen, 2007). Similarly, techniques designed to elicit diagnostic confessions from criminal suspects would likely speed the conviction process for guilty persons and protect the innocent from wrongful conviction within the criminal justice system.

Although there has been a notable surge in the frequency of false confessions discussed in the media, the actual rate of false confessions in practice is difficult to determine (chap. 2, this volume; Leo & Ofshe, 1998). According to data from the Innocence Project Web site (http://www.innocenceproject.org), between 20% and 25% of the more than 200 cases of wrongful conviction were due, at least in part, to a false admission or confession on the part of the defendant (see also Drizin & Leo, 2004). As discussed by Gudjonsson (chap. 2, this volume), survey data suggest that between 7% and 12% of individuals who have been interrogated by police report having provided a false confession. In a recent survey, police investigators in the United States who regularly conduct interrogations estimated that approximately 5% of innocent suspects provide a false confession (Kassin et al., 2007). In what is likely the most powerful evidence that false confessions occur, Drizin and Leo (2004) recently documented 125 cases of proven false confession in the Unites States. Their data suggest that significant consequences for the innocent are associated with providing a false confession. For example, 81% of those who went to trial having provided a false confession were convicted of the crime— a figure that speaks to the power of confession evidence in the courtroom (Kassin & Neumann, 1997)—whereas an additional 11% actually chose to accept a plea bargain to avoid the death penalty (see chap. 3, this volume). Furthermore, 61% of those convicted spent over 5 years in prison prior to exoneration.

Taken together, these data demonstrate that the false confession phenomenon occurs in our criminal justice system to a significant degree and that it is associated with severe consequences for both the innocent suspect and for the community that remains at risk. Several decades of research have now examined false confessions both from the field and, more recently, within the laboratory. Although researchers apparently know much about the causes of this phenomenon (see Kassin & Gudjonsson, 2004; chap. 1, this volume), further research that might assist in the development of techniques that would promote the elicitation of diagnostic information (i.e., a greater proportion of true confessions as compared with false confessions) in the interrogation room appears warranted. Furthermore, although several theoretical models have been proposed to account for the influence of psychologically coercive interrogation techniques, little research has provided a venue for the validation and development of such theories under controlled, laboratory conditions. We begin by highlighting what is currently known regarding the false confession phenomenon, provide a review of current theoretical models of confession, and finally discuss research from our laboratory using a novel experimental paradigm that we believe can effectively model the social and cognitive psychological processes involved in the interrogative process. In this context, we describe a series of studies that we have conducted attempting to empirically assess the diagnostic value of certain interrogative approaches.

What Are the Likely Causes of the False Confession Phenomenon?

Social science researchers have begun to systematically examine the false confession phenomenon over the past several decades both from the field and within the laboratory (see Kassin & Gudjonsson, 2004). The overwhelming data from these studies suggest that two primary factors appear to be associated with the elicitation of false confessions: namely, the implementation of psychologically manipulative interrogation techniques and individual differences that make some suspects more vulnerable to interrogation than others.

Interrogation Techniques

Throughout history, investigators have resorted to a wide variety of techniques intended to break down a suspect's resistance and yield a confession. Interrogation techniques have evolved from overtly coercive, third-degree tactics (e.g., beatings, sleep deprivation; see Leo, 2004) to modern-day practices that involve more subtle, yet effective, psychologically based techniques. One of the most heralded and readily used interrogation procedures in the United States is known as the Reid technique of investigative interviewing. Now in its fourth edition, the Reid technique manual (Inbau, Reid, Bukley, & Jayne, 2001) serves as an important resource for police investigators. The Reid technique encourages investigators to initiate an interview by using a nonaccusatorial interview (known as the Behavioral Analysis Interview) to assess verbal and nonverbal indicators of deception prior to conducting the actual interrogation. A growing body of research, however, suggests that the average individual and law enforcement officer performs only slightly better than chance when attempting to distinguish truth from deception (Bond & DePaulo, 2006; Vrij, 2008; chap. 6, this volume). Furthermore, research in our laboratory suggests that police investigators demonstrate a guilt bias in their perception of suspects (Meissner & Kassin, 2002, 2004), including their perception of true versus false confession statements (Kassin, Meissner, & Norwick, 2005), indicating that they are more likely to view suspects as deceptive. Further, a study by Vrij, Mann, and Fisher (2006) found that the Behavioral Analysis Interview technique, in particular, produced a pattern of behaviors counter to that predicted by Inbau et al., which could mean false presumptions of guilt were being placed on innocent suspects (see also chap. 6, this volume).

Nevertheless, it is only following a finding of deception in the preinterrogation interview that investigators are encouraged to apply the nine-step Reid technique of interrogation. As Kassin and Gudjonsson (2004) noted, the nine-step Reid technique can be readily reducible to three general phases involving the following: *custody and isolation,* in which the suspect is detained in a small room and left to experience the anxiety, insecurity, and uncertainty associated with police interrogation; *confrontation,* in which the suspect is presumed guilty and told (often falsely) of the evidence against him or her, is warned of the consequences associated with his or her guilt, and is prevented from denying his or her involvement in the crime (i.e., a process of maximization consistent with that proposed by Kassin & McNall, 1991); and *minimization,* in which a now sympathetic interrogator attempts to gain the suspect's trust, offers the suspect face-saving excuses or justifications for the crime, and implies more lenient consequences should the suspect provide a confession.

The Reid technique is effective in eliciting confessions largely as a result of social influence processes that have been shown to produce powerful effects in psychological studies of conformity (Asch, 1956), obedience to authority (Milgram, 1974), and compliance with requests (Cialdini, 2001). But could such a technique also yield false confessions? Inbau et al. (2001) argued that innocent suspects will not be compelled to confess with these methods, primarily because of the belief that such individuals will be excluded from interrogation on the basis of a successful pre-interview (Kassin & Gudjonsson, 2004). It is unfortunate that Inbau et al. have yet to produce any scientific data supporting this claim, and numerous researchers have expressed concern that some of these techniques may in fact place innocent suspects in danger (Gudjonsson, 2003; Kassin, 2005; Kassin & Gudjonsson, 2004; Redlich & Meissner, 2009). For example, Kassin and Kiechel (1996) have shown that the presentation of false evidence can significantly increase the likelihood of false confession, whereas research in our laboratory (Russano, Meissner, Narchet, & Kassin, 2005) has demonstrated that minimization techniques can increase the likelihood of both true and false confessions.

Individual Difference Characteristics

Research has suggested that some individuals are more vulnerable than others in the interrogation room. Specifically, there appear to be certain characteristics that render an individual more susceptible to interrogation, including the age, mental capacity, suggestibility, and physical or psychological state of the suspect at the time of the interrogation (chaps. 2 and 12, this volume). First, a number of field studies (Baldwin & McConville, 1980; Leiken, 1970; Phillips & Brown, 1998; Softley, 1980; for a review, see Drizin & Colgan, 2004) and laboratory studies (Billings et al., 2007; Redlich & Goodman, 2003) have demonstrated that younger suspects, and in particular children, are more likely to confess during an interrogation than older persons or adults (see chap. 4, this volume). Indeed, 32% of the false confessions discussed by Drizin and Leo (2004) involved juveniles under the age of 18 years.

Second, studies have suggested that police routinely interrogate persons of low intelligence or IQ (Gudjonsson, 1993) and that such individuals may be more suggestible and less able to cope with the pressures of the interrogation room (chap. 12, this volume; Gudjonsson, 2003). For example, Drizin and Leo (2004) found that 19% of their sample of false confessors could be classified as "mentally retarded." Third, interrogative suggestibility has been suggested to be associated with false confessions (chap. 12, this volume; Gudjonsson, 2003;

Gudjonsson & Clark, 1986). The Gudjonsson Suggestibility Scale (Gudjonsson, 1984) has been used to assess suggestibility in a number of studies, with suggestibility often being associated with poor memory, low self-esteem, high levels of anxiety, and a greater likelihood of confession. Finally, the psychological state (e.g., because of mental illness or drug use) of a suspect at the time of interrogation may also be linked to the likelihood of false confession (Pearse, Gudjonsson, Clare, & Rutter, 1998; Redlich, 2004); 10% of the Drizin and Leo (2004) sample of false confessors were described as "mentally ill."

Can We Reduce the Likelihood of False Confessions in Practice?

Identifying interrogation strategies that minimize the likelihood of obtaining false confessions without compromising the ability of interrogators to elicit true confessions is a challenge faced by law enforcement and researchers alike. Research identifying such strategies is sorely lacking. In examining what progress law enforcement has made in this area, it is informative to examine the interrogation practices of other countries. Although interviewing practices in the United States and Great Britain were on par with one another through the 1980s, these two nations now differ greatly in their approaches (Bull & Milne, 2004). As detailed by Bull and Soukara (chap. 5, this volume), high-profile wrongful conviction cases and subsequent research in Great Britain led to the development of the Police and Criminal Evidence Act of 1984 (Home Office, 1985), which prohibited the use of psychologically manipulative techniques and mandated the recording of custodial interrogations.

In 1993, the Royal Commission on Criminal Justice further reformed British interrogation methods by introducing the PEACE model. Contrary to the U.S. accusatorial style of interrogation, this interview has the goal of fact finding rather than that of obtaining a confession (with an emphasis on the use of open-ended questions), and investigators are expressly prohibited from deceiving suspects (Milne & Bull, 1999; Mortimer & Shepherd, 1999). Evaluation research conducted by Clarke and Milne (2001) suggests that the PEACE method has been effective in changing the culture of police interviewing without significantly reducing the likelihood of obtaining confessions in practice (see chap. 5, this volume). Police in New Zealand have now also adopted the PEACE protocol following the successes in Great Britain.

Another related strategy that has been suggested for improving the diagnosticity of interrogative evidence is the use of the cognitive interview (CI) in an interrogation context. The CI was originally developed as a strategy for interviewing cooperative witnesses and has proven useful for increasing the amount of information recalled (see Fisher & Geiselman, 1992). Recently, Fisher and Perez (2007) suggested that the principles of the CI may also be applied to suspect interviews. It is unfortunate, as noted by Hartwig, Granhag, and Vrij (2005), that no empirical laboratory research has examined the potential of either the inquisitorial or cognitive interview as an effective interrogative method. In the following, we discuss our initial attempts at validating such an interrogative approach.

What Theoretical Models Have Been Proposed to Understand Confessions?

As mentioned previously, psychologically based interrogation techniques are believed to elicit confessions largely as a result of social influence processes that have been shown to produce powerful effects in psychological studies of conformity (Asch, 1956), obedience to authority (Milgram, 1974), and compliance with requests (see Cialdini, 2001). However, several specific theories have been developed to account for the cognitive and social psychological processes leading to confession (Berggren, 1975; Gudjonsson, 1989; Hilgendorf & Irving, 1981; Moston, Stephanson, & Williamson, 1992; Ofshe & Leo, 1997; for a review, see Gudjonsson, 2003).

One of the most frequently cited theories involves the decision-making model put forth by Hilgendorf and Irving (1981). In essence, the authors applied a form of subjective expected utility theory (Ajzen & Fishbein, 1980; Malpass, 1990) to the confession phenomenon and took into consideration the role of certain environmental stressors that can influence decision-making performance. According to Hilgendorf and Irving, suspects undergo three phases when evaluating whether they should confess to a crime. In the first phase, suspects appraise their perceptions of the available courses of action by considering their options and weighing the likely consequences attached with those options. In the second phase, the suspect is said to assess the likelihood of the various consequences attached to the courses of action by estimating their subjective probabilities (or what they believe will happen), whereas in the final phase the suspect evaluates the utility values or gains attached to the various courses of action. In the case of false confessors, the authors argued that a suspect may accept the immediate instrumental gain of ending the interrogation and mistakenly determine that the truth of his or her innocence will be revealed or that no jury would ultimately convict them. Hilgendorf and Irving further contended that various social and environmental factors associated with interrogations can impair a suspect's ability to make an informed decision, particularly as interrogators manipulate a suspect's perceptions regarding the likely outcome about a certain course of action (e.g., by minimizing the seriousness of the alleged offense) or their level of fear, anxiety, or ability to rationalize a decision through sleep deprivation and fatigue.

Gudjonsson (1989, 2003; chap. 2, this volume) has expanded on the work of Hilgendorf and Irving (1981) in his cognitive–behavioral model of confession and has argued that five factors should be considered when understanding why suspects confess. First, *social* factors refer to the suspect's feelings of isolation and their need for approval or affiliation. Second, *emotional* factors refer to the suspect's feelings of distress or anxiety, whereas *cognitive* factors refer to the suspect's thoughts and interpretations of the interrogation situation (e.g., does the suspect perceive the evidence against him or her to be strong or weak). Fourth, *situational* factors refer to pre-existing circumstances associated with the suspect (e.g., does the suspect have experience with the legal system) or environmental factors (e.g., does the suspect have an attorney present during the interrogation). Finally, *physiological* factors refer to the suspect's aroused physical state (i.e., heart rate, blood pressure, perspiration, and respirations). Gudjonsson further proposed that certain antecedents may exacerbate the influence of any given factor. In addition, although it is possible that a suspect could evaluate both the immediate and long-term consequences associated with confessing, it would appear that focusing a suspect on *immediate consequences* (e.g., feeling of approval or being permitted to visit with family or friends) would more likely yield a confession.

Although the theoretical models proposed to date have provided rather intuitive explanations of the social and cognitive psychological processes associated with confession, little empirical research has been conducted to examine their validity or to assess the extent to which such models might appropriately explain both true and false confessions. In the following, we describe recent research in our laboratory that has provided a foundation for assessing the validity of these models via a controlled, experimental paradigm.

Why Use a Laboratory Paradigm to Investigate True Versus False Confessions?

Two broad methods have been used to study interrogations and confessions: field observations and laboratory research. *Field research* (e.g., observational studies of actual police interrogations or archival reviews of wrongful convictions) carries the distinct advantage of high external validity (i.e., the extent to which findings can be applied beyond those of the specific study) and generalizability. For example, in a seminal study of U.S. police interrogations, Leo (1996) observed more than 300 live and videotaped interviews in an effort to systematically document the techniques used by investigators. Similar studies have been conducted in Great Britain (Baldwin, 1993; Irving; 1980; Irving & McKenzie, 1989; Moston et al., 1992; Softley, 1980). Although archival and observational studies have certainly increased our understanding of police interrogations, like most field research methodologies these studies suffer from issues of internal validity (i.e., the extent to which a researcher is assessing a true causal relationship between two or more factors) because they lack the experimental controls necessary to eliminate all confounds that might enable researchers to draw causal conclusions.

Because of the limitations of field research methods, a number of researchers have begun to use experimental laboratory research methods. Although generally limited by issues of external validity, laboratory research benefits from a high degree of experimental control. This advantage of internal validity allows researchers to explore cause-and-effect relationships and thereby to draw causal conclusions regarding the influence of certain interrogation techniques on the likelihood of true versus false confessions. It is important that laboratory paradigms also permit researchers to validate proposed psychological models of confession in a controlled fashion: Postconfession questionnaires and experimental manipulations that distinguish psychological processes of interest can be administered across a normative sample of individuals in the laboratory. To the extent that the psychological processes of interest are transposed to the laboratory paradigm, experimental methods provide an effective means for investigating the psychology of confessions and interrogation.

Although each research type has inherent advantages and disadvantages, ultimately both field and laboratory research approaches are necessary to understand the process of interrogation and the psychology of confessions. As Behrman and Davey (2001) noted regarding research on eyewitness identification, "A diversity of methods is needed if we are to provide the legal profession with practical advice regarding eyewitness memory. It is from a combination of methods, controlled experiments, field studies, and archival studies that conclusions should be drawn" (p. 489). The success of field and laboratory research on eyewitness memory, and its contribution to practice, are now well known (Wells et al., 2000), and this multimethod approach would appear to provide an appropriate model for research on interrogations and confessions.

The interrogation room certainly presents a challenge to laboratory researchers who attempt to recreate the elements of police interrogation in a controlled environment. Ethical constraints likely always preclude researchers from creating situations in which participants believe they are under suspicion and are being interrogated for an actual criminal act. As such, it is impossible to precisely replicate the circumstances that a criminal suspect faces during interrogation (e.g., the potential consequence of incarceration, the stigma of criminal behavior). The challenge for researchers, then, is to design research studies that maximize both internal and external validity and to ensure that the cognitive and social psychological processes under investigation are transposed to the laboratory in a context that preserves their natural elements and thereby substantiates their application to the real world of police interrogation. In the following section, we briefly review the predominant laboratory paradigm that has been used over the past decade, discuss its benefits and limitations, and propose an alternative paradigm that we believe improves both the internal and external validity with which we can explore psychological theories of confession in the laboratory.

What Can Laboratory Research Tell Us About the Psychology of Confessions?

Over the past decade, researchers have engaged in experimental studies both to assess the extent to which certain interrogation methods might elicit false confessions and more recently to empirically evaluate the diagnostic utility of certain interrogative approaches. We describe in the following the two experimental paradigms that have been used for these purposes, respectively.

The Kassin and Kiechel Paradigm

Kassin and Kiechel (1996) designed the first paradigm to demonstrate the false confession phenomenon in the laboratory. In this study, innocent participants were accused of accidentally hitting a forbidden key on a keyboard during a computer-based task, causing the computer to crash and important data to be lost. In their demonstration of this paradigm, the authors manipulated the presentation of false evidence: In half of the conditions, a confederate confirmed seeing the participant hit the *Alt* key (when, in reality, no participants actually hit the *Alt* key), whereas for others the confederate said he or she had not seen what happened. The pace of the typing task (fast vs. slow) also served to manipulate participants' level of memory vulnerability: In the fast-paced condition, participants were less confident about whether they had hit the *Alt* key than participants in the slow-paced condition.

Kassin and Kiechel (1996) collected three dependent measures. In particular, they measured *compliance* by assessing whether participants would sign a handwritten confession, *internalization* by determining whether participants actually came to believe that they had hit the *Alt* key, and *confabulation* by assessing whether participants began to generate false memories of the event. Although all participants initially denied hitting the *Alt* key, 69% eventually exhibited compliance, 28% internalized, and 9% confabulated. In the most intense interrogation condition (high memory vulnerability and presentation of false evidence), 100% exhibited compliance, 65% internalized, and 35% confabulated. Researchers have continued to use the Kassin and Kiechel paradigm to investigate other possible influences, such as a preexisting state of stress (Forrest, Wadkins, & Miller, 2002), the gender of the interrogator or suspect (Abboud, Wadkins, Forrest, Lange, & Alavi, 2002), the suspect's age (Redlich & Goodman, 2003), individual difference variables such as locus of control and authoritarianism (Forrest, Wadkins, & Larson, 2006), the consequences of confession (Horselenberg, Merckelbach, & Josephs, 2003), and the use of minimization and maximization techniques (Klaver, Rose, & Lee, 2008).

Although false confession research conducted using Kassin and Kiechel's (1996) *Alt* key paradigm was an important first step into this research area, the paradigm fails to capture a number of important elements present in real-world interrogation situations that may limit the ecological validity (i.e., the extent to which laboratory research on interrogations resembles real-world interrogations) and generalizability of the research findings. For example, participants in the paradigm were accused of accidentally committing a highly plausible crime, leaving open the possibility that many participants were unsure whether they were innocent or guilty. In contrast, real-world suspects are typically accused of intentionally committing a criminal act and are certain of their own culpability. Second, in the real world, the accused may or may not have actually committed the crime; however, participants in the Kassin and Kiechel paradigm are always innocent. We believe it is important that researchers attempt to understand the influence of various techniques in eliciting both true and false confessions to assess the diagnostic value (i.e., the elicitation of true versus false confessions) of an interrogation and to validate proposed theoretical models of confession. Finally, the real-world consequences of confessing to a crime are usually severe for the suspect, although the interrogator may minimize the perceived consequences during the course of the interrogation. In the Kassin and Kiechel paradigm, the consequence for confessing has typically been relatively mild (e.g., a phone call from the primary investigator of the study or a small monetary loss in Horselenberg et al., 2003). The failure of researchers to move beyond this now classic paradigm has been due, in part, to the difficulty in creating a paradigm that might better approximate real-world conditions while treating participants in accordance with current ethical standards.

A Novel Laboratory Paradigm

In an effort to enhance both internal and external validity and to preserve the ethical treatment of research participants, we have recently developed a novel laboratory paradigm that can be used to assess the effects of interrogation techniques on the likelihood of both true and false confessions (Russano et al., 2005). In our paradigm, participants are accused of breaking an experimental rule, an act that is later characterized as "cheating." Participants are recruited to participate in a study on team versus individual problem solving in which they are asked to solve a series of logic problems, sometimes working individually and sometimes working with a confederate. In his instructions to the participant and confederate, the researcher makes clear that they are not to work together on designated individual problems, which is the critical rule of the experiment that is subsequently manipulated. In the guilty condition, the confederate asks for help on a target individual problem; participants who provide an answer violate the rule of the experiment and are thus considered guilty of cheating on the task. In the innocent condition, the confederate does not make this request and so participants remain innocent of violating the experimental rule. Later, all participants are accused of cheating (with the academic implications thereof), are interrogated by an experimenter who remains blind to the participants' actual guilt or innocence, and are ultimately asked to sign a confession statement.

We believe there are several strengths to this paradigm. First, the crime used may be considered by students as a fairly severe act, as it is portrayed as a form of cheating within the context of an academic setting. In addition, as in the real world, committing the crime requires intent, and participants clearly know whether they are guilty or innocent of the behavior. Finally, in this paradigm, as in the real world, some of the individuals being interrogated are innocent and some are guilty, enabling researchers to assess the effects of interrogation factors on the likelihood of both true and false confessions. It is important that this allows us to examine not only those factors that might lead to false confession but also those techniques that might improve the diagnostic value of police interrogations.

In our first demonstration of this paradigm (Russano et al., 2005), we varied the interrogation techniques used by our experimenters, including an explicit offer of leniency (or a deal) and exposure to minimization tactics (i.e., the interrogator expressed sympathy, provided face-saving excuses, and emphasized the importance of cooperation). Our results indicated that guilty participants were significantly more likely to confess than innocent participants and that both an explicit offer of leniency and minimization techniques independently increased both true and false confession rates. Moreover, diagnosticity (i.e., the ratio of true to false confessions) was significantly reduced when either the deal technique or minimization was used or when the two tactics were combined when compared with that of the no-tactic control condition. It is interesting that the use of both the deal and minimization techniques increased participants' perceptions of the social pressure that the interrogator was placing on them to provide a confession. Because of the ethically sensitive nature of the paradigm and the use of deception, we administered a follow-up questionnaire to a subset of participants from our original study to assess their reactions to the study. Participants reported that they felt moderately stressed during the interrogation, they thought the use of deception was justified, and in the end, they had a somewhat positive and educational experience.

In a second study using the paradigm (Narchet, Meissner, & Russano, 2009), we examined the extent to which investigator knowledge or biases (Kassin, Goldstein, & Savitsky, 2003; Meissner & Kassin, 2002, 2004) might influence the process of interrogation leading to confession. Furthermore, we were interested in assessing whether Gudjonsson's (1989) five-factor model might account for the psychological processes leading to confession in our paradigm. To examine these issues, we trained our interrogators in 15 different interrogation techniques (including aspects of maximization and minimization) and permitted them freedom to apply these techniques within the context of a 15-minute interrogation. We also provided the experimenters with some information regarding participants' likely guilt or innocence prior to interrogation. Finally, following each interrogation, we provided participants with a questionnaire to assess the influence of Gudjonsson's cognitive, social, affective, physiological, and situational factors on confession. As expected, guilty persons were more likely to confess than innocent persons (consistent with Russano et al., 2005); however, investigator biases also influenced the nature of the interrogation, particularly for those participants who were factually innocent. More specifically, experimenters who were led to believe that the participant was guilty were more likely to apply strong accusatorial interrogation methods, leading to an increase in both true and false confessions. In addition, the use of accusatorial methods (i.e., minimization and maximization approaches) produced confessions that were significantly less diagnostic when compared with interrogations involving noncoercive, investigative interviewing approaches. With regard to assessing theories of confession, our results suggested that participants' who perceived greater social pressure to confess from the experimenter (Gudjonsson's social factor) and for whom the consequences of not confessing led them to believe that there was no way out of the situation (Gudjonsson's cognitive factor) were more likely to confess. Finally, postinterrogation interviews of experimenters revealed that those led to believe that the participant was guilty were more likely to believe (postinterrogation) that the participant was in fact guilty, thereby demonstrating a process of behavioral confirmation (see Meissner & Kassin, 2004).

It should be noted that our ultimate goal in using this paradigm has been to identify interrogative approaches that might provide a viable alternative to traditional methods of interrogation and specifically to demonstrate that noncoercive methods can improve the diagnostic value of interrogative information. The Narchet et al. (2009) study provided an important account of the potential benefit of a noncoercive (inquisitorial) style of interrogation when compared with methods of minimization and maximization that are often used in modern interrogations. In an effort to confirm this trade-off in diagnosticity, we recently conducted two additional studies in which we exerted greater control over the tactics used by our interrogators and examined the specific benefits of an inquisitorial approach compared with that of maximization and minimization techniques (Meissner, Russano, Rigoni, & Horgan, 2009).

The inquisitorial approach used in these studies was modeled after the approach advocated in Great Britain (chap. 5, this volume). It included developing rapport, explaining the allegation and the seriousness of the offense, emphasizing the importance of honesty and truth gathering, and requesting the suspect's version of events. The suspect was permitted to explain the situation without interruption as the experimenter demonstrated active listening skills. Following the suspect's narrative, the experimenter was permitted to identify discrepancies or contradictions in the account but was not permitted to falsify evidence or contradictions. Finally, the suspect was provided an opportunity to sign a confession statement. The results of both studies (Meissner et al., 2009) demonstrated a significant advantage in using inquisitorial methods over that of accusatorial approaches; in particular, the inquisitorial approach produced significantly fewer false confessions and, when combined with the cognitive interview in the second study, significantly increased true confessions. Thus, the inquisitorial approach was significantly more diagnostic in producing superior confession evidence! In addition, the inquisitorial approach distinguished itself from the other techniques such that innocent participants in this condition perceived significantly less social pressure to confess, whereas guilty participants showed elevated levels of social pressure consistent with that of an accusatorial approach. Given that the perception of pressure is most often associated with interrogative confessions, this finding is important to our attempts at identifying techniques that target guilty suspects.

Conclusions

Laboratory research on confessions has yielded valuable information regarding the extent to which certain interrogation tactics can lead to false confessions and, most important, the identification of techniques (e.g., the inquisitorial method) that can increase the diagnostic value of confession evidence. Furthermore, the laboratory paradigm presented in this chapter has provided an opportunity to assess the role of psychological theory in the interrogation room, and as such has provided support for the influence of social pressure and cognitive decision-making processes as key factors leading to true versus false confessions.

In this chapter, we have emphasized that the bulk of research on interrogations and confessions has focused on factors associated with the false confession phenomenon. Although this research has been important in highlighting cases of wrongful conviction that stem from the interrogation room, we believe that it is also important to explore the development of techniques that might improve the diagnostic value of confession evidence and thereby also account for true confessions. Not only is this approach important for the development of theoretical models that might distinguish between true versus false confessions, but it will also enable the provision of alternative interrogation methods to law enforcement that have been empirically validated and supported by the broader scientific community. As noted by Redlich and Meissner (2009), interrogative methods currently available to law enforcement have no scientific foundation but rather have been offered (or better sold) by former investigators who purport that the validity of those techniques is based on their success in yielding confession statements, independent of veracity or ground truth. As we further develop our scientific understanding of interrogations and confessions, we should be prepared to offer alternative methods of interrogation to law enforcement, as opposed to simply discouraging their use of various tactics that now have a foothold in everyday practice.

With these objectives in mind, we have begun a systematic research effort designed to lay the groundwork for identifying techniques that promote the elicitation of guilty knowledge and simultaneously reduce the likelihood of obtaining false confessions from innocent individuals. We recognize that once this laboratory research has been completed, further research using field tests of the proposed techniques will be important for documenting the success of the proposed alternative approaches in everyday practice. It is to this end that we are currently working with law enforcement entities in an effort to take our findings beyond the laboratory and into the field (see Evans et al., in press). In our view, a scientific approach to understanding interrogations and confessions involves collaboration between both the laboratory and the field, and we hope that our current work might set the stage for further validation and implementation of approaches that promote the diagnostic elicitation of confession evidence.

References

Abboud, B., Wadkins, T. A., Forrest, K. D., Lange, J., & Alavi, S. (2002, March). *False confessions: Is the gender of the interrogator a determining factor?* Paper presented at the biennial meeting of the American Psychology–Law Society, Austin, TX.

Ajzen, I., & Fishbein, M. (1980). *Understanding attitudes and predicting social behavior.* Englewood Cliffs, NJ: Prentice-Hall.

Asch, S. E. (1956). Studies of independence and conformity: A minority of one against a unanimous majority. *Psychological Monographs, 70,* 416.

Baldwin, J. (1993). Police interviewing techniques: Establishing truth or proof? *The British Journal of Criminology, 33,* 325–352.

Baldwin, J., & McConville, M. (1980). *Confessions in crown court trials* (Royal Commission on Criminal Procedure Research Study No. 5). London: Her Majesty's Stationery Office.

Behrman, B. W., & Davey, S. L. (2001). Eyewitness identification in actual criminal cases: An archival analysis. *Law & Human Behavior, 25,* 475–491.

Berggren, E. (1975). *The psychology of confessions.* Leiden, the Netherlands: Brill.

Billings, F. J., Taylor, T., Burns, J., Corey, D. L., Garven, S., & Wood, J. M. (2007). Can reinforcement induce children to falsely incriminate themselves? *Law & Human Behavior, 31,* 25–139.

Bond, C. F., & DePaulo, B. M. (2006). Accuracy in deception judgments. *Personality & Social Psychology Review, 10,* 214–234.

Bull, R., & Milne, R. (2004). Attempts to improve the police interviewing of suspects. In G. D. Lassiter (Ed.), *Interrogations, confessions, and entrapment* (pp. 182–196). New York: Kluwer Academic.

Cialdini, R. B. (2001). *Influence: Science and practice* (4th ed.). Needham Heights, MA: Allyn & Bacon.

Clarke, C. & Milne, R. (2001). *National evaluation of the PEACE investigative interviewing course.* London: Home Office.

Drizin, S. A., & Colgan, B. A. (2004). Tales from the juvenile confessions front. In G. D. Lassiter (Ed.), *Interrogations, confessions, and entrapment* (pp. 127–162). New York: Kluwer Academic.

Drizin, S. A., & Leo, R. A. (2004). The problem of false confessions in the post-DNA world. *North Carolina Law Review, 82*, 891–1007.

Evans, J. R., Meissner, C. A., Brandon, S. E., Russano, M. B., & Kleinman, S. (in press). Criminal versus HUMINT interrogations: The importance of psychological science to improving interrogative practice. *Journal of Psychiatry & Law.*

Fisher, R. P., & Geiselman, R. E. (1992). *Memory enhancing techniques for investigative interviewing: The cognitive interview.* Springfield, IL: Thomas.

Fisher, R. P., & Perez, V. (2007). Memory-enhancing techniques for interviewing crime Suspects (pp. 329–354). In S. Christianson (Ed.), *Offenders' memories of violent crimes.* Chichester, England: Wiley.

Forrest, K. D., Wadkins, T. A., & Larson, B. A. (2006). Suspect personality, police interrogations, and false confessions: Maybe it is not just the situation. *Personality & Individual Differences, 40*, 621–628.

Forrest, K. D., Wadkins, T. A., & Miller, R. L. (2002). The role of pre-existing stress on false confessions: An empirical study. *The Journal of Credibility Assessment & Witness Psychology, 3*, 23–45.

Gudjonsson, G. H. (1984). A new scale of interrogative suggestibility. *Personality & Individual Differences, 5*, 303–314.

Gudjonsson, G. H. (1989). The psychology of false confessions. *The Medico-Legal Journal, 57*, 93–110.

Gudjonsson, G. H. (1993). Confession evidence, psychological vulnerability, and expert testimony. *Journal of Community & Applied Social Psychology, 3*, 117–129.

Gudjonsson, G. H. (2003). *The psychology of interrogations and confessions: A handbook.* West Sussex, England: Wiley.

Gudjonsson, G. H., & Clark, N. K. (1986). Suggestibility in police interrogations: A social psychological model. *Social Behavior, 1*, 83–104.

Hartwig, M., Granhag, P. A., & Vrij, A. (2005). Police interrogation from a social psychology perspective. *Policing & Society, 15*, 379–399.

Hilgendorf, E. L., & Irving, M. (1981). A decision-making model of confessions. In M. Lloyd-Bostock (Ed.), *Psychology in legal contexts: Applications and limitations* (pp. 67–84). London: MacMillan.

Home Office. (1985). *Police and Criminal Evidence Act of 1984.* London: HMSO.

Horselenberg, R., Merckelbach, H., & Josephs, S. (2003). Individual differences and false confessions: A conceptual replication of Kassin and Kiechel (1996). *Psychology, Crime & Law, 9*, 1–8.

Inbau, F. E., Reid, J. E., Buckley, J. P., & Jayne, B. C. (2001). *Criminal interrogation and confessions* (4th ed.). Gaithersberg, MD: Aspen.

Irving, B. (1980). *Police interrogation: A case study of current practice* (Royal Commission on Criminal Procedure Research Study No. 2). London: Her Majesty's Stationery Office.

Irving, B., & McKenzie, I. K. (1989). *Police interrogation: The effects of the Police and Criminal Evidence Act.* London: Police Foundation of Great Britain.

Kassin, S. M. (2005). On the psychology of false confessions: Does innocence put innocents at risk? *American Psychologist, 60*, 215–228.

Kassin, S. M., Goldstein, C. J., & Savitsky, K. (2003). Behavioral confirmation in the interrogation room: On the dangers of presuming guilt. *Law & Human Behavior, 27*, 187–203.

Kassin, S. M., & Gudjonsson, G. H. (2004). The psychology of confession evidence: A review of the literature and issues. *Psychological Science in the Public Interest, 5*, 33–67.

Kassin, S. M., & Kiechel, K. L. (1996). The social psychology of false confessions: Compliance, internalization, and confabulation. *Psychological Science, 7*, 125–128.

Kassin, S. M., Leo, R. A., Meissner, C. A., Richman, K. D., Colwell, L. H., Leach, A.-M., & LaFon, D. (2007). Police interviewing and interrogation: A self-report survey of police practices and beliefs. *Law & Human Behavior, 31*, 381–400.

Kassin, S. M., & McNall, K. (1991). Police interrogations and confessions: Communicating promises and threats by pragmatic implication. *Law & Human Behavior, 15*, 233–251.

Kassin, S. M., Meissner, C. A., & Norwick, R. (2005). "I'd know a false confession if I saw one": A comparative study of college students and police interrogators. *Law & Human Behavior, 29*, 211–228.

Kassin, S. M., & Neumann, K. (1997). On the power of confession evidence: an experimental test of the fundamental difference hypothesis. *Law & Human Behavior, 21,* 469–484.

Klaver, J., Lee, Z., & Rose, V. G. (2008). Effects of personality, interrogation techniques, and plausibility in an experimental false confession paradigm. *Legal & Criminological Psychology, 13,* 71–88.

Leiken, L. S. (1970). Police interrogation in Colorado: The implementation of Miranda. *Denver Law Review, 47,* 1–53.

Leo, R. A. (1996). Inside the interrogation room. *The Journal of Criminal Law & Criminology, 86,* 266–303.

Leo, R. A. (2004). The third degree and the origins of psychological interrogation in the United States. In G. D. Lassiter (Ed.), *Interrogations, confessions, and entrapment* (p. 37–84). Kluwer Academic/Plenum Press.

Leo, R. A., & Ofshe, R. J. (1998). The consequences of false confessions: Deprivations of liberty and miscarriages of justice in the age of psychological interrogation. *Journal of Criminal Law & Criminology, 88,* 429–496.

Malpass, R. S. (1990). An excursion into utilitarian analyses, with side trips. *Behavioral Science Research, 24,* 1–15.

McFadden, R. D., & Saulny, S. (2002, September 6). DNA in Central Park jogger case spurs call for new review. *The New York Times,* p. B1.

Meissner, C. A., & Albrechtsen, J. S. (2007). Interrogation and torture. In *McGraw-Hill 2007 Yearbook of Science & Technology* (pp. 125–127). New York: McGraw-Hill.

Meissner, C. A., & Kassin, S. M. (2002). "He's guilty!": Investigator bias in judgments of truth and deception. *Law & Human Behavior, 26,* 469–480.

Meissner, C. A., & Kassin, S. M. (2004). "You're guilty, so just confess!" Cognitive and behavioral confirmation biases in the interrogation room. In G. D. Lassiter (Ed.), *Interrogations, confessions, and entrapment* (pp. 85–106). Kluwer Academic/Plenum Press.

Meissner, C. A., Russano, M. B., Rigoni, M. E., & Horgan, A. J. (2009). *Is it time for a revolution in the interrogation room? Empirically validating inquisitorial methods.* Manuscript submitted for publication.

Milgram, S. (1974). *Obedience to authority: An experimental view.* New York: Harper & Row.

Milne, R., & Bull, R. (1999). *Investigative interviewing: Psychology and practice.* Chichester, England: Wiley.

Mortimer, A., & Shepherd, E. (1999). Frames of mind: Schemata guiding cognition and conduct in the interviewing of suspected offenders. In A. Memon & R. Bull (Eds.), *Handbook of the psychology of interviewing* (pp. 293–315). Chichester, England: Wiley.

Moston, S., Stephenson, G. M., & Williamson, T. M. (1992). The incidence, antecedents and consequences of the use of the right to silence during police questioning. *Criminal Behavior & Mental Health, 3,* 30–47.

Narchet, F. M., Meissner, C. A., & Russano, M. B. (2009). *Modeling the influence of investigator bias on the elicitation of true and false confessions.* Manuscript submitted for publication.

Ofshe, R. J., & Leo, R. A. (1997). The social psychology of police interrogation. The theory and classification of true and false confessions. *Studies in Law, Politics, & Society, 16,* 189–251.

Pearse, J., Gudjonsson, G. H., Clare, I. C. H., & Rutter, S. (1998). Police interviewing and psychological vulnerabilities: Predicting the likelihood of a confession. *Journal of Community and Applied Social Psychology, 8,* 1–21.

Phillips, C., & Brown, D. (1998). *Entry into the criminal justice system: A survey of police arrests and their outcomes.* London: Home Office.

Redlich, A. D. (2004). Mental illness, police interrogations, and the potential for false confession. *Law & Psychiatry, 55,* 19–21.

Redlich, A. D. (2007). Military versus police interrogations: Similarities and differences. *Peace & Conflict: Journal of Peace Psychology, 13,* 423–428.

Redlich, A. D., & Goodman, G. S. (2003). Taking responsibility for an act not committed: The influence of age and suggestibility. *Law & Human Behavior, 27,* 141–156.

Redlich, A. D., & Meissner, C. A. (2009). Techniques and controversies in the interrogation of suspects: The artful practice versus the scientific study. In J. Skeem et al. (Eds.), *Psychological science in the courtroom: Controversies and consensus* (pp. 124–148). New York: Guilford Press.

Russano, M. B., Meissner, C. A., Narchet, F. M., & Kassin, S. K. (2005). Investigating true and false confessions within a novel experimental paradigm. *Psychological Science, 16,* 481–486.

Scheck, B. (2001). DNA and innocence scholarship. In S. D. Westervelt & J. A. Humphrey (Eds.), *Wrongly convicted: Perspectives on failed justice* (pp. 241–252). New Brunswick, NJ: Rutgers University Press.

Scheck, B., Neufeld, P., & Dwyer, J. (2000). *Actual innocence.* Garden City, NY: Doubleday.

Softley, P. (1980). *Police interrogation: An observational study in four police stations.* London: HMSO.

Vrij, A. (2008). *Detecting lies and deceit: Pitfalls and opportunities.* London: Wiley.

Vrij, A., Mann, S., & Fisher, R. P. (2006). An empirical test of the Behavior Analysis Interview. *Law & Human Behavior, 30,* 329–345.

Wells, G. L., Malpass, R. S., Lindsay, R. C. L., Fisher, R. P., Turtle, J. W., & Fulero, S. M. (2000). From the lab to the police station: A successful application of eyewitness research. *American Psychologist, 55,* 581–598.

8

The Wisdom of Custodial Recording

Thomas P. Sullivan

The men and women who serve in police and sheriff departments contribute to our communities on a daily basis. They have firsthand experience with the many differing personalities they encounter, signs of dangers, and methods of detecting and deterring criminal conduct. Many, especially detectives, routinely interview persons who are suspected of committing crimes, which may result in suspects confessing or making damaging admissions or false exculpatory statements. However, when later testifying about these events in court, many officers have had their recollections and candor questioned by defense lawyers (including myself) about what was said and done by the participants during the closed door sessions.

This chapter concerns a basic improvement in the way interviews of felony suspects are conducted in police facilities. There is a simple, efficient, and relatively inexpensive way to avoid disputes about what was said and done when arrested suspects are interrogated in stationhouses: Make an electronic recording, by audio or video, of the entire interview, from the time the *Miranda* warnings are given to the suspect to the end of the interview. Indeed, recognizing the value of having complete electronic records of custodial interviews, and to protect both suspects and officers from the risk that one or the other will misstate or distort what occurred behind closed stationhouse doors, state legislatures have begun to enact laws to require (and state supreme courts have expressed the preference) that felony suspects, when arrested, are interviewed in police facilities and that electronic recordings are made from the *Miranda* warnings until the completion of the sessions.

A Brief History of Laws and Cases Requiring Recording

Police recordings of custodial interviews of felony suspects are a relatively recent development in the United States. The original court ruling was made in *Stephan v. State* (1985), when the Alaska Supreme Court, relying on the due process clause of the state constitution, held that for statements made by suspects in police facilities to be admitted into evidence, the entire interview must be recorded electronically. The Minnesota Supreme Court followed suit 9 years later, basing its ruling on the court's inherent power over the state's criminal justice process (*State v. Scales*, 1994). Other state-reviewing courts often expressed a preference for complete recordings of custodial interrogations but declined to mandate the practice (e.g., *People v. Raibon,* 1993; *State v. James,* 1996).

That is where the matter stood in 2000, when the governor of Illinois formed the Commission on Capital Punishment to study the state's death penalty system and make recommendations as to how it could be made more accurate, fair, and just. He acted after 13 men on Illinois' death row had been released from prison. In 2002, the commission rendered its report, containing 85 recommendations, one of which (Recommendation 4) was that questioning of homicide suspects who are under arrest in police facilities must be electronically recorded by audio or video. The following year the Illinois General Assembly passed, and the governor signed a law to that effect, thus making Illinois the first state to require by statute that custodial interviews be recorded, beginning to end. The chief sponsor in the Illinois Senate was then Senator, now President, Barack Obama.

Since then, the District of Columbia, Maine, Maryland, Missouri, Montana, Nebraska, New Mexico, North Carolina, Oregon, and Wisconsin have enacted recording statutes covering a variety of custodial felony investigations, and recording bills are pending before many other state legislatures. In addition, as a result of opinions of the Iowa and Massachusetts supreme courts (*Commonwealth v. DiGiambattista,* 2004; *State v. Hajtic,* 2006), and a rule adopted by the Supreme Court of New Jersey (Rule 3:17, 2006), law enforcement officials in those states have begun recording suspects' complete custodial interviews. It is clearly a growing trend in the United States, so much so that in August 2007, the National Conference of Commissioners on Uniform State Laws approved the formation of a drafting committee on electronic recording of custodial interrogations.

The practice of police recording custodial interviews of felony suspects has been endorsed by a number of prestigious legal organizations (e.g., American Law Institute, Justice Project, National Association of Criminal Defense Lawyers, New York State Bar Association) and knowledgeable authors (e.g., Boetig, Vinson, & Weidel, 2006; Drizin & Reich, 2004; Kassin & Gudjonsson, 2004; Leo & Ofshe, 1998; Sullivan, 2005b; see also Conclusion, this volume). In foreign countries, the practice has been required by legislative bodies (e.g., Australia, England, Wales; see chap. 5, this volume), and encouraged and endorsed by courts, legal organizations, and writers (e.g., Canada, Japan), as well as by international tribunals (e.g., International Criminal Tribunal for the Former Yugoslavia).

Law Enforcement's Hesitancy to Accept the Wisdom of Custodial Recording

As noted earlier, in 2002 the Illinois governor's commission's recommended legislation requiring recording of custodial interviews of homicide suspects (the recommendation was thus limited because the commission dealt only with cases in which a potential penalty was capital punishment), and legislation to that effect was introduced in the Illinois General Assembly and eventually passed, but over the initial vigorous opposition of many Illinois law enforcement organizations. My interest was piqued as to why, when the commission's inquiries indicated that recordings of custodial interviews were immensely helpful to law enforcement officials (e.g., protecting them from claims that they failed to give *Miranda* warnings, abused suspects, or misstated what was said and done) that they nevertheless resisted the proposed recording legislation. Illinois police and sheriff organizations appeared to be taking a position opposed to their own fundamental interests. This led to my decision to speak directly with officers from police and sheriff departments that recorded custodial interrogations, learn of their experiences, and perhaps learn whether and why members of the Illinois law enforcement community were justified in opposing the proposed statute.

Accordingly, beginning in 2003, we began telephoning departments throughout the United States we had reason to believe made it a practice to record their stationhouse custodial interviews. We did not represent any organization, nor did we conduct a standard survey. Rather, beginning with a list of 10 departments that we were informed were recording custodial interviews (not including the departments in Alaska and Minnesota, which have been recording for years under the 1985 and 1994 court rulings mentioned earlier), we asked about their practices and inquired whether they knew of other departments that might be recording on a voluntary basis. After we spoke with a representative of a police or sheriff department, we sent a letter with an attached memorandum summarizing what we were told about the department's policies and experiences with recording custodial interrogations—or the reasons they do not record—and requested that any inaccuracies be brought to our attention. The letters and memoranda and the responses received from both those that do and do not record have been carefully indexed and secured. This was not conducted as a survey, with the customary methodological procedures. We acted solely on our own. Our results are contained in raw, unrecorded data.

We now have spoken with detectives and supervisors in small, medium, and large departments in every state as well as many who record under statutory or court mandates. Our frequently updated list of departments that record a majority of custodial interviews can be accessed online at http://jenner.com/news/pubs_item.asp?id=000014590124. The memoranda and responses we have on file reveal two distinct patterns of responses about the wisdom of recording custodial interviews:

- Those who have a policy of recording custodial questioning give various reasons as to why they endorse the practice, almost always with great enthusiasm, and often with interesting examples of instances in which recordings have proven crucial in convicting guilty suspects and exonerating those who are innocent. No one has expressed a desire to return to nonrecording of custodial interviews.
- Those who have not recorded oppose doing so on the basis of various hypothetical objections and imagined dangers to law enforcement. Most of these arguments have not been mentioned by officers who record nor have been considered to be a reason to cease recording.

To illustrate this dichotomy, I set forth in the following sections of this chapter summaries representative of the responses received from hundreds of departments that customarily record, and in a later section I analyze the responses I received from nonrecording departments about why they are opposed to the practice of recording.

A Summary of the Benefits of Recording Custodial Interviews

Here are the reasons repeatedly voiced by experienced law enforcement personnel from around the country about why they support the practice of making electronic recordings (from the *Miranda* warning to the end) of custodial interviews of felony suspects that take place in police facilities. The basic reason is a truism: Recordings by either audio or video are the only ways in which the actual words, tones, and other details of interviews may be fully and accurately preserved. Videos illustrate the gestures and facial and body movements of the participants that cannot be reproduced orally or in written summaries or in audio recordings. The following explains the more specific benefits of recording custodial interviews with regard to different groups.

Members of the Law Enforcement Community on Both a Local and Statewide Level

Recordings permit the police who are conducting the interviews to focus on suspects rather than taking notes, which distracts both police and suspects. Police become more aware of how their words and actions will later appear to listeners and viewers, and as a result they are more cautious about their actions and language and conduct themselves in a more professional manner. Other police, listening to audio or watching video by remote hookups in nearby rooms, are often able to suggest questions or lines of inquiry to the officers conducting the interviews.

Later review of recordings often reveals previously overlooked inconsistencies and evasive conduct or responses that indicate the suspects are innocent of the crimes under investigation. Suspects have been recorded engaging in incriminating conduct when left alone in the interview room, which would not be revealed without the recordings.

Full custodial recordings make it unnecessary for police to struggle to recall details when later writing reports and testifying about what occurred during the interviews. Decades of psychological research has demonstrated that human memory is not fixed but malleable and constructive; as a result, it is highly susceptible to errors and distortions, including at the extreme the unintentional creation of entirely false recollections (cf. Bartlett, 1932/1995; Loftus, & Ketcham, 1994, 1996).

When police have conducted themselves properly, recordings demonstrate that the required warnings were given, depict precisely what the police and suspects said, and show that the suspects' statements were voluntarily and knowingly made. Recordings played in court to establish what occurred during custodial questioning—whether in pretrial hearings on a motion to suppress or during trials—are usually regarded as conclusive evidence.

When defense lawyers have the opportunity to evaluate audio or videotapes of their clients' interviews, pretrial motions to suppress statements and confessions are drastically reduced because there is usually no room for dispute as to what happened. Police officers do not have to spend time preparing for and engaging in pretrial hearings and are spared hostile cross examinations about failing to give *Miranda* warnings, using coercive tactics, and misstating what occurred.

Recordings are also useful as tools for self-evaluation by those who conducted interviews and for teaching newly recruited detectives about successful interrogation practices.

Prosecutors

Recorded interviews simplify prosecutors' decision-making process, because they are able to experience firsthand precisely what suspects said and how they acted when questioned about the crimes. Prosecutors often observe additional areas for investigation as well as indicators of suspects' innocence. Prosecutors' time and energy are conserved because when recordings verify that proper *Miranda* warnings were given and statements made by suspects were voluntary, pretrial motions to suppress are virtually eliminated and, if made, are quickly dismissed by having the trial judges view the tapes. The risk of the court excluding suspects' statements from evidence because of contradictory and confusing testimony as to what occurred behind closed doors is no longer a concern.

When recordings contain voluntary confessions, damaging admissions, or demonstrably false exculpatory claims, prosecutors' positions are greatly strengthened and are often invulnerable. The result is a dramatic increase in negotiated pleas of guilty, which saves time and expense for all concerned by avoiding contested trials; lengthy, expensive appeals; and other postconviction procedures.

Suspects

When viewed by suspects' lawyers, detectives and their supervisors, prosecutors, judges, and juries, recordings can illustrate the sincerity and reliability of suspects' innocent explanations. When recordings are made from the outset to the end, motions to prohibit (suppress) the use of the suspects' statements as evidence will be granted if the tapes reveal that *Miranda* warnings were not given or the suspects stated they wished to remain silent or requested a lawyer.

Tapes prevent officers misstating or misinterpreting what suspects said or did or omitting suspects' claims of innocence, denials of guilt, and exculpatory explanations. Recordings reveal abusive or coercive treatment, excessively prolonged questioning, and use of other unlawful tactics.

Trial Court Judges

Judges are not called on to spend time conducting pretrial hearings, listening to contradictory testimony from police and defendants, and attempting to determine where the truth lies. The use of recordings has proven to increase the number of guilty pleas, which in turn relieves trial judges from spending time presiding over contested bench or jury trials; hearing arguments and ruling on admissibility of evidence, and the many other issues presented in contested trials; and deciding the outcomes in bench trials.

Reviewing Court Judges

Reviewing court judges are not called on to pore over and evaluate transcripts of conflicting testimony as to what occurred during stationhouse questioning. With reduction in the number of contested trials, fewer appeals are presented to the reviewing courts, relieving appellate judges of having to read the parties' written briefs, hear oral arguments, and write opinions explaining the bases of their rulings.

Jurors

Jurors are relieved of the need to engage in inference and guesswork when called on to determine what occurred during custodial questioning sessions in police and sheriff stationhouses. They can hear—and with video, see—as though they were present in the room from start to finish.

The Public

Because recordings provide a superior source of evidence, they help ensure that guilty persons are convicted and innocent persons are not prosecuted or convicted. Recordings deter police who might engage in improper tactics or misstate what the suspect said or did, and if improper tactics are revealed on tape, the offending officers are subject to discipline or discharge and, perhaps, suits for civil damages and criminal prosecutions. With the increased accuracy and reliability of what occurred during stationhouse interviews and the removal of officers who engage in questionable or unlawful practices during custodial questioning, there is increased public confidence in and approval of police practices. There is a reduced basis for civil rights claims and lawsuits that are expensive to defend and that involve the risk of large settlements or verdicts paid from public funds.

Thus, making complete recordings of custodial interviews is a boon to the criminal justice system, helps to convict the guilty, exonerates the innocent, shields police from false claims of misconduct, protects suspects from improper police behavior, and saves time and expense for all concerned.

Direct Statements of Support

Recounted below are testimonials from police and their supervisors, prosecutors, and judges, illustrating the broad base of support for the practice of recording custodial interviews. Many, many more are contained in the files we have carefully kept of hundreds of interviews.

Police Officers

Quotations from two law enforcement officers are contained in two published articles previously written on this subject (Sullivan, 2004, 2005a). Here are a few recently received from departments in all sizes of communities (PD stands for police department, and CSO for county sheriff's office):

> Recordings can be a tremendous help because they allow you to document suspects' body language. In one instance, the detective left the room to get a glass of water, and the suspect called a friend on his cell phone and confessed to the crime, all of which was recorded. (Pleasanton, CA PD)
>
> It makes no sense not to record. Many local jurors tend to be suspicious of the police, and recordings provide solid evidence of what occurred, what the suspect said and did, and whether detectives conducted themselves properly. (San Francisco, CA PD)
>
> Recording is 100 times better than note taking. It is often more descriptive because, when we are taking notes, we will often miss something, ignore body language, or use abbreviations which mean little when reviewed. There is nothing better in court. The evidence is indisputable, and allows all involved to view body language and reactions to questions. (Collier County, FL CSO)
>
> I'm all for it. Taping shows everybody that you're not browbeating. Juries are stunned that people will talk about killing other people like it's nothing. A serial killer admitted to killings like we talk about buying a car made a hell of a tape. (Fulton County, GA PD)
>
> It is valuable for the jury to see the defendant admit or rationalize his behavior in his own words, as opposed to having an officer recall what occurred during the interrogation. It is also good for the jury to see how the suspect appeared just after the incident occurred. And officers regularly review recordings to refresh their memories and to verify details of interrogations. (Des Moines, IA PD)
>
> I am a big fan of recordings. They are quicker and more accurate than note taking. Defense attorneys challenge everything as a matter of practice, and it's always great to have a solid piece of evidence showing what occurred during the interrogations. (Montgomery County, MD PD)
>
> People can't deny what they said when it's on audio or video. Recordings help detectives learn from each other, and improve their techniques by watching recorded interrogations. (Pittsfield, MA PD)
>
> Video interrogations are especially useful to prosecutors trying to make their cases. Jurors can see firsthand what the suspects' demeanor was during the interrogations. When watching video recordings, it is as though jurors are put inside the interrogation rooms with the officers. This is important, because the appearance and behavior of suspects often show completely different persons from the defendants sitting in court. (Valley City, ND PD)
>
> It is hard to dispute a recorded confession, and when there is a good one on tape, the case will almost never go to trial. (Warren, OH CSO)
>
> Recording interrogations is a great practice. They protect officers from liability and provide proof that suspects received *Miranda* warnings. (Douglas County, OR CSO)
>
> Officers are aware they are being recorded, and this has made them very thorough and professional while conducting interviews. Detectives also

later review recordings to observe suspects' responses and [use them] as training devices. (Cleveland, TN PD)

Many false allegations by suspects have been disproved due to interviews being recorded. (Arlington, TX PD)

When trials occur, there is no question about whether the interrogating officers misunderstood or misrepresented what the suspects were saying, because judges and jurors can see the words coming out of the suspects' mouths. Recordings also allow supervisors to monitor interrogations [by remote hookups], and if necessary[,] aid detectives. (Prince William County, VA PD)

A Special Agent in the Federal Bureau of Investigation's (FBI's) San Francisco Office, together with supervisory police officers from Michigan and New York, authored an article in the FBI Law Enforcement Bulletin explaining in detail the many benefits to all concerned from recording custodial interviews (Boetig et al., 2006). They wrote:

Law enforcement agencies should address the contemporary issue of electronic recording in a progressive manner. The commitment of departments to effectuate change in their investigative practices related to the electronic recording of custodial interrogations will allow them to reap the benefits of an established, effective, and reliable police practice while avoiding a potentially chaotic transition if mandated to do so in the future. (p. 3)

The authors cautioned about the rising expectations on the part of jurors that recordings be made when feasible:

A law enforcement officer's credibility is his most valuable asset when testifying in court. Electronic recordings of suspect confessions help enhance an officer's credibility in several ways. First, it provides unequivocal, unbiased evidence that can support the officer's testimony. Second, it indicates that the officer used the most complete and accurate method available for collecting the confession evidence. Because video-recording technology is readily available in the United States, jurors have difficulty believing that some type of electronic recording equipment was not available to the investigating officer . . . . By recording, the officer can demonstrate commitment to impartiality by collecting and preserving evidence in its most unbiased and unadulterated form. (pp. 5–6)

Prosecutors and Defense Lawyers

A Larimer County, Colorado, prosecutor expressed great enthusiasm for custodial recording, noting that "I prefer to have all interrogations videotaped so the jury can see the suspect and how he reacts. Video is an excellent piece of evidence in homicide cases." Amy Klobuchar (2002), former prosecutor of Hennepin County, Minnesota (now United States senator), stated that "police and prosecutors have little to fear from a requirement to videotape all interrogations. Recording not only protects the innocent, it helps convict the guilty and sustain the public's faith in our criminal justice system" (p. A21). One of Ms. Klobuchar's top assistants said the ruling of the Minnesota Supreme Court requiring recording of custodial interviews was "the best thing we've ever had rammed down our throats."

The state's attorney of St. Clair County, Illinois, gave the following testimony at an Illinois Capital Punishment Reform Study Committee (CPRSC) Public Hearing in November 2006 about Illinois' statutory requirement that custodial interviews of homicide suspects be recorded:

> [Recording] has been so overwhelmingly successful that most of the police departments in my jurisdiction now videotape interrogations in almost every felony investigation. The police, law enforcement, realize that it's better for them. It protects them from false accusations of physical or mental coercion. It's a better end product . . . many of the issues I think were the foundation for some of the exoneration cases are now gone, at least in St. Clair County, and certainly across the State as it relates to homicide cases. (Illinois Capital Punishment Reform Study Committee [CPRSC], 2007, pp. 9–10)

The state's attorney of Peoria County, Illinois, gave the following testimony at a CPRSC Public Hearing in March 2009:

> *State's attorney:* Although I'm not much of an apologist, as you may have learned, I have to tell Mr. Sullivan, Tom, that you were right with regard to that videotaping of suspects in homicide cases. I thought that it would be more chilling, and I thought that it would result in, and it has resulted in hours and hours of videotape. But I think the courts have done a good job in redacting it and paring it down.
>
> You'll remember that that was my fear that we would have jurors falling asleep watching, you know, six hours of a guy eating a Steak n' Shake meal while he was still denying it. But it's, that was a pretty good—and we didn't agree on that, you'll recall. But that's been a healthy addition I think to the—you know the old saying a picture says a thousand words, so there's, a video's a thousand pictures. And I like that so—.
>
> *Mr. Sullivan:* I've always regarded that as a law enforcement, of greater benefit to law enforcement than to the defense.
>
> *State's attorney:* Right.
>
> *Mr. Sullivan:* But overall a benefit to the criminal justice system on both sides.
>
> *State's attorney:* Right. And actually I, I probably am even more agreeable to the expansion of it in other cases.
>
> *Mr. Sullivan:* Right. That was one of the recommendations, 83, in the Governor's Commission that the reforms that are applicable in non-death cases should be adapted in non-death cases. We'll see. I think it's moving in that direction. Many states are now adopting recording statutes and not applying them only to homicides but to other serious felonies.
>
> *State's attorney:* And I'm not going to tell war stories, except that last year I had a case where it was, I mean, it was a fervent denial. Why do you people have me here? And of course, we're watching the entire thing and it was just, you know, why do you keep doing this? And then right before your eyes, I did it. It's a case study in psyche.
>
> *Mr. Sullivan:* Was this a homicide?
>
> *State's attorney:* Yeah. And it was, and it was one of those moments where you could describe that, but to show that to any person of conscience,

and you would say, good heavens, I was believing that lie right up until that moment. So if I, if it works for me on those cases, then I think it should work the other way too. And it shows it was a good suggestion and, well, that's that.

Mr. Sullivan: Thanks.

The CPRSC's Third Annual Report to the Illinois General Assembly (2007) noted that prosecutors were not the only ones to praise the custodial-recording requirement:

> The defense lawyers interviewed about recording custodial interviews of homicide suspects also expressed favorable impressions. One told of a client who allegedly confessed on videotape, but the prosecutor dismissed the indictment because after watching the video he agreed that the "confession" was not credible. The defense lawyers found that the recordings "keep the police honest" by allowing viewers to focus on coercive treatment of suspects that is not reflected in police reports . . . . The Chief of the Cook County Public Defender's Homicide Task Force . . . said that, overall, custodial recordings in homicide investigations have been helpful in advancing the truth seeking process. (CPRSC, 2007, pp. 10–11)

State and Federal Trial Court Judges

A Michigan state court trial judge coauthored an article in which he wrote:

> Recording increases conviction rates, improves case preparation by investigators, allows supervisors to monitor and weed out inappropriate interrogation techniques, and permits the tapes to be used in training. The benefit to the wrongly accused is far greater . . . . Victims of false confessions also tend to be illiterate, mentally deficient, young and/or a member of a minority population . . . . Yet, some local police departments still rely on confessions that are handwritten by the police and signed by the accused. Although it may be rare, this practice nevertheless has the potential for police abuse. (Randon & Gardner, 2005)

In several cases (e.g., *United States v. Ford,* 2006; *United States v. Hensley,* 2007), federal district court judges have criticized both federal and state law enforcement personnel for not recording custodial interviews, and in several cases they have mentioned the importance of recordings when ruling confessions inadmissible. Their views about law enforcement agencies that can easily record custodial interviews, but fail to do so, was summarized by a federal judge in Indiana (*United States v. Bland,* 2002): "I don't know why I have to sit here and sort through the credibility of what was said in these interviews when there's a perfect device available to resolve that and eliminate any discussion about it . . . ."

State Reviewing Courts

After the Supreme Court of Iowa (*State v. Hajtic,* 2006) expressed a strong preference that custodial recordings be made when feasible, a county attorney wrote the law enforcement officers in his county that his office and the Iowa attorney general's office believe the court's ruling should be read as essentially mandating the practice from this time forward.

In 2004, the Supreme Judicial Court of Massachusetts held that when statements from unrecorded custodial interrogations are admitted into evidence, the trial judge must instruct the jury that "the state's highest court has expressed a preference that [custodial] interrogations be recorded whenever practicable." If the defendant claims the statement was made involuntarily, the instruction must also state that the jury may (but need not) conclude from the police's failure to record the interrogation that the State has not met its burden of proof that the statement was made voluntarily (*Commonwealth v. DiGiambattista,* 2004). This decision has caused most Massachusetts police to begin recording custodial interviews.

In May 2007, pursuant to a recommendation of a Special Committee appointed by the New Jersey Supreme Court, the court adopted Rule 3:17, which provides that all custodial interrogations that occur in a "place of detention" (which is defined) must be electronically recorded when the suspect is charged with named crimes, unless a stated exception applies. There are seven exceptions that excuse recording; the prosecution must establish the applicability of the exception by a preponderance of the evidence at a pretrial hearing. If an unrecorded custodial statement is admitted during trial, the presiding judge must give a prescribed jury instruction that could lead the jury to seriously question the reliability of any confession evidence presented by the State.

In 2005, the Wisconsin Supreme Court was presented with a case in which a statement was taken by police from a juvenile in a police station about an armed robbery without recording. Having reviewed the literature and cases on the subject, the court (*In re Jerrell,* 2005) stated, "We agree that electronic recording is an efficient and powerful tool in the administration of justice." The advantages specifically identified were "a recording requirement will provide courts with a more accurate and reliable record of a juvenile's interrogation"; "an accurate record will reduce the number of disputes over *Miranda* and voluntariness issues for juveniles"; "recording will protect the individual interest of police officers wrongfully accused of improper tactics"; "a recording requirement will enhance law enforcement interrogation of juveniles"; and recording will "protect the rights of the accused." The court ruled that henceforth all custodial interrogations of juveniles "shall be electronically recorded where feasible, and without exception when questioning occurs at a place of detention." This ruling led to the enactment of, and was superseded by, the comprehensive mandatory recording statute mentioned earlier and is applicable throughout Wisconsin to all suspects, both juveniles and adults.

A few years ago, the Supreme Court of Arizona opined in *State v. Jones* (2002):

> Recording the entire interrogation process provides the best evidence available and benefits all parties involved because, on the one hand it protects against the admission of involuntary or invalid confessions, and on the other, it enables law enforcement agencies to establish that their tactics were proper.

In *People v. Fike,* (1998), Judge P. J. Fitzgerald of the Michigan Appellate Court (concurring in part and dissenting in part with the ruling) emphatically noted:

> I . . . urge the Legislature to promulgate a statute mandating the electronic recording of prestatement conversation and actual interrogation and, unless and until that time, I urge law enforcement officers to make recordings voluntarily.

And in 2001, the Tennessee Supreme Court (*State v. Godsey,* 2001) found:

> There can be little doubt that electronically recording custodial interrogations would reduce the amount of time spent in court resolving disputes over what occurred during investigation. As a result, the judiciary would be relieved of much of the burden of resolving these disputes . . . sound policy considerations support its adoption as a law enforcement practice.

Thus, knowledgeable participants at all levels of the criminal justice system support custodial recordings so that the truth may more accurately be ascertained. In August 2007, the National Conference of Commissioners on Uniform State Laws approved formation of a drafting committee to formulate a uniform state statute on electronic recording of custodial interrogations. Legislation that applies throughout the state providing uniform rules and funding is far preferable to having each police department formulate its own regulations (Sullivan, 2005b). Similarly, all federal investigative agencies should record custodial interviews (Sullivan, 2006, 2008).

Common Objections to Recording

Members of departments that do not record custodial interrogations of felony suspects, including the federal investigative agencies, voice a recurring pattern of reasons why they believe that recording is not in the best interests of law enforcement. When mandatory recording legislation is proposed in various state legislatures, representatives of local police and sheriff organizations have often made their opposition to recording known. As observed above, this leads to an incongruous irony: The members of the law enforcement community who are the major opponents of recording custodial interrogations are usually its major beneficiaries.

As publicity has spread from the many experienced officers who enthusiastically endorse the practice, the objections of police organizations have begun to shift from outright opposition to cautious, qualified acceptance of the practice but opposition to mandatory legislation. A recently formulated contention is that each department should be permitted to decide whether to record, and it should not be imposed by statute or court ruling of statewide application. Here are the reasons most often given by those who oppose custodial recording and my observations:

1. *Officers' testimony about unrecorded interrogations is almost always accepted, hence there is no need for electronic recordings.*

   It is correct that in the past the testimony of officers has usually been accepted by trial court judges over that of defendants as to what occurred during unrecorded custodial interviews. But as shown above, many police officers, sheriff deputies, judges, and prosecutors have begun to voice their strong preference for recordings to put an end to testimonial disputes and uncertainties about what occurred during custodial interviews, to the end that the truth may be more accurately and efficiently ascertained. There is clearly a growing understanding that there is no legitimate excuse for not recording and that unrecorded interviews are unsatisfactory and suspicious when they take place in stationhouses in which the officers have control of the surroundings and ready availability of recording equipment.

2. *Recordings will interfere with our efforts to build rapport with suspects, and those who know they are being recorded will be less likely to speak candidly.*

   These are two hypothetical objections posited by nonrecording departments that we have heard from neither the hundreds of experienced detectives and supervisors with whom we have spoken nor from the prosecutors who handle the cases. In 38 of the 50 states, suspects need not be informed that a recording is being made, and many departments in those states nevertheless make it a practice to advise suspects of the intent to record or place the equipment in plain view. And, of course, there are suspects who will realize that certain departments make it a practice to record. The statutes that require recordings deal with this potential problem by providing that if suspects decline to speak if a recording is made, the officers should record their refusals, turn the equipment off, and proceed with handwritten notes.

   The vast majority of the police officers say that the suspects' knowledge that a recording is being made has no effect on the relationship between interviewers and suspects or the content of the sessions. To the contrary, the use of recording devices has become so prevalent that many suspects expect to be recorded and it is not unusual for suspects to express a preference for an accurate, complete electronic record. When the equipment is in view, most suspects pay no attention to it once the interview is underway, just as witnesses in court ignore the court reporters after they begin testifying.

   We have not heard from police that making recordings of interviews, beginning to end, has impaired them from building rapport with suspects, whatever that may mean. When officers fail to record the beginning of a custodial interview and turn the equipment on at a later point, they expose themselves to being charged with having failed to give required *Miranda* warnings, or using threats and abusive tactics, or providing details of the crime later adopted by the suspects in their statements. This in turn results in defense counsels' efforts to suppress confessions or admissions—even if recorded on equipment activated later in the session—which in turn plunges the participants into contested testimonial factual disputes at hearings on pretrial motions to suppress and at trial. The resulting expenditure of the time, effort, and expense of police, prosecutors, defense lawyers, judges, and jurors can be completely avoided by the simple act of recording the interviews from the outset to the end.

Thus, the so-called rapport-building excuse for postponing or omitting recordings is illusory. The conservative and wise course for law enforcement personnel is to make complete recordings of their custodial interviews, from *Miranda* to the end, thus precluding factual disputes and exonerating officers who have conducted themselves properly.

3. *Recordings will disclose certain lawful interviewing techniques that may seem inappropriate to jurors.*

This is a troublesome rationale for not recording because it contains a suggestion that members of the law enforcement community want the freedom to avoid exposing certain things they said or did during the closed interview sessions. The law is that when witnesses are asked to describe what occurred, but they deliberately omit relevant facts, they have committed the crime of perjury and obstruction of justice, and persons who encourage them to do so may be guilty of subornation of perjury or accessory to obstruction. Both federal and state courts have placed restrictions on the kinds of tactics that are permissible for law enforcement personnel to use during custodial interrogations. The federal Constitution provides the minimum standard, and each state is permitted to establish more stringent rules. If and when officers go over the line of legality, they risk not only the loss of a case but also removal from their positions and exposure to criminal charges and civil damage suits by the suspects.

Two of the chief benefits of recordings are that the vast majority of officers who do not engage in unlawful tactics will be protected from false accusations of misconduct by suspects they have questioned and that the few officers who do engage in unlawful tactics will be exposed and removed.

4. *There may be partial or total loss of recordings because of equipment failures or mistaken operation of the equipment, resulting in suppression of unrecorded confessions or admissions.*

The various statutes and court rulings that require recordings make exceptions to the need for a recording if there are inadvertent mistakes in the use of the equipment or inadvertent equipment failures. These problems seldom arise and have not proven to be a hindrance in getting unrecorded statements into evidence. This is another concern about a "ghost under the bed" raised by those who have not given recording a fair try.

5. *If recordings are required but for some legitimate reason are not made, suspects' statements may be excluded from evidence or jury instructions may be given cautioning about the inferior reliability of unrecorded statements.*

As noted previously, the statutes and court rulings requiring recordings of custodial interviews contain exceptions that excuse recordings under various circumstances, so long as the failure to record does not result from officers' willful effort to avoid compliance. On the other hand, several of the statutes and court rulings provide that if there is no reasonable excuse for the failure to record custodial interrogations, the court may exclude the resulting unrecorded statements or warn the jury about unrecorded statements compared with those that are recorded.

Those are the direct consequences of officers' conduct. Law enforcement officers are trained in proper procedures, and almost all make sincere efforts to comply. But, just like the rest of the citizenry, the law requires that police suffer the consequences of deliberate failures to comply with the law. This is similar to the *Miranda* rule—statements made by suspects may be suppressed by the court if the rule is knowingly violated by the police—and to the rule excluding from evidence the fruits of unreasonable searches and seizures.

6. *The costs associated with mandatory recordings are too great.*
    The costs involved are for equipment, preparation of rooms for recordings, training of officers, courtroom facilities, preparation of transcripts, and storage of tapes and discs. The matter of expense has rarely been mentioned to us and then almost always relating to the cost of preparing typewritten transcripts. But all of these expenses, taken together, pale in comparison with savings that result: for example, the time of officers, public defenders, prosecutors, trial and appellate judges, jurors, and court personnel in pretrial motions to suppress, in trials, and in appeals from denials of motions to suppress and convictions as well as the expense involved in defending civil rights suits for damages for alleged unlawful police conduct and payment of settlements or adverse judgments in those cases.

Conclusion

Given the multiple benefits to all concerned in the criminal justice system from recording custodial interviews of felony suspects, especially the increased assurances of convicting the guilty and not the innocent and exposing improper police conduct, it is heartening to note that the law enforcement community is coming around to the acceptance of this significant reform.

References

Bartlett, F. C. (1995). *Remembering.* Cambridge, England: Cambridge University Press. (Original work published 1932)

Boetig, B. P., Vinson, D. M., & Weidel, B. R. (2006). Revealing incommunicado: Electronic recording of police interrogations. *FBI Law Enforcement Bulletin, 75,* 1–8.

Commonwealth v. DiGiambattista, 813 N.E. 2d 516, 533-34 (Mass., 2004).

Drizin, S. A., & Reich, M. J. (2004). Heeding the lessons of history: The need for mandatory recording of police interrogations to accurately assess the reliability and voluntariness of confessions. *Drake Law Review, 52,* 619–646.

Illinois Capital Punishment Reform Study Committee. (2007, April). Third annual report to the Illinois General Assembly. Retrieved August 28, 2009, from http://www.icjia.org/public/pdf/dpsrc/CPRSC%20Third%20Annual%20Report.pdf

In re Jerrell, 699 N.W.2d at 110, 121-23 (2005).

Kassin, S. M., & Gudjonsson, G. H. (2004). The psychology of confessions: A review of the literature and issues. *Psychological Science in the Public Interest, 5,* 33–67.

Klobuchar, A. (2002, June 10). Eye on interrogations: How videotaping serves the cause of justice. *Washington Post,* p. A21.

Leo, R. A., & Ofshe, R. J. (1998). The consequences of false confessions: Deprivations of liberty and miscarriages of justice in the age of psychological interrogation. *Journal of Criminal Law & Criminology, 88,* 429–496.

Loftus, E. F. (1996). *Eyewitness testimony* (Rev. ed.). Cambridge, MA: Harvard University Press.

Loftus, E. F., & Ketcham, K. (1994). *The myth of repressed memory: False memories and allegations of sexual abuse.* New York: St. Martin's Press.

People v. Fike, 577 N.W.2d 903, 908 (1998).

People v. Raibon, 843 P.2d 46, 49 (Colo. Ct. App., 1993).

Randon, M., & Gardner, T., Jr. (2005, March 6). A point well made: Taped interrogations would benefit all parties. *Detroit Free Press,* p. 31.

Rule 3:17, N.J. Sup. Ct. (2006).

State v. Godsey, 60 S.W.3d 759, 772 (Tenn. 2001).

State v. Hajtic, 724 N.W.2d 449, 454-56 (Iowa, 2006).

State v. James, 678 A.2d 1338, 1360 (Conn., 1996).

State v. Jones, 203 Ariz. 1, 49 P.3d 273, 279 (Ariz. 2002).

State v. Scales, 518 N.W.2d 587, 591 (Minn., 1994).

Stephan v. State, 711 P. 2d 1156, 1162 (Alaska, 1985).

Sullivan, T. P. (2004). *Police experiences with recording custodial interrogations.* Chicago: Northwestern University School of Law, Center on Wrongful Convictions. Retrieved August 28, 2009, from http://www.jenner.com/news/pubs_item.asp?id=000012636224

Sullivan, T. P. (2005a). Electronic recording of custodial interrogations. *The Chief of Police, 19,* 17–19.

Sullivan, T. P. (2005b). Electronic recording of custodial interrogations: Everybody wins. *Journal of Criminal Law & Criminology, 95,* 1127–1144.

Sullivan, T. P. (2006). Federal law enforcement should record custodial interrogations. *The Federal Lawyer, 53,* 44–48.

Sullivan, T. P. (2008). Recording of federal custodial interviews. *American Criminal Law Review, 45,* 1297.

United States v. Bland, No. 1:02-CR-93 (N.D. Ind. Dec. 13, 2002).

United States v. Ford, 2006 WL 3533080 (D. Kan.).

United States v. Hensley, 2007 U.S. Dist., LEXIS 10692 (D. Ind. 2007).

9

Videotaping Custodial Interrogations: Toward a Scientifically Based Policy

G. Daniel Lassiter, Lezlee J. Ware, Matthew J. Lindberg, and Jennifer J. Ratcliff

Wisdom consists of the anticipation of consequences.

—Norman Cousins

This chapter draws on the psychological literature to emphasize some important issues that would be prudent for lawmakers to keep in mind in their pursuit of a sound videotaping policy. Such a scientifically based policy would not only require that custodial interrogations be videotaped in their entirety but would also provide guidance on how interrogations should be videotaped to best protect the innocent from the possibility of wrongful conviction. Moreover, we argue in this chapter—again from the standpoint of relevant science—that even under the best of circumstances, evaluations of defendants' videotaped statements obtained during a typical police interrogation conducted in the United States (see chap. 1, this volume) are subject to the same biases that often undermine the quality of judgments of in vivo interactions between people (e.g., the fundamental attribution error; Ross, 1977). Consequently, the ultimate success of the videotaping reform will only be as good as fact finders' decision-making processes. It is not the point of this chapter to disparage the videotaping movement; rather, as the chapter's epigraph suggests, the hope is to further its success by identifying potential unintended consequences and offering recommendations, sooner as opposed to later, for avoiding them (cf. Lassiter & Dudley, 1991).

Camera Perspective Bias in Videotaped Confessions and Interrogations: A 25-Year Program of Research

The impetus behind the body of scholarship on videotaped confessions and interrogations was a single-page article appearing in *Time* magazine in June 1983 ("Smile, You're On," 1983). The article described how law enforcement in parts of New York City and in other locations throughout the United States was successfully using videotape to record suspects' confessions obtained during custodial interrogations. It was noted that videotaping had "resulted in a guilty-plea rate of 85% and a conviction rate of almost 100%" (p. 61). Then Bronx district attorney Mario Merola, whose office was credited with being the first to use videotaped confessions in the mid-1970s, was quoted as saying that videotaping was such a powerful tool in the war on crime that it "is taking the gamesmanship out of the process; it tells the truth." The article pointed out, however, that not everyone in the criminal justice system embraced the advent of this new use of videotape technology with open arms. For example, a Chicago defense attorney was reported as saying, "Let's face it. Some confessions are elicited not by beating but by trickery." The implication of this comment was that even videotape would not necessarily make obvious to later fact finders the operation of more subtle coercive pressures.

In a photograph accompanying the *Time* article, two staff members of the Bronx district attorney's office were flanking a video monitor that was displaying a videotaped confession of a 22-year-old suspect. The front of the suspect from the waist up was visible, but because of the camera perspective it was not possible to view the interrogators, which the article indicated included a detective and a prosecutor. To the present day, this camera perspective (focused entirely on the suspect, providing little, if any, opportunity to observe the interrogators) is typically how confessions and interrogations are videotaped in the United States (Geller, 1992; Kassin, 1997; Lassiter, Ware, Ratcliff, & Irvin, 2009). For more than 2 decades now, Lassiter (2002) and his colleagues (Lassiter, Geers, Munhall, Handley, & Beers, 2001) have argued that positioning the camera such that it directs attention exclusively onto suspects could have an unanticipated detrimental influence on fact finders' evaluations of videotaped confessions and interrogations because of, among other things, illusory causation—a well-documented phenomenon in the psychological literature.

This chapter briefly reviews some of the research that initially established the existence of what is now known as the *camera perspective bias* (Lassiter, 2002). It then turns to a more detailed presentation of the most recent findings that provide the strongest evidence to date that policymakers should heed the scientific data to ensure that the videotaping reform advances, rather than impedes, the cause of justice.

Theoretical Basis and Early Empirical Evidence for the Camera Perspective Bias in Videotaped Confessions and Interrogations

Common sense suggests that the camera should be focused on the suspect during questioning, as it is this person's statements, demeanor, and overall behavior that presumably will be most informative to later trial fact finders in rendering correct assessments of the voluntariness and validity of any confession. Therefore, it is understandable that a suspect-focus camera perspective is the default in the United States with regard to videotaping police interrogations (Geller, 1992; Kassin, 1997). Psychological science, however, indicates that people's perceptions of the causes of another's behavior are not simply a function of the relevant information available to them. That is, factors that may not be truly causing a person's behavior have been shown nonetheless to be perceived as causal simply because they are more visually prominent or salient to observers than other factors (Briggs & Lassiter, 1994; Lassiter, Geers, Munhall, Ploutz-Snyder, & Breitenbecher, 2002; McArthur, 1981; Taylor & Fiske, 1978).

This phenomenon, known as *illusory causation* (McArthur, 1980), suggests the possibility that videotapes of interrogations in which the suspect is more visually conspicuous than the interrogator by virtue of the camera perspective (i.e., the suspect is facing the camera, with at best only the back of the interrogator visible) could bias observers' evaluations. More specifically, the visual prominence of the suspect could lead observers to conclude that incriminating statements made by him or her are largely volitional rather than a consequence of excessive pressure being exerted by the interrogator, irrespective of the reality of the situation. (For many years, there was considerable uncertainty about the mechanisms underlying illusory causation. For example, one view was that the phenomenon resulted from the tendency to remember more about a visually conspicuous person than a visually inconspicuous person, with this asymmetry in memory leading observers to conclude that the former individual was more causally influential; cf. Fiske, Kenny, & Taylor, 1982. Recent research, however, has shown that illusory causation is more closely tied to perceptual than to reasoning processes and as such is extremely difficult for people to overcome; Lassiter, Geers, Munhall, et al., 2002; Ratcliff, Lassiter, Schmidt, & Snyder, 2006; Ware, Lassiter, Patterson, & Ransom, 2008.) Basic research has examined illusory causation in contexts that are very different from custodial police interrogations; for example, many studies of illusory causation focused on judgments regarding which of two college students set the tone in an observed, get-acquainted conversation (see Taylor & Fiske, 1978). Therefore, convincing policymakers that the camera perspective bias described above is a serious threat to the integrity of the criminal justice system is likely to require considerable direct evidence of its existence and generalizability to actual legal contexts.

The seminal demonstration that camera point of view could influence evaluations of a videotaped confession was reported by Lassiter and Irvine (1986). Participants viewed one of three versions of a videotaped mock confession concerning the crime of shoplifting that differed only in terms of the camera perspective taken when the confession was initially recorded. In the suspect-focus version, the front of the suspect from the waist up and the back of the detective (part of the head and one shoulder) were visible; in the interrogator-focus version, the front of the detective from the waist up and the back of the suspect (part of the head and one shoulder) were visible; and in the equal-focus version, the profiles of both the suspect and detective from the waist up could be seen equally well. After the presentation of the confession, participants were asked to indicate the degree to which they believed it was voluntary. The confession was judged to be the most voluntary in the suspect-focus condition, less voluntary in the equal-focus condition, and the least voluntary in the interrogator-focus condition. Regardless of condition, participants expressed high confidence in the correctness of their judgments.

Since its initial demonstration, the camera perspective bias has also been found to influence judgments of a suspect's likelihood of guilt and sentencing recommendations in the same linear fashion (Lassiter, Beers, et al., 2002). Moreover, numerous investigations attest to the considerable robustness and generalizability of the bias. For example, individual differences in the motivation to think effortfully (Lassiter, Slaw, Briggs, & Scanlan, 1992) and in the capacity to reason specifically about complex causal relationships (Lassiter et al., 2005) do not moderate the camera perspective bias, nor is it reduced by situationally increasing observers' sense of accountability for their judgments

(Lassiter, Munhall, Geers, Weiland, & Handley, 2001). The bias has also been shown to occur across various types of crime (Lassiter, Slaw, Briggs, & Scanlan, 1992), in the context of realistic trial simulations (Lassiter, Geers, Handley, Weiland, & Munhall, 2002), and with samples of college students and community members from disparate backgrounds (Lassiter, Geers, Handley, et al., 2002).

On the positive side, multiple studies (Lassiter et al., 1992; Lassiter, Beers, et al., 2002) have reported that when the camera is positioned so that the profiles of the suspect and the interrogator are similarly visible (i.e., an equal-focus perspective), videotaped confessions generate judgments that are comparable to those based on more traditional presentation formats, that is, audiotapes and transcripts. Assuming audio recordings and transcripts of interrogations and confessions are largely unbiased presentation formats, such results indicate that the videotaping procedure per se is not inherently prejudicial; rather, the manner in which it is actually implemented seems to determine its potential to convey bias. It appears, then, that the advantages associated with the videotape method—for example, a more detailed record of the interrogation is provided to fact finders— can be maintained without introducing bias if an equal-focus perspective is used to preserve the interrogation for subsequent viewing. (For more detailed coverage and discussion of the early literature on the camera perspective bias in videotaped confessions, see Lassiter, Geers, et al., 2001; Lassiter & Geers, 2004; Lassiter, Ratcliff, Ware, & Irvin 2006.)

The Most Recent Findings on the Camera Perspective Bias and Their Implications for Emerging Reform in the Criminal Justice System

Several scholars (e.g., Bornstein, 1999; Bray & Kerr, 1982; Diamond, 1997) have noted that research programs in the area of legal psychology must aspire to a high standard with regard to issues of ecological validity, that is, the extent to which the methodology used captures the look and feel of the real world. For example, Bornstein (1999) pointed out that "courts have not welcomed psycho-legal research findings with open arms, especially when derived from methods that are neither very realistic nor representative of actual legal processes" (p. 88). Bray and Kerr (1982) suggested that a reasonable approach to addressing ecological validity "is to conduct a series of carefully planned studies that collectively provide data that determine the limits of generalizability" (p. 304). The latest studies in this ongoing program of investigation, like those reviewed earlier, adopted this approach, with the aim to continue moving the research on the camera perspective bias in videotaped confessions even closer to the high standard of ecological validity needed to ultimately impact the legal system.

CONVINCING A TRADITIONALLY GUARDED LEGAL COMMUNITY OF THE IMPORT OF PSYCHOLOGICAL SCIENCE. All of the foregoing research examined the judgments of laypersons who would be eligible to serve on juries. However, in *Jackson v. Denno* (1964), the United States Supreme Court ruled that a judge in a pretrial hearing must decide that a confession was voluntary before it can be properly introduced at trial. Because judges play such a critical role in determining what confession evidence juries are actually allowed to consider, a question of great significance to the criminal justice community is whether the decisions of judges are similarly influenced by camera perspective. It is possible that their greater knowledge, experience, and understanding of the law pertaining to confessions could immunize them against such an effect.

Guthrie, Rachlinski, and Wistrich (2002) noted that systematic, controlled studies of judicial decision making are rare. They therefore conducted an important investigation of judges' susceptibility to various cognitive illusions (e.g., the hindsight bias, the inverse fallacy). Guthrie et al. reported that although judges were as susceptible to some illusions as laypersons and other professionals, their relative performance with regard to other illusions was noticeably better. More recently, it has been shown that judges' perceptions of a witness's credibility—in contrast to those of laypersons—are unaffected by the witness's potentially misleading emotional expression (Wessel, Drevland, Eilertsen, & Magnussen, 2006). Findings such as these suggest the possibility that judges may be able to overcome the camera perspective bias. More specifically, judges, unlike laypersons, may be better at focusing their attentional resources on the information that is most revealing in terms of reaching an accurate assessment of the voluntariness of a given confession. Although laypersons in several of the previous studies were no doubt highly motivated to reach an accurate assessment, their lack of expertise with regard to deciding the voluntariness question may have made them gravitate to the most salient cues (e.g., the suspect makes a self-incriminating statement) rather than the most useful information (e.g., the suspect's self-incriminating behavior immediately followed a pragmatically implied promise of leniency).

To directly examine this possibility, Lassiter, Diamond, Schmidt, and Elek (2007) presented a group of judges possessing considerable relevant expertise (i.e., all had many years of previous experience as prosecutors, criminal defense attorneys, and trial court judges hearing criminal cases) with either a suspect-focus, equal-focus, or interrogator-focus version of a mock interrogation and confession regarding a sexual assault. Results revealed that judges' evaluations of the voluntariness of the confession, like those of laypersons, were significantly affected by the camera perspective. (Lassiter et al., 2007, also investigated whether the expertise of highly trained and experienced police interrogators made them any less susceptible than laypersons to the camera perspective bias. Like the judges, police interrogators proved to be no exception.)

The many merits of the studies already described notwithstanding, the likelihood of the legal establishment heeding the existing scientific evidence for a camera perspective bias could be diminished by the fact that none of the experiments reviewed so far exposed participants to authentic confessions obtained during real police interrogations. That is, the prior work used mock interrogations and confessions that were designed to be composites of various elements known to occur in true interrogations or that were constructed reenactments developed from transcripts of specific police interrogations. These simulations were required because of the need to produce multiple camera perspectives of the same confession. Because simulated confessors faced no serious consequences, it is possible that their behavior diverged in important ways from that of actual confessors. As such differences could, in turn, affect judgments, it cannot be assumed that observers viewing authentic videotaped interrogations and confessions will also manifest the camera perspective bias.

Some recent work in the area of deception detection (Mann, Vrij, & Bull, 2004; Mann & Vrij, 2006) in fact raises the possibility that observers might render less biased evaluations when viewing authentic videotaped interrogations and confessions. Mann et al. (2004) argued that studies (e.g., DePaulo & Pfeifer, 1986; Meissner & Kassin, 2002) demonstrating that laypersons and even professionals (e.g., police and customs officers) who generally fare not much better than chance at judging whether a person is lying or telling the truth suffer from a potential drawback, namely, the stakes (i.e., the negative consequences of being caught and the positive consequences of getting away with the lie) may not have been high enough for liars to exhibit clear cues of their deception (cf. DePaulo, Lanier, & Davis, 1983; DePaulo, Stone, & Lassiter, 1985). Mann et al. (2004), therefore, had participants view clips from videotapes of real-life police interviews in which actual criminal suspects were sometimes telling true, rather than simulated, lies. (Statements from reliable, independent witnesses and forensic evidence were used to establish whether any given statement of the suspects' was true or false.) Their results revealed that observers were able to achieve higher rates of accuracy at differentiating deception from truth than is typically found in studies in which the lies are told in a less realistic context.

The implications of the Mann et al. (2004) research are straightforward: In real-world, high-stakes situations, a person may behave in ways that cannot easily be evoked or reproduced in mere simulations, no matter how well the latter are constructed. Moreover, such behaviors may provide vital information capable of improving observers' judgments of the person. With regard to videotaped interrogations, the availability of more potentially diagnostic cues in the behavior of actual suspects and detectives might help observers avoid being influenced by tangential and possibly misleading aspects of the videotape, including the camera perspective from which it was initially recorded.

As described earlier, prior studies (Lassiter et al., 1992; Lassiter, Beers, et al., 2002) have shown that audiotapes and transcripts of simulated confessions generally produce evaluations comparable with those obtained with equal-focus videotapes. On the basis of this pattern of results, Lassiter et al. (2009) argued that comparing an authentic suspect-focus videotape with audio only and transcript presentations of the same interrogation and confession would constitute a reasonable test of the camera perspective bias under conditions of high ecological validity. That is, if the bias truly occurs with real interrogations and confessions, then an authentic suspect-focus videotape should produce judgments of greater voluntariness than either an audio only or a transcript presentation.

To test this prediction, Lassiter et al. (2009) conducted an experiment in which two authentic videotaped police confessions and interrogations were used. One involved a case of sexual assault and was originally recorded with the camera trained on the suspect (suspect-focus confession). The other involved a murder-by-arson case and was originally recorded with the camera trained on both the suspect and interrogator (equal-focus confession). Audio only and transcript versions of each interrogation were derived from the videotapes. The inclusion of an authentic equal-focus confession allowed Lassiter et al. (2009) to rule out the possibility that the predicted differences between the suspect-focus videotape and its corresponding audio only and transcript presentation formats is simply due to a general tendency to judge the confession as more voluntary when presented on videotape. If, as predicted, the original camera perspective per se is the source of the bias, then in contrast to the authentic suspect-focus confession no differences in voluntariness judgments as a function of presentation format (video and audio, audio only, transcript) should occur for the authentic equal-focus confession.

The anticipated pattern of results was obtained: Participants who evaluated the suspect-focus confession in the original video and audio format judged it to be more voluntary than did participants who either read a transcript or only listened to the audio, whereas no effect of presentation format on evaluations of the equal-focus confession was observed. The fact that the impact of presentation format diverges for the two confessions makes it likely that camera perspective, rather than the video and audio format, was responsible for the relatively high assessments of voluntariness made by participants viewing the suspect-focus videotape.

Lassiter et al. (2009) acknowledged the possibility that the crucial interaction between authentic confessions (suspect focus vs. equal focus) and presentation format (video and audio vs. audio only vs. transcript) may have resulted from content differences across the two confessions, rather than from the varying camera perspectives specifically. To eliminate this potential confound, in a second experiment they transformed the authentic equal-focus confession into two new versions. By editing the original videotape, they were able to create a version in which only the suspect was visible (suspect focus) and a version in which only the interrogator was visible (interrogator focus). The essential content in these two versions is thus identical, with only the visual conspicuousness of the suspect and interrogator differing. If, as they argued, the interaction pattern obtained in their initial experiment was caused by changes in camera perspective and not changes in content, then observers viewing the new suspect-focus version of the videotape should judge the confession to be more voluntary than those viewing the new interrogator-focus version.

The results revealed the predicted effect of camera perspective: Participants who viewed the suspect-focus version rendered assessments of voluntariness and judgments of likely guilt that were greater than those rendered by participants who viewed the interrogator-focus version. These findings, then, definitively demonstrate that even when the same authentic interrogation is being considered, which person (suspect or interrogator) is more visually salient affects observers' evaluations in a manner consistent with the many prior studies that have documented the camera perspective bias in simulated videotaped confessions.

The above investigations showing that experienced judges are not immune to the camera perspective bias in videotaped confessions and that the bias persists even when observers view authentic, rather than simulated, videotaped confessions further strengthen the case for developing and adopting a policy that would prevent suspect-focus videotaped confessions from being used as evidence at trial.

TESTS OF THE ACCURACY ISSUE WITH REGARD TO VIDEOTAPED CONFESSIONS AND INTERROGATIONS. There is at least an implicit assumption that an actual videotape of an interrogation and confession should make it possible for trial fact finders to assess more accurately the reliability of any admission of guilt or other self-incriminating statements (cf. Gudjonsson, 1992; Leo & Ofshe, 1998). Yet, such an assumption has not heretofore been empirically tested. The fact that camera point of view has been shown to bias observers' evaluations of a videotaped confession might seem to suggest that just the opposite may in fact be true—that is, videotaping leads to less accurate assessments of reliability.

But the presence of a bias in judgment does not necessarily impugn the accuracy of that judgment (cf. Funder, 1987). For example, it has been repeatedly demonstrated that people consistently favor dispositional explanations for an observed other's behavior over situational explanations (the aforementioned fundamental attribution error; Ross, 1977). However, the question of whether this attributional bias increases, decreases, or has no effect on the accuracy of causal judgments typically has not been addressed (cf. Harvey, Town, & Yarkin, 1981). Similarly, the research reviewed so far was designed to allow for an examination of possible judgment bias but not for an assessment of judgment accuracy. Proponents of videotaping interrogations with the camera zeroed in on the suspect could argue that if observers make accurate judgments under such circumstances, then the evidence of a camera perspective bias is in essence moot. What matters in the end, they may say, is whether fact finders can separate the reliable confessions from the unreliable confessions. We now discuss a series of studies that was specifically designed to address the important issue of accuracy in the evaluation of videotaped confessions.

Lassiter, Clark, Ware, Schmidt, and Geers (2008) argued that one approach to examining the effect of camera perspective on the ability of observers to accurately differentiate true from false confessions would be to use events from an actual trial in which the truth regarding the guilt or innocence of a defendant is known for certain. That is, which camera perspective best allows mock jurors to render judgments that most closely match the known facts of a case? One real case that fits this requirement is the trial of Peter Reilly. Reilly was wrongfully convicted of the manslaughter of his mother on the basis of a coerced and false confession he made to police after intensive interrogation. Two years following his conviction, evidence was discovered that demonstrated that Reilly could not have been the actual killer. As a result, his conviction was overturned, and all charges against him were dismissed.

In an initial experiment, Lassiter et al. (2008) used detailed accounts of the Reilly case provided by Barthel (1976) and Connery (1977) to recreate portions of the actual interrogation (of which there is an audiotaped record). This partial recreation of the interrogation and confession of Peter Reilly was videotaped simultaneously by three cameras: one taking a suspect-focus position, another taking a interrogator-focus position, and the last taking an equal-focus position. On the basis of the Barthel and Connery accounts, a reenactment of key events occurring in Reilly's trial was also staged. This resulting trial simulation was highly realistic and was professionally videotaped in an actual courtroom.

Jury-eligible community volunteers, recruited via an ad placed in a local newspaper, served as mock jurors. Participants viewed the trial simulation in which was embedded one of the three versions of the confession. At the conclusion of the trial, all participants individually provided assessments of the voluntary status of the confession as well as ratings of the likelihood that Reilly was guilty. The results revealed a most interesting pattern: Participants more accurately judged that Reilly was less likely to be guilty and that his statements were less likely voluntary when they viewed an interrogator-focus version of the confession as opposed to a suspect-focus or an equal-focus version of the confession. These data suggest the possibility that observers were able to detect and better appreciate the external pressure to confess experienced by Reilly when the camera perspective made the source of that pressure, the interrogator, visually conspicuous (cf. Arkin & Duval, 1975).

Lassiter et al. (2008) noted that a drawback to the preceding study was that observers viewed only a single, simulated false confession. What, if any, influence would camera perspective have on judgments when observers are asked to evaluate real confessions, some of which are false and others of which are true? To address this issue, Lassiter et al. (2008) first obtained actual true and false confessions from several different individuals. Using a modification of the methods of Kassin and Kiechel (1996) to induce false confessions, researchers asked pairs of college students to work together on a computer task. The computer ostensibly crashed and the cause was that either the actual participant (men in all cases) or a confederate (women in all cases) hit a certain key. The experimenter (interrogator) questioned the participant (suspect) about his role in crashing the computer, extracting a true confession in cases in which the participant did hit the critical key (at the urging of the confederate). In instances in which the confederate was guilty, she pleaded with the participant to take the blame so as not to hurt her chances of obtaining a research position with the faculty member conducting the experiment. This method was effective in getting some participants to give a false confession.

Participants' confessions were videotaped and later presented to new groups of observers whose task was to rate the truthfulness of four confessions (two were true and two were false). Camera perspective was systematically varied in the usual way—suspect focus, interrogator focus, and equal focus—so it could be determined which format promotes the highest degree of judgmental accuracy.

Observers' ratings of truthfulness for the two false confessions were subtracted from their truthfulness ratings for the two true confessions to yield a relative accuracy index. The overall results were sobering: Observers fared no better than chance at differentiating true from false confessions. However, consistent with the findings of their first study, Lassiter et al. (2008) found that an interrogator-focus perspective produced relatively greater accuracy than did an equal-focus perspective, which in turn produced relatively greater accuracy than did a suspect-focus perspective.

To establish a baseline level of accuracy, in a third study Lassiter et al. (2008) added audio only and transcript presentation formats. Furthermore, to gain insight into why a suspect-focus camera perspective was producing the poorest accuracy, they also added a format in which the camera zoomed in on the suspect so that only his face was visible and a format in which only his body from the neck down could be seen. The rationale for these latter two presentation formats was based on the deception detection literature, which indicates that facial cues, despite commonsense notions, are generally not very helpful to observers in detecting falsehoods (DePaulo et al., 1985; chap. 6, this volume).

However, what people say (verbal content) and, to some extent, how they say it (tone of voice) tend to be more informative and revealing with respect to distinguishing deceit from truth. However, Lassiter et al. (2008) suggested that when people have access to facial expressions, they may put far too much emphasis on their ability to judge another's veracity primarily from these expressions and thus pay less attention to more diagnostic cues (e.g., verbal content) that are available to them. If their assumption were indeed correct, then it should be the case, Lassiter et al. (2008) argued, that presentation formats that deny access to suspects' facial cues (i.e., interrogator-focus video, transcript, audio only, and suspect body only video) should do better at telling the difference between a true confession and a false confession than formats that make suspects' facial expressions readily discernable (i.e., suspect face only video, suspect-focus video, and to a lesser extent equal-focus video).

The results were in line with the foregoing argument: The interrogator-focus video produced greater accuracy than did the suspect face only video, the suspect-focus video, and the equal-focus video. The interrogator-focus video produced levels of accuracy that were comparable with those obtained with the suspect body only video, audio only, and transcript. These data support the idea that confession presentation formats that provide access to suspects' facial cues seem to hinder rather than help observers' accuracy with regard to differentiating true from false confessions.

In a fourth and final experiment, Lassiter et al. (2008) took an entirely different tack in examining the accuracy question. They investigated observers' ability to detect the most explicit and legally impermissible tactic in the interrogator's arsenal—a direct threat—as a function of confession presentation format. This, Lassiter et al. (2008) reasoned, would constitute the strongest test yet of the power of confession presentation format to influence evaluations of videotaped confessions. That is, in the best of all worlds, fact finders would detect the presence of an illegal threat regardless of the format in which the interrogation was presented. Lassiter et al. (2008) set out to determine if this is indeed the case.

Two simulated interrogations dealing with a hit-and-run accident based on materials used initially by Kassin and McNall (1991) were developed. In the first of these, the interrogator at one point issues a very strong and direct threat to elicit an admission of guilt from the suspect, and in the other, this tactic is omitted. Aside from this difference, the two versions of the interrogation, which ended with the suspect confessing, were identical. The two versions were each videotaped from one of three camera perspectives: suspect focus, equal focus, and interrogator focus. Kassin and McNall had previously found that observers could detect a threat and adjust their evaluations accordingly when reading a transcript of an interrogation. Therefore, Lassiter et al. (2008, Study 4) included a transcript of each of the two versions of the interrogation as a point of comparison. Observers viewed or read about one of the two interrogations (threat vs. no threat) in one of the four presentation formats (suspect-focus video vs. equal-focus video vs. detective-focus video vs. transcript) and subsequently rendered a verdict of guilty or not guilty.

Analysis of the verdict data indicated that although the overall conviction rate was lower for the version of the interrogation that included the threat, presentation format still exerted a powerful influence on the extent to which verdicts were appropriately adjusted for the threat. Whereas only 38% and 33% of participants who read the transcript and viewed the interrogator-focus video, respectively, found the suspect guilty, the conviction rate was 67% for participants who viewed the equal-focus video and an astonishing 78% for participants who viewed the suspect-focus video. The results of this study, taken together with the findings of Lassiter et al.'s (2008) first three experiments, leave little doubt that a suspect-focus camera perspective fails to enhance accurate evaluations of videotaped confessions, and perhaps of even greater concern, appears to actually diminish the capability of decision makers to arrive at objectively correct assessments.

A FINAL ATTEMPT TO REACH A COMPROMISE. Another counterintuitive implication arising from the series of studies described above is that the best approach to videotaping interrogations might be to focus the camera on the detective (cf. Lassiter et al., 2006). However, this perspective is unlikely to be adopted by law enforcement as it does not provide a clear view of the suspect. Snyder, Lassiter, Lindberg, and Pinegar (2009) investigated a compromise: a dual-camera perspective, in which observers see the suspect-focus and the detective-focus videos side by side on a split screen. This perspective differs from the equal-focus perspective in that it allows observers to view both the suspect and detective face-on rather than in profile. In an initial experiment, Snyder et al. (2009, Study 1) sought to determine whether a dual-camera perspective eliminates the well-established camera perspective bias in judgments of voluntariness.

Participants were randomly assigned to one of five conditions: suspect-focus video, equal-focus video, detective-focus video, dual-camera video, or audio only. The detective- and suspect-focus videos were spliced together to create the dual-camera perspective. After viewing or hearing the confession and interrogation (a simulation based on the actual interrogation of Bradley Page, a college student who was convicted of the manslaughter of his romantic partner primarily because of self-incriminating statements that many experts regard as coerced and false; e.g., Leo & Ofshe, 1998), participants responded to measures of guilt and voluntariness.

Results showed that the traditional suspect-focus video yielded higher guilt and voluntariness judgments than all other presentation formats. Particularly promising, ratings based on viewing the dual-camera video were comparable with those found for the equal-focus video and audio only. These findings, then, indicate that the biased judgments typically associated with a suspect-focus videotaped confession could be mitigated by using a dual-camera approach that permitted simultaneous face-on views of both the suspect and detective.

In a second study, Snyder et al. (2009) addressed the important question of whether a dual-camera approach also improves accuracy in differentiating true from false confessions. The stimulus materials used in this investigation were the same as those used in Lassiter et al.'s (2008) Study 3, except that their suspect body only video was replaced with a newly created dual-camera video. The procedure duplicated that of Lassiter et al. (2008, Study 3), with participants viewing four confessions (two true, two false) and rating each in terms of its apparent veracity.

Following Lassiter et al. (2008, Study 3), an accuracy index was created by subtracting truthful ratings of the two false confessions from the ratings of the two true confessions. The results failed to confirm an advantage for the dual-camera approach. In fact, there was no difference in accuracy among the dual-camera video, suspect-focus video, and suspect face only video, which collectively produced lower accuracy than did the equal-focus video, detective-focus video, audio only, and transcript formats.

Snyder et al. (2009) noted that this discrepancy across studies was not entirely unexpected. It makes sense, they argued, that illusory causation and biased voluntariness judgments would be eliminated because in a dual-camera perspective the suspect and interrogator are equally salient, just as with an equal-focus perspective. However, for judgments of truthfulness, observers seem to be led astray by their apparent overreliance on suspects' facial expressions (as suggested by the findings of Lassiter et al., 2008). In general, people apparently have strong ideas about how someone should look when lying versus telling the truth, but as discussed earlier, decades of research on deception detection has shown that these perceived cues are in fact not very diagnostic (cf. DePaulo et al., 1985; chap. 6, this volume).

Therefore, the failure of the simultaneous, face-on presentation of the detective with the suspect in the dual-camera perspective to improve accuracy beyond the presentation of only the suspect (i.e., suspect-focus perspective) is not so surprising. Accuracy, it once again appears, is only improved beyond the suspect-focus perspective when a clear view of the suspect's face is not available (e.g., detective-focus video, audio only) and therefore cannot mislead the viewer. Snyder et al. (2009) concluded, then, that the dual-camera perspective is not an appropriate alternative format to use as a means to appease both police (who favor a face-on view of the suspect) and researchers (who are concerned about the problems associated with a view of only the suspect) because observers viewing this particular perspective are relatively inaccurate at determining whether the suspect is being truthful with regard to self-incriminating statements made during an interrogation.

Translating the Research Into Scientifically Based Policy

In the end, a sound policy regarding the videotaping of custodial interrogations must meet the concerns of all relevant constituents: defendants, prosecutors, police, defense counsel, trial and appellate judges, and ultimately the public at large. To aid criminal justice practitioners and legal policy makers in achieving this objective, we present the following recommendations distilled from the research reviewed in this chapter and then discuss some additional issues of concern based on the findings of other pertinent scientific investigations.

Some Specific Recommendations for How Custodial Interrogations Should be Videotaped

1. Custodial interrogations should be recorded in their entirety with the camera positioned so that the resulting videotape displays an equal-

focus perspective or, still better, an interrogator-focus perspective (both as described herein). Although intuitively, a suspect-focus perspective seems to make the most sense, time and time again the research demonstrates that this perspective leads to biased and inaccurate assessments of videotaped interrogations, which could increase the possibility of an innocent person being wrongfully prosecuted and ultimately wrongfully convicted.

2. In instances in which an interrogation has already been videotaped from a suspect-focus camera perspective, it is recommended that the resultant videotape not be used as evidence at trial. Rather, the audio track only or a transcript derived from the videotape should be used instead. Either of these presentation formats circumvents the well-established drawbacks of suspect-focus videotapes.

3. Although two cameras, one focused on the suspect and the other focused on the interrogator(s), increase the amount and variety of visual details that can be recorded, splicing the resultant videotapes together to produce a split-screen presentation of face-on views of both the suspect and interrogator is not advised. The research indicates that this dual-camera perspective minimizes the effect of illusory causation on voluntariness judgments but does nothing to remedy the problems associated with a suspect-focus perspective in regard to the actual accuracy of judgments (i.e., the extent to which true and false confessions are correctly identified as such).

The Best-Laid Plans: Limits on What Videotaping Alone Can Realistically Accomplish

Over the years, calls for requiring the complete videotaping of custodial interrogations have come from virtually every camp on the political spectrum: from the most pro-defendant to the most pro-law enforcement. The one thing these groups have in common is their unreserved endorsement of videotaping as a surefire solution to the problem of false confessions leading to the wrongful conviction and imprisonment of innocent people. One proponent's faith in the videotaping movement is so absolute that he has gone to the extreme of arguing that legally required *Miranda* warnings to suspects concerning their rights to silence and counsel can be dispensed with if interrogations are routinely videotaped (Cassell, 1996). His reasoning is that the voluntariness question can be adequately answered without the need for *Miranda* once fact finders have the opportunity to view for themselves an interrogation in its entirety.

Although less extreme, similar assertions implying that videotapes "reveal the truth" are abundant. Several of the testimonials recounted by Sullivan (chap. 8, this volume) included references to how videotape is a superior method of documenting interrogations because it allows observers to examine suspects' so-called body language, that is, their gestures and facial and body movements. The implication of such statements is that the meaning of various nonverbal behaviors is invariant and understood equally well by all potential observers. For example, it is virtually a truism that people shift their eyes when telling a lie. The only problem is that this truism is not true. Multiple meta-analyses of hundreds of scientific studies fail to support this belief and many other naïve theories of the meaning of various nonverbal behaviors (e.g., Bond & DePaulo, 2006), yet confidence in their validity persists among laypersons as well as highly trained criminal justice professionals.

In the example just cited, most people are in agreement about what "shifty eyes" say about a person's veracity. They all just happen to be incorrect. In other instances, however, different observers may ascribe different meanings to the same behavior. For example, at a recent conference in which the first author of this chapter described his concerns about suspect-focus videotaped confessions, he was asked if seeing a suspect slumped over during an interrogation could indicate anything other than the fact that the suspect was experiencing great fatigue, and therefore his incriminating statements would be interpreted more cautiously by any reasonable observer, which the questioner was presumably touting as an example of how a suspect-focus videotaped confession could actually protect an innocent suspect. Lassiter responded that a prosecutor could easily argue that the slumping was an indication of how much shame the suspect was experiencing as a result of his overwhelming feelings of guilt. Similarly, nervous and agitated behavior on the part of suspects could be seen by one observer as clearly confirming their guilt and by another observer as the reasonable reaction of innocent persons confronted with an intolerable situation. Our point is that the "truth" in videotaped interrogations that so many advocates proclaim is self-evident may be more elusive than first thought.

As our system of criminal justice is adversarial in nature, when examining a videotaped interrogation the prosecution will be looking for proof that a defendant is guilty, whereas the defense will be looking for some indication that he or she is not. Psychological research indicates that people expecting or desiring to see different things very often end up seeing different things (e.g., Massad, Hubbard, & Newtson, 1979; Zadny & Gerard, 1974). A particularly relevant example is a study demonstrating that when observers with diametrically opposed expectancies viewed the same videotaped sample of a person's behavior, their subsequent evaluations of the person became more extreme in line with whichever expectancy they held, despite the fact that the information contained in the video was entirely inconclusive, that is, some of it supported and some it contradicted each of the expectancies (Darley & Gross, 1983). This and more recent work (Balcetis & Dunning, 2006; Balcetis & Lassiter, in press; Lassiter, Lindberg, Ratcliff, & Ware, in press) suggests that expectancies, hopes, and desires lead people to unintentionally register information from an event selectively; thus, in instances in which the information available for forming judgments is not 100% conclusive (which for contested confessions is likely to be the case), people are literally more likely to perceive or notice the very information that fits with what they expect or wish to find.

In some cases, the information contained in videotaped confessions should be so conclusive that it is not possible for reasonable observers to come to disparate conclusions. Even here, though, the science suggests one cannot be confident that this will be the case. Work on the fundamental attribution error (Ross, 1977) indicates that in contexts in which the external constraints on an observed other's

behavior are at their most severe, people still will often fail to identify those constraints as the cause of the behavior; instead, they will persist in perceiving the
behavior as having its roots in aspects of the person (for a review, see Gilbert
& Malone, 1995). Recall that in Study 4 of the Lassiter et al. (2008) research
described earlier, even after viewing what turned out to be the best confession
presentation format for achieving accurate judgments (i.e., the interrogator-
focus video), a full third of the mock jurors convicted the suspect despite the fact
that he was threatened explicitly by the interrogator if he did not confess. This
result is not an aberration, as Kassin and Sukel (1997) reported a similar finding:
After reading a transcript describing a high-pressure interrogation in which the
defendant was handcuffed, verbally abused, and threatened with a weapon, 50%
of mock jurors still voted him guilty.

While writing this chapter an especially relevant, real-world event that
parallels the aforementioned research came to our attention. In a 2007 ruling
(*Scott v. Harris*), the U.S. Supreme Court was persuaded (although not unanimously) primarily as a result of viewing a videotape of a car chase. Justice
Scalia noted on behalf of the majority that "we are happy to allow the videotape to speak for itself." The implication of this statement is that there was
only one way the videotape could possibly be interpreted. However, in his dissenting opinion, Justice Stevens indicated that the videotape led him to draw
the exactly opposite conclusion of the majority. It is interesting that the majority felt the "truth of matter" was so clear in the videotape that they took the
unusual step of posting it online for citizens to draw their own (presumably
identical) conclusions.

A trio of legal researchers availed themselves of this opportunity and collected the reactions of over a thousand individuals who were asked to view
the posted videotape (Kahan, Hoffman, & Braman, 2009). Although the majority
of these individuals agreed with the court's ruling, the researchers reported
that race, gender, income, party affiliation, ideology, region of residence, and cultural orientation all produced sharp differences in opinion. These results clearly
showed that different people, with different experiences, can see different things,
even in a purportedly definitive videotape (Kahan et al., 2009).

Videotaping custodial interrogations is indeed a wise thing to do, but
alone it will not solve the problem of false confessions occurring, nor will it
ensure that false confessions will be detected before an innocent life is ruined.
More needs to be done with regard to reforming how police go about interviewing and interrogating suspects in the first place. The pioneering efforts
in England and Wales over the last 2 decades in this regard are admirable
and, more important, have been by all accounts highly effective (see chaps. 5
and 7, this volume). We recommend, then, that the United States follow the
lead of these countries in changing "the ethos of interviewing [suspects] from
that of seeking a confession to a search for information—from a blinkered,
close-minded, oppressive, and suggestive interviewing style to one involving
open-mindedness, flexibility, and the obtaining of reliable evidence" (Bull &
Milne, 2004, p. 186). Such a sea change in combination with the guidelines we
have presented here for videotaping custodial interrogations should go a long
way toward reducing the likelihood of false confessions and the wrongful convictions that would almost certainly follow.

References

Arkin, R., & Duval, S. (1975). Focus of attention and causal attributions of actor and observers. *Journal of Experimental Social Psychology, 11,* 427–438.

Balcetis, E., & Dunning, D. (2006). See what you want to see: Motivational influences on visual perception. *Journal of Personality & Social Psychology, 91,* 612–625.

Balcetis, E., & Lassiter, G. D. (Eds.). (in press). *The social psychology of visual perception.* New York: Psychology Press.

Barthel, J. (1976). *A death in Canaan.* New York: Thomas Congdon.

Bond, C. F., Jr., & DePaulo, B. M. (2006). Accuracy of deception judgments. *Personality & Social Psychology Review, 10,* 214–234.

Bornstein, B. H. (1999). The ecological validity of jury simulations: Is the jury still out?" *Law & Human Behavior, 23,* 75–91.

Bray, R. M., & Kerr, N. L. (1982). Methodological considerations in the study of the psychology of the courtroom. In N. L. Kerr & R. M. Bray (Eds.), *The psychology of the courtroom* (pp. 287–323). New York: Academic Press.

Briggs, M. A., & Lassiter, G. D. (1994). More evidence for the robustness of salience effects. *Journal of Social Behavior & Personality, 9,* 171–180.

Bull, R., & Milne, B. (2004). Attempts to improve the police interviewing of suspects. In G. D. Lassiter (Ed.), *Interrogations, confessions, and entrapment* (pp. 181–196). New York: Kluwer/Plenum.

Cassell, P. G. (1996). All benefits, no costs: The grand illusion of Miranda's defenders. *Northwestern University Law Review, 90,* 1084–1124.

Connery, D. S. (1977). *Guilty until proven innocent.* New York: Putnam.

Darley, J. M., & Gross, P. H. (1983). A hypothesis-confirming bias in labeling effects. *Journal of Personality & Social Psychology, 44,* 20–33.

DePaulo, B. M., Lanier, K., & Davis, T. (1983). Detecting the deceit of the motivated liar. *Journal of Personality & Social Psychology, 45,* 1096–1103.

DePaulo, B. M., & Pfeifer, R. L. (1986). On-the-job experience and skill at detecting deception. *Journal of Applied Social Psychology, 16,* 249–267.

DePaulo, B. M., Stone, J. I., & Lassiter, G. D. (1985). Deceiving and detecting deceit. In B. R. Schenkler (Ed.), *The self and social life* (pp. 323–370). New York: McGraw-Hill.

Diamond, S. S. (1997). Illuminations and shadows from jury simulations. *Law & Human Behavior, 21,* 561–571.

Fiske, S. T., Kenny, D. A., & Taylor, S. E. (1982). Structural models for the mediation of salience effects on attribution. *Journal of Experimental Social Psychology, 18,* 105–127.

Funder, D. C. (1987). Errors and mistakes: Evaluating the accuracy of social judgment. *Psychological Bulletin, 101,* 75–90.

Geller, W. A. (1992). *Police videotaping of suspect interrogations and confessions: A preliminary examination of issues and practices* (A report to the National Institute of Justice). Washington, DC: U.S. Department of Justice.

Gilbert, D. T., & Malone, P. S. (1995). The correspondence bias. *Psychological Bulletin, 117,* 21–38.

Gudjonsson, G. (1992). *The psychology of interrogations, confessions and testimony.* Chichester, England: Wiley.

Guthrie, C., Rachlinski, J. J., & Wistrich, A. J. (2002). Judging by heuristic: Cognitive illusions in judicial decision making. *Judicature, 86,* 44–50.

Harvey, J. H., Town, J. P., & Yarkin, K. L. (1981). How fundamental is the "Fundamental Attribution Error"? *Journal of Personality & Social Psychology, 43,* 345–346.

Jackson v. Denno, 378 U. S. 368 (1964).

Kahan, D., Hoffman, D. A., & Braman, D. (2009). Whose eyes are you going to believe: *Scott v. Harris* and the perils of cognitive illiberalism. *Harvard Law Review, 122,* 837–906.

Kassin, S. M. (1997). The psychology of confession evidence. *American Psychologist, 52,* 221–233.

Kassin, S. M., & Kiechel, K. L. (1996). The social psychology of false confessions: Compliance, internalization, and confabulation. *Psychological Science, 7,* 125–128.

Kassin, S. M., & McNall, K. (1991). Police interrogations and confessions: Communicating promises and threats by pragmatic implication. *Law & Human Behavior, 15,* 233–251.

Kassin, S. M., & Sukel, H. (1997). Coerced confessions and the jury: An experimental test of the "harmless error" rule. *Law & Human Behavior, 21,* 27–46.

Lassiter, G. D. (2002). Illusory causation in the courtroom. *Current Directions in Psychological Science, 11,* 204–208.

Lassiter, G. D., Beers, M. J., Geers, A. L., Handley, I. M., Munhall, P. J., & Weiland, P. E. (2002). Further evidence of a robust point-of-view bias in videotaped confessions. *Current Psychology, 21,* 265–288.

Lassiter, G. D., Clark, J. K. Ware, L. J., Schmidt H. C., & Geers, A. L. (2008). *Accuracy in assessing confession evidence: Effects of presentation format.* Manuscript in preparation.

Lassiter, G. D., Diamond, S. S., Schmidt, H. C., & Elek, J. K. (2007). Evaluating videotaped confessions: Expertise provides no defense against the camera perspective effect. *Psychological Science, 18,* 224–226.

Lassiter, G. D., & Dudley, K. A. (1991). The a priori value of basic research: The case of videotaped confessions. *Journal of Social Behavior & Personality, 6,* 7–16.

Lassiter, G. D., & Geers, A. L. (2004). Bias and accuracy in the evaluation of confession evidence. In G. D. Lassiter (Ed.), *Interrogations, confessions and entrapment* (pp. 197–214). New York: Kluwer/Plenum.

Lassiter, G. D., Geers, A. L., Handley, I. M., Weiland, P. E., & Munhall, P. J. (2002). Videotaped interrogations and confessions: A simple change in camera perspective alters verdicts in simulated trials. *Journal of Applied Psychology, 87,* 867–874.

Lassiter, G. D., Geers, A. L., Munhall, P. J., Handley, I. M., & Beers, M. J. (2001). Videotaped confessions: Is guilt in the eye of the camera? In M. P. Zanna (Ed.), *Advances in experimental social psychology* (Vol. 33, pp. 189–254). New York: Academic.

Lassiter, G. D., Geers, A. L., Munhall, P. J., Ploutz-Snyder, R. J., & Breitenbecher, D. L. (2002). Illusory causation: Why it occurs. *Psychological Science, 13,* 299–305.

Lassiter, G. D., & Irvine, A. A. (1986). Videotaped confessions: The impact of camera point of view on judgments of coercion. *Journal of Applied Social Psychology, 16,* 268–276.

Lassiter, G. D., Lindberg, M. J., Ratcliff, J. J., & Ware, L. J. (in press). Top–down influences on the perception of ongoing behavior. In E. Balcetis & G. D. Lassiter (Eds.), *The social psychology of visual perception.* New York: Psychology Press.

Lassiter, G. D., Munhall, P. J., Berger, I. P., Weiland, P. E., Handley, I. M., & Geers, A. L. (2005). Attributional complexity and the camera perspective bias in videotaped confessions. *Basic & Applied Social Psychology, 27,* 27–35.

Lassiter, G. D., Munhall, P. J., Geers, A. L., Weiland, P. E., & Handley, I. M. (2001). Accountability and the camera perspective bias in videotaped confessions. *Analyses of Social Issues & Public Policy, 1,* 53–70.

Lassiter, G. D., Ratcliff, J. J., Ware, L. J., & Irvin, C. R. (2006). Videotaped confessions: Panacea or Pandora's box? *Law & Policy, 28,* 192–210.

Lassiter, G. D., Slaw, R. D., Briggs, M. A., & Scanlan, C. R. (1992). The potential for bias in videotaped confessions. *Journal of Applied Social Psychology, 22,* 1838–1851.

Lassiter, G. D., Ware, L. J., Ratcliff, J. J., & Irvin, C. R. (2009). Evidence of the camera perspective bias in authentic videotaped interrogations: Implications for emerging reform in the criminal justice system. *Legal & Criminological Psychology, 14,* 157–170.

Leo, R. A., & Ofshe, R. J. (1998). The consequences of false confessions: Deprivations of liberty and miscarriages of justice in the age of psychological interrogation. *Journal of Criminal Law & Criminology, 88,* 429–496.

Mann, S., & Vrij, A. (2006). Police officers' judgements of veracity, tenseness, cognitive load and attempted behavioural control in real-life police interviews. *Psychology, Crime & Law, 12,* 307–319.

Mann, S., Vrij, A., & Bull, R. (2004). Detecting true lies: Police officers' ability to detect suspects' lies. *Journal of Applied Psychology, 89,* 137–149.

Massad, C. M., Hubbard, & Newtson, D. (1979). Selective perception of events. *Journal of Experimental Social Psychology, 15,* 513–532.

McArthur, L. Z. (1980). Illusory causation and illusory correlation: Two epistemological accounts. *Personality & Social Psychology Bulletin, 6,* 507–519.

McArthur, L. Z. (1981). What grabs you? The role of attention in impression formation and causal attribution. In E. T. Higgins, C. P. Herman, & M. P. Zanna (Eds.), *Social cognition: The Ontario symposium* (Vol. 1, pp. 201–241). Hillsdale, NJ: Erlbaum.

Meissner, C. A., & Kassin, S. M. (2002). "He's guilty!": Investigator bias in judgments of truth and deception. *Law & Human Behavior, 26,* 469–480.

Ratcliff, J. J., Lassiter, G. D., Schmidt, H. C., & Snyder, C. J. (2006). Camera perspective bias in videotaped confessions: Experimental evidence of its perceptual basis. *Journal of Experimental Psychology: Applied, 12,* 197–206.

Ross, L. (1977). The intuitive psychologist and his shortcomings: Distortions in the attribution process. In L. Berkowitz (Ed.), *Advances in experimental social psychology* (Vol. 10, pp. 174–220). New York: Academic Press.

Scott v. Harris, 550 U. S. 372 (2007).

"Smile, you're on the D.A.'s camera." (1983, June 27). *Time,* p. 61.

Snyder, C. J., Lassiter, G. D., Lindberg, M. J., & Pinegar S. K. (2009). Videotaped interrogations and confessions: Does a dual-camera approach yield unbiased and accurate evaluations? *Behavioral Sciences & the Law, 27,* 451–466.

Taylor, S. E., & Fiske, S. T. (1978). Salience, attention, and attribution: Top of the head phenomenon. In L. Berkowitz (Ed.), *Advances in experimental social psychology* (Vol. 11, pp. 249–288). New York: Academic Press.

Ware, L. J., Lassiter, G. D., Patterson, S. M., & Ransom, M. R. (2008). Camera perspective bias in videotaped confessions: Evidence that visual attention is a mediator. *Journal of Experimental Psychology: Applied, 14,* 192–200.

Wessel, E., Drevland, G. C. B., Eilertsen, D. E., & Magnussen, S. (2006). Credibility of the emotional witness: A study of ratings by court judges. *Law & Human Behavior, 30,* 221–230.

Zadny, J., & Gerard, H. (1974). Attributed intentions and informational selectivity. *Journal of Experimental Social Psychology, 15,* 513–532.

10

The Supreme Court on *Miranda* Rights and Interrogations: The Past, the Present, and the Future

Lawrence S. Wrightsman

The purposes of this chapter are the following: first, to describe what led up to the *Miranda v. Arizona* decision rendered by the United States Supreme Court in 1966 (that is, to review not only those earlier Supreme Court decisions that dealt with interrogations but also the nature of police questioning at that time); second, to identify the goals of the justices in the *Miranda* decision; third, to evaluate whether those goals have been achieved; and last, to describe what needs to be done to achieve those goals in light of more recent Supreme Court decisions.

What Were the Policy Goals of the *Miranda* Decision?

Throughout the United States' more than 200-year history as a nation, the courts have struggled over a dilemma: how to provide law enforcement agencies with the resources and procedures to investigate crimes and punish criminals while still protecting the rights of individuals (including suspects) to due process. The decision by the Court in *Miranda v. Arizona* (1966) sought to bring into balance a criminal justice system that in the view of the majority of the justices, had given priority to police investigation at the sacrifice of the rights of possibly innocent suspects. But this tension between two goals remains in our society more than 40 years later; in fact, it is present among the justices currently on the Court and even serves as an explanation for the seemingly inconsistent decisions by the Court before and after the *Miranda* decision.

The State of Interrogation at the Time of Miranda

One does not have to search further than the *Miranda* opinion itself to find a record of what police interrogations were often like a half century ago. Part I of the decision described the nature of interrogations in the middle of the 20th century and then summarized:

> The use of physical brutality and violence is not, unfortunately, relegated to the past or to any part of the country. Only recently in Kings County, New

York, the police brutally beat, kicked, and placed lighted cigarette butts on the back of a potential witness under interrogation for the purpose of securing a statement incriminating a third party. (*Miranda v. Arizona,* 1966, p. 442)

In its opinion the Court noted that although this example is "undoubtedly the exception now . . . [such events still] are sufficiently widespread to be the object of concern" (p. 447). Chapter 10 of White (2001) also reviews claims that torture still existed 40 years later "in at least one pocket of the country" (p. 128).

The Essence of the Miranda Opinion

The *Miranda* opinion showed a sophisticated awareness of the impact of the interrogation on fragile suspects. "Coercion can be mental as well as physical," wrote Chief Justice Warren (*Miranda v. Arizona,* 1966, p. 448), noting that mental degradation can be massively destructive to human dignity. The opinion analyzed the practices advocated in the various police manuals then available, such as Inbau and Reid (1962), and illustrated their deliberate use of procedures designed to discourage the suspect's will to resist. The bottom line, in the view of the Court, was that regardless of whether intimidation was physical or psychological, the police often did not "undertake to afford proper safeguards at the onset of the interrogation to ensure that the statements were truly the product of free choice" (*Miranda v. Arizona,* 1966, p. 457).

The Court thus gave credibility to speculations in the media regarding abusive police practices—beating with fists or rubber hoses, whippings, the use of "water boarding"—occurring throughout the country. It stated that "unless a proper limitation upon custodial interrogations is achieved . . . there can be no assurance that practices of this nature will be eradicated in the foreseeable future" (*Miranda v. Arizona,* 1966, p. 443).

In forming its majority opinion, the Court in *Miranda* emphasized the centrality of voluntariness in determining the admissibility of a confession. The Court's decisions that led up to *Miranda* (described in the next section) had struggled with the relationship of coercion to the voluntary nature of a suspect's admissions. But voluntariness is a subjectively assessed phenomenon, and this aspect makes psychology relevant. From the decisions by the Court in the 1940s to those in the last few years, some justices have displayed different conceptions of human nature than have others. They have differed specifically with respect to how much coercion a person can withstand and, hence, whether a confession that occurs in response to coercion is an act of free will. Justices as eminent as Robert Jackson in the 1940s and Sandra Day O'Connor, who was on the Court until 2006, have assumed that the typical person can withstand extreme degrees of coercion, and hence admissions of guilt induced by such police actions are voluntary.

Decisions Prior to Miranda

As noted, throughout the period of its concern with interrogation procedures, the Supreme Court has demonstrated an inconsistent, shifting policy toward what it considers police behavior that is congruent with constitutional protections (White, 2001). Early on, in the 1930s, the Court condemned the use of "third-degree tactics" (see Leo, 2008, for a detailed history of such physically assaultive tactics and how they eventually gave rise to modern, psychologically oriented, interrogation tactics). An example was its decision in *Brown v. Mississippi* (1936), a case in which the police not only used severe whippings and other brutal methods but also told the suspects that these would continue until they confessed. Eventually, the three Black suspects complied, but the Court invalidated their confessions because of the excessive nature of the interrogation methods. In 1940, in *Chambers v. Florida,* the Court extended its prohibition to less violent forms of intimidation, including a prolonged and exhaustive interrogation, frequent threats, and isolation of the suspects from their relatives. (In this case, the suspects had resolutely refused to confess during 5 days of questioning, only to succumb after an all-night interrogation.)

But the inconsistent position of the Court prior to its *Miranda* decision is reflected in its reaction to two cases in 1944, cases that were decided by the Court only 1 month apart. In the first (*Ashcraft v. Tennessee,* 1944), E. E. Ashcraft was questioned in regard to his wife's death continuously for 36 hours; the detectives came at him in relays, and he was given only 5 minutes' respite from questioning during this entire day and a half period. He then, it is claimed, admitted to the murder of his wife, a confession that he recanted at his trial. Justice Hugo Black wrote the opinion for the Court, declaring that the intensity and duration of the interrogation constituted a "situation . . . so inherently coercive that its very existence is irreconcilable with the possession of mental freedom by a lone suspect against whom its full coercive force is brought to bear" (*Ashcraft v. Tennessee,* 1944, p. 154). But not all justices were by any means in agreement with this position; Justice Robert Jackson wrote a minority opinion (endorsed by Justices Felix Frankfurter and Owen Roberts) that reflected the traditional assumption that those suspects who were truly innocent possessed the ability and the will to withstand even this excessive pressure. In his dissent, Justice Jackson wrote:

> If the constitutional admissibility of a confession is no longer to be measured by the mental state of the individual confessor but by a general doctrine dependent on the clock, it should be capable of statement in definite terms. If 36 hours is more than permissible, what about 24? Or 12? Or six? Or one? All are "inherently coercive." (*Ashcraft v. Tennessee,* 1944, pp. 161–162)

The forward-looking decision authored by Justice Black did not remain operative for very long. The appeal in *Lyons v. Oklahoma* (1944), decided by the same nine justices just a little more than a month after *Ashcraft,* had a radically different outcome. Justice Jackson was able to persuade a majority of justices in the *Lyons* case to uphold the use of continued questioning as long as the individual suspect possessed "mental freedom" at the time of his or her confession. The defendant, Lyons, and an accomplice were suspected of the murder of a man, a woman, and their 4-year-old son. Lyons was arrested, questioned for 2 hours, and held incommunicado for 11 days. Then, he was questioned again for at least 8 hours, during which he was physically abused and threatened. He was even shown the bones of a murder victim. He then confessed.

Even though the *Lyons* decision was a setback for those concerned with the invidious nature of interrogations, the use of mental freedom put an issue on the table. Yes, the two decisions, *Ashcraft* and *Lyons,* so close and yet so disparate, illustrated how much justices could differ in their assumptions about the capacity of possibly innocent suspects to withstand coercive procedures. But they also opened the door for the justices in the *Miranda* appeal to reconsider the centrality of mental freedom.

How to Correct Abuses: The Choices Available to the Miranda *Justices*

The hope held by the justices contributing to the *Miranda* decision was that the institution of what came to be called "the *Miranda* rights" would curtail those abuses by the police that violated the Fifth Amendment right against self-incrimination. Directing this development was their belief that in the absence of safeguards, custodial interrogation was, as Justice Black had written, inherently coercive (White, 2001). The Court chose among several corrective procedures; for example, it could have required that an attorney representing the suspect be present at all interrogations, or it could have mandated the electronic recording of all questioning. But it chose to require that police ensure that the suspect knew of his or her constitutional rights, including those of remaining silent or demanding an attorney.

The Effect of *Miranda*

The justices who endorsed the *Miranda* warnings were concerned primarily about false confessions that resulted from police coercion. One wonders if in their private conferences they speculated about what percentage of suspects would waive their rights to remain silent or to have an attorney present. They probably would have been surprised to learn that about 80% would come to waive such rights (Leo, 1996a; Schulhofer, 1999). They doubtless assumed that some decrease in the number of confessions would occur, but they probably considered that a salutary outcome because the *Miranda* warning would be a safeguard against false self-incrimination. However, it should be noted that of the nine-person Court, only five of the justices adopted the *Miranda* warnings, and one of the minority justices, in a dissent, expressed an assumption that it would impede effective law enforcement, a viewpoint that was endorsed by a number of conservative scholars, journalists, and judges. Justice John Marshall Harlan II wrote:

> There can be little doubt that the Court's new code would markedly decrease the number of confessions . . . . How much harm this decision will inflict on law enforcement cannot fairly be predicted with accuracy . . . . We do know that some crimes cannot be solved without confessions . . . and that the Court is taking a real risk with society's welfare in imposing its new regime on the country. (*Miranda v. Arizona,* 1966, pp. 516–517)

Almost immediately, some law enforcement officials decried the decision, claiming it would stranglehold the police in their quest to solve crimes. Has the availability of *Miranda* warnings thwarted the police and reduced the conviction rate? Several viewpoints exist; these are described in detail by G. C. Thomas (1998). The first argues that the police have learned how to accommodate to the warning; some ways of doing so will be described in the last section of this chapter. Specifically, it has been observed that police became adept at introducing the warning so casually that suspects waive their rights without full knowledge; other police find ways to continue questioning suspects even after they refuse to answer. Observers of interrogations have concluded that one of the goals is to prevent the suspect from invoking his or her right to an attorney (Simon, 1991).

But two other positions have generated a long-running and acrimonious dispute. A former law clerk to Justice Scalia, Paul Cassell (1996a, 1996b; Cassell & Fowles, 1998; Cassell & Hayman, 1996), while a law professor at the University of Utah, accumulated extensive data that he interpreted as reflecting a reduced clearance rate after the institution of the *Miranda* warnings, meaning that a greater percentage of suspects (or, in the eyes of the police, criminals) are out on the streets. Cassell, who later became a federal district judge, maintained on the television program *60 Minutes* that *Miranda* was the most harmful decision to law enforcement in the last 50 years (White, 2001). One of Cassell's (1996b) articles concluded that *Miranda* "has resulted in a lost confession in one out of every six cases" (p. 417). He has also claimed that the incidence of false confessions is largely limited to those suspects who are mentally retarded or disturbed (Cassell, 1999). Others have disagreed, arguing that Cassell's conclusions are based on selective cases and that the actual declines in clearance rate are not so large (Schulhofer, 1996; White, 2001). Furthermore, as noted earlier, the majority of suspects—rightly or wrongly—waive their Miranda rights (Leo, 1996a; Schulhofer, 1999).

Another position, posited by G. C. Thomas (1998), is a *steady-state* theory that "*Miranda* persuades some suspects to make voluntary statements that sometimes turn out to be incriminating, at the same time that it permits roughly the same number of suspects to resist the inherent compulsion of police interrogation" (p. 323). As Kassin (1997) and G. C. Thomas (1998) have observed, differences in the data samples used and in the ideological viewpoints of the advocates have driven an extensive exchange in the literature about just how much *Miranda* has affected rates of confessions and convictions (Cassell, 1998, 1999; Cassell & Hayman, 1996; Leo & Ofshe, 1998; Ofshe & Leo, 1997). Although we all seek a society in which most criminals are apprehended and convicted, we differ with regard to the extent of costs and sacrifices we are willing to pay to achieve this goal. And we should not forget, as Leo (1996b) reminded us, that the presence of the *Miranda* rule has led to a civilizing effect on police practices and has increased the public's awareness of defendants' rights.

The Supreme Court's Response to the False Confession Phenomenon

The hope reflected in the Court's *Miranda* decision—that ensuring suspects their rights would eradicate the incidence of coerced false confessions—has not been fulfilled. Recent cases of wrongfully convicted persons who later are found innocent because of DNA analyses indicate that anywhere from 15% to 50% of the time such individuals falsely confessed after an interrogation. It may be assumed that many of these are a result of coercion (chaps. 1 and 2, this volume).

What can be done to control the continuing excesses of the police, and what has the Supreme Court done since *Miranda* to do so? In a recent review of research and expert testimony on interrogations and confessions, Costanzo and Leo (2007) suggested six possible solutions based on psychological research to the problems of coercion-instigated false confessions. These are the following: reform interrogation training, impose time limits on interrogations, videotape the entire interrogation process, limit lying about evidence and psychological trickery, require an appropriate adult to be present when interrogating a vulnerable suspect, and provide expert testimony on interrogations and confessions. The reader may note that these reforms deal with interrogation practices in general, so what do they have to do with *Miranda?* Each does; for example, trickery can surface in the timing or the method of giving the warning, experts can testify to the difficulties vulnerable suspects have in understanding their rights, and an advocate can be present to ensure the suspect fully comprehends his or her rights. The Supreme Court has recently made decisions relevant to these three proposed reforms (the last three on the above list are from Costanzo & Leo, 2007), so I will concentrate on these. In keeping with the theme of inconsistency in the Court's decisions, some of these Court decisions are congenial with psychological recommendations, and some are not.

Prohibiting Lying and Trickery by the Police

For many years, the Supreme Court failed to deal with the use of trickery by the police. Until 2004, the only decision that was anywhere close to relevant was that of *Frazier v. Cupp* (1969), decided more than 30 years ago. In this case, the police did lie to the defendant, Martin E. Frazier, telling him that his cousin Jerry Rawls had confessed and implicated Frazier in a murder. Frazier did eventually confess, only later to recant. One of the grounds for the appeal of his conviction was the trickery used by the police detectives. The decision by the Court is noteworthy, if that is the word, because Frazier's appeal was rejected in an opinion written by Justice Thurgood Marshall, who argued that the "totality of circumstances" led to a conclusion that Frazier's confession was voluntary even though the police had misrepresented what Rawls had said to them (*Frazier v. Cupp,* 1969, p. 739). For example, the interrogation was rather brief (45 minutes), it was tape-recorded, and the lie by the police did not seem to be the aspect that instigated Frazier to confess (Sasaki, 1988; J. G. Thomas, 1979).

What is most important about this decision, however, is that lower courts came to rely on it as a definitive ruling that police trickery is "a mere factor to be included in a court's assessment of a confession's voluntariness under a totality of circumstances analysis" (Sasaki, 1988, p. 1608). And the Inbau and Reid manual regarded the *Frazier* decision as tacit approval of trickery, claiming that *Frazier* and many other cases, state and federal, upheld the legal validity of trickery and deceit. The latest edition of the manual (Inbau, Reid, Buckley &

Jayne, 2001) continues to provide police with tricks like those in *Frazier* as well as other types to be illustrated later in this chapter.

Recently, the Supreme Court took steps to stifle at least certain types of trickery by the police; the case was that of *Missouri v. Seibert,* decided in 2004. Patrice Seibert, of Rolla, Missouri, was considered by the police to be an accomplice in an act of arson of her own trailer home that caused the death of Donald Rector, age 17, who lived with the family and took care of Seibert's disabled son. When a police officer was sent to arrest Seibert, his supervisor specifically instructed the officer not to advise her of her *Miranda* rights. She was taken to the police station, placed in a small interrogation room, and questioned. After about 20 to 30 minutes, she confessed to her role in setting the fire. Then, after a brief break, the interrogation was continued, now with a tape recorder, and Seibert was at this point advised of her *Miranda* rights. She signed the waiver form and confessed once again. The trial judge did not allow the first confession into evidence but did allow the second. After Seibert's conviction and sentence of life in prison, she appealed. On June 28, 2004, the Supreme Court, by a 5 to 4 vote, ruled in Seibert's favor. Justice David Souter, in the opinion for the Court, wrote that the facts of the case "by any objective measure reveal police strategy adapted to undermine the *Miranda* warnings" (*Missouri v. Seibert,* 2004, p. 2612). It would be natural for a suspect, having confessed once, to confess again, Souter reasoned. Furthermore, she "would not have understood that she retained a choice about continuing to talk" (p. 2613).

For many of us, this sounds like a sensible decision as well as one that preserves the original intent of providing *Miranda* rights to suspects, but I remind you that it passed by the narrowest of margins: 5 to 4. The dissenting opinion in this case written by Justice O'Connor and joined by Justices Rehnquist, Scalia, and Thomas, carried no weight as legal precedent, but it is worthy of note because it gave a different rationale for deciding the case. Justice O'Connor wrote that the intent of the police officers should make no difference "because a suspect could not know what was in the officer's mind" (*Missouri v. Seibert,* 2004, p. 2618). Rather, the test should be the voluntariness of the second set of statements: If Seibert gave them voluntarily, they should have been admitted.

Thus, the reproach given by the majority of the justices in the *Seibert* decision was in many respects a tenuous victory for *Miranda.* There is no guarantee it will survive as a precedent, given the present composition of the Court. In fact, on the same day that the Court decided *Seibert,* it ruled on another case involving *Miranda* warnings and ruled in the opposite direction. In the case of *United States v. Patane* (2004), federal agents went to Samuel Patane's house in Colorado Springs because they had a report that he illegally possessed a gun. Before they could finish reading Patane his *Miranda* rights he interrupted them, saying he knew his rights. So the agents stopped giving the warning and asked—persistently—about the location of the gun. Patane then directed them to the gun in the bedroom. After his conviction, he appealed. But the Supreme Court ruled (again, by a 5 to 4 vote) that physical evidence should not be thrown out simply because it was obtained from a suspect who had not waived his *Miranda* rights.

The Admissibility of an Expert Witness

I wish now to turn to the second of Costanzo and Leo's (2007) recommendations for which the Supreme Court has made a relevant ruling. At a trial, confession evidence introduced by the prosecution has a powerful influence on the decisions made by the jury, even if the defendant takes the stand to recant (Leo, 1996a; Wrightsman & Kassin, 1993). Costanzo and Leo listed four ways in which an expert witness can aid a jury:

1. By describing the psychological research literature indicating the possibility—and estimated prevalence of—police-induced false confessions;
2. By demonstrating the impact of particular interrogation methods (removal of support, minimization, apparent sympathy, lying, suggesting benefits from confessing, etc.) on the result of confessing falsely;
3. By identifying qualities within the suspect that increase the risk of false confession (youth, mental limitations, naiveté, etc.);
4. By questioning the fit between the suspect's story and the actual facts of the crime (p. 94).

In its decision in the case of *Crane v. Kentucky* (1986), the Supreme Court opened the door for the admissibility of expert testimony in cases with a disputed confession. The facts of the crime and the subsequent investigation are all too familiar to those of us concerned with the abundance of coerced false confessions. During the robbery of a liquor store in Louisville, a clerk was killed. The absence of physical evidence stifled the police in their search for a suspect. But a week after the murder, Major Crane, age 16, was arrested in connection with an unrelated robbery, that of a filling station. After a long interrogation, Crane confessed to committing several robberies and the shooting of a police officer. He initially denied any participation in the murder of the liquor store clerk but eventually confessed to that crime as well. He later recanted his confession.

In a preliminary hearing, the judge ruled the confession to be voluntary, so when Crane's defense attorney sought to introduce evidence at the trial about the coercive nature of the interrogation, the request was denied. This ruling came in the face of much ambiguity about the validity of the confession, which not incidentally was not taped (Fulero, 2004). Costanzo and Leo (2007) wrote:

> Mr. Crane [claimed that he] had been held in a small, windowless room, interrogators denied his repeated requests to telephone his mother, he was interrogated for several hours, as many as six police officers in the interrogation room at the same time, and the police interrogators behaved in an intimidating manner. (p. 83)

Many of the details of the robbery that were given by Crane were inconsistent with the facts of the case; for example, he said it occurred during the day, when in fact it occurred at 10:40 p.m.; he said he took money from the cash register, when in fact none was taken (Fulero, 2004).

When Crane appealed, the Kentucky Supreme Court ruled that the trial judge did not err in excluding this testimony, but the United States Supreme

Court disagreed and ordered a new trial. The decision, authored by Justice O'Connor, was brief—only six pages—and was unanimous. The Court held that "certain interrogation techniques, either in isolation, or as applied to the unique characteristics of a particular suspect, are so offensive for a civilized system of justice that they must be condemned under the Due Process Clause of the Fourteenth Amendment" (*Crane v. Kentucky,* 1986, p. 684). Recognizing the power of confession evidence on jurors' verdicts, Justice O'Connor's opinion for the Court went on to say:

> A defendant's case may stand or fall on his ability to convince the jury that the manner in which the confession was obtained casts doubt on its credibility . . . . Stripped of the power to describe to the jury the circumstances that prompted his confession, the defendant is effectively disabled from answering the one question every rational juror needs answered: If the defendant is innocent, why did he previously admit his guilt? (*Crane v. Kentucky,* 1986, p. 688)

Thus, the Supreme Court said that the state may not exclude "competent, reliable evidence bearing on the credibility of a confession when such evidence is central to the defendant's claim of innocence" (p. 683). But it left unresolved what form the evidence could take (Fulero, 2004). Since that decision, trial courts and lower appellate courts have differed with regard to their admissibility of expert witnesses. Fulero's chapter (13) in this volume and other recent publications (Fulero, 2008; Fulero & Everington, 2004) deal with this issue.

Appropriate Adult Present at Interrogations of a Vulnerable Suspect

Costanzo and Leo (2007) noted that in England and Wales the Police and Criminal Evidence Act of 1986 requires that an appropriate adult be present when the police are interrogating a vulnerable suspect. *Vulnerable* would include juveniles as well as suspects known to have mental illness or mental retardation. Several other chapters in this volume, including those by Gudjonsson (chap. 2), Leo and Drizin (chap. 1), and Reppucci, Meyer, and Kostelnik (chap. 4), identify the problems of ensuring that confessions from vulnerable suspects are legitimate. It is unfortunate that the United States Supreme Court has not been responsive to such concerns. The decision in *Yarborough v. Alvarado* (2004) is a recent example.

Like Major Crane, Michael Alvarado was a minor. Alvarado was involved in an attempt to steal a truck, during which Alvarado's accomplice, Paul Soto, shot and killed the truck's owner. Alvarado helped hide the gun used by Soto. The Los Angeles County detective who was investigating the crime asked Alvarado to come to the sheriff's office for questioning. He dutifully appeared, with his parents, who waited in the lobby while he was questioned. After first denying involvement, during a 2-hour interrogation Alvarado eventually confessed to his role in the crime. He was not read his *Miranda* rights at any time during the questioning. At trial, both he and Soto were found guilty of first-degree murder and attempted robbery, but Alvarado's crime was later reduced to second-degree murder because of his lesser role in the act. On appeal, Alvarado's case was first rejected at the district court level; here, the judge concluded that Alvarado was not in custody and hence did not require being Mirandized while he was questioned. But the United States Court of Appeals for the Ninth Circuit reversed this decision, concluding that Alvarado's youth and inexperience should have been taken into account when deciding whether a reasonable person in such a situation would feel free to leave the interview. Thus, the State of California appealed the matter to the United States Supreme Court.

The Supreme Court, by a 5 to 4 vote, reinstated Alvarado's murder conviction, concluding that the original California court was not in error. According to the opinion of the Supreme Court, he was not in custody and hence issues of youth and inexperience were irrelevant. Justice Kennedy's majority opinion noted that "our court has not stated that a suspect's age or experience is relevant to the *Miranda* custody analysis" (*Yarborough v. Alvarado,* 2004, p. 2150). In a dissent with which most psychologists would agree, Justice Stephen Breyer wrote that the majority opinion defied "ordinary common sense." He asked:

> What reasonable person in the circumstances—brought to a police station by his parents at police request, put in a small interrogation room, questioned for a solid two hours, and confronted with claims that there is strong evidence that he participated in a serious crime—could have thought to himself, 'Well, anytime I want to leave I can just get up and walk out'? (p. 2153)

Let us grant that the original *Miranda* decision dealt solely with questioning that occurred while the suspect was in custody. But at least for lay people, *custody* is a vague concept. Even Justice Kennedy's majority opinion in the *Alvarado* case acknowledged that "fair-minded jurists could disagree over whether Alvarado was in custody" (p. 2143). In previous decisions, the Court has used the *reasonable person* standard: Does a reasonable person feel at liberty to terminate the interrogation and leave? Always the fair-minded jurist himself, Justice Kennedy, in his opinion for the Court, listed facts on either side of the custody or not custody question. The following facts, in his view, "weigh against a finding that Alvarado was in custody":

1. The police did not transport him to the police station or require him to appear at a particular time.
2. They did not threaten him or suggest he would be placed under arrest.
3. His parents remained in the lobby during the questioning, suggesting that the interview would be brief.
4. The detective appealed to Alvarado's interest in telling the truth and being helpful to a police officer.
5. The detective twice asked him if he wanted a break.
6. At the end of the interview he went home.

Other facts point in the opposite direction:

1. Alvarado was interviewed at the police station.
2. He was not told he was free to leave.

3. He was brought to the police station by his legal guardians, rather than appearing of his own accord.
4. His parents were rebuffed when they asked to sit in on the interview (*Yarborough v. Alvarado,* 2004).

The Short-Term Future of Miranda *Rights in the Courts*

Whereas the Warren Court, in the *Miranda* decision, expanded the protections to suspects undergoing a custodial interrogation, the general thrust of the Burger and Rehnquist Courts was to diminish the breadth and applicability of these protections. In a chapter published in 1978, Geoffrey Stone foretold the pattern for the next 2 decades:

> It would be an understatement to say that the Burger Court has taken a dim view of *Miranda.* The Court has stated that the principles underlying *Miranda* are not to be extended beyond the sort of custodial interrogation involved in *Miranda* itself, and it has narrowly defined the concept of "custodial interroga-tion." It has declared that evidence obtained without compliance with the *Miranda* safeguards is admissible in any proceeding other than a criminal prosecution, and it has held that such evidence is admissible even in a crimi-nal prosecution if used for the purpose of impeachment. It has embraced an uncertain standard for determining when the police may renew efforts to inter-rogate an individual who previously asserted his right to remain silent, and it has impliedly undercut *Miranda's* requirement of a "knowing and intelligent" waiver. It has hinted that evidence obtained in violation of *Miranda* will be excluded only if the police did not act in good faith, and it has announced that the *Miranda* safeguards are not derived from the privilege against compelled self-incrimination. Although the results in these cases are consistent, in that the Court has steadfastly declined to exclude even a single item of evidence on the authority of *Miranda,* the decisions do not appear to rest on any unifying, coherent principle other than a fundamental rejection of the premises of *Miranda* and an apparent desire to return, ultimately, to the "voluntariness" standard. (p. 168)

The Dickerson *Case*

The conservative Rehnquist Court did, in the year 2000, have an opportunity to eliminate a *Miranda* requirement entirely. The appeal was *Dickerson v. United States* (2000), based on an action by the police that relied on a little-known and generally ignored act of Congress, which had made voluntariness the sole test for the admissibility of confessions in federal trials; this law stated that the presence or absence of a warning of the suspect's right to remain silent and a right to assis-tance of counsel "need not be conclusive on the issue of voluntariness of confes-sions" (18 U.S. C. #3501[b]).

Thus, the intent was to substitute a due process test for the *Miranda* warn-ings. It should be noted that this statute had its origin in President Nixon's 1968 criticism of *Miranda;* in a position paper he urged Congress to enact leg-islation that "would leave it to the judge and jury to determine both the volun-tariness and the validity of any confession" (White, 2001, p. 57). In 1999, the

Fourth Circuit, in a decision inconsistent with the position of the Department of Justice, held that the law was constitutional, thus affirming an interrogation of Charles Dickerson that had been carried out without giving him his *Miranda* warnings.

When this matter came before the Supreme Court, most observers felt the decision could go either way. Justices Stevens, Souter, Ginsburg, and Breyer seemed quite likely to support Dickerson's appeal and uphold the *Miranda* warnings as constitutional. Justices Rehnquist, Scalia, and Thomas seemed likely to uphold the act of Congress, given their lack of sympathy for the rights of defendants. Justices O'Connor and Kennedy were less predictable; their votes on previous cases described in this chapter reflect how they were less ideology driven than the other justices. Thus, Court watchers expected a 5 to 4 vote, but it was uncertain in which direction.

The actual vote was a surprise: 7 to 2 to uphold *Miranda* and reject the act of Congress. The opinion for the Court was written by Chief Justice Rehnquist, who had been on the record as a staunch opponent of broadening defendants' rights. Only Justices Scalia and Thomas were in the minority. As Yale Kamisar (2000) observed, Justice Rehnquist's opinion reads "almost as if he had reread the original *Miranda* opinion recently and discerned facts about it and its companion cases and language that he had not noticed before" (p. A18).

Why did this surprising outcome happen? Three themes emerge from Chief Justice Rehnquist's opinion. First, *Miranda* "warnings have become a part of our national culture" (*Dickerson v. United States*, 2000, p. 2336). Second, erosions in the *Miranda* warnings made since its adoption in 1966 have made it a more acceptable procedure. But the third theme (and perhaps the determinative one) reflected a desire to squelch Congress's efforts to make laws that reflect its interpretation of what the Constitution says (Greenhouse, 2000). The opinion seemed to be saying to Congress: Don't tell the Supreme Court what is or is not in the Constitution—that's the Court's job, not yours. In that sense, the thrust of the *Dickerson* decision was consistent with other decisions by the Court while Rehnquist was Chief Justice—those that restricted or even rejected acts of Congress that violated articles of the Constitution and especially the sovereign immunity of the individual states (Greenhouse, 2002).

Thus, *Miranda,* in the year 2000, survived for the time being. But the composition of the Court has changed, and new cases bubbling up from the lower courts always pose a threat to its endurance. Two justices who participated in the *Dickerson* decision are no longer on the Court, replaced by Chief Justice Roberts and Justice Alito. On the basis of their votes in recent criminal cases, they appear to be unsympathetic to defendants' rights.

Miranda is Not Enough

The United States has had *Miranda* rights for more than 40 years. Certainly some excesses by the police have been abolished or reduced. For example, videotaped interrogations (or at least confessions) are required by six states in some or all felony cases, and a number of jurisdictions are voluntarily taping interrogations (see chap. 8, this volume). This permits jurors to see if browbeating, lying, or other unseemly tactics are used. But some police continue to circumvent the *Miranda* rights of suspects, as recent examples reflect. One technique is to encourage the waiver of rights by presenting them in a palatable manner. Chapter 7 of White's (2001) book classifies these into four categories and presents examples:

1. Delivering *Miranda* warnings in a neutral or low-keyed manner;
2. De-emphasizing the significance of the *Miranda* warnings (for example, implying they are an unimportant bureaucratic ritual);
3. Providing suspects opportunities to tell their side of the story; and
4. Convincing suspects that the interrogator is acting in their best interests.

But what if the suspect wants to remain silent? How does a police officer respond? Some interrogators simply leave the suspect alone for a while "to stew in his cell" in the hopes that the suspect will have a change of mind. The Inbau and Reid (1962) manual, for example, advises "to concede him the right to remain silent" but then suggests that the police officer should point out the significance of a failure to talk:

> Joe, you have the right to remain silent. That's your privilege and I'm the last person in the world who'd try to take it away from you. If that's the way you want to leave this, ok. But let me ask you this. Suppose you were in my shoes and I were in yours and you called me in to ask me about this and I told you, "I don't want to answer any of your questions." You'd think I had something to hide, and you'd probably be right in thinking that. That's exactly what I'll have to think about you, and so will everybody else. So let's sit here and talk this whole thing over. (p. 111)

According to Inbau and Reid (1962), when handled in this manner, "except for the career criminal, there are very few persons who will persist in their refusal to talk" (p. 112).

One of the most pernicious decisions by the Supreme Court post-*Miranda* dealt with a situation in which the suspect invoked his right to remain silent. The police terminated the conversation, but a few minutes later the suspect said to the officer, "Well, what's going to happen to me now?" The detective then attempted once more to get a waiver. In *Oregon v. Bradshaw* (1983), the Court ruled that the suspect's question reflected a re-initiation of an interaction and "although ambiguous . . . [it] evinced a willingness and desire for a generalized discussion about the investigation" (*Oregon v. Bradshaw,* 1983, pp. 1043–1044).

What if the suspect asks for an attorney? Inbau and Reid (1962) also had a rejoinder in this situation. The interrogator should suggest that the suspect can save himself or herself the expense of this professional service, "particularly if he [sic] is innocent of the offense under investigation." They suggested that the police officer might add, "Joe, I'm only looking for the truth, and if you're telling me the truth, that's it. You can handle this by yourself" (Inbau & Reid, 1962, p. 112).

Several sets of scholars (Drizin & Colgan, 2004; Wiggins & Wheatman, 2004) have suggested how psychological research can be brought to bear on policy issues. Here, I offer three recommendations for action by the Supreme Court.

Awareness of Vulnerable Suspects

Empirical work, specifically the detailed analysis of factors that produce false confessions by Leo and Ofshe (1998) and Drizin and Leo (2004), leads to the conclusion that two factors are especially important: a lengthy interrogation and a mentally handicapped or youthful suspect (see also White, 2001). The Court needs to reconsider the issue that it dispensed with too casually in *Yarborough v. Alvarado* (2004). It needs to recognize, as illustrated by earlier studies (Drizin & Colgan, 2004; Fulero & Everington, 2004; Redlich, Silverman, Chen, & Steiner, 2004) and in other chapters of this book, that interrogations play on the vulnerabilities of the mentally disabled and the young. The Court needs to remind itself of its conclusion in *Ashcraft v. Tennessee* (1944), more than 60 years ago, that interrogations are "inherently coercive" (p. 154) and thus extended interrogations "will automatically render a confession involuntary" (White, 2001, p. 203). From Leo and Ofshe's (1998) analysis, an interrogation of 6 hours appears to be the "tipping point." The problem of vulnerable suspects is compounded by the fact that the Court has never regulated the wording of the warnings, and among the 17,000 police jurisdictions in the United States there are now literally hundreds of different variations, some as long as 400 words, many of which have a required reading level much above that of the typical suspect (see Rogers, Hazelwood, Sewell, Shuman, & Blackwood, 2008).

Taking a Stand Against Deceit

Back in the 1950s, the Supreme Court in two cases (*Leyra v. Denno,* 1954; *Spano v. New York,* 1959) expressed its disapproval of the use of deception and manipulation of emotions to elicit a confession. Although it has been suggested that the rationale for the Court's overturning convictions may have stemmed from other aspects (Grano, 1993; Hancock, 1996), still, as White (2001) observed, these cases "could provide a starting point for identifying improper police practices" (p. 47). It should be recognized that even some conservatives who have been on the Court recently have expressed concern (Justice O'Connor's decision in *Crane v. Kentucky,* 1986, recognized the possibility of a confession being coerced). In the majority opinion in a frequently cited case, *Colorado v. Connelly* (1986), Chief Justice Rehnquist acknowledged that "certain interrogation techniques, either in isolation or as applied to the unique characteristics of a particular suspect, are so offensive to a civilized system of justice that they must be condemned" (p. 163).

Psychologists can help by determining public opinion about deceptive police tactics (Wiggins & Wheatman, 2004; Zimbardo, 1967, 1971). At what point do police tactics become morally abhorrent to a majority of citizens? What types of trickery have a greater potential for generating a false confession? What tricks are most offensive? Telling a suspect he lied on a polygraph test? That fictitious witnesses identified him in a lineup? That his wife and children will be interrogated if he fails to confess?

If the justices were made aware of the concern of the public about police deception, they might be willing to act. It takes only four of the justices to grant certiorari to an appeal. If cert is granted to a case in which a defendant has been convicted after having been lied to by the police, it is possible that Justice Kennedy, currently the justice least entrenched in an ideology, might side with the four relative liberals. For example, even though Justice Kennedy sided with the conservatives two thirds of the time in 5 to 4 decisions (2006–2007 term), he sided with the liberals in all five of the cases that involved appeals from defendants on death row.

Requiring an Attorney to Be Present

When the justices, back in 1966, considered remedies for the abuses of police interrogations, one that they considered but discarded was the requirement that an attorney be present. The Sixth Amendment permits the right to counsel. But the Court in 1966 essentially "abandoned [requiring this] as a solution to pre-indictment interrogation" (Leo & Thomas, 1998, p. 37) and instead substituted the Fifth Amendment right to avoid answering questions. The presence of an attorney would facilitate the goal of the suspect knowingly undertaking his or her options as aspired to by the Court's *Miranda* decision. It is interesting that in the decision in *Spano v. New York* (1959), several justices had suggested that an arrested suspect should have an attorney present at pretrial questioning. The British system now requires this. What if the Court had adopted this requirement?

Two objections would immediately be made. First, it would be said that most suspects who are arrested are guilty, and many of them are willing to confess without prompting. So why not have an attorney meet with each privately, and if the suspect voluntarily indicates a desire to confess, the attorney withdraws. Second, this requirement would place a burden on overworked public defenders and other defense attorneys. But suspects have a right to attorneys at lineups, a time-consuming activity for the defense counsel. It is time to reconsider this option.

Conclusion

The previous section considered revisions of *Miranda* that might be initiated by a Court that was sensitive to a defendant's rights. But the current court is not; in the just completed term, of 11 cases involving defendants' rights, eight of the rulings were against the defendant (these included the use of the insanity plea, incompetence of representation, and search-and-seizure issues). So it is appropriate to ask, What is the likelihood of the Court completely overturning *Miranda,* perhaps in response to one of the appeals described earlier that were recently decided at the circuit-court level?

Miranda avoided an overturn in 2000 in the *Dickerson v. United States* case, but perhaps for turf war issues more than anything else. The two justices who were in the minority in 2000, Justices Scalia and Thomas, are still on the Court, and one of the results of the conservative surge on the Court in last year's term was greater audacity by each of these two justices (expressed in concurring opinions) in which they sought a complete overturn of established liberal precedents.

Predicting future votes and decisions by the Court is a tricky enterprise, but I believe that for the time being the Court will continue to endorse *Miranda* and will support a position expressed in the Court's opinion in *Moran v. Burbine* (1986), written by Justice O'Connor, that the use of *Miranda* warnings offers a good balance between the needs of society and the rights of suspects.

References

Ashcraft v. Tennessee, 322 U.S. 143 (1944).

Brown v. Mississippi, 297 U.S. 278 (1936).

Cassell, P. G. (1996a). All benefits, no costs: The grand illusion of *Miranda's* defenders. *Northwestern University Law Review, 90,* 1084–1124.

Cassell, P. G. (1996b). *Miranda's* social costs: An empirical reassessment. *Northwestern University Law Review, 90,* 387–499.

Cassell, P. G. (1998). Protecting the innocent from false confessions and lost confessions—and from *Miranda. Journal of Criminal Law & Criminology, 88,* 497–556.

Cassell, P. G. (1999). The guilty and the "innocent": An examination of alleged cases of wrongful conviction from false confessions. *Harvard Journal of Law & Public Policy, 22,* 523–603.

Cassell, P. G., & Fowles, R. (1998). Handcuffing the cops? A thirty-year perspective on *Miranda's* harmful effects on law enforcement. *Stanford Law Review, 50,* 1055–1146.

Cassell, P. G., & Hayman, B. S. (1996). Police interrogation in the 1990s: An empirical study of the effects of *Miranda. UCLA Law Review, 43,* 839–931.

Chambers v. Florida, 309 U.S. 227 (1940).

Colorado v. Connelly, 479 U.S. 157 (1986).

Costanzo, M., & Leo, R. A. (2007). Research and expert testimony on interrogations and confessions. In M. Costanzo, D. Krauss, & K. Pedzek (Eds.), *Expert psychological testimony for the courts* (pp. 69–98). Mahwah, NJ: Erlbaum.

Crane v. Kentucky, 476 U.S. 683 (1986).

Dickerson v. United States, 120 S.Ct. 2326 (2000).

Drizin, S. A., & Colgan, B. A. (2004). Tales from the juvenile confession front. In G. D. Lassiter (Ed.), *Interrogations, confessions, and entrapment* (pp. 127–162). New York: Kluwer Academic/ Plenum.

Drizin, S. A., & Leo, R. A. (2004). The problem of false confessions in the post-DNA world. *North Carolina Law Review, 82,* 891–1007.

Frazier v. Cupp, 394 U.S. 731 (1969).

Fulero, S. M. (2004). Expert psychological testimony on the psychology of interrogations and confessions. In G. D. Lassiter (Ed.), *Interrogations, confessions, and entrapment* (pp. 247–263). New York: Kluwer Academic/Plenum.

Fulero, S. M. (2008, August). *Case law of expert testimony regarding Miranda competency and suggestibility.* Paper presented at the meeting of the American Psychological Association, Boston, MA.

Fulero, S, M., & Everington, C. (2004). Mental retardation, competency to waive Miranda rights, and false confessions. In G. D. Lassiter (Ed.), *Interrogations, confessions, and entrapment* (pp. 163–174). New York: Kluwer Academic/Plenum.

Grano, J. D. (1993). *Confessions, truth and the law.* Ann Arbor: University of Michigan Press.

Greenhouse, L. (2000, June 28). A turf battle's victim. *New York Times,* pp. A1, A20.

Greenhouse, L. (2002, July 2). Court had Rehnquist's initials intricately carved on docket. *New York Times,* p. A14.

Hancock, C. (1996). Due process before *Miranda. Tulsa Law Review, 70,* 2195–2222.

Inbau, F. E., & Reid, J. E. (1962). *Criminal interrogation and confessions.* Baltimore: Williams & Wilkins.

Inbau, F. E., Reid, J. E., Buckley, J. P., & Jayne, B. C. (2001). *Criminal interrogation and confessions* (4th ed.). Gaithersburg, MD: Aspen Publishers.

Kamisar, Y. (2000, July 17). Your sort-of right to remain silent. *National Law Journal,* p. A18.

Kassin, S. M. (1997). The psychology of confession evidence. *American Psychologist, 52,* 221–233.

Leo, R. A. (1996a). *Miranda's* revenge: Police interrogation as a confidence game. *Law & Society Review, 30,* 259–288.

Leo, R. A. (1996b). The impact of *Miranda* revisited. *Journal of Criminal Law & Criminology, 88,* 557–577.

Leo, R. A. (2008). *Police interrogation and American justice.* Cambridge, MA: Harvard University Press.

Leo, R. A., & Ofshe, R. J. (1998). The consequences of false confessions: Deprivations of liberty and miscarriages of justice in the age of psychological interrogation. *Journal of Criminal Law & Criminology, 88,* 429–496.

Leo, R. A., & Thomas, G. C., III. (Eds.). (1998). *The Miranda debate: Law, justice, and policing.* Boston: Northeastern University Press.

Lyons v. Oklahoma, 322 U.S. 596 (1944).

Miranda v. Arizona, 384 U.S. 436 (1966).

Missouri v. Seibert, 124 S.Ct. 2601 (2004).

Moran v. Burbine, 475 U.S. 412 (1986).

Ofshe, R. J., & Leo, R. A. (1997). The social psychology of police interrogation: The theory and classification of true and false confessions. *Studies in Law, Politics, & Society, 16,* 189–251.

Oregon v. Bradshaw, 462 U.S. 1039 (1983).

Redlich, A. D., Silverman, M., Chen. J., & Steiner, H. (2004). The police interrogation of children and adolescents. In G. D. Lassiter (Ed.), *Interrogations, confessions, and entrapment* (pp. 107–125). New York: Kluwer Academic/Plenum.

Rogers, R., Hazelwood, L. L., Sewell, K. W., Shuman, D. W., & Blackwood, H. L. (2008). The comprehensibility and content of juvenile Miranda warnings. *Psychology, Public Policy, & Law, 14,* 63–87.

Sasaki, D. W. (1988). Guarding the guardians: Police trickery and confessions. *Stanford Law Review, 40,* 1593–1616.

Schulhofer, S. J. (1996). *Miranda's* practical effect: Substantial benefits and vanishingly small social costs. *Northwestern University Law Review, 90,* 500–564.

Schulhofer, S. J. (1999, March 1). "Miranda" now on endangered species list. *National Law Journal,* p. A22.

Simon, D. (1991). *Homicide: A year on the killing streets.* New York: Ivy Books.

Spano v. New York, 360 U.S. 315 (1959).

Stone, G. R. (1978). The *Miranda* doctrine in the Supreme Court. In P. B. Kurland & G. Casper (Eds.), *The Supreme Court review 1977* (pp. 99–169). Chicago: University of Chicago Press.

Thomas, G. C., III. (1998). The twenty-first century: A world without *Miranda?* In R. A. Leo & G. C. Thomas, III. (Eds.), *The Miranda debate: Law, justice, and policy* (pp. 314–328). Boston: Northeastern University Press.

Thomas, J. G. (1979). Police use of trickery as an interrogation technique. *Vanderbilt Law Review, 32,* 1167–1213.

United States v. Patane, 124 S.Ct. 2620 (2004).

White, W. S. (2001). *Miranda's waning protections: Police interrogation practices after Dickerson.* Ann Arbor: University of Michigan Press.

Wiggins, E. C., & Wheatman, S. R. (2004). What's a concerned psychologist to do? Translating the research on interrogations, confessions, and entrapment into policy. In G. D. Lassiter (Ed.), *Interrogations, confessions, and entrapment* (pp. 265–280). New York: Kluwer.

Wrightsman, L. S., & Kassin, S. M. (1993). *Confessions in the courtroom.* Newbury Park, CA: Sage.

Yarborough v. Alvarado, 124 S.Ct. 2140 (2004).

Zimbardo, P. G. (1967). The psychology of police confessions. *Psychology Today, 1,* 17–20.

Zimbardo, P. G. (1971). Coercion and compliance: The psychology of police confessions. In R. Perruci & M. Pilisuk (Eds.), *The triple revolution emerging* (pp. 492–508). Boston: Little.

11

Oral *Miranda* Warnings: A Checklist and a Model Presentation

Gregory DeClue

This chapter presents tools that should be useful for psychologists conducting assessments relevant to legal questions in criminal cases in which a defendant disputes an admission or confession taken during police questioning (see also chap. 12, this volume). It briefly considers broad issues in psychological assessments in disputed confession cases as well as general approaches to questions relevant to *Miranda* warning and waiver. In light of these considerations, the chapter then introduces a new checklist and model presentation for use in cases in which the *Miranda* warnings and waiver were electronically recorded.

Broad Considerations

A review of psychological and legal literature (DeClue, 2005a, 2005b) suggests that disputed confession cases will most likely require psychologists to provide relevant testimony on the following legal issues:

- Did the state fail to prove, by a preponderance of the evidence, that the defendant knowingly, intelligently, and voluntarily waived his or her *Miranda* rights?
- Did the state fail to prove, by a preponderance of the evidence, that the defendant's supposed confession was freely and voluntarily made under the totality of the circumstances?
- Should the court suppress the defendant's coerced statements to the police because they are so highly unreliable and virtually uncorroborated?
- Should the jury give little or no weight to the defendant's statements because they are so highly unreliable?

These questions are in the form that would be presented to the judge. The questions posed to a testifying psychologist would be in a different form, but they would be designed to produce testimony that would be relevant to the question ultimately considered by the judge or jury.

Some psychologists, by virtue of their knowledge, training, and experience, are able to assist the court in each of the following areas:

1. Gather and analyze information regarding "the physical and psychological environment in which the [waiver] was obtained" (*Crane v. Kentucky,* 1986, p. 684).
2. Assess the defendant's current mental status, including intelligence, memory, reading comprehension, listening comprehension, and psychopathology, if any.
3. Reconstruct the defendant's mental state at the time of the waiver, similar to the type of assessment in insanity and other evaluations of mental state at the time of the offense (see Rogers & Shuman, 2000).
4. Assist the judge in understanding interactions among the above.

(For recommended assessment procedures, see DeClue, 2005a, especially chap. 8, including Assessment Procedures beginning on p. 147 and the "Soddi Jones" sample report in the appendix.)

Miranda Waiver: General Approaches

The U.S. Supreme Court decided more than 40 years ago that interrogation of a person in police custody can only occur if police advise the person of certain rights guaranteed by the Constitution and warn the suspect that the police are about to embark on an enterprise that without the person's permission would clearly violate those constitutional rights (*Miranda v. Arizona,* 1966). *Miranda* requires that the contents of the warnings be stated in "clear and unambiguous language" lest the process devolve into "empty formalities" (p. 468).

Requirements for a valid waiver of *Miranda* rights are described in *Colorado v. Spring* (1987):

> First, the relinquishment of the right must have been voluntary in the sense that it was the product of a free and deliberate choice rather than intimidation, coercion, or deception. Second, *the waiver must have been made with a full awareness both of the nature of the right being abandoned and the consequences of the decision to abandon it* [italics added]. Only if the "totality of the circumstances surrounding the interrogation" reveals both an uncoerced choice and the requisite level of comprehension may a court properly conclude that the Miranda rights have been waived. (p. 573)

Orally Presented *Miranda* Warnings

Psychologists can play an important role in gathering evidence regarding a defendant's current understanding of *Miranda* rights, along with current intelligence, achievement, and various personality test scores (DeClue, 2005a). But more and more interrogations are being recorded, allowing an opportunity for detectives to create a record that clearly shows whether and to what extent a suspect understands his or her *Miranda* rights. The remainder of this chapter focuses on how psychologists can assist in cases in which the *Miranda* warning and waiver were electronically recorded.

Examples

Three recent cases illustrate interrogators' opportunity to show whether a suspect waived his rights, and if so, whether it was a knowing, intelligent, and voluntary waiver. These cases show that police vary considerably in the extent to which they elicit pertinent information. In each case, the interrogation was video recorded. (Each case involves different police in different jurisdictions.)

C. is a 43-year-old man with average intelligence. Police suspected him of capital sexual battery. The audio portion of the video-recording equipment was not working during the initial part of the interview, and it was during that time that the detective read *Miranda* rights to C. The police were aware of the problem with the audio equipment (it produced white noise) and fixed it after about 10 minutes. Just after the noise abated, the detective commented about the audio difficulty, announced that C. had been read his rights, and moved on. This illustrates how little importance some police officers place on the opportunity to create a record that shows whether and to what extent a suspect's "waiver [was] made with a full awareness both of the nature of the right being abandoned and the consequences of the decision to abandon it" (*Colorado v. Spring,* 1987, p. 573). Suspect C. had signed a *Miranda* form, and that was that. Although the video- and audio-recording equipment was now working properly, the detective made no effort to memorialize C.'s understanding regarding his rights; he proceeded with the interrogation. See Exhibit 11.1 for a transcript of the relevant portion from the video recording.

T. is a 16-year-old male with average intelligence, attention-deficit disorder, and a learning disability. Police suspected him of committing murder. A detective deliberately downplayed the importance of the *Miranda* rights,

---

Exhibit 11.1.   Excerpt From the Transcript of the Interrogation of C.

Detective A: All right, we'll go ahead and get started. . . . C, raise your right hand. You swear the statement you're about to give is gonna be the truth, nothing but the truth?

    C.:   Yes.

Detective A: Okay. (to Detective B) I got him to sign here. He signed his *Miranda.* So that's good. Can you witness this for me real quick?

Detective B: (to C) This is your signature right here?

    C.:   Yes.

Detective B signs the "Witness" section of the *Miranda* form, and there is no further discussion regarding *Miranda* rights.

Note.   From "Oral *Miranda* Warnings: A Checkist and a Model Presentation," by G. DeClue, 2007, *Journal of Psychiatry & Law, 35,* pp. 421–441. Copyright 2007 by the Journal of Psychiatry and Law. Reprinted with permission.

described the procedure as a formality, read the rights quickly (interspersed with comments that would be more likely to confuse than enlighten), and then told T., "You can just sign it right there." T. was never asked to demonstrate his understanding of the rights, and the record did not provide much useful data about whether he understood his rights or not. Neither T. nor his parents were given an opportunity to read the rights form. See Exhibit 11.2 for a transcript of the relevant portion from the video recording.

L. is a 17-year-old female adolescent with average intelligence and behavioral problems and no other significant psychiatric symptoms or history. Police suspected her of committing murder. A detective asked her to explain her understanding of each right as it was read to her. The detective asked L. to rephrase the right in her own words, and then he clarified apparent misconceptions. See Exhibit 11.3 for a transcript of the relevant portion from the video recording. (Audio clips of these orally presented *Miranda* warnings are available in the Presentations section of the Reprints of Publications page accessible from http://gregdeclue.myakkatech.com/.)

Checklist

What should psychologists look for and listen for as they analyze a recording of an orally presented *Miranda* warning? I prepared a preliminary checklist based on my review of legal decisions (DeClue, 2005a) and my experiences in current forensic cases, which I then submitted to some colleagues for their input (including suggested additions, corrections, deletions, style changes, etc.). Appendix 11.1 is the resulting version of the checklist, which should be useful to psychologists and others who analyze recordings of orally presented *Miranda* warnings to assist judges in deciding whether a suspect's waiver meets the full awareness standard specified in *Colorado v. Spring* (1987).

Model Warning

Miranda warnings devolve into empty formalities if the suspect does not understand them. Rogers, Harrison, Shuman, Sewell, and Hazelwood (2007) collected 560 different versions of the *Miranda* warnings and found that their reading skills varied from elementary school to postgraduate levels (using the Flesch–Kincaid Comprehension Scale; Flesch, 1950). The version of *Miranda* that was easiest to read was at the second-grade, 8th-month (2.8) level.

Rogers et al. (2007) reported, anecdotally, that

> college students do not understand the term 'right' as a *protection*. Instead, the large majority of students construed 'right' as simply an *option*, but an option for which they will be severely penalized (i.e., their non-cooperation will be used in court as incriminating evidence) (p. 190)

They noted further:

> The *Miranda* decision articulates several mechanisms to protect the Constitutional privilege against self-incrimination, including (a) the assertion

Exhibit 11.2.   Excerpt From the Transcript of the Interrogation of T.

Detective: I am just going to explain this, this rights waiver form to you and your folks. We kinda talked about it before. But, um, you know I want you to know, now that I mean we read you your rights so people understand your rights and so you know anytime you are interviewed by the police for the most part and you come down to the station or interview room here, um, people sometimes get the impression that maybe they are in custody and they are not free to leave. So, it's a good time to give you your rights so you understand you know your rights are per *Miranda.* I'm going to go ahead and read them to you. If you have any questions, just let me know. It says before you are asked any questions, you must understand your rights, okay? You have the right to remain silent. However, anything you do say can and will be used against you in court, okay? You have the right to talk to a lawyer for advice before you are asked any questions and have him with you during questioning, okay? You have this right to the advice and presence of a lawyer even if you cannot afford to hire one. That means if you cannot afford to hire one, that you get a public defender is what that means, okay, so one will be appointed to you. If you wish to answer questions or make a statement at this time without a lawyer being present, you have the right to refuse to answer any questions, okay, and to have this interview terminated at any time, okay? Do you understand those rights?

T.: Yeah.

Detective: In a nutshell, it means that you understand anything you say can and will be used against you. At the same token, if we ask you something you do not like, you are not being forced to answer any questions, okay?

T.: Okay.

Detective: The second part of this is just merely a waiver and the waiver says that I read you the form, that I have read you the statement of your rights, and I have shown you, and I have told you what your rights are, okay? I desire to answer questions and to make a statement without first consulting an attorney, which I think you have today, and without having a lawyer present at this time, okay? But you have your parents here because you are a juvenile and you know they have rights over you there. This decision is voluntary on your part and your parents', right, and no promises and threats of force of any nature have been made against you to get you to come in here and talk, okay?

T.: Okay.

Detective: So again it's voluntary, it's totally on your own free will and we are just going to sit and it will be basically five people in here talking, and you can just sign it right there, just your signature that you understand your rights.

T. signs or does not sign the form at this point.

Note.   From "Oral *Miranda* Warnings: A Checkist and a Model Presentation," by G. DeClue, 2007, *Journal of Psychiatry & Law, 35,* pp. 421–441. Copyright 2007 by the Journal of Psychiatry and Law. Reprinted with permission.

Exhibit 11.3.   Excerpt From the Transcript of the Interrogation of L.

Detective G.: There's a couple things that we want you to know. I understand that since you've been here you've been great. You've been talking to everybody and trying to tell your side of the story. Our job is to gather all of the facts, okay, and try to put this whole picture together. It's kind of like a big jigsaw puzzle. We try to put it together. We had to talk to a bunch of people and get a whole bunch of information and you're kind of the last person on the list to talk to, so we can get your side. But there's some things I want to go over first before we talk about any of that stuff. How old are you?

L.: Seventeen.

Detective G.: Okay, um, do you go to school?

L.: No.

Detective G.: . . . How far did you go in school? . . . What kind of grades did you get? . . . Do you drive? . . . Did you ever get a driver's license? . . . Have you ever been in trouble with the police before? . . . Have you ever been to court before? . . . Do you think you understand the court system a little bit? . . . I'm sure you've watched television and seen different things. When somebody gets arrested for a crime there's certain rights that they have. I'm gonna go over those rights with you because I want to make sure that you understand them. The first right that they talk about is: I understand that I have a right to remain silent. Do you understand that?

L.: Mm-hm [yes].

Detective G.: What does that mean?

L.: I'm not s'pose to say anything.

Detective G.: Is it you're not supposed to say anything or you don't have to say anything?

L.: I don't have to say anything.

Detective G.: Okay. So if you want to say something you could, but if you didn't want to, you also have that right.

L.: Okay.

Detective G.: I understand that anything I say can be used against me in a court of law. Do you understand that?

L.: Mm-hm [yes].

Detective G.: What does that mean?

L.: That mean anything I say, that could be brought up again in court.

Detective G.: Correct. I understand that I have a right to talk to an attorney and have him or her present with me while I'm being questioned. Do you understand that?

L.: Mm-hm [yes].

Detective G.: What does that mean to you?

L.: That I could hire a lawyer and that, um, discussing it, he be right there.

Detective G.: He could be with you, or she could be with you, when you're talking.

L.: Mm-hm [yes].

Detective G.: Okay. I understand that if I want an attorney and cannot afford one that an attorney will be appointed to represent me free of charge before any questioning. Do you understand that?

L.: Mm-hm [yes].

Exhibit 11.3.   Excerpt From the Transcript of the Interrogation of L. (*Continued*)

Detective G.: What does that mean?

      L.: Like a public defender.

Detective G.: Okay, um, if you came in here today and you had no money to afford, to pay for an attorney, would you still have the right to have one before we talked?

      L.: Mm. I don't know. Yeah. I don't know.

Detective G.: Okay. Let's go over that. It says [pointing to the page] if I want an attorney and cannot afford one that an attorney will be appointed to represent me free of charge before any questioning.

      L.: Okay.

Detective G.: Okay. So in other words if you came in here and you didn't have the money for an attorney but you wanted one, you could get one before you talked. Is that right or wrong?

      L.: Right.

Detective G.: Okay. And feel free to correct me if I say something that's not correct. Okay. I understand that at any time I can decide to exercise these rights and not answer any questions or make any statements. Do you understand that?

      L.: Yeah.

Detective G.: What does that mean?

      L.: If you ask me a question, that I don't have to answer it.

Detective G.: Correct. If we talked for however long we talked and all of a sudden you decided, you know what, I don't want to talk anymore, do you have that right?

      L.: Mm-hm [yes].

Detective G.: Yes you do. Okay. Understanding these rights explained to me I wish to make a statement at this time. Would you like to talk about what happened today?

L. answers yes or no at that point.

Note.   From "Oral *Miranda* Warnings: A Checkist and a Model Presentation," by G. DeClue, 2007, *Journal of Psychiatry & Law, 35,* pp. 421–441. Copyright 2007 by the Journal of Psychiatry and Law. Reprinted with permission.

of rights will stop further interrogation and (b) the exercising of rights cannot be used as incriminating evidence. The Supreme Court did not specify whether these protections needed to be expressed to custodial suspects. We found that they remain unexplained in almost all *Miranda* warnings (98.2%). (p. 186)

In the recent case of T. (mentioned previously), I was asked to assist the court in determining whether a teenager with average intelligence, a learning disability, and attention-deficit disorder gave a knowing, intelligent, and voluntary waiver of his *Miranda* rights. The interrogation, including the *Miranda* warnings and waiver, was electronically recorded, providing a good quality audiovisual record of the proceedings, and there was a *Miranda* rights form with the youth's signature on it. Nevertheless, there was a serious dispute about whether the young man understood his rights. The rights were presented orally, with interspersed comments that appeared to minimize the importance of the rights, distract T. from recognizing exactly what rights he was waiving, suggest that his parents might somehow substitute for a lawyer, and convey that not signing the form would be an indication of refusal to cooperate with the police, with the implication that failure to cooperate would have negative consequences. After the rights were rapidly read to T., he was told to "sign here," with no clear indication of what his signature meant: That he was read his rights? That he understood them? That he wished to waive his rights and talk to the police?

Testifying at a hearing in which the judge was asked to suppress T.'s interrogation and his responses therein, I described how the manner of presentation of the *Miranda* rights appeared likely to exploit the adolescent's weaknesses, as shown in his school records and as measured by relevant psychological tests (DeClue, 2005a, 2005b). I further explained that the comprehension level of the rights and waiver used was higher than T.'s comprehension level on several relevant tests. That raised a serious question as to whether T. could understand his rights at the time they were read to him. T.'s lawyer reminded the Court that the state has a burden to show that he understood his rights, and I testified that, in my opinion, the adolescent's responses during the recorded interview failed to show that he understood his rights. On cross-examination, the prosecutor tried to insist that I answer that T. either did understand his rights or did not. Instead, I explained that the manner in which T.'s rights were presented failed to elicit responses from him that showed whether, and to what extent, he understood his rights, and whether he was truly waiving them. (Voluntariness of the waiver was not challenged in this case. The reader is encouraged to use the checklist in Appendix 11.1 to analyze T.'s interview, Exhibit 11.2.)

How could a *Miranda* warning be administered in a case like this to provide a clear record of whether a suspect gives a knowing, intelligent, and voluntary waiver? Using principles identified by Rogers et al. (2007), I developed a model oral *Miranda* warning (see Appendix 11.2). This warning is presented in "clear and unambiguous language" as the text of *Miranda* appears to require. It uses simple language, understandable at a second-grade level. (This *Miranda* warning has a Flesch–Kincaid reading comprehension level of 2.6, slightly lower than that of the easiest of the 560 warnings studied by Rogers et al., 2007. Reading comprehension and listening comprehension are significantly correlated; Hoover & Gough, 1990; Jackson & McClelland, 1979; Savage, 2001.) It incorporates clear promises that exercising one's constitutional rights does not constitute a failure to cooperate and that exercising one's rights cannot be used against the suspect. It also includes clear directions on how to exercise the rights.

The model oral *Miranda* warning is intended to be presented orally, and the presentation should be electronically recorded (Innocence Project, 2007; Ofshe and Leo, 1997; see also chaps. 8 and 9, this volume). A law enforcement agency could adapt this oral warning to match the agency's written form, or the agency could adapt its written form to match this oral warning. Agencies are encouraged to check the comprehension level (e.g., Flesch–Kincaid) of whatever written form they use. If an agency decides to alter the wording of this oral warning, the effect on the comprehension level of the new oral warning should be checked (for additional recommendations, see Rogers et al., 2007).

Summary

In custodial interrogations, police are required to advise suspects of their consti-tutional rights, as described in *Miranda*. Unless a suspect waives his or her *Miranda* rights, nothing the suspect says can be used in court. The state carries the burden of showing that the suspect understood his or her rights and volun-tarily waived them. As more police interrogations are electronically recorded (see chap. 8, this volume; Weigl, 2007), police have increasing opportunities to create a clear record of whether and to what extent a suspect understands his or her rights at the time the suspect is advised of his or her rights.

When police have electronically recorded the entire interrogation, includ-ing the *Miranda* warning, the checklist presented as Appendix 11.1 should aid in analyzing whether and to what extent the suspect understood his or her rights. This is a rationally derived checklist consisting of items that are consid-ered subjectively. This checklist should be a useful tool to enhance a comprehen-sive assessment, along with ability and achievement testing, clinical interview, school records, and so forth. Of course, it is the judge who makes the final decision about whether a particular suspect made a knowing and intelligent waiver of his *Miranda* rights.

It is increasingly recognized that it is unfair and inadequate for police to interrogate a suspect in secret and only turn on electronic recording devices after the suspect has been persuaded to confess to a crime (DeClue, 2005a, 2005b; Gudjonsson, 2003; Kassin, 2005; Kassin & Gudjonsson, 2004). In the United States, we are living in an interesting time: Police are increasingly recording entire interrogations, now revealing techniques that were formerly conducted in secret. In many police departments, current cases constitute the first time that their detectives' work is being exposed to scrutiny by peo-ple from outside the department. Perhaps some police practices are cleaned up as the police know that their actions are being recorded, but to a large extent police are doing what they always did and are just now in a position to get useful feedback.

My experience with T.'s case, for example, is that the police genuinely believed—and, perhaps, still believe—that because T. signed the form, that proves that he understood all of his *Miranda* rights and all of the consequences of waiving those rights (see Exhibit 11.2). The prosecutor argued as much in the suppression hearing, giving every impression that he, too, considered a sig-nature on a form to be proof that T. understood his rights and the consequences of waiving them.

What more could a judge expect from a video-recorded interchange as police advise a suspect of his or her *Miranda* rights and ask the suspect to knowingly and intelligently waive those rights? Quite a bit, it turns out, though nothing complicated or time consuming. The checklist presented in this chap-ter can help when analyzing an already recorded interrogation, and the model oral warning can guide detectives as they advise a suspect of his or her rights during their next interrogation. Future research, of course, should be conducted on both of these tools to establish empirically whether they repre-sent an advance over current approaches to *Miranda* warning and waiver (see chap. 7, this volume).

Appendix 11.1. Oral *Miranda* Warning Checklist

Did the suspect show, in his or her own words, understanding of the following? (If so, list page and line numbers from the transcript.)

1. I am/am not free to leave.
2. I do not have to talk to the police.
3. If I do talk to the police, anything I say can be used against me in court.
4. If I do not talk to the police, my choice not to do so cannot be used against me in court.
5. I can talk to an attorney.
6. If I cannot afford an attorney, an attorney will be provided for free.
7. I can talk to an attorney before I decide whether to talk to the police.
8. If I decide to talk to the police, I can talk to an attorney before talking to the police.
9. If I decide to talk to the police, I can talk to an attorney while I talk to the police.
10. If I decide to talk to the police, I do not have to answer every question. I can choose not to answer any question. If I choose not to answer a question, that cannot be used against me in court.
11. If I decide to talk to the police, I can decide at any time to stop talking to the police, and the decision to stop talking cannot be used against me in court.
12. If I say, "I do not want to talk to you anymore," the police will stop asking me questions and the interview is over.
13. If I say, "I want a lawyer," the police will stop asking me questions and the interview is over.

In addition to the above specific items, the following general items should also be considered:

A. Did the police make any statements before, during, or after advising the suspect of *Miranda* warnings that directly contradict any of the above? (If so, list page and line numbers from the transcript.)

B. Did the police make any statements before, during, or after advising the suspect of *Miranda* warnings that (perhaps implicitly) may contradict any of the above? (If so, list page and line numbers from the transcript.)

Note: Checklist from "Oral *Miranda* Warnings: A Checkist and a Model Presentation," by G. DeClue, 2007, *Journal of Psychiatry & Law, 35,* pp. 421–441. Copyright 2007 by the Journal of Psychiatry and Law. Reprinted with permission.

Appendix 11.2. Model Oral *Miranda* Warning

We would like to talk to you today. We would like to ask you some questions. You do not have to talk to us. You do not have to be here today. You do not have to stay here. You can leave if you want. You can leave any time you want. If you do not talk to us, that cannot be used against you in court. If you do talk to us, anything you say can be used against you in court.

Now, I'm going to read you your rights. These are important rights. The U.S. Supreme Court says that these apply to every suspect in a criminal case. Right now you are a suspect in a criminal case, and that's why I'm going to read you your rights.

It is important that you understand your rights. I know you're probably feeling nervous right now. I'm going to read these to you slowly and carefully. I'm going to ask you to tell me in your own words what each right means. So I'll read each right to you. And then I would like you to show me whether you understand or not. Tell me in your own words what the right is. Ready?

You have the right to remain silent. Tell me in your own words what that means. . . . And being silent is your right. You don't have to talk to us. And if you don't talk to us, we can't hold that against you. We can't use it against you in any way. You can say "no" right now, and that's it. We'll stop. We will not hold it against you that you chose not to talk to us. If you do choose to talk to us, at any time you can say the magic words. "Stop, I don't want to talk anymore." And that's it. We'll stop. And we won't hold that against you.

Anything you say can and will be used against you in court. Tell me in your own words what that means. . . . So if you do talk to us, anything you say can be used against you in court.

You have the right to talk to a lawyer for advice before you are asked any questions. Tell me in your own words what that means. . . . So you could say, "Stop, I want to talk to a lawyer." Those are magic words, too. And if you say those magic words, "Stop, I want to talk to a lawyer," we will stop. We won't ask you any more questions. We won't say or do anything to try to get you to talk more. And the fact that you told us to stop cannot be used against you. You can say that before we ever start. If you do, we won't ask you any questions. You can say that right now, and we will stop right now. Or if you do agree to start answering questions, it is up to you when we stop. All you have to do is say those magic words. "Stop, I want to talk to a lawyer."

Also, you have the right to have a lawyer present with you during questioning. Tell me in your own words what that means. . . . So, if you want to have a lawyer present right now while we talk, that's fine. Or if you want to talk to a lawyer first, and then also have a lawyer present while we talk, that's fine, too. And if you choose to talk to a lawyer or to have a lawyer present while we talk, that's fine. That's a fine way for you to cooperate with us in the investigation. There is nothing uncooperative about talking with a lawyer. There is nothing uncooperative about having a lawyer present while you talk to us. If you'd like to have a lawyer present, we won't hold that against you in any way.

You have the right to the advice and presence of a lawyer even if you cannot afford to hire one. Tell me in your own words what that means. . . . So if you do not have the money to pay for a lawyer, you can still say, "Stop, I want a lawyer." And we stop. And you get a lawyer for free. And you can talk to the lawyer and decide whether you want to talk to us. And if you do decide to talk to us, you can have a lawyer present, even if you don't have the money to pay for a lawyer.

If you talk to me, you do not have to answer every question. Tell me in your own words what that means. . . . So if I ask you something that you don't want to answer, all you have to say is, "I don't want to answer that." Or, "I don't want to talk about that." And we won't hold it against you.

You have the right to stop this interview at any time. Tell me in your own words what that means. . . . Like I said, just say the magic words. "Stop, I don't want to talk anymore." Or, "Stop, I want a lawyer." And we'll stop. And we won't hold it against you.

Now, do you understand all of those rights? Do you have any questions? . . . Like I said, you don't have to talk to us. And we won't hold it against you if you don't talk to us. Do you want to talk to us now? [If yes.] If you understand each of these rights, please put your initials next to each right. But listen, if you put your initials there, that means that we went over these rights, *and you're saying that you understand the right.* So, here's the first one. You have the right to remain silent. *If you understand that,* please put your initials here, next to that one. [Continue for each of the rights.]

And now I'm asking you, having these rights in mind, do you want to talk to us? . . . Do you have any more questions? Okay, then, if you want to talk to us, then sign here. Your signature here means that you understand the rights, and you are choosing to talk to us. . . . Okay, now remember, you can talk to us as long as you want. But any time you want to stop, all you have to do is say the magic words. Okay, here we go.

Note: From "Oral *Miranda* Warnings: A Checkist and a Model Presentation," by G. DeClue, 2007, *Journal of Psychiatry & Law, 35,* pp. 421–441. Copyright 2007 by the Journal of Psychiatry and Law. Reprinted with permission.

References

Colorado v. Spring, 479 U.S. 564 (1987).

Crane v. Kentucky, 476 U.S. 683 (1986).

DeClue, G. (2005a). *Interrogations and disputed confessions: A manual for forensic psychological practice.* Sarasota, FL: Professional Resources Press.

DeClue, G. (2005b). Psychological consultation in cases involving interrogations and confessions. *Journal of Psychiatry & Law, 33,* 313–366.

Flesch, R. (1950). Measuring the level of abstraction. *Journal of Applied Psychology, 34,* 384–390.

Gudjonsson, G. H. (2003). *The psychology of interrogations and confessions: A handbook.* West Sussex, England: Wiley.

Hoover, W. A. & Gough, P. B. (1990). The simple view of reading. *Reading and Writing, 2,* 127–160.

Innocence Project. (2007). *False confessions & recording of custodial interrogations.* Retrieved May 7, 2007, from http://www.innocenceproject.org/Content/314.php#

Jackson, M. D., & McClelland, J. L. (1979). Processing determinants of reading speed. *Journal of Experimental Psychology: General, 108,* 151–181.

Kassin, S. M. (2005). On the psychology of confessions: Does innocence put innocents at risk? *American Psychologist, 60,* 215–228.

Kassin, S. M. & Gudjonsson, G. H. (2004). The psychology of confessions: A review of the literature and issues. *Psychological Science in the Public Interest, 5,* 33–67.

Miranda v. Arizona, 384 U.S. 436 (1966).

Ofshe, R., & Leo, R. (1997). The social psychology of police interrogation: The theory and classification of true and false confessions. *Studies in Law, Politics, and Society, 16,* 189–251.

Rogers, R., Harrison, K. S., Shuman, D. W., Sewell, K. W., & Hazelwood, L. L. (2007). An analysis of Miranda warnings and waivers: Comprehension and coverage. *Law and Human Behavior, 31,* 177–192.

Rogers, R., & Shuman, D. (2000). *Conducting insanity evaluations* (2nd ed.). New York: Guilford.

Savage, R. S. (2001). The "simple view" of reading: Some evidence and possible implications. *Educational Psychology in Practice, 17,* 17–33.

Weigl, A. (2007, May 17). Bill would bolster homicide inquiries. *News & Observer.* Retrieved May 18, 2007, from http://www.newsobserver.com/politics/politicians/legislature/story/574894.html

12

Evaluations of Competency to Waive *Miranda* Rights and Coerced or False Confessions: Common Pitfalls in Expert Testimony

I. Bruce Frumkin

Forensic psychologists have been increasingly used by the court in cases in which the admissibility of a confession is disputed. False confessions occur with some frequency (e.g., Drizin & Leo, 2004; chap. 2, this volume). There is ample discussion on the effects of various interrogation methods on the reliability and validity of a confession (e.g., Leo, 1996; Ofshe & Leo, 1997; Philipsborn, 2001; chap. 1, this volume). Social psychologists and sociologists are generally allowed to testify on the effects of interrogation on the accuracy of a confession (chap. 13, this volume). The forensically trained clinician, however, offers the court something different. A forensic psychological evaluation of a specific defendant can provide relevant data to the court regarding those psychological characteristics that heighten the risk of a false confession and impact the voluntariness of a confession or *Miranda* waiver. Also, an evaluation oriented toward a defendant's ability at the time of the police interrogation to understand and appreciate the *Miranda* warnings can assist the court in determining the competency of a defendant to have made a knowing and intelligent waiver of those rights.

A number of evaluation protocols have been proposed in the literature (DeClue, 2005; Frumkin, 2008; Frumkin & Garcia, 2003; Oberlander, Goldstein, & Goldstein, 2003; chap. 11, this volume) for conducting such evaluations. There are many more similarities than differences in how these evaluations should be conducted. Yet, to date, there has not been a detailed analysis of the common errors or pitfalls psychologists make when conducting these evaluations and their subsequent testimony in court. This chapter is divided into five parts. It discusses psychologists' involvement in the evaluation of competency to waive *Miranda* rights and the use of the so-called Grisso tests. There is a discussion on evaluations relevant to issues of the voluntariness of a *Miranda* waiver and confession, the validity of a confession, and in particular, the use of the Gudjonsson Suggestibility Scales (GSS). The chapter also discusses potential errors or pitfalls psychologists make when using and testifying about both the Grisso tests and the GSS, respectively. The chapter closes with a discussion of admissibility issues pertinent to expert testimony.

Competency to Waive *Miranda* Rights

A psychologist must conduct a comprehensive evaluation of a defendant's psychological functioning when addressing competency to waive *Miranda* rights. This evaluation involves a retrospective analysis of the defendant's mental state at the time of the police interrogation. Third-party data, such as *Miranda* waiver forms, police reports, interrogation transcripts, or audio- or videotape of the interrogation, school records, treatment records, and other relevant data should be requested by the psychologist to the referral source. Once most of those data are reviewed, the clinical interview is conducted. This interview includes a thorough psychosocial history, including arrest history and a mental status examination. Attention is focused on a defendant's version of events the moment he or she had contact with law enforcement up through the end of the interrogation. It is important that the psychologist not overstep the boundaries of the evaluation but gather only information directly relevant to the issue being addressed. For example, one does not want the defendant to indicate whether he or she committed the offense, just what was stated to law enforcement.

If the defendant does not spontaneously discuss the *Miranda* warnings, the psychologist may need to ask specific questions regarding whether any papers were asked to be signed or whether the police read any statement of rights to the subject. The psychologist then either reads the actual *Miranda* rights given by law enforcement or asks the defendant to read such rights, depending on how the rights were administered by the police. If the defendant is unable to read the rights, then they can be read to the defendant. After the rights are read, the defendant is asked to recall what he or she remembers of the rights. It must be emphasized that remembering the rights does not equate with understanding or appreciating the significance of the rights. Nevertheless, if one's legal rights may be invoked at any time, it is relevant whether one can remember the rights.

Although there is no single IQ cut-off or diagnostic category that automatically renders one unable to competently waive the *Miranda* rights at the time of the interrogation, research is clear in showing a negative correlation between *Miranda* comprehension and appreciation and intelligence (e.g., Cloud, Shepherd, Barkoff, & Shur, 2002; Fulero & Everington, 1995, 2004; Grisso, 2003). Thus, it is important to administer valid intelligence tests, not only to obtain IQ scores that are useful in and of themselves, but more so to emphasize a defendant's verbal intelligence relative to those his or her age. The various verbal subtests measure such areas as vocabulary knowledge, verbal abstract reasoning skills, general information about the world, judgment and common sense, and working memory. All of these data provide useful information relative to a knowing and intelligent waiver of rights. Reading comprehension tests may be given if the defendant was asked to read the rights.

Personality tests may provide important information regarding a defendant's psychological functioning. Issues of reality testing, accommodation, assertiveness, submissiveness, impulse control, coping skills, and other states and traits are highly relevant to how a defendant is able to process information in a typical high-stress interrogation. These tests may later become relevant in examining the voluntariness or susceptibility of a defendant to police influence.

If there is any evidence of cognitive limitations or psychopathology, it is essential for the psychologist to administer effort or malingering tests.

Grisso (1981, 1986, 2003), as part of a project funded by the National Institute of Mental Health, studied adults' and juveniles' comprehension (knowing waiver) and appreciation (intelligent waiver) of *Miranda* rights. Four separate tests, often referred to as the *Grisso tests,* were developed from this research (see Grisso, 1998): the Comprehension of *Miranda* Rights (CMR), the Comprehension of *Miranda* Rights–Recognition (CMR-R), the Comprehension of *Miranda* Vocabulary (CMV), and the Function of Rights in Interrogation (FRI).

The CMR and CMR-R help measure current understanding or knowledge of the *Miranda* constructs; they do not measure understanding of the rights at the time of the police questioning. With the CMR, the subject is shown four cards, each containing one of the four *Miranda* rights from the test. The defendant is read each right and is asked to state in his or her own words what that right means. In Grisso's research, a national panel of judges, lawyers, and legal scholars decided what type of response indicated a full understanding of the right (2-point response), a partial understanding of the right (1-point response), or no understanding of the right (0-point response). A scoring manual was created to allow one to objectively score the items. A subject obtains a score of 0 to 8, and that score can be compared with various normative groups in the standardization sample. These tests help the psychologist to provide a functional assessment of the constructs of a knowing and intelligent waiver of rights.

The CMR-R was developed as a less verbally expressive means of assessing *Miranda* comprehension. The subject is shown one of the four *Miranda* warnings. Each right is paired with three comparison statements. The subject states whether each comparison statement has the "same" or "different" meaning as the *Miranda* right. Thus, a total score ranges from 0 to 12.

The CMV was developed to examine a defendant's understanding of the meaning of six words often contained in a *Miranda* warning. One can obtain a score of 2, 1, or 0 for an individual word, depending on whether full understanding, partial understanding, or no understanding of the word is conveyed. Scoring is facilitated with the scoring manual.

The FRI, unlike the CMR and the CMR-R, was developed to help assess one's current ability to make an intelligent waiver of rights. An intelligent waiver was defined by Grisso, on the basis of case law, as a decision-making capacity involving an appreciation of the meaning and effect of waiving the rights. On the FRI, a subject is presented with brief vignettes paired with illustrations. These vignettes depict an individual being interrogated by law enforcement, another involving a suspect meeting with his attorney, and other vignettes involving an individual being interrogated by police and later appearing in court. After each vignette, questions are asked about the story. The questions tap into one of three areas: a subject's grasp of the nature and significance of the interrogation process, the intelligent use of the right to counsel, and the intelligent use of the right to silence. Again, a manual is used to determine whether a response indicates full appreciation, partial appreciation, or no appreciation of the significance of the right.

Pitfalls in the Use of the Grisso Tests

Whereas the use of the Grisso tests is a necessary component of a functionally based, psychological assessment of a defendant's ability to have made a knowing and intelligent waiver at the time of the police questioning, the use of these tests alone, or with a clinical interview, is not a sufficient component of such an assessment. In my experience, a major mistake occurs when psychologists place too much weight on the results from the Grisso tests and misunderstand what is being measured.

First, the Grisso tests are standardized instruments. The *Miranda* warnings contained in the test were those that were used in St. Louis County, Missouri in the late 1970s. The *Miranda* warnings given in any jurisdiction are likely to vary in actual wording and complexity from those on the test (cf. Rogers, Harrison, Shuman, Sewell, & Hazelwood, 2007). Generally, *Miranda* rights, such as those contained in the Grisso tests, are written at the seventh-grade level. Yet, Kahn, Zapf, and Cooper (2006) found that word comprehension and reading level play a significant role in a defendant's ability to knowingly waive *Miranda* rights. Thus, it is important for the psychologist to not only test the defendant on the rights contained in the Grisso tests but also assess the defendant's understanding of the specific rights given by law enforcement. One should also analyze the readability of the *Miranda* waiver form (chap. 11, this volume). A Flesch–Kincaid readability score (Flesch, 1994) is easily obtained by typing the *Miranda* passage in a Microsoft Word document.

Second, the Grisso tests measure only current understanding and appreciation of the rights. The legal issue is the knowing and intelligent waiver of the rights at the time of the police questioning. An individual may now understand and appreciate the rights but perhaps did not at the time of the police questioning. This could be for many reasons. Since the interrogation, the defendant may have been educated about his or her rights by legal counsel, family members, jailhouse lawyers, or other inmates or self-educated by visits to the jail library or taking classes in jail. The manner in which law enforcement administered the rights may also differ from how the rights are administered in the Grisso tests. If the defendant was asked by the police to read the rights, and the defendant cannot read, then it may not matter that the defendant obtained good scores when administered the Grisso tests.

Additionally, the defendant's mental state at the time of the interrogation might be different than during the evaluation process. The stress of the interrogation, influence of alcohol or drugs, sleep deprivation, or effects of pain or discomfort may all influence how well one can process, understand, and appreciate such concepts as those contained in the *Miranda* warnings. Severe mental illness may also play a role, although one has to look at the defendant as an individual. Viljoen, Roesch, and Zapf (2002) found that defendants who had primary psychotic disorder had greater impairment than other defendants in their understanding of Canadian rights (similar to *Miranda*). Yet psychosis itself was not the primary predictor, as psychotic defendants with low intelligence were less able to understand the rights compared with those with higher intelligence.

Another pitfall occurs when psychologists view each of the Grisso tests, and the individual components of the tests, as if they measured a single construct. As mentioned previously, the CMR and the CMR-R help measure knowing waiver of the rights and the FRI helps measure the intelligent waiver of the rights. The FRI in particular measures something different from the CMR and CMR-R. In fact, psychologists and lawyers often equate a knowing waiver of rights with an intelligent waiver of rights. A defendant may be capable of making a knowing waiver of the right to counsel; he or she may understand that he or she has the right to an attorney before and during questioning and that a lawyer can be provided at no cost if there is no money to pay for one. Yet, if the defendant erroneously believes a lawyer will defend only someone who is innocent, an intelligent waiver of that right cannot be made. Likewise, a defendant may understand the right to silence: that he or she does not have to speak to the police. Yet if the defendant erroneously believes that invoking one's right to silence would be perceived by the judge or jury as indicative of guilt or that one must testify in court to what he or she did that was wrong, the defendant cannot make an intelligent use of the right to silence. In contrast, it should be noted that in the United Kingdom, a defendant is informed as part of his legal warnings that invoking the right to silence may be perceived as indicative of guilt.

A defendant may perform well on the CMR and CMR-R but not perform particularly well on the FRI. A typical cross-examination question is, "Doctor, do you believe that anyone who waives their rights is not making an intelligent waiver?" Often, the psychologist responds affirmatively. Yet, the absence of an intelligent waiver does not refer to using good or bad judgment in waiving the rights. It refers to waiving one's rights on the basis of a misconception of how the legal system functions. It is important for the psychologist to understand this distinction.

Psychologists also often misinterpret what the scores mean on the Grisso tests and place too much weight on the scores themselves. To begin with, the CMV becomes irrelevant if most of the six words are not actually contained in the *Miranda* warnings given to the defendant. The Vocabulary subtest of the Wechsler Intelligence Scales provide a much better, objective measure of an individual's overall knowledge of the meaning of vocabulary words. If one wants to assess understanding of the actual words from the rights given by the police, one can question the defendant regarding the meaning of each of the words.

The psychologist may testify that a defendant has a slightly less than average current understanding of the rights because the CMR score was 6, which falls a little below the mean score of the normative group. This reasoning is fallacious. How was the score of 6 obtained? Did the defendant obtain a score of 6 because he or she showed partial understanding (1-point response) on two of the rights and full understanding (2-point response) on the other two rights? Or did the defendant demonstrate full understanding on three of the rights and no understanding (0-point response) on one of the rights. The latter would indicate the defendant did not at all understand one of the rights. It is misleading to opine that he or she is a little below average in *Miranda* understanding. Also, in that the number of test items is very small (only four rights), placing too much weight on percentile ranges is problematic. A slight difference in scoring may drastically alter how the individual performs compared with others. Should there be a comparison with others anyway? Does one want to look at *Miranda* comprehension in a relative fashion (compared with others) or in an absolute fashion? Does the person understand or doesn't he? *Miranda v. Arizona* (1966) does not speak about a defendant being able to make a knowing, intelligent, and voluntary waiver of rights compared with others but speaks about the abilities of the defendant in an absolute fashion. Ultimately, this is a legal issue that needs to be weighed by the court.

Another problem is how the psychologist interprets the score on the CMR-R. The CMR-R is a forced-choice test, whereby the subject has to respond "same" or "different" to the 12 comparison statements, three comparison statements for each of the four rights. Often, a score of 3 or lower is erroneously interpreted by the psychologist as reflective of poor comprehension of the rights. In fact, if the defendant were guessing randomly for each item (assuming the items are of equal difficulty), there is only a 7% chance of a subject obtaining a total score of 3 or less, and there is only a 2% chance of a subject obtaining a total score of 2 or less. Thus, scores close to 6 are reflective of no understanding of the rights. Scores of 3 or less are more suggestive of malingering.

It is important not to apply the above analysis in too simplistic a fashion. A particular defendant may be more prone to miss items at below chance levels because of a misconception of how the rights apply in the comparison statements. For that subject, the comparison statements pull for an incorrect response. Also, one needs to look at the pattern of responding on the CMR-R. For example, did the defendant miss all the items associated with a particular right but obtained perfect scores on the other three rights? Finally, it is possible for a defendant to obtain a low, nonmalingered score (e.g., 5, 6, 7, or 8) but still have a fairly good understanding of the rights. If the CMR score is high and the CMR-R score is low, this may mean that a defendant was unable to compare and contrast statements, or that he or she did not fully understand the instructions. The issue here is that the psychologist, in addressing *Miranda* comprehension using the Grisso tests, must look at the quality of responses and the patterns of scores, not just the absolute score and resultant percentiles.

Scoring on the FRI can also be misinterpreted by the psychologist. Three different constructs are assessed on the FRI: nature of the interrogation process, intelligent use of right to counsel, and intelligent use of right to silence. Someone may obtain a relatively high score on the total FRI (compared with others), but several responses indicate the individual has a misconception of how the rights apply. For example, if a defendant gets a perfect score on 13 of the 15 questions on the test (each of the items obtaining a maximum of 2 points) and gets a 0-point response on two of the questions, the total score would be 26. This is an average total score. Yet, if the responses on the two 0-point items indicate that the defendant believes the judge will punish the defendant for not speaking to the police and that the defendant must incriminate himself in court, the defendant is unlikely to have been able to make an intelligent use of the right to silence. Thus, the overall average score on the FRI is misleading. Again, it is incumbent upon the psychologist not to place undue weight on the scores but to look at the quality of the responses and the pattern of scores. This is particularly true because each subtest of the FRI contains only five items.

Psychologists sometimes change the standardized administration of the test. For example, they may substitute the actual *Miranda* warnings given by law enforcement for the Grisso version of *Miranda* on the test. The psychologist certainly will want to question the defendant on the actual version administered by the police, but if one changes the test stimuli too dramatically the test is changed in ways that prevent the scoring manual and normative data to have any real meaning. I sometimes may substitute the word *questioning* for the word *interrogation* if the defendant does not understand the word *interrogation* and that word does not appear in the actual rights administered by law enforcement. This is done only once and only on the CMR test. From a clinical perspective, it makes sense to do this. However, comparing the subject's CMR score with others becomes problematic because a question on the test was changed. Moreover, sometimes it is important to test the limits on some of the items, that is, ask follow-up questions that are not specified in the administration manual. This is done to better clinically assess what the defendant understands or appreciates, particularly if ambiguous responses are given. Also, "I don't know" responses are almost always followed up with an encouragement to try to answer the question as best one can. Although the protocol is scored on the basis of the responses prior to testing of the limits, this clinically relevant information is useful, sometimes more than the scores themselves, in forming an overall opinion of a defendant's ability to have made a knowing and an intelligent waiver at the time of the police questioning. For further critical discussion of the Grisso tests, the interested reader is referred to Rogers, Jordan, and Harrison (2004) and Rogers and Shuman (2005). Detailed responses to these critiques have been provided by Grisso (2004) and Frumkin (2008).

Validity and Voluntariness of a *Miranda* Waiver and Confession

Psychologists have been used to assist the court in cases in which the admissibility of a confession is disputed. Apart from providing data relevant to a knowing and intelligent waiver of *Miranda* rights, psychologists can assist the fact finder by providing data that compare the vulnerabilities or susceptibility to influence of one defendant with others. This is highly relevant to a determination of the voluntariness of a rights waiver or the examination of the voluntariness or validity of a confession. In other words, one can provide the court with a description of a defendant's psychological characteristics that heighten the risk of him or her succumbing to police demands or providing less than accurate or false statements to law enforcement.

One needs to be familiar with the types of interrogation procedures used by law enforcement (see Inbau, Reid, Buckley, & Jayne, 2001), the literature critiquing such methodology as one that produces false confessions in vulnerable populations (e.g., Leo, 1996), and the types of false confessions that occur (e.g., chap. 2, this volume; Kassin & Wrightsman, 1985; McCann, 1998; Ofshe & Leo, 1997).

Kassin and Wrightsman (1985) described three types of false confessions. A *voluntary false confession* occurs when a suspect willingly provides police with untrue statements because of a desire for notoriety, a need to protect a friend or relative, or some pathological need to be punished. This type of false confession rarely comes to the attention of the forensic clinician, as law enforcement generally eliminates the individual from serious consideration as a suspect, and the individual does not get charged with a crime. A *coerced-compliant false confession* occurs when a suspect confesses to avoid a stressful interrogation or to achieve some immediate goal, such as less punishment or a reward for cooperating (e.g., being allowed to make a phone call to a family member, getting a cigarette break, being promised placement in a nicer correctional facility). Finally, a *coerced-internalized false confession* is one in which a suspect who has been subjected to intense police questioning and misinformation about incriminating evidence begins to internalize or believe he or she, in fact, committed a crime. These individuals generally do not trust their own memories or have little memory of their actions around the time of the offense. McCann (1998) suggested a fourth category, that of a *coerced-reactive false confession*. This is an involuntary confession in which a suspect is pressured or coerced, not by the police, but by another entity, to falsely confess to a crime. A psychologist may evaluate a battered spouse whose husband threatens her to falsely confess or a gang member who is threatened with violence from other gang members. Not all false confessions fit neatly into these four categories (for further discussion of different models of false confessions, see chap. 2, this volume).

Another type of false confession should be considered: the *coerced-substituted false confession* (Frumkin, 2007). In this confession, a suspect who has committed a finite number of similar offenses (e.g., stealing cars, burglarizing homes), all within a short, specific time period, confesses to a greater quantity of like offenses than actually committed. This generally happens because law enforcement presents the suspect with a number of unsolved similar offenses, some of which were committed by the suspect, and some not committed by the suspect. It is unfortunate that the suspect cannot remember the specifics of the offenses (such as the model of each of the cars or the address of each of the homes). The suspect essentially confesses to most of the like offenses, knowing he committed some of them, just not which ones. Some of the confessions happen to be true, and some happen to be false. The suspect, who is pressured by law enforcement to cooperate, confesses to most of these unsolved similar crimes. In essence, he or she substitutes true involvement in crimes committed with ones not committed.

Gudjonsson (1986, 2003) described three general processes related to false confessions: suggestibility, compliance, and acquiescence. Gudjonsson defined *interrogative suggestibility* as the extent to which an individual comes to accept messages or information communicated during formal questioning as true. A defendant may falsely confess to a crime because he or she comes to believe the police version of their criminal conduct. This closely corresponds to the coerced-internalized false confession. *Compliance* is moderately correlated with suggestibility. It differs from suggestibility in that the individual does not have to privately accept the premise presented by police officers as true. The defendant knows he or she is giving a false confession. This closely corresponds to the coerced-compliant false confession. *Acquiescence* is the tendency to act in accordance with the preferences of others, essentially to affirm information regardless of the content (Cronbach, 1946). Acquiescence shows little correlation with compliance or suggestibility (Gudjonsson & Clare, 1995).

In conducting evaluations relevant to the voluntariness of a *Miranda* waiver and false or coerced confessions, as was the case with *Miranda* competency assessments, the astute clinician conducts a comprehensive clinical interview, performs a thorough record review, and administers relevant psychological testing. Gudjonsson (2003), Kassin and Gudjonsson (2004), Frumkin (2008), and others have provided good summaries of the case law, research, and methodology for conducting psychological evaluations in this arena.

The GSS is a test specifically designed to help measure interrogative suggestibility. Although relatively simple to administer, it is easily misused and misunderstood by clinicians. It is important that the psychologist carefully read the test manual (Gudjonsson, 1997). Administration of the GSS, which is presented as a test of memory, involves reading a complex narrative story consisting of 40 bits of factual information. After reading the story to the subject, he or she is told, "Tell me everything you remember about the story." The test's purpose is not to measure short-term memory. For subjects with relatively good recall, after a 50-minute delay they are asked to recall everything they can about the story (for those with poor initial recall, there is no 50-minute delay). Then, 20 standardized questions are asked about the story, 15 of them are designed to be leading or misleading. A Yield 1 score is obtained on the basis of the number of times the subject yields to these leading questions. Regardless of performance, the subject is told that he or she made a number of errors and that it is necessary to go over each question again, and this time to be "more accurate." Yield is measured a second time, referred to as Yield 2, as well as a *shift score,* the number of times the individual shifts from one response, right or wrong, to a different response. The Yield 1 is combined with shift to produce a total suggestibility score.

The psychologist incorporates empirical data into his or her opinion, all the while understanding there are individual differences between defendants. Research from Gudjonsson (2003) and others has shown an inverse relationship between intelligence and suggestibility. Thus, it would be wise to administer to the defendant a valid intelligence test. Individuals with memory impairment, particularly those who may mistrust their own judgments and rely on others, will generally have high suggestibility scores. Yield is related more to these cognitive variables, whereas shift is related to interpersonal and social factors (Gudjonsson, 2003). Other research (e.g., Gudjonsson, Rutter, & Claire, 1995) has shown that poor assertiveness, evaluative and state anxiety (and possibly trait anxiety), and avoidance coping strategies are correlated with both yield and shift scores. Sleep deprivation is also correlated with suggestibility (Blagrove, 1996; Blagrove & Akehurst, 2000; Blagrove, Cole-Morgan, & Lambe, 1994). Prior convictions are negatively correlated with suggestibility, that is, those who have convictions are generally less suggestible than those never arrested before (Gudjonsson, 2003). There are a host of other variables correlated with suggestibility, and the prudent clinician should be familiar with those studies summarized in Gudjonsson (2003).

Gudjonsson (2003) summarized the research regarding suggestibility and juveniles. Children who are 12 years of age and older, although no more likely to give in to leading questions than adults, are more affected by negative feedback or interrogative pressure to change their responses. Younger children are more suggestible than older children and tend to be not only more susceptible to negative feedback and pressure but also more likely to yield to leading questions, in comparison with both older juveniles and adults. This, of course, has implications for how juveniles are interrogated.

There is no simple relationship between mental illness and suggestibility (e.g., Sigurdsson, Gudjonsson, Kolbeinsson, & Petursson, 1994; Smith & Gudjonsson, 1995). Thus, tests such as the Minnesota Multiphasic Personality Inventory–2 have less utility except to examine psychopathology, introversion, ability to manage stress, or malingering of psychotic symptoms. Yet, personality tests, such as the 16 Personality Factor (Cattell, Cattell, Cattell, 1993), provide information regarding more normal aspects of personality, like an accommodating versus an independent personality, a deferential versus a dominant style of relating, and shyness versus social boldness. A number of other relevant personality factors are measured on the 16 Personality Factor. When necessary, tests should be administered to help assess for malingering.

Pitfalls in the Use of the Gudjonsson Suggestibility Scales

Psychologists must be aware of the normative population on which a test was developed. One potential pitfall when using the GSS is that the clinician is unable to adequately address issues related to the normative sample for which the GSS was derived. The GSS was developed using normative data from Great Britain and Iceland. One could argue that use of the GSS with populations in the United States is not warranted. Yet research has shown (Gudjonsson, Rutter, & Claire, 1995) that ethnicity contributes to relatively minor variance in GSS scores (factors such as intelligence, memory, and anxiety create much more variance). There is no reason to believe that an American population would perform substantially differently from populations in Great Britain or Iceland. In fact, Frumkin and Garcia (2003) argued that even if one does not make use of the normative data with an American population, the GSS provides good behavioral data on ways in which a defendant responds when confronted with leading questions, both with and without pressure, and how easily the individual shifts to different responses under pressure.

Just as important, psychologists need to give thought to which normative population in the test manual (Gudjonsson, 2003) should be used for comparison of a defendant's scores. For example, Table 5.1 (Gudjonsson, 2003, p. 21) and the resulting Appendix 1 (p. 34), which lists percentile ranks, are labeled *adults in the general population*. Yet the age range of the adults is 16 to 62, with a mean age of 29. More problematic are the juveniles' normative data (see Table 5.4, p. 23, and the resulting Appendix 4, p. 35). The so-called juveniles have an age range of 15 to 23 years, with a mean age of 18 years. It is important that the psychologist carefully assesses the appropriate comparison group and not merely rely on the table headings.

The clinician, particularly if testing American populations, should be very conservative in assessing what is considered to be a high score. The standard deviation for each mean score is high enough that a difference of a point or two on the obtained score may drastically influence a defendant's percentile rank, particularly at scores closer to the mean. Although I do not advocate that a score reach statistical significance (95% range) for an interpretation of high suggestibility, a score lower than the 80th or 85th percentile range may not have much clinical significance. A successful cross-examination can be made with the psychologist unfamiliar with these various issues. Also, although the total suggestibility score provides general information about a defendant's overall interrogative suggestibility, Yield 1, Yield 2, and shift scores can and should be interpreted separately and in combination.

A common misconception is that GSS scores can only be used in cases in which a defendant erroneously believes he or she committed the crime. The implication is that the GSS has relevance only in coerced-internalized false memory cases. A coerced-reactive false confession, arising from compliance, in which the defendant knows he or she did not commit the crime but confesses anyway, has been considered less relevant to the GSS given that the defendant does not have an episodic or autobiographical memory impairment (Beail, 2002). This is a fallacy. First, Henry and Gudjonsson (2003) have shown that shift scores (changing responses based on subtle pressure) are less influenced by memory processes than Yield 1 (giving in to leading questions). Also, it is important that a high GSS score reflects a potential vulnerability to influence and, as with all test data, must be interpreted by the totality of circumstances for a particular defendant and case.

Gudjonsson (1989, 1997) also developed the Gudjonsson Compliance Scale to help measure the construct of compliance. The Gudjonsson Compliance Scale comprises a 20-item, self-report questionnaire. The subject answers "true" or "false" to questions such as "I give in easily when I am pressured," or "I find it very difficult to tell people when I disagree with them." Knowledgeable informants, such as friends or family members, can be given a slightly modified version of the test. This provides the clinician with additional data regarding a subject's compliance. Frumkin (2000) stated that the test must be used very cautiously because, as a self-report measure, it is susceptible to inaccurate response sets. An individual may consciously or unconsciously want to present as less or more compliant. In contrast, the GSS is relatively free from malingering. First, subjects believe it is a memory test. Also, Baxter and Bain (2002) told an experimental group prior to administering the GSS that their suggestibility was to be measured and were then given instructions to feign suggestibility. Only the Yield 1 score was affected.

Even though the GSS provides useful information regarding how a defendant may respond to police interrogation procedures, it is important that the psychologist not place undue weight on the scores. GSS scores should be used in conjunction with other clinically relevant data and empirical findings. Although research has shown that there are significant differences in suggestibility scores between alleged false confessors in criminal trials and those who resisted giving a statement (e.g., Gudjonsson, 1984, 1991), it is a major mistake for a psychologist to testify that because of a high GSS score the defendant likely gave a false confession. An individual may be quite suggestible and compliant, yet committed the offense, confessed to that offense, and then later retracts the confession. In addition, one can have a low suggestibility score for a defendant who falsely confessed to a crime. The issue is not whether the person gave a false confession, but what aspects of the defendant's statement are true and what aspects are false. A defendant may have committed the offense but the stated version of the crime provided during interrogation makes the defendant's criminal act appear more heinous than what actually transpired. This would have relevancy for mitigation at the time of sentencing. Thus, the mental health professional may want to interpret the GSS and couch later testimony in terms of risk factors. If a defendant gave less than accurate statements to the police, what personality characteristics place him or her at high risk for doing so?

To date, no studies have directly examined the relationship between poor *Miranda* comprehension and interrogative suggestibility. Both seem to be influenced by low intelligence, but apparently for different reasons. With respect to comprehending and appreciating *Miranda* rights, poor verbal reasoning skills, judgment, vocabulary knowledge, general knowledge about the world, and processes affecting working memory (all measured by the Wechsler intelligence tests) would seem to have a direct relationship to capacities one would need to successfully understand and make use of *Miranda* warnings. Moreover, in that individuals with low intelligence often have more difficulty reading, this could also impact comprehension if the rights were read by the subject.

Whereas interrogative suggestibility, particularly the yield score, is also correlated with low intelligence, this correlation is likely due in large part to personality dynamics associated with lower intelligence. Individuals of lower intelligence often mask intellectual deficiencies and are less trusting of their own memory. Thus, when presented with misleading or erroneous information, they are more likely to believe the examiner (or law enforcement officer). According to Gudjonsson (1990), their shifting to different responses when told they made errors seems less likely to be due to low intelligence but rather related to avoidance coping, eagerness to please, and anxiety associated with how well one copes with pressure. Frumkin (2007) has begun to analyze test data from the Grisso tests and from the GSS in more than 400 forensic subjects who have undergone evaluations related to confessions. In light of the theoretical formulations outlined above, it would be surprising if *Miranda* comprehension did not significantly correlate with interrogative suggestibility because both are influenced by intelligence but in different ways.

Admissibility of Expert Testimony

Psychologists can be expected to be cross-examined not only on their use or misuse of the Grisso and GSS tests but also on their overall interview and psychological testing procedures. Although it is beyond the scope of this chapter to discuss in detail the problems of various other psychological tests used in a confession-related evaluation, it is important that the psychologist use all the test results and interview data to make a functional assessment. The psychologist needs to integrate the clinically relevant information with the appropriate legal criteria. For example, for a *Miranda* waiver to be valid, the fact finder is concerned with the totality of circumstances surrounding the interrogation, including the nature of the interrogation process and those individual characteristics that may increase or decrease a defendant's understanding and appreciation (e.g., *Fare v. Michael C.*, 1979).

As stated previously, no one IQ score or diagnosis would automatically render a defendant incompetent to waive *Miranda*. Thus, undue weight should not be placed on test results in and of themselves. The test results add to an overall description of a defendant's functioning, yet the test results must be integrated with what one knows of how the rights were administered by law enforcement and the particular environment in which the rights were given. Interrogative suggestibility is based not only on the results of the GSS but also on the manner in which the interrogation was conducted and the defendant's mental state at the time. Mental health professionals should not offer opinions regarding whether a confession is true or false. That is for the trier of fact to decide. Rather, the psychologist strives to provide a detailed description of how the special psychological characteristics of the defendant interact with the specific interrogation procedure used in the particular case.

Intelligence tests, such as the Wechsler scales, are useful not only in obtaining various IQ scores, scale scores, and indices but also in providing behavioral samples for observing how a defendant responds to various types of tasks (Frumkin, 2008). It is unfortunate that some psychologists use brief or abbreviated versions of intelligence tests. Axelrod (2002) and others have cautioned against the use of short forms of intelligence, such as the Wechsler Abbreviated Scale of Intelligence (WASI). There is poor correlation with Wechsler Adult Intelligence Scale–III, and WASI scores show poor accuracy in predicting true scores. For example, research suggests that one out of seven WASI scores vary greater than 10 points in either direction.

It is problematic and exceeding psychological expertise for one to offer direct testimony regarding whether a defendant's *Miranda* waiver or confession was voluntarily produced (see chap. 13, this volume). In *Colorado v. Connelly* (1986), the United States Supreme Court reversed a trial court's suppression of a confession. The lower court had based its ruling on a psychiatrist's testimony that a defendant's psychosis (i.e., the defendant had heard the voice of God demanding he confess to a murder) interfered with his ability to make a free and rational choice and motivated him to confess and waive his legal rights. The Supreme Court found there is no requirement that for a waiver to be voluntary, it must be a product of free will. Rather, for a waiver to be involuntary, there has to be a showing that the police were unduly coercive in extracting the confession and *Miranda* waiver. The coerciveness of police conduct, or whether the police overstepped their bounds, is a legal determination. Psychologists ought not to determine whether police conduct has crossed the line in rendering a waiver or confession involuntary. Yet one often hears a mental health professional opine that the defendant made a knowing, intelligent, and voluntary waiver of rights.

The Grisso tests and the GSS are specialized forensic assessment tests that are unknown to many psychologists and attorneys. On occasion, particularly when the expert places undue weight on the scores of the tests themselves, their use may be challenged on *Frye v. United States* (1923) or *Daubert v. Merrell Dow Pharmaceuticals, Inc.* (1993) grounds. The *Frye* standard, which is commonly referred to as the *general acceptance principle,* requires that "the thing from which the deduction is made must be sufficient to have gained general acceptance in the particular field which it belongs." The *Daubert* standard superseded *Frye* in federal court, and now a number of states also use its criteria for admissibility of expert testimony. In *Daubert,* the United States Supreme Court provided guidance to the lower courts by enumerating four nonexhaustive or dispositive factors trial judges could consider when evaluating the admissibility of expert testimony. Admissibility according to the Court requires a determination of whether the principles and methods governing the expert's opinion are based on the scientific method. The factors to be considered in arriving at this determination are (a) whether the methodology or principle for which the opinion is based was testable, (b) whether the methodology had been published in peer-reviewed literature, (c) the known degree of error when using the particular methodology, and (d) whether the principle or methodology in question had gained general acceptance in the scientific community. The *Kumho Tire Company v. Carmichael* (1999) ruling expanded *Daubert* to social science and technical testimony.

Frumkin (2008) provided a detailed analysis of the admissibility issues of the Grisso tests and the GSS. This analysis is not repeated here. Nevertheless, if there is a *Frye* or *Daubert* challenge, the psychologist should be prepared to discuss in detail how the GSS and the Grisso tests were developed, the reliability and validity data discussed in the test manuals and elsewhere, and the peer-reviewed literature discussing these tests. Error rates become problematic to discuss because neither the Grisso tests nor the GSS were designed to address the ultimate legal issues. They were meant to be used as one part of an overall extensive and integrative assessment. A high score on the CMR, for instance, provides information related to a defendant's current ability to understand *Miranda*. It does not allow a psychologist to make a decision, on the basis of the scores alone, regarding whether the defendant understood the rights when questioned by the police. This should be based on many additional factors, including how the rights were administered during interrogation, the totality of the circumstances during the interrogation, whether the defendant was educated about his or her rights subsequent to the interrogation, and a host of other defendant-specific variables including cognitive and emotional states.

Although there is a correlation between those who have given false confessions and GSS scores, a high total GSS score does not mean the defendant produced a false or involuntary confession. The GSS score provides one piece of information regarding a defendant's functioning. The psychologist must integrate those results with other psychological data, what is known about the interrogation process, and whether the defendant's statements are consistent with facts known about the case. The psychologist who uses the GSS is advised not to offer ultimate opinion testimony on the voluntariness or validity of a confession. If the psychologist heeds this recommendation, then there is no such thing as an error rate, or false positive divided by false negative data. Even then, a judicial determination of whether a rights waiver was made knowingly, intelligently, and voluntarily or whether a confession was voluntary or false is and should be made on the basis of a host of factors, some of which have little to do with psychology.

In those court cases in which the Grisso tests were deemed not to meet *Frye* or *Daubert* standards for admissibility (*Carter v. State,* 1997; *State v. Griffin,* 2003), the defense did not lay adequate foundation for the use of the Grisso tests. In the *Carter* case, the defense psychologist testified that the Grisso test is not commonly used nor nationally recognized. The psychologist appeared unaware of the widespread use of these tests and its acceptance for those who do these specialized *Miranda* evaluations. With the *Carter* case, the psychologist appeared to do an excellent, thorough, and integrative job in evaluating a defendant's competency to waive *Miranda,* using data from the Grisso tests and incorporating those results with other psychometric and behavioral data. Yet during a *Daubert* challenge, the psychologist testified under cross-examination that she knew of only a "couple of organizations" that use the test and testified that although she recalled a law review article written about the Grisso tests, apart from Grisso's own writings she could not recall any others who have peer-reviewed the tests.

In a recent *Frye* decision, *People v. Hernandez* (2007), the appellate court concluded that a trial court did not abuse its discretion in disallowing expert testimony from a forensic psychologist regarding administration and results of a Grisso test, which was used "as a device to measure a defendant's ability to comprehend *Miranda* warnings." The trial court did not allow testimony, in part, because the vocabulary from the Grisso test used to gauge a defendant's understanding of the rights differed from those rights actually administered by law enforcement. Although it is difficult to assess from reading the appellate decision what the psychologist testified to, the court did state that the defense counsel "had substantial opportunity to challenge a defendant's ability to understand and waive *Miranda* warnings." It appears that the psychologist's testimony put too much weight on the Grisso test itself and did not integrate those scores with the totality of circumstances.

Conversely, in *People of the State of Illinois v. Jeanette Daniels* (2009), the appellate court ruled that the trial court erroneously denied a defendant's motion to suppress a videotaped confession on the basis she did not knowingly, intelligently, and voluntarily waive her *Miranda* rights. The appellate court referenced some of the data obtained from my use of the Grisso tests in demonstrating that the defendant was unable to make a knowing and intelligent waiver of her rights.

The GSS was judged to meet *Daubert* standards in *United States v. Raposo* (1998) and *Frye* standards in *State v. Romero* (2003). There is also case law that disallowed the use of the GSS. For example, in *Misskelley v. State* (1996) the trial court's decision not to allow a psychologist to testify on the GSS was upheld by the Arkansas Supreme Court. In that case, the psychologist offered the opinion that the defendant was "quite suggestible" and that the confession was the product of coercion. The psychologist acknowledged this was the first time he had administered the GSS. Describing the defendant as "quite suggestible" is appropriate when the GSS results are integrated with other data. Yet, in the *Misskelley* case the psychologist provided ultimate opinion testimony that the confession was the product of coercion. This was for the trier of fact to decide.

In *Commonwealth v. Soares* (2000), a psychologist testified that although the defendant was suggestible as measured by the GSS, "application of results from that test to a custody situation might not be valid." The psychologist also said his opinion would change if it was shown that the interrogation was devoid of physical force or yelling. The trial's courts refusal to allow the GSS was upheld by the higher court. In *Soares,* the psychologist seemed unaware that the GSS is highly relevant to police custodial situations and that law enforcement personnel routinely ask leading questions and pressure a suspect to produce a different response. Perhaps if the expert had testified differently, the results of the GSS may have been admitted.

The exclusion of my testimony on a defendant's interrogative suggestibility was recently upheld in *People of the State of Illinois v. Aaron Bennett* (2007). The trial court refused to allow a *Frye* hearing and did not allow testimony at the time of trial, believing the defendant's interrogative suggestibility "was not beyond the common knowledge of lay persons and would not aid the trier of fact in reaching its conclusions." Although *Crane v. Kentucky* (1986) seems to allow such testimony, the appellate court opined that the trial court did not abuse its discretion by excluding this expert testimony. The appellate court also indicated that had the expert opined that the defendant suffered from a "personality disorder," then testimony may have been admitted because "juries are unlikely to know that social scientists and psychologists have identified a personality disorder that will cause individuals to make false confessions" (*United States v. Hall*, 1996). In all due deference to the court's opinion, research does not show a simple correlation between personality (or mental disorders) and suggestibility. The key is the term *disorder*, which implies a formal *Diagnostic and Statistical Manual of Mental Disorders* (4th ed., text rev.) diagnosis. Rather, it was the defendant's personality characteristics, combined with low intelligence and integrated with what was known about the totality of the interrogation process, that would have been testified to at the time of trial. Also, testimony would not have stated that those characteristics would have caused the defendant to make a false confession but rather would have suggested risk factors. This could be important data for a jury to consider (see chap. 13, this volume).

Summary

A psychological assessment of a defendant's competency to waive *Miranda* rights or psychological characteristics that heighten the risk of a false, inaccurate, or involuntary confession involves a comprehensive evaluation comprising an extensive interview, psychological testing (including the use of specialized tests, such as the Grisso tests and the GSS), and a review of relevant third-party data. Generally, mental health experts have seen success in getting their testimony admitted in court. Psychologists who place undue weight on test scores or make unfounded interpretations because they are not thoroughly familiar with what the tests measure are less likely to have their testimony given much weight (if they are allowed to testify at all). It is important for the psychologist to perform a functional assessment, looking at the totality of circumstances that led to a *Miranda* waiver or confession. Such circumstances include assessing not only the manner in which the interrogation or *Miranda* administration was conducted but also personality characteristics, mental states, and cognitive variables present during the police questioning or interrogation. Psychological testimony is less likely to be admitted when an opinion is directly offered that a confession was involuntary, coerced, or false.

References

Axelrod, B. (2002). Validity of the Wechsler abbreviated scale of intelligence and other very short forms of estimating intellectual functioning. *Assessment, 9,* 17–23.

Baxter, J., & Bain, S. (2002). Faking interrogative suggestibility: The truth machine. *Legal & Criminological Psychology, 7,* 219–225.

Beail, N. (2002). Interrogative suggestibility, memory, and intellectual disability. *Journal of Applied Research in Intellectual Disability, 15,* 129–137.

Blagrove, M. (1996). Effects of length of sleep deprivation on interrogative suggestibility. *Journal of Experimental Psychology: Applied, 2*(1), 48–59.

Blagrove, M., & Akehurst, L. (2000). Effects of sleep loss on confidence–accuracy relationships for reasoning and eyewitness memory. *Journal of Experimental Psychology: Applied, 6*(1), 59–73.

Blagrove, M., Cole-Morgan, D., & Lambe, H. (1994). Interrogative suggestibility: The effects of sleep deprivation and relationship with field dependence. *Applied Cognitive Psychology, 8,* 169–179.

Carter v. State, 697 So.2d. 529 (Fla. App. 1 Dist. 1997).

Cattell, R. B., Cattell, A. K., & Cattell, H. E. P. (1993). *Sixteen Personality Factor Questionnaire* (5th ed.). Champaign, IL: Institute for Personality and Ability Testing.

Cloud, M., Shepherd, G., Barkoff, A., & Shur, J. (2002) Words without meaning: The constitution, confessions, and mentally retarded suspects. *University of Chicago Law Review, 69,* 495–624.

Colorado v. Connelly, 479 U.S. 157 (1986).

Commonwealth v. Soares, 51 Mass.App.Ct. 273, 745 N.E.2d 362 (2001).

Crane v. Kentucky, 476 U.S. 683, 106 S.Ct. 2142 (1986).

Cronbach, L. (1946). Response sets and test validity. *Educational & Psychological Measurement, 6,* 475–494.

Daubert v. Merrell Dow Pharmaceuticals, Inc., 509 U.S. 579 (1993).

DeClue, G. (2005). *Interrogations and disputed confessions: A manual for forensic psychological practice.* Sarasota, FL: Professional Resource Press.

Drizin, S. A., & Leo, R. A. (2004). The problem of false confessions in the post-DNA world. *North Carolina Law Review, 82,* 894–1007.

Fare v. Michael C., 442 U.C. 707 (1979).

Flesch, R. (1994). *The art of readable writing* (reissue ed.). New York: Macmillan General Reference.

Frumkin, I. B. (2000). Competency to waive *Miranda* rights: Clinical and legal issues. *Mental and Physical Disability Law Reporter, 24,* 326–331.

Frumkin, I. B. (2007, September). *Competency to waive Miranda rights and coerced/false confessions: Common pitfalls in expert testimony and the use/misuse of normative data.* Paper presented at Interrogations & Confessions: A Conference Exploring Current Research, Practice, and Policy, El Paso, TX.

Frumkin, I. B. (2008). Psychological evaluation in *Miranda* waiver and confession cases. In R. L. Denny & J. P. Sullivan (Eds.), *Clinical neuropsychology in the criminal forensic setting* (pp. 135–175). New York: Guilford Press.

Frumkin, I. B., & Garcia, A. (2003). Psychological evaluations and competency to waive *Miranda* rights. *The Champion, 27,* 12–23.

Frye v. United States, 54 App. D.C. 47 (1923).

Fulero, S. M., & Everington, C. (1995) Assessing competency to waive *Miranda* rights in defendants with mental retardation. *Law & Human Behavior, 19,* 533–543.

Fulero, S. M., & Everington, C. (2004). Mental retardation, competency to waive Miranda rights, and false confessions. In G. D. Lassiter (Ed.), *Interrogations, confessions, and entrapment* (pp. 163–174). New York: Kluwer Academic/Plenum.

Grisso, T. (1981). *Juveniles waiver of rights: Legal and psychological competence.* New York: Plenum Press.

Grisso, T. (1986). *Evaluating competencies: Forensic assessments and instruments.* New York: Plenum Press.

Grisso, T. (1998) *Instruments for assessing understanding & appreciation of Miranda rights.* Sarasota: Professional Resource Press.

Grisso, T. (2003). *Evaluating competencies: Forensic assessments and instruments* (2nd ed.) New York: Kluwer Academic Press.

Grisso, T. (2004). Reply to "A critical review of published competency-to-confess measures." *Law & Human Behavior, 28,* 719–724.

Gudjonsson, G. H. (1984). Interrogative suggestibility: comparison between "false confessors" and "deniers" in criminal trials. *Medicine, Science, & the Law, 24,* 56–60.

Gudjonsson, G. H. (1986). The relationship between interrogative suggestibility and acquiescence: Empirical findings and theoretical implications. *Personality & Individual Differences, 7,* 195–199.

Gudjonsson, G. H. (1989). Compliance in an interrogation situation: A new scale. *Personality & Individual Differences, 10,* 535–540.

Gudjonsson, G. H. (1990). The relationship of intellectual skills to suggestibility, compliance and acquiescence. *Personality & Individual Differences, 11,* 227–231.

Gudjonsson, G. H. (1991). Suggestibility and compliance among false confessors and resisters in criminal trials. *Medicine, Science, & the Law, 31,* 147–151.

Gudjonsson, G. H. (1997) *The Gudjonsson Suggestibility Scales manual.* Hove: Psychology Press.

Gudjonsson, G. H. (2003). *The psychology of interrogations and confessions: A handbook.* West Sussex, England: Wiley.

Gudjonsson, G. H., & Clare, I. (1995). The relationship between confabulation and intellectual ability, memory, interrogative suggestibility and acquiescence. *Personality & Individual Differences, 19,* 333–338.

Gudjonsson, G. H., Rutter, S., & Clare, I. (1995). The relationship between suggestibility and anxiety among suspects detained at police stations. *Psychological Medicine, 25,* 875–878.

Henry, L., & Gudjonsson, G. H. (2003). Eyewitness memory, suggestibility, and repeated recall session with children with mild and moderate intellectual deficiencies. *Law & Human Behavior, 27,* 481–505.

Inbau, F., Reid, J., Buckley, J., & Jayne, B. (2001). *Criminal interrogation and confessions* (4th ed.). Gaithersburg, MD: Aspen.

Kahn, R., Zapf, P., & Cooper, V. (2006). Readability of *Miranda* warnings and waivers: Implications for evaluating *Miranda* comprehension. *Law & Psychology Review, 30,* 119–142.

Kassin, S. M., & Gudjonsson, G. H. (2004) The psychology of confessions: A review of the literature & issues. *Psychological Science in the Public Interest, 5,* 31–67.

Kassin, S. M., & Wrightsman, L. (1985). Confession evidence. In S. Kassin & L. Wrightsman (Eds.), *The psychology of evidence and trial procedures* (pp. 67–94). London: Sage.

Kumho Tire Company v. Carmichael, 526 U.S. 137 (1999).

Leo, R. A. (1996). Inside the interrogation room. *Journal of Criminal Law & Criminology, 86,* 266–303.

McCann, J. (1998). A conceptual framework for identifying various types of false confessions. *Behavioral Sciences & the Law, 16,* 441–453.

Miranda v. Arizona, 384 U.S. 436 (1966).

Misskelley v. State, 323 Ark. 449, 915 S.W.2d 702 (1996).

Oberlander, L., Goldstein, N., & Goldstein, A. (2003). Competence to confess. In A. Goldstein (Ed.), *Handbook of psychology: Forensic psychology* (Vol. 11, pp. 335–357). New York: Wiley.

Ofshe, R., & Leo, R. (1997). The social psychology of police interrogations. The theory and classification of true and false confessions. *Studies in Law, Politics, & Society, 16,* 189–251.

People of the State of Illinois v. Aaron Bennett, N.E.2d, 2007 Westlaw 2669550 (Ill.App. 1 Dist.).

People of the State of Illinois v. Jeanette Daniels, No. 1-06-3514, 2009 (Ill. App. 1 Dist.).

People of New York v. Hernandez, 2007 NY slip op. 9604: 2007 N.Y. App. Div. LEXIS 12351.

Philipsborn, J. (2001, January/February). Interrogation tactics in the post-Dickerson era. *The Champion,* pp. 18–22, 75–78.

Rogers, R., Harrison, K. S., Shuman, D. W., Sewell, K. W., & Hazelwood, L. L. (2007). An analysis of *Miranda* warnings and waivers: Comprehension and coverage. *Law & Human Behavior, 31,* 177–192.

Rogers, R., Jordan, M. J., & Harrison, K. S. (2004). A critical review of published competency-to-confess measures. *Law & Human Behavior, 28,* 707–718.

Rogers, R., & Shuman, D. (2005). *Fundamentals of forensic practice: Mental health law and criminal law.* New York: Springer.

Sigurdsson, E., Gudjonsson, G., Kolbeinsson, H., & Petursson, H. (1994). The effects of ECT and depression on confabulation, memory processing, and suggestibility. *Nordic Journal of Psychiatry, 48,* 443–451.

Smith, P., & Gudjonsson, G. (1995). The relationship of mental disorder to suggestibility and confabulation among forensic inpatients. *The Journal of Forensic Psychiatry, 6,* 499–515.

State v. Griffin, 78 Conn. App. 646, 656-57, 828 A.2d 65 (2003).

State v. Romero, 191 Or. App. 164, 81 P.3d 714 (2003).

United States v. Hall, 93 F.3d 1337 (7th Cir. 1996).

United States v. Raposo, 1998 WL 879723 (S.D.N.Y. Dec. 16, 1998).

Viljoen, J., Roesch, R., & Zapf, P. (2002). An examination of the relationship between competency to stand trial, competency to waive interrogation rights, and psychopathology. *Law & Human Behavior, 26,* 481–506.

13

Tales From the Front: Expert Testimony on the Psychology of Interrogations and Confessions Revisited

Solomon M. Fulero

As research in the field of the psychology of interrogations and confessions has grown and post-DNA exoneration cases have made the phenomenon of false confessions an indisputable fact (see Drizin & Leo, 2004; Garrett, 2008; chap. 2, this volume), defense attorneys have increasingly called upon legal psychologists to provide expert testimony to triers of fact in cases in which a false confession is alleged to have been made. It is critical for attorneys and experts in the area to be familiar with the developing case law regarding the admissibility of such testimony.

The jurisprudence of expert testimony on confessions would seem to begin with the case of *Crane v. Kentucky* (1986), decided by the United States Supreme Court. The facts of the case, as set forth in the Supreme Court opinion, are rather typical of many confession cases (for a detailed description, see Fulero, 2004). The question that remains after *Crane* is not whether defendants may contest the accuracy or the weight to be given to a confession before the jury. Instead, the question is what sort of evidence may be presented and whether expert testimony is admissible. Just as with expert testimony on eyewitness identification, such a determination is subject to a threshold determination by the trial judge as to admissibility under Evidence Rule 702 (in federal court and in most state courts that have a version of this rule), known in some states as the so-called *Frye* rule (Inwinkelreid, 1992) or in other states and in federal courts as the *Daubert* rule (Penrod, Fulero, & Cutler, 1995). Recent articles such as Kageleiry (2007) have concluded that expert testimony on interrogations and confessions should be admissible (for earlier opposing views, see Agar, 1999; Kastenberg, 2003).

The classic but conservative *Frye* test (1923), which is still used in states such as New York to judge the admissibility of expert testimony, emphasizes that expert testimony must conform to a generally accepted explanatory theory (for a critical discussion of the rule, see Inwinkelried, 1992). By the mid-1970s, in response to criticism of the *Frye* rule, the new Federal Rules of Evidence focused on other issues. Thus, Rule 702 states that expert testimony is admissible if the expert is qualified, the testimony assists the trier of fact, and the expert's testimony is sufficiently reliable. In 1993, the United States Supreme Court decided the *Daubert* case, which explicitly rejected *Frye* and complemented the Federal Rules of Evidence requirements by admonishing trial courts to consider research-related factors such as falsifiability of the theories, peer review, and publication; known or potential error rate; and general acceptance (see Faigman, 1995, 1999; Penrod et al., 1995). It will be these standards by which expert testimony on interrogations and confessions will be judged, depending on the jurisdiction.

In 1991, the First District of California Court of Appeals decided *California v. Page,* involving what appears to be the first use of expert testimony in a confession case. Fulero (2004) discussed this case in detail (see also Costanzo & Leo, 2007) because it appears to be virtually a prototype for the types of issues and arguments that have come up repeatedly since then in cases involving expert testimony on interrogations and confessions. Although there are threshold issues under the tests of admissibility of general acceptance and scientific reliability and validity (see the following), the extent of the expert's testimony in such cases is also an issue. This is true because—unlike the case of the expert on eyewitness reliability who (like the judge, jury, and attorneys) was not at the scene and therefore does not have first-hand knowledge of the circumstances under which the eyewitness made the identification—the interrogations and confessions expert often gets a detailed look at the process leading up to the confession. It is clear from case law (e.g., *State v. Buell,* 1986) as well as from logic that eyewitness experts are not permitted (nor should they) render opinions about a specific eyewitness' accuracy or inaccuracy. In eyewitness cases, it is up to the defense attorney to link the general scientific principles and factors discussed by the expert to the specific facts of the case and to argue the link to the jury. But similarly, in confession cases, experts should avoid the temptation to render opinions about the particular confession. Going beyond the general principles and available empirical research runs the risk of having the testimony objected to or not admitted and creating a dangerous precedent for other judges to see. This is because it is, by and large, only cases in which the expert testimony is limited or excluded entirely (and the defendant is convicted) that reach appellate courts and generate opinions, making the body of opinions on this question essentially a biased sample that lacks cases in which the expert was admitted at trial. In the next sections, I review the available federal and state cases involving interrogations and confessions experts that have been reported since Fulero (2004).

Recent Case Decisions Involving Expert Testimony on Interrogations and Confessions: Federal Court

As just noted, because of the biased sample of cases that reach appellate courts, one must be careful in discussing case decisions in any area of expert testimony. The seminal federal case thus far is *United States v. Hall* (1996), a federal Seventh Circuit case (see Fulero, 2004). In addition, a recent important decision reversing a federal district court judge who did not allow expert testimony on interrogations and confessions came from the Fourth Circuit Court of Appeals, in *United States v. Belyea* (2004). Indeed, in that case, the trial judge later ruled in a *Daubert* hearing that the expert testimony would be admitted, but the government offered a plea bargain prior to trial that was accepted.

Generally, the case law since 2004 has been mixed. Some cases approve the admission of the testimony, whereas others find it not to be an abuse of discretion to exclude. The reasoning varies across cases. A Fifth Circuit court recently upheld a trial court ruling that expert testimony on interrogations and confessions was not admissible in *United States v. Dixon* (2008). The trial court, in an apparent but common misunderstanding about the thrust of such expert testimony, had ruled that because the expert was not going to opine about the truth or falsity of the confession in the case but was only going to add "nothing more than abstract scientific nostrums," the testimony would not assist or be helpful to the jury. The appellate court ruled that this was not "manifestly erroneous."

Daubert factors themselves have sometimes been used to reject proffered expert false confession testimony as unreliable (*United States v. Hebah,* 2006; *United States v. Mamah,* 2003). The defendant in *Hebah* claimed that the district court erred in refusing his proffered expert false confession testimony, which was intended to show the defendant's tendency to falsely confess based on his "compliant nature and tendency to acquiesce to the wishes of others" (*Hebah,* 164 Fed. Appx. at 690). The government relied on articles suggesting that the tests of suggestibility developed in Great Britain should not be used in American courts because the British criminal justice system does not afford *Miranda* rights or an exclusionary rule for evidence suppression (on the courts' acceptance of these sorts of tests, see Fulero, in press). The district court, after a *Daubert* hearing, denied the proffered testimony at least in part because the Court found that the expert's procedures were not shown to be reliable, were based in the fundamentally different British criminal justice system, and had no established rate of error, although the primary basis appeared to be the lack of qualification of the proposed witness. The 10th Circuit affirmed, finding the trial court did not abuse its discretion in applying the reliability prong of the *Daubert* or *Kumho* test.

Recent Case Decisions Involving Expert Testimony on Interrogations and Confessions: State Courts

State courts have also addressed the admissibility of false-confession expert testimony. Perhaps the most important of these is *People v. Kogut,* a 2005 New York case. On November 10, 1984, the victim, a 16-year-old girl named Teresa Fusco, disappeared after leaving her job at a roller rink at 9:45 p.m. On December 5, 1984, her body was found, naked, in a wooded area of Lynbrook, New York. The body had been covered by leaves and debris and was located a short distance from the roller rink. The autopsy revealed that the victim had died as a result of ligature strangulation. Vaginal swabs taken during the autopsy revealed the presence of semen and spermatozoa. However, serology tests to determine the semen donor's blood type were never performed.

The Nassau County Police Department was under enormous pressure to solve this crime, particularly because there had been several other disappearances of young girls in the area in recent years. John Kogut, Dennis Halstead, and John Restivo were all initially interrogated as part of an investigation into the disappearance of another girl. After three polygraph examinations, detectives began to focus on Kogut as a suspect in the Fusco case. Though he was told that he failed the polygraph, Kogut continued to maintain his innocence. After nearly 18 hours of interrogation, however, the police produced a confession from Kogut. The confession was handwritten by the interrogating officer for Kogut's signature, allegedly after five other versions of the confession that were never transcribed. According to the confession, Restivo, Halstead, and Kogut were all in Restivo's van. They approached the victim, who was on foot, and she entered the van voluntarily. When the victim demanded to be let out of the van, she was stopped, stripped, and raped by Halstead and Restivo. They drove to a cemetery, where the victim was taken out of the van and Kogut strangled her with a piece of rope. The victim's body was then rolled into a blanket and dumped in another location.

On the basis of the confession, investigators procured a warrant to search Restivo's van. They claimed to have found two hairs in the van that were microscopically similar to the victim's, including indications of chemical treatment. Kogut was then taken to the crime scene, though he could not point the police to any evidence from the crime that was missing, such as the victim's clothes, jewelry, or murder weapon. The next day, the confession was recorded on videotape. It contained no details that were not previously known by law enforcement.

DNA testing in this case went through many rounds over a period of 10 years, despite repeated exclusions of all three men. The prosecution initially argued that the samples tested (vaginal slides) were not the best samples available and could have failed to detect semen from the defendants that was present on the original swabs. However, in 2003, the defense team obtained property records from the police department that led to the discovery of an intact vaginal swab that had never been tested. DNA testing on the spermatozoa on the vaginal swab matched the single unknown male profile from the prior testing and again excluded all three men.

In addition, defense attorneys also secured a new affidavit from former Detective Nicholas Petraco, who had testified for the state in 1986 regarding the hairs allegedly found in Restivo's van. Detective Petraco concluded, on the basis of 20 years of research and expertise, that the hairs displayed "post-mortem root-banding." Because the victim was alleged to have been in the van only for a few minutes after death, he concluded that the hairs could not have been shed during that time and were instead autopsy hairs that were commingled with others from the van, whether through police negligence or misconduct.

On the basis of these results, all three convictions were vacated in June 2003, and all three defendants were released. John Kogut, however, faced retrial, largely because of his confession. At trial, the prosecution sought to rebut the DNA evidence by arguing that the victim, who was said by her mother and best friend to be a virgin, had consensual sex with an unknown male prior to her rape and murder. Kogut's lawyer argued that the confession was false and filed a motion to have expert testimony on false confessions and the role that the polygraph played admitted at the trial. Saul M. Kassin, Richard Ofshe, and Solomon M. Fulero all testified in the *Frye* hearing, which lasted for almost 2 weeks. Judge Ort ruled that expert testimony on false confessions was admissible for what was apparently the first time in the state of New York, generating an important written opinion. Judge Ort's reasoning in admitting the expert testimony of Kassin at trial is both important and interesting to consider (see Exhibit 13.1). Subsequently, after a 3-month bench trial at which Kassin testified, Judge Ort found Kogut not guilty on all counts on December 21, 2005. The verdict included specific findings that numerous aspects of the confession were contradicted by DNA and other forensic evidence and that the decomposed hairs from the victim were not shed by her in Restivo's van.

Other cases have begun to appear, using the reasoning of *Crane* to allow testimony from experts about the general phenomenon of false confessions, interrogation techniques that might increase false confessions, and characteristics of suspects that might make them more likely to confess falsely. By and large, the cases still disallow testimony about the specifics of a given confession, though they do (and should) allow particularized testimony from clinical psychologists about the makeup of a defendant, absent an opinion that the confession by that defendant was or was not false (see chap. 12, this volume).

In *Downs v. Virginia* (2008), the defendant appealed after being convicted of killing her child. The opinion clearly notes that a false confession expert testified in the case and discusses that testimony. Trial courts in California have also allowed such testimony (e.g., *People v. Cota,* 2007; *People v. Madrigal,* 2008; *People v. Muratalla,* 2007; *People v. Wroten,* 2007). A published Ohio case similarly reports that a false confession expert testified at trial (see *State v. Tapke,* 2007). In a Colorado case (*People v. Flippo,* 2007), it is clearly stated that expert testimony on interrogations and confessions would have been admissible despite an exclusion of the expert on procedural grounds.

A number of trial court decisions have allowed experts but with no published opinions (see the following for discussion of how this occurs). For example, I have testified before juries in three cases in Connecticut since 2005 (*State v. Sullivan,* 2005; *State v. Blakeslee,* 2006; *State v. Wells-Jordan,* 2008; for newspaper accounts, see Siegel, 2006; Beach, 2008) as well as in cases in Louisiana (see Purpura, 2007), Michigan (*People v. Brown,* 2007), and a number of other states (see also Fulero, 2004). A newspaper account in the Indiana case of *State v. Wilkes* (Braser, 2007) indicates that Richard Leo testified at trial in that case, and similar newspaper accounts are available for other cases and experts.

On the other hand, some trial courts have, in the exercise of their discretion, refused to allow interrogation and confession expert testimony of any sort. In *People v. Crews* (2008), the trial court refused to allow expert testimony on false confessions. The Court held that "the subject of whether a person has falsely confessed 'does not depend upon professional or scientific knowledge or skill not within the range of ordinary training or intelligence,' and therefore, 'there is no occasion to resort to expert testimony.'" It is not clear whether this decision is on appeal. A recent Georgia case (*Lyons v. State,* 2007) also held that the denial of expert testimony by the trial judge was not an abuse of discretion. In Massachusetts, the denial of expert testimony at the trial level was similarly upheld (*Commonwealth v. Robinson,* 2007).

In a recent California case, a trial court denial of expert testimony was upheld as not an abuse of discretion (*People v. Rathbun,* 2007). It is interesting that the Court's rationale was that there was no evidence in the trial that any

Exhibit 13.1.   Excerpt From *People v. Kogut* (2005)

... [T]he fact that police officers use various psychological techniques to elicit confessions from suspects is within the ken of lay jurors. However, as with psychological studies regarding the accuracy of eyewitness identification, it cannot be said that the typical juror is familiar with psychological research concerning the voluntariness of confessions or the tendency of certain techniques to contribute to a false confession.

While the question may be debated whether Dr. Kassin's research with simulated criminals and investigators should be applied to any specific real life interrogation, the court concludes that Dr. Kassin's analysis and methodology are generally accepted in the social psychology community. The fact that social psychology is not yet able to plot the curve showing the relationship between the decision to confess and the variables involved does not rebut the significance of Dr. Kassin's findings. Indeed, the universal agreement that more research needs to be done based upon Dr. Kassin's work confirms that his findings are generally accepted in the scientific community.

The application to permit testimony with respect to psychological studies concerning false confessions generally, is not unlike that considered by the courts when the issue of rape trauma syndrome first arose. Evidence of a "syndrome," or recognized pattern of behavior, including psychological reactions, if generally accepted within the relevant scientific community, may be admissible in order to dispel misconceptions that jurors might be expected to possess. *People v. Taylor,* 75 N.Y.2d 277, 552 N.E.2d 131, 552 N.Y.S.2d 883 (1990). After analyzing the approaches taken by various other jurisdictions, a unanimous Court of Appeals held that "the reason why the testimony is offered will determine its helpfulness, its relevance and its potential for prejudice." Id. at 292. In Taylor, the court noted the popular misconception that a rape victim will always promptly report a rape. The court found that expert testimony would aid a lay jury and allowed evidence of the general phenomenon of rape trauma syndrome to dispel this misconception and explain why a victim might delay in reporting the rape or naming her attacker. Similarly, jurors might be expected to assume that an innocent person will not confess to a crime he did not commit. Therefore, a study based upon generally accepted social psychology principles, establishing that the phenomenon of false confessions does occur, should be admissible to explain behavior that might appear unusual to a lay juror not familiar with the phenomenon.

Quite obviously, the voluntariness of Mr. Kogut's confession is central to this case because of the absence of corroborating evidence other than the hair sample allegedly found in co-defendant John Restivo's vehicle. In these circumstances, the court concludes, as a matter of discretion, that the nature of Dr. Kassin's psychological studies on the voluntariness of confessions generally and the phenomenon of eliciting false confessions will be admissible at trial. It will be for the jury to decide whether to accept Dr. Kassin's analysis and whether it is sufficiently reliable to be applied to the facts in this case.

However, the court will not permit Dr. Kassin to offer any opinion on the ultimate issue, namely whether John Kogut's confession was in fact involuntary. The court notes in this regard that Dr. Kassin's analysis, when applied directly to Mr. Kogut's interrogation, takes on the form not of psychological research but rather purely legal argument. The risk of crossing the line from scientific study to legal advocacy may be inherent when research is conducted at the intersection of law and other disciplines.

Note.   From *People v. Kogut,* 2005 NY Slip Op 25409, 2005 N.Y. Misc. LEXIS 2126 (September 15, 2005). In the public domain.

of the interrogation techniques discussed by the expert had been used by the police. Of course, because the police had taped only the last part of the interrogation, such evidence was unavailable. This rationale sets up a potentially dangerous precedent: With no requirement to tape the entire interrogation, expert testimony could be routinely avoided by the state by simply not collecting any evidence about how the confession was obtained (see chaps. 8 and 9, this volume).

The Five Arguments Against Experts, and the Responses to Them

It is typical and understandable that prosecutors reflexively oppose false confession experts. Though the confession expert would testify identically should he or she be called by the prosecution, the testimony is usually proffered by the defense because by the time the case gets to the expert, the confession has already been obtained, and it is in the defense's interest to provide the scientific basis of their argument that the confession was false. In most instances, the prosecution objection to the expert testimony focuses on one of five arguments: (a) The testimony is not scientific, or not reliable and valid (thereby not meeting a *Daubert* or *Frye* test); (b) the testimony invades the province of the jury; (c) the points that an expert would make are all within the ken of the average layperson and therefore not a proper subject for expert testimony; (d) the points that an expert makes can be addressed in cross-examination or by jury instructions; or (e) the prejudicial effect of the testimony outweighs its probative value. In the following, I examine each of these arguments in turn.

Argument 1: Not Scientific or Not Reliable and Valid

This, of course, was the argument made in Kogut. The record in that case, and Judge Ort's summary of it, are the best sources for counterarguments, along with *United States v. Hall* (1997) and *United States v. Belyea* (2004). In the eyewitness arena, the best cases for the parallel argument (which applies equally to false confession expert testimony) are found in *United States v. Smithers* (2000), *United States v. Sullivan* (2003), and *United States v. Smith* (2009). The *Daubert* criteria by which admissibility is judged include the following: a body of scientific work published in peer-reviewed scientific journals, general acceptance of the work in the field, a known or potential error rate, and the amenability of the conclusions to scientific test.

DEVELOPMENT OF A SCIENTIFIC LITERATURE. Scientific research on false confession is one of the oldest areas of research within the field of psychology, dating back to the writing of Hugo Münsterberg (1908) in his book *On the Witness Stand*. The body of work is large (see Gudjonsson, 2003; Lassiter, 2004), and as Kassin (2008) noted, the relevant work is not just directly on false confessions but includes bodies of work from social psychology (e.g., attitude change and persuasion, obedience, conformity) and from psychology in general (e.g., principles of reinforcement). The studies are conducted in accord with generally accepted scientific principles of research, and when tested in court the body of scientific knowledge should easily pass the *Daubert* test of reliability and validity (for similar arguments on eyewitness expert testimony, see Penrod et al., 1995; Leippe, 1995).

GENERAL ACCEPTANCE WITHIN THE FIELD. It is clear that this work is generally accepted. But how does one quantify this? Again, it is instructive to look at the work in the area of eyewitness reliability. There, surveys of experts have been conducted to determine what people in the field agree on as accepted findings appropriate for testimony (Kassin, Ellsworth, & Smith, 1989; Kassin, Tubb, Hosch, & Memon, 2001). Researchers in the interrogation and confessions area need to do the same (for a recent survey of police beliefs and practices in this area, see Kassin et al., 2007). Coverage of this topic in basic psychology textbooks in introductory psychology, social psychology, and forensic psychology (e.g., Fulero & Wrightsman, 2008) is also a good measure. Other measures of general acceptance include publication of the research in peer-reviewed scientific journals, the number of citations of that work, coverage of the topic in graduate programs or courses in psychology and law, and discussion of the topic in major handbooks or encyclopedias (Oberlander, Goldstein, & Goldstein, 2008; Torkildson & Kassin, 2008).

Other indices of general acceptance in the field are found in the fact that the American Psychological Association (APA) recently gave a presidential citation to Saul M. Kassin for his work in this area. In addition, the APA funded the conference on which this volume is based and then published the resulting edited volume. Finally, the APA recently filed an amicus brief in a 2008 Pennsylvania case, *Wright v. Commonwealth,* relying on the body of scholarly work in this area (http://www.apa.org/releases/wright-pa-brief.pdf), and Division 41 of the APA (the American Psychology–Law Society) has recently approved a white paper as a state-of-the-art statement of the science in this area, which will be published in the flagship journal of this field, *Law and Human Behavior* (Kassin, Drizin, Grisso, Gudjonsson, Leo, & Redlich, in press).

KNOWN OR POTENTIAL ERROR RATE. Prosecutors often focus on this point by suggesting that one cannot know the error rate of the conclusions without knowing the total number of confessions in the United States and the percentage of those that are false, which are clearly not obtainable (see chap. 2, this volume). The best discussion of this factor is in *United States v. Sullivan* (2003), an eyewitness case. The trial judge ruled that this factor is not relevant in the eyewitness context because the expert is not going to opine about the accuracy of a particular witness. For that matter, what does *error rate* actually mean? Is it the .05 level of significance in a study? (Maybe.) The number of times the confession is true or false? (No.) In my view, Judge Coffman got it right in *Sullivan.* This factor is simply not relevant in the determination.

AMENABLE TO TEST? It is clear that the answer is yes. All studies are conducted in accord with generally accepted scientific principles. Researchers set up a hypothesis, collect data, analyze data, and draw conclusions. The best discussion of this, again in the eyewitness context, is by Cutler and Penrod (1995). All of the same arguments apply to the false confession context.

Argument 2: Invades the Province of the Jury

This appears to be an absurd argument on its face. The interrogation and confession expert does not invade the province of the jury, which is to determine whether the confession is true or false. The expert does not opine on this point. Instead, the testimony is designed under Rule 702 to be helpful to the jury in making that determination.

Argument 3: Within the Ken of the Average Layperson?

There is now a good deal of evidence that the science provides knowledge that is beyond the ken of judges, much less lay jurors. Again, the eyewitness area is instructive (see Fulero, 2004). A recent study of actual jury-eligible persons in the District of Columbia by the Public Defender Service explored juror knowledge of the factors affecting eyewitness identification (Schmechel, O'Toole, Easterly, & Loftus, 2006). The overall conclusion was that laypersons appear to be aware of some factors but tend to underestimate their impact (e.g., cross-racial identifications) and to overestimate the impact of others (e.g., confidence). Wise and Safer (2003, 2004) offered a provocative study of judges' knowledge of the factors affecting eyewitness testimony showing essentially the same. Additional work of this sort would be helpful in the interrogations and confessions area (for one attempt, see e.g., Kassin, Meissner, & Norwick, 2005, finding that mock jurors and trained investigators both have trouble distinguishing true from false confessions).

Argument 4: It All Can Be Handled on Cross-Examination

In the eyewitness arena, considerable empirical evidence indicates that cross-examination is not effective for revealing memory errors and problems with evidence-gathering techniques. Similar arguments apply in the interrogation and confession arena. One might ponder how a defense attorney would effectively cross-examine about interrogation techniques. A hypothetical colloquy would go as follows: Q: "Officer Krupke, are you familiar with the methods taught in the Reid technique?" A: "What's the Reid technique?"

Even if the officer acknowledged some familiarity with the technique, it is likely that he or she would not know of the research on the impact of the techniques on false confessions: Q: "Officer, are you aware of psychological research showing that the use of the evidence ploy increases the likelihood of false confessions?" A: "No."

And when the entire interrogation is not taped, the prosecution is free to argue that "there is no evidence that anything of that sort was done," and the defense has no rebuttal. This is a troubling development as it means that there is little incentive for the police to record an interrogation, as doing so in theory would only make it easier for a defense expert's testimony to be admitted (though see chap. 8, this volume). Although one might attempt to adopt the strategy of presenting testimony about how detectives are generally trained, in most cases such testimony is not allowed on the grounds that it is irrelevant to the case at hand (unless one could show that such techniques were actually used in the case at issue).

Argument 5: Probative Value Versus Prejudicial Effect

This is essentially a Rule 403 argument, in which the prosecutor suggests that the expert testimony should be kept out because it is prejudicial (query to whom). Footnote 5 in the *United States v. Smithers* (2000) case (an eyewitness expert case) mentioned earlier offers a rebuttal to this claim:

> Presumably, the district court was trying to express that the expert testimony would be unduly prejudicial. This conclusion is flawed. First, as the *Smith* Court noted, "in reviewing a 403 balancing [in a criminal case], the court must look at the evidence in the light most favorable to the proponent, maximizing its probative value and minimizing its prejudicial effect . . . . " The district court did not apply this standard here. Second, it appears the trial court thought the expert nature of the testimony would unduly impress the jury; this is an improper factor upon which to exclude expert testimony, for if this were the test, no expert could ever testify. The court erred in concluding that merely because testimony is given by an expert, it must be excluded. (*United States v. Smithers,* 2000)

The *Smithers* opinion continued later:

> In addition, the district court could have concluded that this testimony . . . could have been applied to the facts at issue in this case . . . . Had the district court conducted a proper evaluation of this testimony, we believe it may have found that Dr. Fulero's testimony met the first requirement of the *Daubert* test. The district court [stated] that "a jury can fully understand" its "obligation to be somewhat skeptical of eyewitness testimony." . . . The court's statement, however, is simply wrong . . . . Today, there is no question that many aspects of perception and memory are not within the common experience of most jurors and, in fact, many factors that affect memory are counter-intuitive. (*United States v. Smithers,* 2000)

State v. Echols (1998) is another instructive opinion from the eyewitness realm. The Court, in reversing a trial judge for not allowing expert testimony, stated as follows:

> The trial court in this case determined that Dr. Fulero's testimony concerning such areas as common misconceptions of laypersons about eyewitness identification, the effect of salient details on the accuracy of identifications, factors affecting a witness' ability to recall, the processes by which a person acquires, retains, and retrieves visual information, and the effect of post-event information on identification invaded the province of the jury. It is unclear whether the trial court believed that such testimony would invade the jury's domain because the information could affect the jury's determination of credibility or because the testimony would not help the jury reach an accurate decision. *In either case, the trial court was wrong* [italics added].
>
> Evidence Rule 704 allows for expert testimony even if it "embraces an ultimate issue to be decided by the trier of fact." Dr. Fulero's testimony concerned, generally, the variables that may affect eyewitness identification. Thus, the jury would have been free to make its own credibility determinations and draw its own inferences, using all, part, or none of the testimony

presented by Dr. Fulero. His testimony would not have invaded the jury's province as the arbiter of fact and credibility. Further, Dr. Fulero's testimony would have been very helpful to the jury because his knowledge . . . was outside the scope of a layperson's knowledge and could dispel misconceptions about eyewitness identification. (*State v. Echols*, 1998)

The conviction was reversed and remanded. Two similar opinions from Ohio are *State v. Sargent* (2006) and *State v. Bradley* (2009).

Summary and Conclusions

There is no doubt that these cases are the tip of the iceberg and that many more will appear. It is unfortunate that the published cases are a biased and skewed sample (Fulero, 2004). As noted earlier, only those cases in which the expert is excluded or limited reach the appellate level; if the expert is admitted, there is no record created. Saul M. Kassin, Richard Ofshe, and Richard A. Leo, among others, have also testified numerous times, perhaps hundreds, usually without generating a record (see *State v. Tapke,* 2007, in which it is reported that Ofshe testified that he had testified as an expert in 243 cases at that time). It is important in these cases that experts who are admitted to testify keep careful records of the case names, jurisdictions, case numbers, and judges, so that others who are proposed as experts can provide attorneys with this information to use as precedent in their motions to admit expert testimony. I have proposed the creation of a data bank in which all of the cases in which expert testimony is admitted can be accessed so as to facilitate this process (see Fulero, 2004), and law professor Edward Cheng (personal communication, June 24, 2008) is doing just that.

The case law is also becoming clear on the parameters of expert testimony in such cases. Testimony about the phenomenon of false confessions, social psychological testimony about police interrogation procedures that are commonly used, clinical psychological testimony about personality or clinical factors that might be linked to confessions, and even specific clinical testimony about a particular defendant, are likely to pass muster. In contrast, testimony that purports to determine if a particular confession is true or false does not. For example, Ofshe, in a 2004 hearing in Marty Tankleff's case, reportedly testified in part that "the confession, whoever created it, is false." Of course, it is always true that expert testimony must be relevant to the facts of the particular case (in the eyewitness context, see *United States v. Downing,* 1985). But testimony about the truth or falsity of a particular confession goes beyond the appropriate scope of expert testimony in this area, invading the province of the jury and running the risk that a judge will throw the baby out with the bathwater by disallowing otherwise appropriate and relevant expert testimony. In other words, it is for the expert to lead the jurors to water, but it is for the attorneys to make them drink.

All of this expert testimony will be judged according to the *Daubert* or *Frye* standard, depending on the rule that is applied in the jurisdiction in which the case arises. It is clear that the trend favors admissibility under either standard, and as the scientific literature increases, so too do general acceptability, scientific reliability, and validity. In that sense, both the law—the arguments and the rulings—and the science in this area seem to be following the career path of eyewitness identification research and expert testimony identified in Fulero (2004).

References

Agar, J. (1999, August). The admissibility of false confession expert testimony. *The Army Lawyer,* 26–43.

Beach, R. (2008, April 22). Judge rules jurors can hear teen's statement to police. *New Haven Register,* p. A1.

Braser, K. (2007, December 11). Jury to decide Wilkes' case on Wednesday. *Evansville Courier and Press.* Retrieved August 29, 2009, from http://www.courierpress.com/news/2007/dec/11/prosecution-rests-now-defense-begins/

California v. Page, 2 Cal.App.4th 161 (1991).

Commonwealth v. Robinson, Supreme Judicial Court of Massachusetts, No. SJC-08015 (April 26, 2007). Retrieved August 29, 2009, from http://www.suffolk.edu/sjc/archive/opinions/SJC_08015.pdf

Costanzo, M., & Leo, R. A. (2007). Research and expert testimony on interrogations and confessions. In M. Costanzo, D. Krauss, & K. Pezdek (Eds.), *Expert psychological testimony for the courts* (pp. 69–98). Mahwah, NJ: Erlbaum.

Crane v. Kentucky, 476 U.S. 683 (1986).

Cutler, B. L. & Penrod, S. D. (1995). *Mistaken identifications: The eyewitness, psychology, and law.* New York: Cambridge University Press.

Downs v. Virginia, Virginia Court of Appeals, No. 1604-06-1 (May 6, 2008). Retrieved August 29, 2009, from http://www.courts.state.va.us/opinions/opncavwp/1604061.pdf

Drizin, S. A., & Leo, R. A. (2004). The problem of false confessions in the post-DNA world. *North Carolina Law Review, 82,* 891–1007.

Faigman, D. L. (1995). The evidentiary status of social science under *Daubert:* Is it "scientific," "technical," or "other" knowledge? *Psychology, Public Policy, & Law, 1,* 960–979.

Faigman, D. (1999). *Legal alchemy: The use and misuse of science in the law.* New York: Freeman.

Fulero, S. (2004). Expert psychological testimony on the psychology of interrogations and confessions. In G. D. Lassiter (Ed.), *Interrogations, confessions, and entrapment* (pp. 247–262). New York: Kluwer Academic/Plenum.

Fulero, S. (in press). Admissibility of expert testimony based on the Grisso and Gudjonsson scales in disputed confession cases. *Journal of Psychiatry & Law.*

Fulero, S., & Wrightsman, L. (2008). *Forensic psychology* (3rd ed.). Belmont, CA: Wadsworth.

Garrett, B. (2008). Judging innocence. *Columbia Law Review, 108,* 55–142.

Gudjonsson, G. H. (2003). *The psychology of interrogations and confessions: A handbook.* Chichester, UK: Wiley.

Inwinkelreid, E. (1992). Attempts to limit the scope of the *Frye* standard for the admission of scientific evidence: Confronting the real cost of the general acceptance test. *Behavioral Sciences & the Law, 10,* 441–454.

Kageleiry, P. (2007). Psychological police interrogation methods: Pseudoscience in the interrogation room obscures justice in the courtroom. *Military Law Review, 193,* 1–51.

Kassin, S. M. (2008). Expert testimony on the psychology of confessions: A pyramidal model of the relevant science. In E. Borgida & S. Fiske (Eds.), *Beyond common sense: Psychological science in the courtroom* (pp. 195–218). London: Blackwell.

Kassin, S. M., Drizin, S. A., Grisso, T., Gudjonsson, G. H., Leo, R. A., & Redlich, A. D. (in press). Police-induced confessions: Risk factors and recommendations. *Law & Human Behavior.*

Kassin, S. M., Ellsworth, P. C., & Smith, V. L. (1989). The "general acceptance" of psychological research on eyewitness testimony: A survey of the experts. *American Psychologist, 44,* 1089–1098.

Kassin, S. M., Leo, R. A., Meissner, C. A., Richman, K. D., Colwell, L. H., Leach, A. M., & La Fon, D. (2007). Police interviewing and interrogation: A self-report survey of police practices and beliefs. *Law & Human Behavior, 31,* 381–400.

Kassin, S. M., Meissner, C. A., & Norwick, R. J. (2005). "I'd know a false confession if I saw one": A comparative study of college students and police investigators. *Law & Human Behavior, 29,* 211–228.

Kassin, S., Tubb, V., Hosch, H., & Memon, A. (2001). On the "general acceptance" of eyewitness testimony research: A new survey of the experts. *American Psychologist, 56,* 405–416.

Kastenberg, J. (2003). A three-dimensional model for the use of expert psychiatric and psychological evidence in false confession defenses before the trier of fact. *Seattle University Law Review, 26,* 783–839.

Lassiter, G. D. (Ed.). (2004). *Interrogations, confessions, and entrapment.* New York: Kluwer Academic/Plenum.

Leippe, M. (1995). The case for expert testimony about eyewitness memory. *Psychology, Public Policy, & Law, 1,* 909–959.

Lyons v. State, 652 S.E.2d 525, 07 FCDR 3299 (Georgia 2007).

Münsterberg, H. (1908). *On the witness stand: Essays on psychology and crime.* Garden City, NY: Doubleday.

Oberlander, L. B., Goldstein, N. E., & Goldstein, A. M. (2008). Competence to confess. In A. Goldstein & I. Wiener (Eds.), *Handbook of psychology: Forensic psychology* (Vol. 11, pp. 335–358). New York: Wiley.

Penrod, S., Fulero, S., & Cutler, B. (1995). Eyewitness expert testimony before and after *Daubert:* The state of the law and the science. *Behavioral Sciences & the Law, 13,* 229–259.

People v. Cota, 2007 WL 3360054 (Cal.App. 4 Dist.).

People v. Crews, 2008 NY Slip Op 50145(U), 18 Misc 3d 1120(A), decided Jan. 24, 2008.

People v. Flippo, Colorado Supreme Court, No. 05SC794 (Colo. June 11, 2007).

People v. Kogut, 2005 NY Slip Op 25409, 2005 N.Y. Misc. LEXIS 2126 (September 15, 2005).

People v. Madrigal, 2008 WL 192310 (Cal.App. 5 Dist.).

People v. Muratalla, 2007 WL 4376374 (Cal.App. 2 Dist.).

People v. Rathbun, 2007 WL 2391258 (Cal.App. 2 Dist.).

People v. Wroten, 2007 WL 4501776 (Cal.App. 2 Dist.).

Purpura, P. (2007, September 14). St. Rose man guilty in Kenner slaying. *The Times Picayune.*

Schmechel, R. S., O'Toole, T. P., Easterly, C., & Loftus, E. F. (2006). Beyond the ken? Testing jurors' understanding of eyewitness reliability evidence. *Jurimetrics Journal, 46,* 177–214.

Siegel, L. (2006). Defense expert makes encore appearance. *Connecticut Law Journal,* p. 5.

State v. Buell, 22 Ohio St. 3d. 124 (1986).

State v. Bradley, 2009-Ohio-460 (2009).

State v. Echols, 128 Ohio App.3d 677 (1998).

State v. Sargent, 169 Ohio App.3d 679 (2006).

State v. Tapke, 2007-Ohio-5124 (2007).

Torkildson, J. M., & Kassin, S. M. (2008). False confessions. In B. Cutler (Ed.), *Encyclopedia of Psychology and Law.* Thousand Oaks, CA: Sage.

United States v. Belyea, Fourth Circuit Court of Appeals, No. 04-4415 (Dec. 28, 2005). Retrieved August 29, 2009, from http://pacer.ca4.uscourts.gov/opinion.pdf/044415.U.pdf

United States v. Dixon, Fifth Circuit Court of Appeals, No. 06-31234 (Slip Op Jan. 16, 2008). Retrieved August 29, 2009, from http://www.ca5.uscourts.gov/opinions%5Cunpub%5C06/06-31234.0.wpd.pdf

United States v. Downing, 753 F.2d 1224 (3d Cir. 1985).*United States v. Hall,* 93 F.3d 1337 (7th Cir. 1996).

United States v. Hall, 974 F.Supp. 1198 (1997).

United States v. Hebah, 164 Fed. Appx. 678 (10th Cir. 2006), *cert.* denied, 126 S.Ct. 1934 (2006).

United States v. Mamah, 332 F.3d 475 (7th Cir. 2003).

United States v. Smith, —F.Supp2d—, 2009 U.S. Dist. LEXIS 43879 (M.D.Ala. 2009).

United States v. Smithers, 212 F.3d 306 (6th Cir. 2000).

United States v. Sullivan, 246 F.Supp.2d 696 (E.D.Ky. 2003).

Wise, R. A., & Safer, M. A. (2003). A survey of judges' knowledge and beliefs about eyewitness testimony. *Court Review, 40,* 6–16.

Wise, R. A., & Safer, M. A. (2004). What U.S. judges know and believe about eyewitness testimony. *Applied Cognitive Psychology, 18,* 427–443.

Wright v. Commonwealth, Supreme Court of Pennsylvania, Eastern Division, Allocatur Docket 2008, No. 21 EAP 2008.

Conclusion: What Have We Learned? Implications for Practice, Policy, and Future Research

Christian A. Meissner and G. Daniel Lassiter

Throughout this volume, readers have learned of the tragic stories of innocent persons who found themselves in the interrogation room being exposed to psychologically manipulative interrogation practices for lengthy periods of time. All too often, these innocent suspects become victims of a system in which they are compelled to provide a false confession, leading to a trial in which they are frequently convicted on the basis of little other evidence (and even despite the presence of exculpatory evidence that might otherwise exonerate them). Faced with the possibility of a death sentence or life in prison and receiving little hope from their defense attorneys, others will take a deal presented by the prosecutor and falsely plead guilty to a crime they did not commit. Yet from these tragedies of injustice, scientists have begun to understand the psychological factors leading to false confession. This volume offers a rather comprehensive description of this research, both past and present, as the authors document the role of certain interrogation practices and the importance of individual differences (or vulnerabilities) that produce this phenomenon. So what can be learned from this volume with regard to policy and practice reforms that might ebb the wave of false confessions being uncovered in the U.S. criminal justice system? And how must researchers focus their efforts in future research to improve practice in the interrogation room? Below, we briefly review the implications and future directions offered by the authors of this volume.

Recommendations for Reforming Police Interrogation Practice and Policy

In each chapter, the authors describe how a scientific understanding of false confessions can lead to reforms that both improve practice and safeguard the innocent persons who may one day find themselves in the interrogation room. Consensus appears for five key reforms to current practice and policy, discussed next.

1. *Record all interrogations from beginning to end.*
   If researchers were asked for the one reform they might advocate over all others, videotaping of interrogations from beginning to end would

undoubtedly be recommended. Thomas P. Sullivan (chap. 8) provides an important perspective on the recording of interrogations: Law enforcement respondents in his study who regularly record interrogations promoted its benefits with great enthusiasm and reported few negatives to its implementation. It is important that recording allows for a measure of transparency to the interrogation process, permitting the courts to assess the voluntariness of the statement, the coercive nature of the interrogation, and the extent to which the details contained in the statement emanate directly from the suspect as opposed to having been provided by law enforcement (the *contamination error;* see chaps. 1 & 2). Sullivan also rebuts the objections to recording most often cited by those in the criminal justice system, including the perceived costs of such a policy and the belief that recording of interrogations will reduce confession rates. Finally, G. Daniel Lassiter, Lezlee J. Ware, Matthew J. Lindberg, and Jennifer J. Ratcliff (chap. 9) describe their detailed analysis of the importance of recording from an equal focus (i.e., one that includes both the suspect and the interrogator).

2. *Prohibit the use of psychologically manipulative interrogation tactics that have been shown to produce false confessions.*
   Chapters by Richard A. Leo and Steven A. Drizin (chap. 1) and Christian A. Meissner, Melissa B. Russano, and Fadia M. Narchet (chap. 7) document the role of psychologically based interrogation methods in producing false confessions. Such tactics include the use of minimization approaches that imply leniency in exchange for a confession and the presentation of false evidence that can lead innocent suspects to believe that no other option exists for them but to confess. As discussed in both chapters, the use of these techniques is often accompanied (or preceded) by a strong belief of guilt on the part of the investigator (referred to as *investigative bias*) that leads to the use of pressure-filled interrogation methods and lengthy interrogations. Throughout this volume, the authors suggest that the use of such tactics that are known to produce false confessions should be prohibited and that alternative approaches to interrogation, such as those introduced in Great Britain (see chap. 5) should be encouraged. As discussed in the following, offering police alternative, empirically derived interrogation approaches is an important direction for future research in this area.

3. *Protect vulnerable persons in the interrogation room.*
   The contributions by Gisli H. Gudjonsson (chap. 2), N. Dickon Reppucci, Jessica Meyer, and Jessica Kostelnik (chap. 4), and I. Bruce Frumkin (chap. 12) discuss the various individual difference characteristics that can make a person more vulnerable to providing a false confession, including age (i.e., juveniles are more vulnerable to interrogation), cognitive or intellectual capacity (i.e., persons with diminished capacity or lower IQ are more vulnerable to interrogation), and physical or psychological state (e.g., alcohol or drug intoxication or certain psychological disorders can increase a person's vulnerability to interrogation). To protect such individuals, law enforcement investigators need to be made

aware of these risk factors (see the following discussion; see also chaps. 1 & 4), and agencies should consider both providing for the assessment of an at-risk individual (see chap. 12) and requiring that legal counsel be present to advise such individuals prior to or during the process of interrogation (see chap. 10).

4.   *Ensure the appropriate administration (knowing and intelligent waiver) of Miranda rights prior to interviewing a suspect.*
The contributions by Gregory DeClue (chap. 11) and Lawrence S. Wrightsman (chap. 10) discuss the importance of ensuring that *Miranda* warnings are provided in a clear, consistent, and comprehensible manner. DeClue notes the great degree of variability across law enforcement's administration of the warnings, both in the particular language used and the reading level required for understanding the warnings. He provides an important checklist for ensuring a suspect's comprehension of *Miranda* and details a model warning that might be adopted by law enforcement agencies. DeClue, among others, also argues that the administration of *Miranda* should be videotaped; as Wrightsman notes, investigators will often use subtle tactics to obtain a waiver and if recorded the appropriateness of such approaches could be evaluated by the court. Finally, Frumkin (chap. 12) describes clinical approaches to assessing a defendant's comprehension of *Miranda* at the time of trial.

5.   *Train law enforcement investigators regarding factors that contribute to false confessions.*
Leo and Drizin (chap. 1) and Gudjonsson (chap. 2) argue that the criminal justice community and law enforcement investigators in particular, need to be made aware of the potential for false confessions and the factors that contribute to this phenomenon, including the role of investigative biases that lead to enhanced, pressure-filled interrogations (chaps. 1 and 7), the inability of investigators to reliably distinguish truth and deception (chaps. 1 and 6), the role of certain interrogation tactics that have been shown to produce false confessions (chaps. 1 and 7), and the importance of certain individual difference characteristics that make some persons more vulnerable to interrogation (chaps. 2, 4, and 12). To this end, university-based criminal justice programs and agency-based police academies should include course content on interrogations and false confession that might be derived from volumes such as this.

Recommendations for Protecting Against Wrongful Conviction in the Courtroom

As noted by Leo and Drizin (chap. 1), an innocent person who has provided a false confession is at significant risk of being wrongfully convicted. As such, the authors have suggested several important recommendations for protecting the innocent defendant who is now faced with defending their actions in the interrogation room.

1. *Allow for the provision of expert testimony on (a) the psychological and situational factors leading to false confessions and (b) the vulnerability of a particular defendant as assessed by a licensed forensic psychologist.*
   Solomon M. Fulero (chap. 13) provides a detailed perspective on both the most appropriate (and admissible) forms of expert testimony in this area and case precedence that allows for the admissibility of such testimony. Expert testimony on false confessions may involve both a normative perspective on the risk factors associated with false confessions or a clinical–forensic assessment of the defendant and her or his psychological vulnerabilities. Frumkin (chap. 12) details the latter approach, including assessments of an individual's comprehension of *Miranda,* interrogative suggestibility, psychological state at the time of interrogation, and general mental capacity. It is important that these authors emphasize that experts should never proffer a direct opinion regarding the veracity of the confession statement; rather, experts should bring to the court a scientific understanding of the factors that may lead an individual to provide a false confession and allow the court to render any ultimate opinion regarding the alleged confession.
2. *Train lawyers (both defense and prosecution) and judges regarding factors that contribute to false confessions.*
   Leo and Drizin (chap. 1) argue that trial judges and attorneys should be educated regarding factors that contribute to false confessions, particularly given the growing number of claims involving disputed confession evidence. Courses on actual innocence and wrongful conviction are increasingly being offered in law schools around the country, and many of the authors in this volume provide continuing legal education to groups of attorneys and judges around the country. Still, many professionals within the criminal justice system remain naïve regarding the prevalence of false confessions and the factors that may be associated with this phenomenon.

Directions for Future Research

Finally, it is important to note that knowledge gained through scientific endeavors, such as that described in this volume, is an incremental and ever-evolving process. New discoveries and proposed theoretical models will always require further evaluation, qualification, and revision through the scientific process. So, too, does our understanding of the problem of false confessions and, in particular, approaches that might improve police interrogation practices. In the following, we describe three key directions for future research.

1. *Identify techniques that improve deception detection performance in the context of investigative interviews.*
   As detailed by Aldert Vrij, Ronald P. Fisher, Samantha Mann, and Sharon Leal (chap. 6), popular training programs in deception detection offered to law enforcement have little or no scientific validity, with trained investigators performing at chance levels and no better

(sometimes worse) than untrained participants. Vrij and his colleagues have begun to identify approaches to credibility assessment that improve performance; however, further research is required (both under controlled, laboratory conditions and in the field) before introducing these methods to law enforcement investigators.

2. *Identify interrogative approaches that improve the diagnostic value of confession evidence and, importantly, reduce the likelihood of false confessions.*

    Meissner and colleagues (chap. 7) argue that if researchers are to advocate prohibiting the use of certain psychologically coercive interrogative methods, then the scientific community should work to identify alternative methods that improve the diagnostic value of confession evidence and reduce the likelihood of false confessions in practice. One alternative approach discussed by Ray Bull and Stavroula Soukara (chap. 5) involves the PEACE approach to investigative interviewing (*P*lanning and Preparation, *E*ngage and Explain, Obtain an *A*ccount, *C*losure, and *E*valuation) used in Great Britain. Bull and Soukara describe four field studies evaluating the approach, whereas Meissner and colleagues discuss several empirical laboratory studies evaluating a similar, noncoercive method of interrogation. Together, these chapters converge to suggest that alternative approaches to interrogation may be developed that both preserve the ability of investigators to elicit confessions and protect the innocent from providing a false confession. Further research in this area is necessary to provide law enforcement investigators with effective, empirically derived methods of interrogation.

3. *Investigate the prevalence of, and factors contributing to, false guilty pleas.*

    Allison D. Redlich (chap. 3) calls attention to the heretofore largely unrecognized problem of false guilty pleas, which, like police-induced false confessions, represent a grave injustice in our society. There is reason to suspect that false guilty pleas are even more prevalent than false confessions, but currently there are no systematic data that address this issue. Moreover, unlike false confessions that arise from police interrogations, to our knowledge there are no safeguards (e.g., *Miranda* warnings or prohibitions against the use of threats) in place to protect individuals subjected to the plea bargaining process. Thus, future research should be directed at both understanding false guilty pleas and developing scientifically based approaches to plea bargaining that will better protect innocent individuals.

Afterword: Deconstructing Confessions—The State of the Literature

Saul M. Kassin

When Marty Tankleff set his alarm for 5:35 a.m. on September 7, 1988, he looked forward to the first day of his senior year. But by 1 p.m. the next afternoon, Marty's life had changed forever. He found himself in a cubicle in a local police station, shoeless, half-dressed, and in shock. His mom was dead; his dad was in a coma. His family had no idea that he was sitting barefoot in the police station, flanked by 400-plus pounds of Suffolk County detectives. They had no idea that some detective would be handwriting a confession for Marty: "They wanted me to drive the crummy old Lincoln," he said of his parents. "I decided I wanted to kill them both." The assault vividly described in the resulting confession was brutal.

Marty Tankleff was a self-described killer, and for that he spent more than 17 years, roughly half his life, behind the walls of a maximum security prison. He was in prison even though there was never any other evidence against him. He was in prison despite numerous witnesses, amply noted by the state appeals court, that his parents were killed in a premeditated break-in by two hired men and their getaway driver. He was in prison, despite innocence, for only one reason: He confessed.

Marty confessed while grieving over the death of his mother and worrying about his father, in the hospital fighting for his life. Marty was badgered and called a liar, tactics pulled right out of the interrogator's playbook. Every denial was challenged, every alibi he tried to give was a lie, and every facet of his story was opened up, dissected, contradicted, and pulled apart. Then police lied about the evidence, telling Marty that his hair was found on his mother and that a "humidity test" in the shower proved he had washed himself clean. As if these fabrications were not disorienting enough, the lead detective then used the "big lie" to lower the boom. Faking a phone call from the hospital, he reported that Seymour Tankleff emerged from his coma and identified Marty as his assailant. In fact, the elder Tankleff never did regain consciousness and died 1 month later.

To Marty, at this moment in his life, this news stung like a proverbial knockout punch. "My dad never lied to me," he thought. "If he said I did it, I must have done it." He and his interrogators went on to speculate, as innocent confessors sometimes do, that somehow he must have "blacked out" and that "another Marty" seized control. The seeds of false confession were planted. The lead detective proceeded to handwrite a confession that he says summarized the crime in Marty's words. In relation to the crime scene analysis that followed, the facts of the confession were all wrong. For his part, Marty never signed or even saw the confession that would forever alter the course of his life.

As is par for the course, Suffolk County police chose not to record this crucial interrogation. This means that neither the judge nor the jury could observe Marty's physical and mental state, his concern about his dying father, detectives calling him a liar, their outright deceit about evidence, and their manufacturing of a narrative statement filled with exquisite details of what Marty allegedly did and how and why he did it. Without videotape replay, the session could only be pieced together through imperfect—and biased—secondhand recollections.

After 20 years, on the basis of a mountain of new evidence, including a number of witnesses who independently reported on the secondhand confessions of the alleged perpetrators to friends and family members, Tankleff's conviction was vacated. On July 22, 2008, all charges against him were dropped.

Marty Tankleff's story may sound surreal, but as detailed in the pages of this book, he is not alone. His false confession betrays a phenomenon that is not new in history or unique to America. It is a phenomenon that social scientists and legal scholars, like those represented in this volume, are fast coming to understand.

In September 2007, I had the good fortune to participate in a 3-day conference on interrogations and confessions. Set on the beautiful campus of the University of Texas at El Paso, surrounded by spectacular mountain vistas and under a large Southwest sky, more than 200 academics, lawyers, judges, law enforcement professionals, and other attendees assembled to address questions of science, law, and practice on the subject of confession evidence. I have been interested in this topic for 30 years now, ever since Larry Wrightsman and I published a research article in 1980 on juror perceptions of coerced confessions. Since that time, I have repeatedly urged (some might say nagged) my colleagues in psychology to focus their theories and empirical research on this golden— sometimes gold-plated—form of evidence. Thanks to advances in DNA technology, a rash of actual innocence cases involving false confessions (many of which were discovered and publicized by the Innocence Project), and a growing research literature both in the United States and abroad, a spotlight of attention was finally cast on the subject. The resulting work can now be found in a wide range of psychology journals, criminology journals, and law reviews. Yet to my knowledge, this conference was the first ever to bring this community of researchers and some practitioners together under one roof. Representing recent work, the presentations covered a great deal of ground. That is why, for 3 days, there was a perceptible buzz on the University of Texas at El Paso campus. That is why this book is so important.

A number of important points are covered in this volume. First, it is clear that confessions occur in a political, cultural, and legal–institutional context, not in a vacuum. Hence, whereas confession rates have generally ranged from 40% to 60% in the contemporary United States and Great Britain, that rate has consistently exceeded 90% in Japan, where fewer restraints are placed on police and where social norms favor confession in response to the shame brought by transgression. Within countries as well, context changes in response to historical, political, and legal events.

In the United States, the Supreme Court had regularly set and reset guidelines concerning various police tactics and whether the confessions they produce are admissible in court. Lawrence S. Wrightsman's chapter (chap. 10) on the role played by the U.S. Supreme Court—in *Miranda v. Arizona* (1966) and in other rulings of relevance to law enforcement practices—provides the legal backdrop against which police interrogate, suspects confess, trial judges admit these voluntary confessions, juries vote to convict, and appellate courts affirm the convictions. It is important that Wrightsman points to *Frazier v. Cupp* (1969), in which the Supreme Court sanctioned a specific form of trickery, the false evidence ploy, by which police are permitted to misrepresent the evidence to suspects to leverage a confession. Indeed, this ruling is what enabled one Suffolk County detective to tell 17-year-old Marty Tankleff that his hair was found in his dead mother's grasp, that a special test proved he had showered that morning, and that his father had regained consciousness to identify Marty as his assailant: all egregious lies. In this volume and elsewhere, many researchers have argued that certain interrogation methods, such as the false evidence ploy and minimization tactics that covertly promise leniency, should be curtailed or altogether banned. Yet police will continue to train and use these tactics, despite any risks they pose to the innocent, to the extent that they are sanctioned by the courts (i.e., that the confessions they produce are admitted into evidence).

Within the broader context of the criminal justice system, the parallels between false confessions and false guilty pleas are particularly striking and potentially disturbing. In her chapter, Allison D. Redlich (chap. 3) notes that confessions and guilty pleas are similar in many ways. Yet whereas police are prohibited from coercing confessions by threats of punishment and promises of leniency, prosecutors routinely induce suspects to plead guilty by forcing them to choose between the uncertainty of trial and a reduced sentence or probation. And whereas police often conduct their interrogations in secrecy, in sessions that are seldom recorded, defendants who plead guilty will undergo a plea colloquy during which time a judge must determine that the defendant agreed to the plea agreement voluntarily, knowingly, and intelligently. At this point, research is needed to determine whether the plea agreement process puts innocents at risk in the same ways and for the same reasons as does the process of interrogation. In light of the numerous critiques of this aspect of criminal justice system described by Redlich, readers of this book should be mindful that the research literature on false confessions may provide an important starting point for understanding the related phenomenon of false guilty pleas.

A perusal of cases involving proven false confessions suggests that this counterintuitive phenomenon cannot be simply explained. Rather, it occurs as a product of a multistep process by which police misidentify innocent but potentially malleable suspects for interrogation by perceiving them to be deceptive during a preinterrogation interview and then use an array of powerful social influence techniques that can sometimes convince these innocent suspects to confess. Many of the chapters contained within this volume are rich in research, much of it quite recent, that both identifies the sources of these problems and proposes some possible solutions.

On the question of why innocent suspects are often targeted for interrogation, Aldert Vrij, Ronald P. Fisher, Samantha Mann, and Sharon Leal (chap. 6) describe the pitfalls in human lie detection, and, more specifically, the failure of existing police interview techniques that purport to produce accurate truth and lie detection, exceeding the virtually chance levels of deception detection accuracy consistently found in research laboratories all over the world. The problem begins with the inherent fallibility of the assumption that perpetrators who lie to police during their interviews are more anxious—and hence more likely to exhibit behavioral symptoms of deception—than innocents who tell the truth but stand falsely accused. Drawing from recent laboratory experiments, Vrij et al. propose an alternative and more promising approach. On the basis of the fact that lying is more cognitively effortful than telling the truth, they recommend that interviewers should tax a suspect's cognitive load and attend to cues that betray effort. Hence, when interviewers had truth tellers and liars recount their stories in reverse chronological order, they became more accurate in their ability to distinguish between the truthful and deceptive accounts.

Turning from the lie detection interview phase of an investigation to the processes of interrogation, a range of approaches are described. In a chapter on "pathways to false confession and wrongful conviction," Richard A. Leo and Steven A. Drizin (chap. 1) describe the chain of events that is set into motion when a detective misclassifies an innocent truth teller as a lying perpetrator. Citing actual cases involving proven false confessions, they describe police interrogation tactics such as stated or implied promises and threats that increase the risk of *coercion error* (i.e., tactics, as they put it, that function as psychological equivalents of the rubber hose). They also describe suspect vulnerability factors such as youth, cognitive impairment, and mental illness that also increase the risk of coercion error, sometimes even in the absence of highly egregious tactics.

No one would dispute the claim that a modern American police interrogation is by definition a guilt-presumptive and highly confrontational process, aspects of which, I believe, put innocent people at risk. One possible approach to reform is to completely reconceptualize interrogation. In their chapter, Ray Bull and Stavroula Soukara (chap. 5) note that beginning in the 1980s, after a number of high-profile false confessions, England and Wales transitioned police from a classic confrontational interrogation to a process of investigative interviewing. As a result, the use of psychologically manipulative tactics significantly declined, apparently without a corresponding decline in confession rates. Several years later, through a collaboration of police officers, psychologists, and lawyers, the Royal Commission on Criminal Justice further reformed the practice of interrogation by proposing the PEACE model that is still in practice and has been adopted throughout New Zealand and Norway (this mnemonic was used to describe the five distinct parts of the new interview approach: *P*lanning and Preparation, *E*ngage and Explain, Obtain an *A*ccount, *C*losure, and *E*valuation). In chapter 5, Bull and Soukara report on four observational studies in which they systematically coded a number of taped police interviews and found that the tactics used conformed to the noncoercive PEACE model and that some number of confessions were still elicited from suspects who initially had denied involvement.

Observations of the PEACE model interviews in England and Wales are encouraging, but other differences between Great Britain and the United States preclude the suggestion that a similar reform of U.S. interrogation practices will have the same beneficial effects. In their chapter on the importance of using laboratory paradigms to create more diagnostic approaches to interrogation, Christian A. Meissner, Melissa B. Russano, and Fadia M. Narchet (chap. 7) describe a recent experiment that compared the effects of confrontational and investigative methods of interrogation on the rates of true and false confessions. They found that the latter produced more diagnostic outcomes: lowering the rate of false confessions without producing a corresponding decrease in the rate of true confessions. Although more systematic research is needed, it is clear that investigative interviewing offers a potentially effective alternative to the classic American interrogation.

Although coercive interrogation tactics can put ordinary innocent people at risk to confess, it is clear that some suspects are uniquely vulnerable to manipulation. In a chapter that overviews the psychological study of false confessions, Gisli H. Gudjonsson (chap. 2) reports on a recent series of self-report studies that he and his associates have conducted involving thousands of students, community participants, and prison inmates across Europe. These studies are part of an effort to estimate the frequency with which people under interrogation confess to crimes they did not commit. Clearly, self-report is an imperfect way to assess false confession rates, but the results indicate that the phenomenon is real, that the numbers are substantial, and that people who are young, relatively uneducated, and psychologically disordered are particularly vulnerable segments of the population.

Basic science in developmental psychology provides ready explanations for why juveniles would be particularly malleable during a police interrogation. Over the years, this research has shown that adolescents are cognitively and psychosocially less mature than adults, as seen in their impulsive decision making, decreased ability to consider long-term consequences, and increased susceptibility to influence from external sources. In a chapter on the custodial interrogation of juveniles, N. Dickon Reppucci, Jessica Meyer, and Jessica Kostelnik (chap. 4) reported on survey research showing that although police know about child and adolescent development, oddly they do not apply that knowledge to interrogation practices, believing instead that juveniles can be treated in the same manner as adults.

It is a testament to the maturity of the literature on confession evidence that social scientists are now in a position to contribute to the administration of justice not only through research but also through forensic clinical assessments and expert testimony in actual cases. In this volume, Gregory DeClue (chap. 11) and I. Bruce Frumkin (chap. 12) offer important insights on how to assess and present a defendant's comprehension and waiver of *Miranda* rights. Frumkin also considers research and assessment of interrogative suggestibility. Solomon M. Fulero (chap. 13) focuses on expert testimony, which is often necessary to educate judges and juries. Noting that federal and state courts have admitted confession experts in some cases but not others, he identifies and refutes a handful of arguments that have been used to exclude this testimony.

In the development of any body of knowledge, the ultimate achievement is to follow up the identification of problems with a proposal for solutions. Implied within many of the chapters in this volume is that certain legal interrogation tactics—such as the false evidence ploy used against Marty Tankleff and certain minimization themes—can put innocents at risk and should be curtailed. Also implied within many chapters is that certain vulnerable suspect populations—such as juveniles and individuals with cognitive impairments or psychological disorders—deserve special protection when placed in custody for interrogation. In my opinion, the single most essential recommendation for reform is to lift the veil of secrecy and demand that all custodial interviews and interrogations of felony suspects should be videotaped in their entirety. Videotaping interrogations will deter police from using the most egregious tactics, discourage offenders who voluntarily confess from claiming that they were coerced, provide a full and objective record of the entire process, and sharpen the fact finding abilities of judges and juries.

Out of ignorance, opponents reflexively argue that a videotaping rule will disable police, inhibit suspects from talking, and make it more difficult to solve crimes by confession. Yet there is not evidence to support these claims. In fact, Thomas P. Sullivan, in his chapter on the wisdom of custodial recording (chap. 8), reports on interviews he has conducted with hundreds of law enforcement officials across the United States who record custodial interrogations. To make a long story short, he found that these police enthusiastically favor the practice and cite several collateral benefits, for example, that recording permits detectives to focus on the suspect rather than on taking notes, provides an instant replay of the suspect's statement that sometimes reveals incriminating comments that were initially overlooked, reduces the time detectives have to spend in court defending their practices, and increases public trust in law enforcement. Countering the objections, those who were interviewed reported that videotaping did not prove costly, inhibit suspects from talking, or prevent confessions.

Following upon Sullivan's call for a mandatory videotaping policy, G. Daniel Lassiter, Lezlee J. Ware, Matthew J. Lindberg, and Jennifer J. Ratcliff (chap. 9) urge that this policy be "scientifically based." Specifically, their chapter describes a programmatic series of studies showing the importance of camera perspective on the way people perceive the transaction between interrogators and their suspects. In studies conducted over the past 20 years, Lassiter and his colleagues have taped mock interrogations from different camera angles so that the suspect, the interrogator, or both were visible. Consistently, people who see only the suspect judge the situation as less coercive than those for whom the interrogator is visible. By focusing all attention on the accused, the camera can thus lead judges and jurors to underestimate the pressure actually exerted by the situation. This research yields the very important policy recommendation that custodial interrogations be videotaped not only from start to finish but with an equal focus perspective. As a result of this bias, Lassiter et al. also argue that suspect-only tapes, even if available, should not be admitted into evidence. On this point, however, on the basis of the numerous false confessions I have seen, I would vehemently disagree. Why? I think of Marty Tankleff who sat in a Long Island interrogation room alone, shoeless, half dressed, and in shock; I think of Barry Laughman, in Pennsylvania, who suffered from an anxiety disorder so disabling that he could tolerate no confrontation and barely manage to answer questions; and I think of Marcellius Bradford, in Chicago, who confessed while suffering a head injury and swelling over the nose from having been beaten. These are images in my mind that were contested at trial and that no judge or jury ever saw before convicting these innocent men.

The scientific study of confessions—how they are induced, when they can be trusted, and what legal consequences are set into motion—has never been more relevant. During the early years of this 21st century, it is now clear that although most known false confessions occur in a criminal justice venue and represent the tip of an iceberg, they also occur with unknown frequency in military intelligence settings (where intensely coercive tactics are sometimes used for information gathering purposes) and in corporate loss-prevention settings (where employees are often prompted by supervisors to confess to theft, whereupon they agree to return the money). Paralleling the empirical work on confessions to police in the criminal justice system, research is also needed within these other venues, where the processes, problems, and likely solutions may or may not be the same. Across settings, one principle looms clear: A concern for justice demands that policy and practice be informed by science, not intuition. Toward this end, *Police Interrogations and False Confessions* provides an invaluable, up-to-date overview of the current literature.

Index

About the Editors

G. Daniel Lassiter, PhD, is a professor of psychology at Ohio University and a fellow of the Association for Psychological Science. He received his doctoral degree in 1984 from the University of Virginia and held a visiting position at the University of Florida before arriving at Ohio University in 1987. For more than 25 years, he has conducted research on perceptual mechanisms in social judgment and decision making. During this same period, he developed one of the first theoretically driven programs of scholarship aimed at examining the effect of presentation format on how mock jurors evaluate confession evidence, which earned him the 2010 Award for Distinguished Contributions to Research in Public Policy from the American Psychological Association. His research on the camera perspective bias in videotaped confessions has influenced model legislation for a videotaping requirement developed by the Innocence Project and is noted prominently in the recent policy paper on interrogations and confessions endorsed by the American Psychology–Law Society Executive Committee. Dr. Lassiter's research has been supported by funds from the National Science Foundation and has resulted in numerous articles in major professional publications. He is the editor of *Interrogations, Confessions, and Entrapment* (2004) and is presently a consulting editor for the journals *Law and Human Behavior, Legal and Criminological Psychology,* and the *Open Access Journal of Forensic Psychology.*

Christian A. Meissner, PhD, is an associate professor of psychology and criminal justice at the University of Texas at El Paso. He holds a doctoral degree in cognitive and behavioral science from Florida State University (2001) and conducts empirical studies on the psychological processes underlying investigative interviews, including issues surrounding eyewitness recall and identification, deception detection, and interrogations and confessions. He has published numerous peer-reviewed journal articles and book chapters, and his research has been funded by the National Science Foundation and the U.S. Department of Defense. He has served on advisory panels for the National Science Foundation, the National Academy of Sciences, the U.S. Department of Defense, and the U.S. Department of Homeland Security, and he currently serves on the editorial boards of several prominent academic journals, including *Applied Cognitive Psychology, Law and Human Behavior,* and *Legal and Criminological Psychology.* He has also consulted on issues of eyewitness misidentification and false confession in numerous state and federal courts in the United States.